NEW HORIZONS IN THE STUDY OF ANCIENT SYRIA

BIBLIOTHECA MESOPOTAMICA

Primary sources and interpretive analyses for the study of Mesopotamian civilization and its influences from late prehistory to the end of the cuneiform tradition

Editor: Giorgio Buccellati

Assistant Editors: John L. Hayes, James H. Platt, Stephen L. Reimer

Published Under the Auspices of
IIMAS
The International Institute for Mesopotamian Area Studies

BIBLIOTHECA MESOPOTAMICA

Volume 25

NEW HORIZONS IN THE STUDY OF ANCIENT SYRIA

edited by

Mark W. Chavalas
John L. Hayes

UNDENA PUBLICATIONS

Malibu 1992

ABSTRACT

This volume contains the revised versions of seven papers delivered to the American Historical Association's two panels on ancient Syria, held in Chicago in 1991. The topics included are: history, archaeology, culture, diplomatic practices, literature, religion, and epigraphic data. The introductory essay outlines the broad course of Syrian history from 3000 B.C. - 1000 B.C., highlights current research activities, and places the seven contributions in their historical context. The volume is supplemented by a comprehensive bibliography and indices.

New horizons in the study of ancient Syria / edited by Mark W. Chavalas, John L. Hayes.
p. cm. -- (Bibliotheca Mesopotamica : v. 25)
Includes bibliographical references and index.
ISBN 0-89003-324-2 (cloth). --ISBN 0-89003-323-4 (pbk.)
1. Syria--Civilization. 2. Syria--History--To 332 B.C.
I. Chavalas, Mark W. (Mark William), 1954- . II. Hayes, John L. (John Lewis), 1946- . III. Series.
DS96.N48 1992
939'.43--dc20 92-42733
CIP

Undena Publications, P.O. Box 97, Malibu, California, U.S.A. 90265

Table of Contents

Preface iii

Contributors v

Map vi

Mark W. Chavalas
Ancient Syria: A Historical Sketch 1

Michael C. Astour
The Date of the Destruction of Palace G at Ebla 23

Gary M. Beckman
Hittite Administration in Syria in the Light of the Texts from Ḫattuša, Ugarit and Emar 41

Daniel E. Fleming
The Rituals from Emar: Evolution of an Indigenous Tradition in Second-Millennium Syria 51

Cyrus H. Gordon
The Geographical Horizons of Ebla 63

William W. Hallo
The Syrian Contribution to Cuneiform Literature 69

Harry A. Hoffner, Jr.
Syrian Cultural Influence in Ḫatti 89

David I. Owen
Syrians in Sumerian Sources from the Ur III Period 107
Appendix by Gordon D. Young
Wabash 1 and a Note on Ur III Syria 176

Abbreviations 177

Bibliography 183

Indices 221

Preface

In December 1991, two panels entitled "New Horizons in the Study of Ancient Syria" were convened at the annual meeting of the American Historical Association in Chicago, chaired by Dennis Pardee and Mark Chavalas. The impetus for the creation of these panels arose from a feeling, often expressed among scholars, that the study of ancient Syria had been somewhat neglected by historical scholarship. The papers in the panels were as follows:

A. *New Horizons in the History of Ancient Syria: The Third Millennium B.C. and Beyond*
Chair: Mark W. Chavalas

1. "Ancient Syria: An Introduction," Mark W. Chavalas
2. "The International Horizons of Syria as Reflected in the Ebla Archives (ca. 2300-2250 B.C.)," Cyrus H. Gordon
3. "The Date of the Destruction of Palace G at Ebla," Michael C. Astour
4. "The Rituals from Emar: Evolution of an Indigenous Tradition in Second Millennium Syria," Daniel E. Fleming

B. *New Horizons in the History of Ancient Syria: Syrian Influence in the Near East.*
Chair: Dennis Pardee

1. "The Syrian Contribution to Cuneiform Learning," William W. Hallo
2. "Syrian Influences on Hittite Culture," Harry A. Hoffner, Jr.
3. "Hittite Administration in Syria in Light of Texts from Ḫattuša, Ugarit, and Emar," Gary M. Beckman
4. "On Reconstructing the Royal Dynasties of Damascus in the Tenth - Eighth Centuries B.C.E.," Diana V. Edelman

The present volume is based upon those panels, but the papers have been modified. In addition, David I. Owen, who was originally scheduled to present a paper in the first session, but was unable to attend the AHA conference, was invited to contribute to the present volume. Gordon D. Young has also added an appendix to Owen's contribution. Because of previous commitments, Diana Edelman was unable to contribute to this volume. A general index and bibliography have been added.

We would like to thank the contributors for the promptness with which they submitted their articles, facilitating the early publication of this volume. We would also like to thank the staff at Undena Publications for all their help and guidance. In particular, we would like to thank Stephen Reimer (Technical Support), who oversaw the typesetting of the volume, and maintained a strict schedule which ensured a rapid completion. Joseph Pagan was instrumental in performing bibliographic research. He along with Romi Keerbs was also responsible for the preparation of the two maps found in the volume. Sandy Armstrong, the typist, overcame a barrage of technical difficulties (including a computer crash) and carefully input these difficult manuscripts. James Platt (Managing Editor of Undena), who was primarily responsible for the rapid completion of this volume, served to ensure quality control, supervised the execution of production, and kept everyone on schedule. He was also a great encouragement and had the foresight to recognize the potential importance of this volume.

The Editors

October 1992

Contributors

Michael C. Astour
Dept. of Historical Studies
Southern Illinois University
Edwardsville, Illinois 62234

Gary M. Beckman
326 Sterling Memorial Library
Yale University
New Haven, Connecticut 06520

Mark W. Chavalas
History Department
University of Wisconsin - La Crosse
La Crosse, Wisconsin 54601

Daniel E. Fleming
Dept. of Hebrew and Judaic Studies
51 Washington Square South
New York University
New York, New York 10012

Cyrus H. Gordon
130 Dean Road
Brookline, Massachusetts 02146

William W. Hallo
Babylonian Collection
Yale University
New Haven, Connecticut 06520

Harry A. Hoffner, Jr.
The Oriental Institute
1155 East 58th Street
Chicago, Illinois 60637-1569

David I. Owen
Dept. of Near Eastern Studies
360 Rockefeller Hall
Cornell University
Ithaca, New York 14853-2502

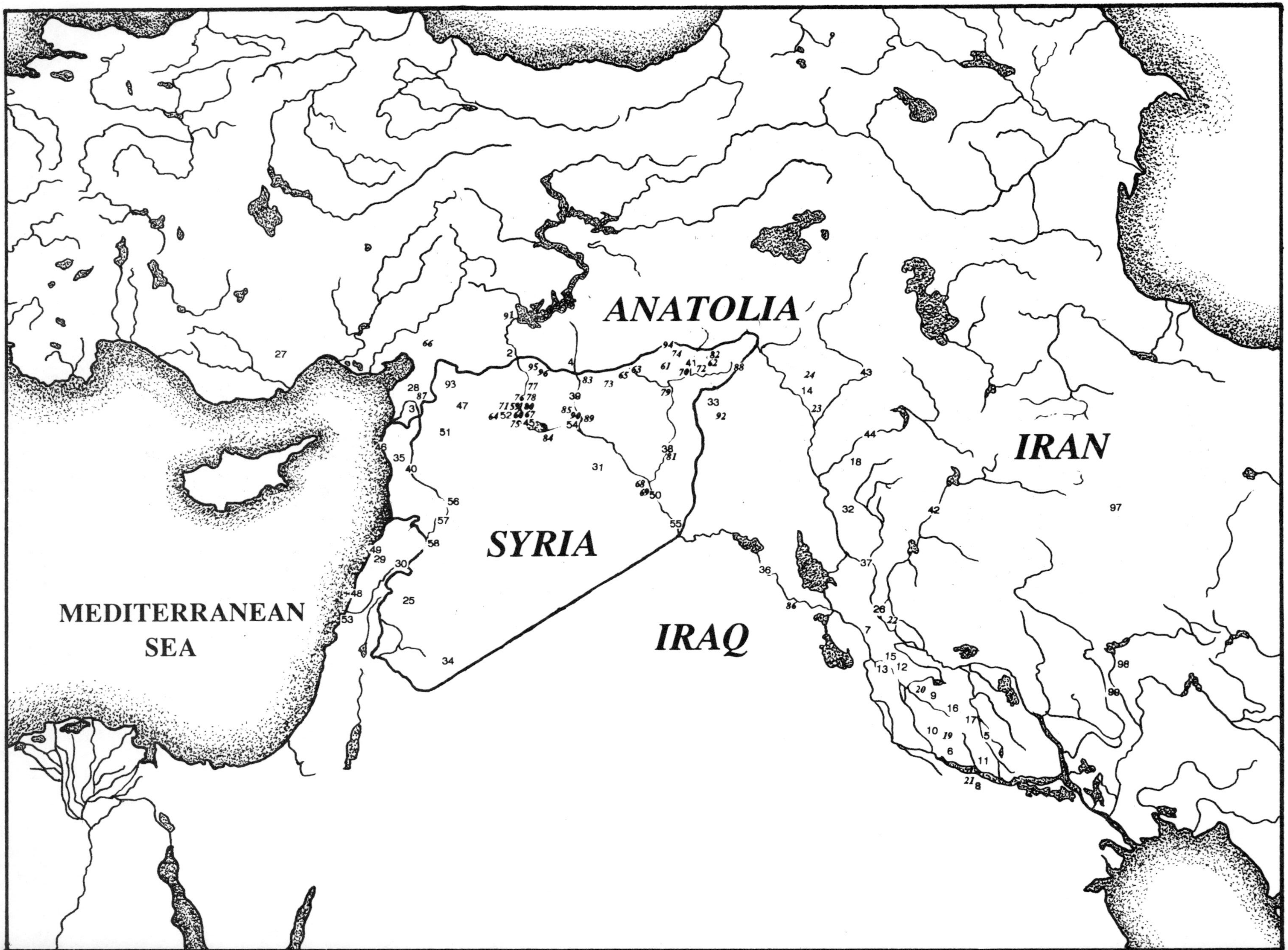
ANATOLIA
IRAN
SYRIA
IRAQ
MEDITERRANEAN
SEA

Map Key

Anatolia

Ancient Cities

1 Ḫattuša
2 Carchemish
3 Alalakh
4 Ḫarran

Iraq

Ancient Cities

5 Lagaš
6 Uruk
7 Sippar
8 Ur
9 Nippur
10 Isin
11 Larsa
12 Agade
13 Babylon
14 Nineveh
15 Kiš
16 Puzriš-Dagan
17 Umma
18 Gasur (Nuzi)

Tells

19 Fara
20 Abu Ṣalabikh
21 Ubayd
22 Khafaje
23 Nimrud
24 Khorsabad

Modern Cities

25 Damascus
26 Baghdad

Mountains

27 Taurus
28 Amanus
29 Lebanon
30 Anti-Lebanon

Jebels

31 Bishri
32 Ḥamrin
33 Sinjar
34 Druz
35 Ansariyeh

Rivers

36 Euphrates
37 Tigris
38 Khabur
39 Balikh
40 Orontes
41 Jaghjagh
42 Diyala
43 Greater Zab
44 Lesser Zab

Lake

45 Assad

Syria

Ancient Cities

46 Ugarit
47 Ḫalab (Aleppo)
48 Sidon
49 Gubla (Byblos)
50 Terqa
51 Ebla
52 Emar
53 Tyre
54 Tuttul
55 Mari
56 Hama
57 Qatna
58 Kadešh

Tells

59 Habuba Kabira
60 Kannas
61 Chagar Bazar
62 Leilan
63 Fakhariyah
64 Faqᵓous
65 Halaf
66 Zinjirli
67 Mureybiṭ
68 Bouqras
69 Qraya
70 Brak
71 Jebel Aruda
72 Barri
73 Chuera
74 Mozan
75 Selenkahiye
76 Hadidi
77 Banat
78 Bazey
79 Gudeda
80 Sweyhat
81 Sheikh Hamad
82 Hamadiya
83 Hammam et-Turkman
84 Abu Hureyra
85 Aswad
86 Ramadi
87 Judaida
88 Hamoukar
89 Zaidan
90 Jebel Belene
91 Samsat
92 Khoshi
93 Ain Dara
94 Amuda
95 Ahmar
96 Arslan Tash

Iran

Ancient Cities

97 Godin Tepe
98 Choga Mish
99 Susa

ANCIENT SYRIA: A HISTORICAL SKETCH[1]

1. Introduction

Until recently, the study of Pre-Classical Syrian history and archaeology was in an 'infant' stage compared to research in Iraq, or Mesopotamia proper. Syrian research has come of age only in the past generation. Scholars have now been forced to reevaluate the geographic limits of 'Mesopotamian' civilization to now include the upper and middle Euphrates regions of Syria, along with its tributaries, the Balikh and Khabur river regions. As a result, the term, 'Syro-Mesopotamia' has been coined.[2] However, the term 'Syria' is ambiguous; ancient and Classical writers were aware of the imprecision of the term.[3] In its broadest sense, Classical Syria comprised the area south of the Taurus mountains in southeast Turkey, west of the Euphrates river,[4] and east of the Amanus mountains and Mediterranean sea. This area was composed of the present states of Syria, Lebanon, and the southern portion of Turkey. Suffice to say there is no general consensus as to what exactly constituted Classical Syria.[5] This ambiguity has contributed to the suffering of Syrian studies in comparison to research concerning Mesopotamia, Anatolia, and Egypt.

---

[1] I wish to thank S. Reimer, member of the editorial board of *Archaeology in the Biblical World* (a publication of the Near East Archaeological Society) for allowing me to reproduce here portions of my article "One Hundred Years of Syrian Archaeology" (Vol 1 [1991] 24-37). I would also like to thank the University of Wisconsin-La Crosse for the 1992-1993 Dahler Faculty Development Fund grant, which aided in the preparation of this contribution.

[2] It is also the name of a journal publication: *Syro-Mesopotamian Studies* (Malibu: Undena; *SMS*; eds. G. Buccellati and M. Kelly-Buccellati); see "Syro-Mesopotamian Studies: A Preface," *SMS* 1 (1977) 1-2.

[3] See P. Hitti, *History of Syria*[2] (London, 1957; first edition 1951) 57-59.

[4] See the discussion in G. Buccellati, *Cities and Nations of Ancient Syria* (Roma, 1967; *SS* 26) 11-24, and Hitti, *Syria* (1957) 57-59, who both use 'Syria' in its broader sense, including even the present states of Jordan and Israel, and M. Drower, "Syria Before 2200 B.C.," *CAH*[3] I/2 (1971) 315, who differentiates Syria from Palestine. Present day Syria beyond the Euphrates was considered part of Mesopotamia proper, but will be included in our discussion.

[5] There is, however, a consensus about the five zones of Syria, as defined by physical geography, vegetation, and climate; cf. E. Wirth, *Syrien: Eine geographische Landeskunde* (Darmstadt, 1971; *Wissenschaftliche Länderkunde* 4/5) 99-107.

Syria was virtually ignored in the early days of archaeological research because it was considered to be without its own personality,[6] with a culture described only in negative terms,[7] merely a cultural dependency of other civilizations, or as unimportant because of the lack of political unity over the entire area in antiquity.[8] This was the case after many decades of seemingly unrelated investigations, including French soundings on the coast at the 'Phoenician' sites of Byblos, Tyre, and Sidon (1860s),[9] the Germans at Zinjirli (1890-94)[10] and Tell Halaf (1911-14, 1927-29),[11] and the British at Carchemish (1911-20).[12] Although some of these excavations were meticulous in nature, Syria still appeared to be relatively unimportant, based upon the fact that no major excavation had exposed any architectural or artistic remains before the period of Hittite and Assyrian domination. Syria was still seen not to have a separate cultural identity, was lacking in any originality, and was shaped only by external circumstances. It was also viewed to have a lack of written sources (partly because of a dearth of references in antiquity), especially when compared to Mesopotamia proper. All of the preceding helped to discourage the financial support that was needed.[13] Syria's historical importance began to be noticed when problems in Iraq during the 1930s encouraged excavators to leave for Syria. This interest has been revived

---

[6] See P. Matthiae, *Ebla: An Empire Rediscovered* (Garden City, 1981) 15-39.

[7] Hitti, *Syria* (1957) 57-59.

[8] The Syrian contribution to ancient Near Eastern civilization will be the subject, in part, of some of the papers in this volume: D. Fleming, "The Rituals from Emar: Evolution of an Indigenous Tradition in Second Millennium Syria"; C. Gordon, "The International Horizons of Syria as Reflected in the Ebla Archives"; W. Hallo, "The Syrian Contribution to Cuneiform Literature"; and H. Hoffner, "Syrian Cultural Influence in Ḫatti".

[9] E. Renan, *Mission de Phénicie* (Paris, 1864).

[10] See the final report by F. von Luschan, *Ausgrabungen in Sendschirli* (Berlin, 1953).

[11] See M. von Oppenheim, *Tell Halaf* I-IV (Berlin, 1943-62), and his more general survey, *Der Tell Halaf: Eine neue Kultur im ältesten Mesopotamien* (Leipzig, 1931). It is certainly true that von Oppenheim did not fully comprehend the stratigraphic relationships found at Tell Halaf, but he did discover 'Halaf ware,' as well as notice the 'metallic' ware at a number of sites, both of which would play large roles in interpreting the chronological sequences in the area. 'Metallic' ware has now been associated more with 'stone' ware; cf. S. Fitz, "Steinzeug vom Tell Ḫuēra: Das früheste Beispiel für die Herstellung dichtgebrannter Keramik," *ZA* 74 (1984) 123-132. For Neo-Hittite artistic styles found at Tell Halaf, see von Oppenheim, *Tell Halaf* II: *Die Bauwerke* (Berlin, 1950), and W. Orthmann, *Untersuchungen zur späthethitischen Kunst* (Bonn, 1971; *Saarbrücker Beiträge zur Altertumskunde* 8). Von Oppenheim appears, however, to have been the first to recognize the double wall system of the Early Bronze age northern Mesopotamian cities; see U. Moortgat-Correns, *Die Bildwerke vom Djeblet el-Bēḍā in ihrer räumlichen und zeitlichen Umwelt* (Berlin, 1972) 26-60, and W.J. van Liere and J. Lauffray, "Nouvelle prospection archéologique dans la Haute Jézireh syrienne," *AAAS* 4-5 (1954-55) 129-148.

[12] See D.G. Hogarth and C.L. Woolley, et al., *Carchemish: Report on the Excavations at Djerablus on Behalf of the British Museum* I-III (London, 1914-52).

[13] See the pertinent survey, D. Warburton, "Previous archaeological work in the Ḫābūr region," in S. Eichler et al., eds., *Tall al-Ḥamīdīya* I (Freiburg, 1985) 13-30, especially p. 15, and B. Hrouda, "Waššukanni, Urkiš, Šubat-Enlil: Ein Beitrag zur historischen Geographie des nördlichen Zweistromlandes," *MDOG* 90 (1958) 22-35. This indifference to research in Syria may have been a blessing in disguise, since early explorations in Iraq suffered from a lack of scientific excavation techniques. Irreparable damage had been done to important sites such as Nimrud, Nineveh, and Khorsabad; Syria may have had an advantage by being excavated later with more precise techniques.

again because of the Iran-Iraq and Gulf Wars of the last dozen years; excavators have again had to leave other Near Eastern areas for Syria, which is now receiving the attention it has richly deserved.

Because of intensified research in the past generation, it is now possible for the first time to envision a synthesis of ancient Syrian history;[14] the articles in this volume will be used as material that will contribute to this goal. Moreover, the present article is but a first step towards that synthesis. Here I will briefly sketch the broad outline of Syrian history. I will concentrate on incorporating recent archaeological and historical research into this sketch, and will attempt to put some of the more spectacular finds from Syria (namely, Ebla, Mari, and Ugarit) into their proper historical context. Syrian relations with Mesopotamia will be discussed to a greater extent than its relations with Egypt. This sketch will be relegated to a discussion of aspects of Syrian history from the Protohistoric period (c. 3500-3000 BCE), the Rise of Urbanization (c. 3000-2100 BCE), the Old Syrian period (c. 2100-1600 BCE), the Middle Syrian period (c. 1600-1200 BCE), and the advent of the New (or Late) Syrian period (c. 1200-900 BCE);[15] the Prehistoric periods, as well as Syria in the first millennium BCE, are outside the scope of this research except in some specific cases.

2. A Brief Survey of Aspects of Syrian History

2.1 Prelude: The Prehistoric Period

Syria has been shown to have been a significant cultural force in the prehistoric Neolithic periods until the urban revolution, with major centers of occupation throughout the area. Both the Khabur and Balikh regions have been systematically surveyed, showing evidence of Neolithic levels at Tell Abu Hureyra,[16] Tell Mureybit,[17] Tell Brak, Tell Chagar Bazar,[18] and Tell Halaf (which generated the name of a prehistoric period in Syro-

---

[14] One can observe just how out of date are the syntheses of Hitti, *Syria* (1957), H. Klengel, *Geschichte Syriens im 2. Jahrtausend v.u.Z.* I-III (Berlin, 1965-70), and idem, *Geschichte und Kultur Altsyriens*[2] (Leipzig, 1979). This can also be seen for the third millennium BCE in particular; see Drower, "Syria Before 2200" (1971) 315-321, 328-362, and J. Bottéro, "Syria at the Time of the Kings of Agade," *CAH*[3] I/2 (1971) 321-327.

[15] See the discussion in H. Weiss, "Introduction," in idem, ed., *Ebla to Damascus: Art and Archaeology of Ancient Syria* (Washington, 1985) 30-31. For recent research concerning Syrian chronology, see G. Schwartz and H. Weiss, "Syria: ca. 10,000-2000 B.C.," in R. Ehrich, ed., *Chronologies in Old World Archaeology* (Chicago, forthcoming; 3rd edition). Another work that will cover the periods in question is P. Matthiae, ed., *L'Archéologie et l'histoire de la Syrie I: De la préhistoire aux royaumes araméens* (Damascus, forthcoming).

[16] A.M.T. Moore, "The Excavation of Tell Abu Hureyra in Syria: A Preliminary Report," *Proceedings of the Prehistoric Society* 41 (1975) 50-77.

[17] M. van Loon, "The Oriental Institute Excavations at Mureybiṭ, Syria: Preliminary Report on the 1965 Campaign. Part I: Architecture and General Finds," *JNES* 27 (1968) 265-282, J. Cauvin, "Les fouilles de Mureybet (1971-1974) et leur signification pour les origines de la sedentarisation au Proche-Orient," in D.N. Freedman, ed., *Archaeological Reports from the Tabqa Dam Project—Euphrates Valley, Syria* (Cambridge, 1979; *AASOR* 44) 19-48, and "Le Moyen-Euphrate au VIIIe millénaire d'après Mureybet et Cheikh Hassan," in J.-C. Margueron, ed., *Le Moyen Euphrate: Zone de contacts et d'échanges* (Leiden, 1980) 21-34.

[18] M. Mallowan, "The Excavations at Tall Chagar Bazar, and an Archaeological Survey of the Ḫabur Region,

Mesopotamia, 'Halafian'). In other parts of Syria there are the important sites of Tell Aswad[19] and Tell Bouqras,[20] among others.[21] There is, however, evidence of southern Mesopotamian influence as early as the Ubaid period (c. 4300-3500 BCE) at various places in Syria (many of which would continue in importance in succeeding periods),[22] including Tell Brak,[23] Tell Leilan, Tell Hammam et-Turkman,[24] Zaidan,[25] Carchemish, Samsat,[26] a number of mounds on the plain of Antioch,[27] and Hama.[28]

2.2 Protohistoric Syria (c. 3500-3000 BCE)

Because of the numerous salvage projects conducted in the last twenty years, it has been found that Syria played a strategic role in the rise of urbanization in the Protohistoric (or Uruk) period (c. 3500-3000 BCE).[29] The sites of Tell Kannas,[30] Tell Habuba

---

1934-5" *Iraq* 3 (1936) 1-86, and "The Excavations at Tall Chagar Bazar and an Archaeological Survey of the Ḫabur Region. Second Campaign, 1936" *Iraq* 4 (1937) 91-177.

[19] H. de Contenson et al., "Tell Aswad (Damascene)," *Paléorient* 5 (1979) 153-156.

[20] H. de Contenson and W.J. van Liere, "Premier sondage à Bouqras en 1965. Rapport préliminaire," *AAAS* 16 (1966) 181-192.

[21] For a general description of the prehistoric period in Syria, see A.M.T. Moore, "The Prehistory of Syria," *BASOR* 270 (1988) 3-12, and H. Weiss, "Archaeology in Syria," *AJA* 95 (1991) 685-698.

[22] See J. Oates, "Ubaid Mesopotamia Reconsidered," in T. C. Young, Jr. et al., eds., *The Hilly Flanks and Beyond: Essays in the Prehistory of Southwestern Asia Presented to Robert J. Braidwood* (Chicago, 1984; *SAOC* 36) 251-281; I. Thuesen, "Diffusion of Ubaid Pottery into Western Syria," in E.F. Henrickson and I. Thuesen, eds., *Upon this Foundation—The ᶜUbaid Reconsidered* (København, 1989) 419-440, and C. Breniquet, "Les origines de la culture d'Obeid en Mésopotamie du nord," ibid., 325-338.

[23] Tell Brak has an abundance of Ubaid period material; see J. Oates, "Tell Brak in the Fourth and Third Millennia: From Uruk to Ur III," in S. Eichler et al., eds., *Tall al-Ḥamīdīya* 2 (Freiburg, 1990) 133-147. A prehistoric chronological sequence has been established for Tell Brak; see K. Fielden, "Tell Brak 1976: The Pottery," *Iraq* 39 (1977) 245-255.

[24] M. van Loon, "Hammâm et-Turkmân on the Balikh: First results of the University of Amsterdam's 1982 Excavation," *Akkadica* 35 (1983) 1-23; "New Evidence for North Syrian Chronology from Hammam et-Turkman," *AJA* 92 (1988) 582-587; idem, ed., *Hammam et-Turkman 1: Preliminary Report on the 1981-84 Seasons* (Istanbul, 1988), and P. Akkermans, "An Updated Chronology for the Northern Ubaid and Late Chalcolithic Periods in Syria: New Evidence form Tell Hammam Et-Turkman," *Iraq* 50 (1988) 109-145.

[25] K. Kohlmeyer, "Euphrat-Survey: Die mit Mitteln der Gerda Henkel Stiftung durchgeführte archäologische Geländebegehung im syrischen Euphrattal," *MDOG* 116 (1984) 108.

[26] M. Özdoğan, *Lower Euphrates Basin 1977 Survey* (Istanbul, 1977) pls. 84-89.

[27] R.J. Braidwood and L.S. Braidwood, *Excavations in the Plain of Antioch I: The Earlier Assemblages Phases A-J* (Chicago, 1960; *OIP* 61) 175-225.

[28] E. Fugmann, *Hama: Fouilles et recherches 1931-38* II (Københaven, 1958) 14-31.

[29] See the discussion by D. Sürenhagen, "The Dry-Farming Belt: The Uruk Period and Subsequent Developments," in H. Weiss, ed., *The Origins of Cities in Dry-Farming Syria and Mesopotamia in the Third Millennium B.C.* (Guilford, 1986) 7-44; G. Algaze, "Mesopotamian Expansion and its Consequences" (Ph.D. diss., University of Chicago, 1986), and his "The Uruk Expansion: Cross-Cultural Exchange in Early Mesopotamian Civilization," *Current Anthropology* 30 (1989) 571-608.

[30] A. Finet, "Les Temples Sumériens du Tell Kannâs," *Syria* 52 (1975) 157-174, and "Bilan provisoire des fouilles belges du Tell Kannâs," in Freedman, *Tabqa* (1979) 79-95.

Kabira,[31] and Jebel Aruda[32] on the middle Euphrates attest to a widespread expansion of the larger urban centers in southern Mesopotamia, notably Uruk. Since there appears to have been no indigenous urbanization in the area, it has been postulated that these sites were colonies, or better enclaves of Mesopotamian urban centers.[33] They display how urbanization was formed in this region of Syria. The central district at Tell Habuba Kabira was a densely settled town with living quarters and workshops and had cult and administrative activities. The site provides the first evidence for town planning in Syria in this period. Long distance trade was of great importance, as many artifacts with styles similar to types from Godin Tepe, Uruk, Susa, and Choga Mish have been found.[34] There is, however, no evidence of any agricultural activities that would have sustained the town. A number of additional small Uruk period sites evidently surrounded the Tell Habuba Kabira complex.[35] The site of Tell Habuba Kabira was occupied for less than two centuries.[36] Uruk period surface finds have also been located at Tell Hadidi.[37] Moreover, further south on the Euphrates there is evidence of small and relatively isolated sites at Tell

---

[31] E. Heinrich et al., "Bericht über die von der Deutschen Orient-Gesellschaft mit Mitteln der Stiftung Volkswagenwerk im Euphrattal bei Aleppo begonnenen archäologischen Untersuchungen, erstattet von Mitgliedern der Expedition," *MDOG* 101 (1969) 27-67; "Zweiter vorläufiger Bericht über die von der Deutschen Orient-Gesellschaft mit Mitteln der Stiftung Volkswagenwerk in Ḥabuba Kabira und in Mumbaqat unternommenen archäologischen Untersuchungen (Herbskampagne 1969), erstattet von Mitgliedern der Mission," *MDOG* 102 (1970) 27-85; "Bericht über die von der Deutschen Orient-Gesellschaft mit Mitteln der Stiftung Volkswagenwerk in Habuba Kabira und in Mumbaqat unternommenen archäologischen Untersuchungen, erstattet von Mitgliedern der Expedition," *AAAS* 20 (1970) 25-47; "Dritter vorläufiger Bericht über die von der Deutschen Orient-Gesellschaft mit Mitteln der Stiftung Volkswagenwerk in Ḥabūba Kabira und in Mumbaqat unternommenen archäologischen Untersuchungen (Herbskampagne 1970), erstattet von Mitgliedern der Mission," *MDOG* 103 (1971) 5-58, and "Vierter vorläufiger Bericht über die von der Deutschen Orient-Gesellschaft mit Mitteln der Stiftung Volkswagenwerk in Ḥabuba Kabira (Ḥububa Kabira, Herbstkampagnen 1971 and 1972 sowie Testgrabung Frühjahr 1973) und in Mumbaqat (Tall Munbaqa, Herbstkampagne 1971) unternommenen archäologischen Untersuchungen, erstattet von Mitgliedern der Mission," *MDOG* 105 (1973) 5-68. See also E. Strommenger, "Fünfter vorläufiger Bericht über die von der Deutschen Orient-Gesellschaft mit Mitteln der Stiftung Volkswagenwerk in Ḥabūba Kabīra unternommenen archäologischen Untersuchungen (Kampagnen 1974, 1974, 1975), *MDOG* 108 (1976) 5-22, and idem, "Ausgrabungen der Deutschen Orient-Gesellschaft in Ḥabuba Kabira," in Freedman, *Tabqa* (1979) 62-78.

[32] G. van Driel, "The Uruk Settlement on Jebel Aruda: a Preliminary Report," in Margueron, *Moyen Euphrate* (1980) 75-93; G. van Driel and C. van Driel-Murray, "Jebel Aruda 1977-1978," *Akkadica* 12 (1979) 2-28, and "Jebel Aruda, The 1982 Season of Excavation, interim report," *Akkadica* 33 (1983) 1-26. For the tablets at Jebel Aruda, see G. van Driel, "Tablets from Jebel Aruda," in idem et al., eds., *Zikir Šumim: Assyriological Studies Presented to F.R. Kraus* (Leiden, 1982) 12-25. For sealings, see idem, "Seals and Sealings from Jebel Aruda 1974-1978" *Akkadica* 33 (1983) 34-62.

[33] Algaze, "Expansion" (1989) 577-579.

[34] See the discussion in Sürenhagen, "Dry-Farming Belt" (1986) 19.

[35] M. van Loon surveyed a few such sites including Tell Mureybiṭ and Tell Abu Hureyra: *The Tabqa Reservoir Survey 1964* (Damascus, 1964).

[36] E. Strommenger, *Habuba Kabira: Eine Stadt vor 5000 Jahren* (Mainz am Rhein, 1980).

[37] R.H. Dornemann, "Tell Hadidi: One Bronze Age Site Among Many in the Tabqa Dam Salvage Area," *BASOR* 270 (1988) 13-42.

Qraya, where Uruk period domestic architecture and artifacts have been found,[38] as well as at Tell Ramadi, near the Iraqi border on the Euphrates.[39]

Different types of settlements have been uncovered in the upper Khabur region,[40] notably at Tell Brak,[41] which had a sequence of Uruk period temples somewhat contemporary to the Sin temples at Khafaje,[42] in addition to a ring of late Uruk period settlements surrounding it.[43] However, Tell Brak had a long pre-Uruk period history and was evidently not an implanted colony similar to what has been postulated for Tell Habuba Kabira.[44] Surface finds dating to the Uruk period have also been found at Tell Barri (ancient Kaḫat) in the upper Khabur region.[45] The distribution of these sites appears to have a pattern similar to the Ubaid sites, and shows a network of settlements along the Orontes, Balikh, and Khabur river basins, as well as the middle Euphrates region.[46] They formed a long chain of towns following the Euphrates river to the north into the Anatolian plateau, apparently consciously placed in strategic locations along lines of communication. Sites that show this distribution include Tell Leilan and surface finds from Tell Hamoukar[47] in northeastern Syria, Tell Hammam et-Turkman,[48] Zaidan,[49] and Jebel Belene[50] along the Balikh river,[51] Carchemish and Samsat[52] in the upper Euphrates region, and Hama

---

[38] See K. Simpson, "Qraya Modular Reports 1: The Early Soundings," *SMS* 4/4 (1989) 1-44, and S. Reimer, "Tell Qraya on the Middle Euphrates," in M.S. Rothman, "Out of the Heartland: The Evolution of Complexity in Peripheral Mesopotamia During the Uruk Period. Workshop Summary," *Paléorient* 15 (1989) 279-290.

[39] See B. Geyer and J.-Y. Monchambert, "Prospection de la moyenne vallée de l'Euphrate: rapport préliminaire: 1982-1985," *MARI* 5 (1987) 318; figs. 8, 10.

[40] Uruk settlements may have existed along the lower Khabur region; see the discussion by Algaze, "Expansion" (1989) 579, J.-Y. Monchambert, "Prospection archéologique sur l'emplacement du futur lac du Moyen Khabour," *Akkadica* 39 (1984) 1-7, and W. Röllig and H. Kühne, "The Lower Habur: A Preliminary Report on a Survey Conducted by the Tübinger Atlas des Vorderen Orients in 1975," *AAAS* 27-28 (1977-78) 115-140.

[41] D. Oates, "The Excavations at Tell Brak, 1976," *Iraq* 39 (1977) 233-244.

[42] See Fielden, "Tell Brak 1976" (1977) 245-255, and M. Mallowan, "Excavations at Brak and Chagar Bazar," *Iraq* 9 (1947) 233-244. For Tell Brak chronology, see J. Oates, "Tell Brak: The Uruk/Early Dynastic Sequence," in U. Finkbeiner and W. Röllig, eds., *Ǧamdat Naṣr: Period or Regional Style?* (Tübingen, 1986) 245-273.

[43] See Oates, "Tell Brak 1976" (1977) 234, and H. Weiss, "Excavations at Tell Leilan and Third Millennium Urbanization," *Paléorient* 9 (1983) 42.

[44] Oates, "Uruk to Ur III" (1990) 143.

[45] P.E. Pecorella and M. Salvini, *Tell Barri/Kahat 1: Relazione preliminare sulle Campagne 1980 e 1981 a Tell Barri/Kahat nel bacino del Habur* (Roma, 1982).

[46] Sürenhagen, "Dry-Farming Belt" (1986) 15.

[47] Weiss, "Origins" (1983) 44.

[48] See van Loon, "Hammam et-Turkman 1982" (1983) fig. 4.

[49] Sürenhagen, "Dry-Farming Belt" (1986) 15 n. 11.

[50] K. Kohlmeyer, "Euphrat-Survey" (1984) 109.

[51] See P. Akkerman's survey of the region: "Archäologische Geländebegehung im Baliḫ-Tal," *AfO* 31 (1984) 188-190.

[52] A. Özten, "Two Pots Recovered in the Excavations at Samsat Belonging to the Late Chalcolitic Period," *Anadolu* 20 (1976-77) 267-271.

and Judaidah along the Orontes river.[53] However, of great import is the fact that there do not appear to be many Uruk period sites away from the major rivers in the outlying regions,[54] although there is some evidence in the Syrian desert.[55] Few sites were founded upon existing socio-political entities, with the exception of Samsat, Carchemish, and Tell Brak.

The abrupt appearance of Uruk type artifacts which are virtually identical to those in the south (i.e., ceramics, cylinder seals, architectural forms, and writing instruments) attest to the possibility of an Uruk 'colonization' along the major river regions of Syria. Most likely, the indigenous native settlements in Syria which were distant from the colonies continued to thrive with the traditions of agricultural and craft productions with which they were accustomed. There is evidence at Tell Habuba Kabira that the local population supported the colonists with foodstuffs. It is still not clear as to whether these centers were directly under southern control, or were dominated by local elites.[56] The function of these so-called colonies affirms the Uruk culture's need for materials which were not present in the south, but only available over great distances. Such commodities may have included copper ores, lapis lazuli, and other semi-precious materials. The nature of the exchanges remains obscure. The Uruk culture was apparently not interested in a broad acquisition of territory or domination of agricultural enterprises.[57] The colonies, however, were relatively short-lived, and none were maintained in the succeeding periods. This abandonment may indicate that either other sources for materials were now available, local communities had successfully thwarted the southern domination of trade routes, or that the need for colonists became obsolete due to the emergence of other forms of exchange.

2.3 The Rise of Urbanization (3000-2100 BCE) (Early Bronze Age)

The Uruk expansion came to an abrupt halt in the succeeding Early Bronze age, and many of the Uruk period sites were abandoned. The indigenous areas in locations peripheral to the Uruk sites became more powerful, and southern Mesopotamian interference did not occur again for at least one half of a millennium. Soon after, there is evidence of Egyptian involvement in western Syria.[58] Indeed, a sharp change in the political landscape had transpired. Whereas the Uruk period culture was able to penetrate the area relatively easily, the Sumerian and Sargonic kings were reduced to using force to

---

[53] Braidwood and Braidwood, *Antioch I* (1960) 226-229, 259-264.

[54] Ibid., 17.

[55] See J. Cauvin and D. Stordeur, "Une occupation d'époque Uruk en Palmyrène: le niveau supérieur d'El Kowm 2-Caracol," *Cahiers de l'Euphrate* 4 (1985) 191-205.

[56] J. Oates has postulated that Tell Brak was under direct southern Mesopotamian control during the latter half of the third millennium BCE ("Tell Brak: Uruk Pottery from the 1984 Season," *Iraq* 47 [1985] 175-186), while H. Weiss has argued for local control (review of J. Curtis, ed., *Fifty Years of Mesopotamian Discovery* [London, 1982]), JAOS 105 [1985] 327-330).

[57] Algaze, "Expansion" (1989) 580.

[58] See Drower, "Syria Before 2200" (1971) 351-362.

control the region, as they subsequently had to overcome local rulers and walled towns.[59] Recent work in Syria in this period has effectively put an end to the 'Pan-Sumerianism' of previous generations.[60] A new type of settlement (c. 3000-2100 BCE) in dry-farming regions began to foster a new relationship with southern Mesopotamia. Both the Khabur region (Tell Hamoukar, Tell Leilan, Tell Mozan, Tell Brak,[61] and Tell Chuera), the plains of Aleppo in coastal Syria (Byblos,[62] Homs, Ebla[63]) and Qatna along the Euphrates permitted the extensive cultivation of wheat and barley without major irrigation, i.e., dry-farming, and extensive raising of sheep and goat herds.[64] The political and economic organization of this region in the first half of the millennium remains virtually unknown, but was probably centered around small towns, but not under any central control.[65]

There were, however, a number of walled towns that were created during this period. It is not clear whether they were initiated by the southerners or were autonomous creations.[66] One of these was Tell Mardikh/Ebla in northwest Syria, the only site in the area that showed signs of sophistication in urbanization equal to any Early Dynastic period site in the south. The city displayed cultural autonomy (an unexpected feature of Proto-Syrian culture), in addition to historical continuity from earlier periods. Thousands of cuneiform tablets have been uncovered predominantly from a major palatial archive, written in a heretofore unknown Semitic language, now called Eblaite, or Eblaic.[67] Clearly Ebla was culturally independent, being far from the Mesopotamian center, and yet, like other sites, showed numerous similarities with Sumer, not the least of which was the usage of the cuneiform script. The major archival remains that have been discovered at Ebla show a wholesale adoption of the Sumerian cuneiform script at a very early date. The extent of Syria's cultural dependence (especially in regards to literature) upon Mesopotamia is not a simple matter.[68] Many of the religious texts at Ebla have their counterparts in the southeast; however, the incantations written predominantly in Eblaite have no attested

---

[59] Algaze, "Expansion" (1989) 601.

[60] See I.J. Gelb, "Mari and the Kish Civilization," in G. Young, ed., *Mari in Retrospect* (Winona Lake, 1992) 122.

[61] Mallowan, "Brak and Chagar Bazar" (1947) 1-266, and more recently, J. Oates, "Tell Brak and Chronology: the Third Millennium," *MARI* 4 (1985) 137-144.

[62] See M. Dunand, *Fouilles de Byblos* I-II (Paris, 1939-58).

[63] The material concerning Ebla is nearly comparable in amount to that of Mari and Ugarit. General works include the previously mentioned Matthiae, *Empire* (1981); G. Pettinato, *The Archives of Ebla: An Empire Inscribed in Clay* (Garden City, 1981), and his *Ebla: A New Look at History* (Baltimore, 1991). Archaeological reports have been included in *Missione archeologica italiana in Siria* (Roma, 1964ff.), while various types of research are found in *Studi Eblaiti* (Roma, 1979ff.).

[64] H. Weiss, "Introduction: The Origins of Cities in Dry-Farming Syria and Mesopotamia in the Third Millennium B.C.," in idem, *Origins of Cities* (1986) 1-6.

[65] Weiss, "Tell Leilan and Shubat Enlil," *MARI* 4 (1985) 269-292.

[66] Weiss, "Origins of Cities" (1986) 2.

[67] G. Pettinato et al., *Materiali Epigrafici di Ebla* (Napoli, 1979ff.), and A. Archi et al., *Archivi Reali di Ebla, Testi* (Roma, 1979ff.). For Eblaite history, see M.C. Astour, "An Outline of the History of Ebla (Part 1)," *Eblaitica* 3 (1992) 3-82.

[68] As W.W. Hallo notes in his contribution to this volume.

parallel,[69] and feature geographic and divine names pointing to a native Syrian context. William Hallo sums up by saying that Syria (and Ebla in particular) was dependent upon Mesopotamia for its literary and scholarly input, but capable of building on the base so derived to serve its own particular needs.[70] Moreover, Ebla surely had a far-flung commercial empire with a wide geographic range of influence in this period, as noted by Cyrus Gordon.[71]

One of the most difficult problems about Ebla is the placing of its texts into the absolute chronology of the ancient Near East; without such chronological precision one cannot, as Michael Astour maintains, understand Ebla's relations with Mesopotamian states.[72] As Ebla's excavator P. Matthiae has stated, the age of the Ebla archives is dependent upon the Royal Palace G, especially its lower limit.[73] The archives therein have been described as 'living.'[74] There are no datable synchronisms with any Mesopotamian ruler. There are, however, inscribed objects in Palace G coming from Egypt.[75] In his closely argued article, Astour claims that the traditional viewpoint that Sargon (or Naram-Sin) of Akkad destroyed Royal Palace G is wrong,[76] and that the conflagration of the Palace preceded the destruction of both Mari (by Sargon) and Kiš (by Lugalzagesi).[77] Coupled with the fact that the palaeography of Ebla is more akin to the period of Lugalzagesi and Urukagina, Astour concludes that there is no evidence that the city was sacked by an invader.[78] This conclusion is suggested by two main factors: 1) the destruction was limited to the area of the Royal Palace, and 2) there was no convincing evidence of looting.[79] He thus holds that the time bracket for the accidental (as he calls it) destruction of the palace was about 2300-2280 BCE, prior to Sargon and Lugalzagesi.[80]

Like Ebla, Mari has expanded our understanding of the limits of 'Mesopotamian' civilization. Although mentioned in the Sumerian King List, this major center has been shown to have exhibited significant cultural independence from the Sumerian south. Recent excavations have shown that the city may have been founded either at the end of the Early

---

[69] Hallo, "Syrian Contribution" 72.

[70] Ibid., 77.

[71] See Gordon, "Horizons" 63-68. For Ebla geography, also see A. Archi, "Notes on Eblaite Geography [I]," *SEb* 2 (1980) 1-16, and idem, "Notes on Eblaite Geography II," *SEb* 4 (1981) 1-17.

[72] This is the subject of M. Astour's article in this volume: "The Date of the Destruction of Palace G at Ebla."

[73] Matthiae, *Empire* (1981) 53.

[74] P.R.S. Moorey, "Abu Salabikh, Kish, Mari and Ebla: Mid-third Millennium Archaeological Interconnections," *AJA* 85 (1981) 448.

[75] See e.g., P. Matthiae, "Recherches archéologiques à Ébla, 1977: le quartier administratif du palais royal G," *CRAIBL* 1978 229-234, and G. Scandone Matthiae, "I vasi egiziani in pietra dal Palazzo Reale G," *SEb* 4 (1981) 99-127.

[76] "Destruction" 33-34.

[77] Ibid., 36.

[78] Ibid., as well as Matthiae, *Empire* (1981) 105.

[79] Astour, "Destruction" 35-36, and J.N. Postgate, "Abu Essalabikh and Tell Mardikh: Sumer and Ebla," *Sumer* 42 (1986) 68-70. This conclusion is partly based upon the quantity of lapis lazuli that was left in the edifice. It is possible, however, that this material could have been overlooked by the proposed invaders.

[80] "Destruction" 37.

Dynastic I or beginning of the Early Dynastic II periods.[81] The excavators have located a possible dike in the line of hills south of the mound, a branching canal which traversed the city obliquely, as well as a number of canal feeders, permitting the production of wheat in this region.[82] The city had a massive wall in this period, as well as three rebuildings of the famed Ishtar temple and a large Sargonic palace. Graves reminiscent of the Ur III period tombs have been uncovered in a small structure of the Šakkanakku period.[83] Both Mari and Ebla appear to have shared a common writing system, language, and calendar in this period.[84] Most likely, the cultural borrowing was from Mari to Ebla, and not the other way around.[85]

North of Mari on the Euphrates river is the site of Tell Ashara, which had a massive defensive system rivaling any other site of this period.[86] Further north in the middle Euphrates region there is also evidence of occupation in the late third millennium BCE at Selenkahiye[87] and Tell Hadidi.[88] Selenkahiye appears to have been founded about 2400 BCE, and was possibly a merchant colony of a Sumerian city. Its destruction coincides with the fall of the Ur III Dynasty.[89] The Early Bronze remains at Tell Hadidi have shown it to also have been a new urban center in the latter half of this period.[90] Further north, the Tishreen Dam salvage project just south of Carchemish on the Euphrates near the Turkish border has revealed occupation in that area, showing an increase in the number of settlements in the second half of the third millennium BCE.[91] These sites include Tell Banat, Tell Bazey, Tell Gudeda,[92] and Tell Sweyhat.[93]

---

[81] The most recent excavation reports and other studies can be found in *MARI* 1-6 (1982-90).

[82] See J.-C. Margueron, "Mari," in Weiss, "Archaeology in Syria" (1991) 709-710.

[83] Ibid., 711.

[84] See Gelb, "Mari" (1992) 197-200. For the similarities in calendars, see D. Charpin, "Mari et le calendrier d'Ebla," *RA* 76 (1982) 1-6.

[85] See I.J. Gelb, "Thoughts about Ibla: A Preliminary Evaluation, March 1977," *SMS* 1 (1977) 15.

[86] There has been as of yet no extensive exposure of third millennium BCE material except for this defensive system; see G. Buccellati, *Terqa Preliminary Reports No. 10: The Fourth Season: Introduction and the Stratigraphic Record* (Malibu, 1979; *BM* 10) 42-83.

[87] M. van Loon, "First Results of the 1974 and 1975 Excavations at Selenkahiye near Meskene, Syria," *AAAS* 27-28 (1975-76) 165-185, and "1974 and 1975 Preliminary Results of the Excavations at Selenkahiye Near Meskene, Syria," in Freedman, *Tabqa* (1979) 97-113.

[88] R.H. Dornemann, "Tell Hadidi: A Millennium of Bronze Age City Occupation," in Freedman, *Tabqa* (1979) 113-151, and "Tell Hadidi: an Important Center of the Mitannian Period and Earlier," in Margueron, *Moyen Euphrate* (1980) 217-234.

[89] van Loon, "Selenkahiye" (1977) 111.

[90] Dornemann, "Tell Hadidi" (1987) 13-42.

[91] See e.g., P. Parr, "The Origins of the Rampart Fortifications of Middle Bronze Age Palestine and Syria," *ZDPV* 84 (1968) 18-45.

[92] M. Fortin, "Rapport préliminaire sur la seconde campagne de fouilles à Tell ᵓAtij et la première à Tell Gudeda (Automne 1987), sur le Moyen Euphrate," *Syria* 67 (1988) 219-256.

[93] Earlier reports on this site include T.A. Holland, "Preliminary Report on Excavations at Tell es-Sweyhat, Syria, 1973-4," *Levant* 8 (1976) 36-70, and his "Preliminary Report on Excavations at Tell es-Sweyhat, Syria 1975," *Levant* 9 (1977) 36-65.

By as early as the mid-third millennium BCE, the Khabur region was populated by the Hurrians, a major ethnic group firmly rooted in the Mesopotamian tradition.[94] In fact, the Hurrian texts reflect a wholly indigenous scribal tradition with autonomy from the south.[95] One of these Hurrian sites was Tell Chuera on the Khabur, which had striking similarities with the Sumerian south.[96] It showed evidence of the large stone architecture of this period, as well as a well-defined upper and lower citadel, typical of many of the northern Syrian centers. Judging from the absence of Uruk period occupation, it is apparent that this site was founded during this period.[97] Another nearby Hurrian center in the last quarter of the millennium appears to have been Tell Barri.[98]

There were other large Khabur region sites in this period, including Tell Mozan, a mound which has the traditional upper and lower citadels.[99] Thus far, a city wall and one of the largest bent-axis temple structures datable to the Early Bronze age of Syria have been located on the high mound. The structure has walls 1.6 meter wide, in addition to a statue of a lion in a building interpreted as a cella.[100] It has been suggested that a Hurrian scribal tradition equivalent to Semitic Ebla may well have existed in this region.[101] Recent excavations have exposed two stratified cuneiform tablets at the site dated to the late third millennium BCE. They appear to be administrative tablets written in Akkadian, but with Hurrian, Sumerian, and Akkadian proper names.[102] In sum, Tell Mozan may have been

---

[94] On the Hurrians, see B. Hrouda, "Zum Problem der Hurriter," *MARI* 4 (1985) 595-613, and for North Syria in particular, M.C. Astour, "Les Hourrites en Syria du Nord: Rapport sommaire," *RHA* 36 (1978) 1-22. On third millennium BCE Hurrian inscriptions and writing, see A. Parrot and J. Nougayrol, "Un document de fondation hurrite," *RA* 42 (1948) 1-20, R.M. Whiting, "Tiš-atal of Nineveh and Babati, Uncle of Šu-Sin," *JCS* 28 (1976) 173-182, W.W. Hallo, "Simurrum and the Hurrian Frontier," *RHA* 36 (1978) 71-83, and idem, "Royal Titles from the Mesopotamian Periphery," *AnSt* 30 (1980) 189-195.

[95] G. Buccellati and M. Kelly-Buccellati, *Mozan 1: The Soundings of the First Two Seasons* (Malibu, 1988; *BM* 20) 31-35.

[96] A. Moortgat, *Tell Chuēra in Nordost-Syrien* (Köln, 1960ff.).

[97] W. Orthmann, "The Origin of Tell Chuera," in Weiss, *Origins of Cities* (1986) 69.

[98] See P.E. Pecorella, "The Italian Excavations at Tell Barri (Kaḫat)," in Eichler et al., *Tall al-Ḥamīdīya* 2 (1990) 48. For Tell Barri in the second millennium BCE, see idem, "Tell Barri/Kahat durante il II millennio," in P. Matthiae, M. van Loon, and H. Weiss, eds., *Resurrecting the Past: A Joint Tribute to Adnan Bounni* (Leiden, 1990) 259-275.

[99] Buccellati and Kelly-Buccellati, *Mozan 1* (1988), and M. Kelly-Buccellati, "Three Seasons of Excavation at Tell Mozan," in Eichler et al., *Tall al-Ḥamīdīya* 2 (1990) 119-132.

[100] See for this and other items, M. Kelly-Buccellati, "A New Third Millennium Sculpture from Mozan," in A. Leonard and B.B. Williams, eds., *Essays in Ancient Civilization Presented to Helene J. Kantor* (Chicago, 1989; *SAOC* 47) 149-155.

[101] See G. Wilhelm, *The Hurrians* (Warminster, 1989) 77-79, and Buccellati and Kelly-Buccellati, *Mozan 1* (1988) 31.

[102] See L. Milano, "Mozan 2: The Epigraphic Finds of the Sixth Season," *SMS* 5/1 (1991) 1-34.

a major Hurrian center.[103] The rise in urbanization in the Khabur region may be attributed to the advent of the Hurrian population.[104]

Near the border of Iraq on the Khabur plains of Syria is Tell Leilan.[105] Tell Leilan's material remains include elements of the Ubaid and Uruk period.[106] Moreover, its lower town shows evidence of third and second millennium BCE settlements, where a number of domestic units, drain filled alleys, and planned streets were encountered.[107] The lower town appears to have been built about 2600-2400 BCE, and the excavators have speculated that there was a profound social transformation that occurred soon after, changing Tell Leilan into a class based society.[108] Indeed, Harvey Weiss has noticed that many walled cities of the type of Tell Leilan (notably those at Tell Mozan, Tell Khoshi, and Tell Hamoùkar) were constructed at this time.[109] He also speculates that these cities were not formed through intimate contact with the southern centralized states (i.e., Sargonic Akkad), but were the result of an indigenous and autonomous process.[110] Indeed, the urbanization in this area may have prompted the southern kingdoms to move into the area during the Sargonic period.[111] Many of these walled towns were larger in size than their southern counterparts.[112] However, the social and economic forces behind this growth are not known.

2.4 The Old Syrian Period (2100-1600 BCE) (Middle Bronze Age)

In what has been termed the Old Syrian period (c. 2100-1600 BCE), Syria continued in the cultural tradition of close relations with the Mesopotamian south, with major political

[103] It has been speculated that Tell Mozan may be the site of ancient Urkiš, one of the major Hurrian capitals in the third millennium BCE; see Buccellati and Kelly-Buccellati, *Mozan 1* (1988) 31-35.

[104] See G. Buccellati, "'River Bank,' 'High Country,' and 'Pasture Land': The Growth of Nomadism on the Middle Euphrates and the Khabur," in Eichler et al., *Tall al-Ḥamīdīya* 2 (1990) 110.

[105] H. Weiss, "Tell Leilan on the Habur Plains of Syria," *BA* 48 (1985) 5-35, and idem et al., "1985 Excavations at Tell Leilan, Syria," *AJA* 94 (1990) 529-582.

[106] Weiss, "Origins" (1983) 42.

[107] H. Weiss, "Tell Leilan 1989: New Data for Mid-Third Millennium Urbanization and State Formation," *MDOG* 122 (1990) 193-218.

[108] H. Weiss, "'Civilizing' the Habur Plains: Mid-Third Millennium State Formation at Tell Leilan," in Matthiae et al., *Bounni* (1990) 387-407, idem, "Archaeology in Syria. Tell Leilan," *AJA* 95 (1991) 706, and D. Parayre, "The Ninevite 5 Period Seal Impressions Retrieved at Tell Leilan in 1987," in Weiss, ed., *The Origins of North Mesopotamian Civilization: Ninevite 5 Chronology, Economy, Society* (New Haven, forthcoming).

[109] H. Weiss, "The Origins of Tell Leilan and the Conquest of Space in Third Millennium Mesopotamia," in idem, *Origins of Cities* (1986) 83. As early as 1963, W.J. van Liere ("Capitals and citadels of Bronze-Iron Age Syria in their relationship to land and water," *AAAS* 13 [1963] 114-115) speculated that these walled towns were not densely occupied, but were protected encampments for pastoralists.

[110] Weiss, "Space" (1986) 98.

[111] H. Weiss, "Third Millennium Urbanization: A Perspective from Tell Leilan," in Eichler et al., *Tall al-Ḥamīdīya* 2 (1990) 163.

[112] Weiss, "Shubat Enlil" (1985) 269.

centers at Mari, Tell Leilan, Terqa, Damascus,[113] and Yamkhad (modern Aleppo). Our main evidence for the early portion of this period (c. 2100-2000 BCE) emanates from the Sumerian Ur III dynasty.[114] Although Amorite presence in Syria (and Mesopotamia) in this and earlier periods is well documented,[115] there is little evidence of Ur III contact with Syria[116] (although western Syria still had close relations with Egypt, similar to the previous Early Bronze age[117]). This is, in part, demonstrated by Owen's cataloging of 67 archival texts which mention Syrian cities and their representatives in Ur III archival sources. This number is strikingly small when considered in light of the abundant Ur III documentation. There is evidence, of course, of contact between Mari and Sumer during this period.[118] Owen notes that neither epigraphic documentation for Ur III and Syrian relations, nor archaeological evidence of Ur III occupation in Syria exist.[119] In fact, no Syrian site to date shows any significant material remains during this dynasty,[120] and no Ur III monarchs record military involvement in the area.[121] It is likely, moreover, that many of the Syrian city states suffered destruction during this era.[122] Thus, there are hardly any references to Syria (except for the Amorites) in the Ur III archives. Owen does list these references to Syrian personal names listed with specific Syrian cities, which contributes to the early evidence for a Semitic presence in Syria.[123]

Subsequent to the fall of Ur (c. 2000 BCE), there is indication of the emergence of a number of powerful states in both Syria and Iraq. The best known of these in Syria is Mari, a fundamental center in the third millennium BCE, which continued to have cultural

---

[113] See W.T. Pitard, *Ancient Damascus: A Historical Study of the Syrian City-State from Earliest Times Until its Fall to the Assyrians in 732 B.C.E.* (Winona Lake, 1987) 27-48.

[114] For an overview of Syrians mentioned in Ur III economic sources, see D. Owen's contribution to this volume. This work is a revision of the research in appendices I-II of (co-authored with R. Veenker) "Me-Gum, the First Ur III Ensi of Ebla," in L. Cagni, ed., *Ebla 1975-1985* (Napoli, 1987) 276-286.

[115] E.g., see G. Buccellati, *The Amorites of the Ur III Period* (Napoli, 1966).

[116] See Owen and Veenker, "Me-Gum" (1987) 263-275, and J. Bottéro, "Syria During the Third Dynasty of Ur," *CAH*³ I/2 (1971) 559-566.

[117] G. Posener, "Syria and Palestine *c.* 2160-1780 B.C.: Relations with Egypt," *CAH*³ I/2 (1971) 532-558.

[118] See Gelb, "Mari" (1992) 121-202, although, as Owen notes, the identification of the Kiš of the Ebla and Mari texts may not be the Babylonian Kiš (see, e.g., P. Michalowski, "Third Millennium Contacts: Observations on the Relationships between Mari and Ebla," *JAOS* 105 [1985] 293-302. Michalowski became convinced, however, that his skepticism concerning Kiš was exaggerated, p. 298, n. 44). Also cf. F. Pomponio, "Exit Kiš dagli orizzonti di Ebla," *Mesopotamia*ᵀ 25 (1990) 175-184.

[119] Both Mallowan ("Brak and Chagar Bazar" ([1947] 69) and C.J. Gadd ("Tablets from Chagar Bazar and Tall Brak, 1937-38," *Iraq* 7 [1940] 61) claimed Ur III presence at Tell Brak, but this has been re-evaluated by Weiss ("Shubat Enlil" [1985] 269-270).

[120] See S. Mazzoni, "Elements of the Ceramic Culture of Early Syrian Ebla in Comparison with Syro-Palestinian EB IV," *BASOR* 257 (1985) 1-18.

[121] See P. Michalowski, "Foreign Tribute to Sumer during the Ur III Period," *ZA* 68 (1978) 45. Gudea did claim to have trade connections with western Syria (See Owen, "Syrians" 5).

[122] See Owen and Veenker, "Me-Gum" (1987) 275 n. 41, Matthiae, *Empire* (1981) 111, and Mazzoni, "Ceramic Culture" (1985) 16 n. 11.

[123] Owen, "Syrians" 114-115.

relations with the south into the next era. It was a major Amorite political power in the early part of the Old Babylonian period (c. 2000-1760 BCE), controlling the middle Euphrates and Khabur river valleys. Vast epigraphic remains have been discovered in the palace archives,[124] which provide us with extensive information concerning nomadism and tribal life,[125] as well as a large corpus of correspondence by feminine writers, virtually unknown in other archives in Syro-Mesopotamia.[126] Ḫammurapi of Babylon destroyed Mari (c. 1760 BCE), bringing its years of power to an end.

There is evidence of occupation at Ebla during this period. A large sacred area has been discovered in the northwestern region of the lower town.[127] A related massive rectangular terrace with stone courses, which may have been a cult terrace, was also found in this area. However, the kingdom of Yamkhad, with its capital at Ḫalab (modern Aleppo), succeeded Ebla in this period and controlled the rich agricultural region bordering the Orontes river. The area was populated by the Amorites, known primarily from the Mari texts. Vassal states existed in Emar, Alalakh, Ugarit, and Carchemish.[128] According to one text from Mari, Yamkhad was more powerful than even Babylon or Larsa, and had a privileged position for trading relations.[129] The Mari letters also depict Qatna and Amurru as being major kingdoms in surrounding areas in this period.[130]

Tell Leilan was a major 'Assyrian' center (Šubat-Enlil[131]) at this time, ruled by Šamši-Adad I (1814-1781 BCE). It is evident that during his reign, the upper Khabur triangle emerged for the first time as a dominant power. The area had not previously been

---

[124] See *Archives royales de Mari* (Paris, 1950ff), and lately, *Mari annales de recherches interdisciplinaires* (Paris, 1982ff.).

[125] J.-R. Kupper, *Les nomades en Mésopotamie au temps des rois de Mari* (Paris, 1956), and J.T. Luke, "Pastoralism and Politics in the Mari Period: A Re-examination of the Character and Political Significance of the Major West Semitic Tribal Groups on the Middle Euphrates, ca. 1828-1758 B.C." (Ph.D. diss., University of Michigan, 1965).

[126] Two important works on this subject are: B.F. Batto, *Studies on Women at Mari* (Baltimore, 1974), and W.H.Ph. Römer, *Frauenbreife über Religion, Politik und Privatleben in Mari* (Kevelaer, 1971; *AOAT* 12).

[127] P. Matthiae, "Mardikh/Ebla," in Weiss, "Archaeology in Syria" (1991) 709.

[128] See G. Dossin, "Le royaume d'Alep au XVIIIe siècle avant notre ère d'après les 'Archives de Mari,'" *Académie royale de Belgique, Bulletin de la Classe des Lettres et des Sciences Morales et Politiques, 5e Série* 38 (1952) 229-239; C.L. Woolley, *A Forgotten Kingdom* (Harmondsworth, 1953) 66-85; S. Smith, "Yarim-Lim of Yamḫad," *RSO* 32 (1957) 155-184, and H. Klengel, "Ḫalab," *RLA* 4 (1975) 50-53.

[129] See G. Dossin, "Les Archives épistolaires du Palais de Mari," *Syria* 19 (1938) 117.

[130] For Qatna, see G. Dossin, "Iamḫad et Qatanum," *RA* 36 (1939) 46-54 and "Le royaume de Qatna au XVIIIe siècle avant notre ère d'après les 'Archives royales de Mari,'" *Académie royale de Belgique, Bulletin de la Classe des Lettres et des Sciences Morales et Politiques, 5e Série* 40 (1954) 417-425. The site has also been excavated; see R. Du Mesnil du Buisson, *Le site archéologique de Mishrifé/Qaṭna* (Paris, 1935). For Carchemish, see G. Dossin, "Aplaḫanda, roi de Carkémiš," *RA* 35 (1938) 115-121; for Amurru, see I. Singer, "A Concise History of Amurru," in S. Izre'el, *Amurru Akkadian*, Vol. 2 (Atlanta, 1991) 135-195. For a general survey of the area, see J.-R. Kupper, "Northern Mesopotamia and Syria," *CAH*[3] II/1 (1973) 1-41.

[131] The identification of Tell Leilan as Šubat-Enlil is generally accepted; see D. Charpin, "Šubat-Enlil et le pays d'Apum," *MARI* 5 (1987) 129-140; Weiss, "Shubat Enlil" (1985) 269-292; R.M. Whiting, "Tell Leilan/Šubat-Enlil: Chronological Problems and Perspectives," in Eichler et al., *Tall al-Ḥamīdīya* 2 (1990) 167-218, and idem, "The Tell Leilan Tablets: A Preliminary Report," in Weiss et al., "1985 Excavations" (1990) 573-575.

integrated into a unified political system; thus his reign marked a political watershed.[132] However, soon after his reign, the area reverted back to small, relatively independent and unintegrated city states, much like the political networks of the third millennium BCE.[133] One of these independent centers was Kaḫat.[134] Much of the Khabur region continued to be occupied by the Hurrians,[135] a fact evidenced, in part, by a large corpus of Hurrian names in texts at Tell Chagar Bazar.[136]

Later in this period Tell Ashara/Terqa acquired importance.[137] There is a body of epigraphic and architectural documentation (a temple complex, an administrative complex, and private houses) coming from this site datable to the so-called 'dark age' between the fall of Mari (c. 1760 BCE) and Babylon (c. 1595 BCE). At this time, Terqa was most likely the capital of the kingdom of Khana on the middle Euphrates. The most recent excavations at Terqa have focused primarily upon Area F, where a large administrative complex testifying to scribal activity has been encountered.[138] Near the original summit of the mound, a large public building has been uncovered and found to contain thus far over thirty Khana period tablets forcing a reevaluation of Khana chronology.[139] Terqa may have remained under Babylonian control during the reigns of Ammiṣaduqa and Samsuditana.[140] The kingdom appears to have been governed by several previously unknown kings bearing Hurrian names, showing that it subsequently passed under Mitanni control in the next period (after 1600 BCE).

During the Old Syrian period, there was an increase in scribal activity, not only at the

---

[132] For the reign of Šamši-Adad I, see M. Anbar, "Le début du règne de Šamši-Addu Ier," *IOS* 3 (1973) 1-33, and P. Garelli, "Les pouvoirs locaux en Assyrie," in A. Finet, ed., *Les pouvoirs locaux en Mésopotamie et dans les regions adjacentes* (Bruxelles, 1982) 76-91. For his importance in the Khabur area, see D.J. Meijer, "An Archaeological Surface Survey: Some Assumptions and Ideas," in Eichler et al., *Tall al-Ḥamīdīya* 2 (1990) 32, and Weiss, "Shubat Enlil" (1985) 269.

[133] Meijer, "Surface Survey" (1990) 41; Kupper, "Northern Mesopotamia" (1973) 29, and Charpin, "Šubat-Enlil" (1987) 136. For a survey of the sites in the Khabur region in this period, see D. Oates, "Walled Cities in Northern Mesopotamia in the Mari Period," *MARI* 4 (1985) 585-594.

[134] See D. Charpin, "A Contribution to the Geography and History of the Kingdom of Kaḫat," in Eichler et al., *Tall al-Ḥamīdīya* 2 (1990) 67-85.

[135] See J.M. Sasson, "Ḫurrians and Ḫurrian Names in the Mari Texts," *UF* 6 (1974) 353-400.

[136] See C.J. Gadd, "Tablets from Chagar Bazar, 1936," *Iraq* 4 (1937) 178-185; idem, "Tablets 1937-1938" (1940) 22-61, O. Loretz, "Texte aus Chagar Bazar," in *Lišān mitḫurti* (1969) 199-260 and his *Texte aus Chagar Bazar und Tell Brak, Teil 1* (Kevelaer, 1969; *AOAT* 3/1).

[137] See G. Buccellati and M. Kelly-Buccellati et al., *Terqa Preliminary Reports* (Malibu, 1977ff.; *SMS* 1ff.) and *Terqa 10* (1979). Concerning the epigraphic remains of Terqa, see O. Rouault, *Terqa Final Reports No. 1: L'Archive de Puzurum* (Malibu, 1984; *BM* 16). A recent synthesis of the second millennium BCE Terqa material can be found in G. Buccellati, "The Kingdom and Period of Khana," *BASOR* 270 (1988) 43-61, and A. Podany, *Kings of Ḫana: An Analysis of their Time and Place in Syro-Mesopotamian History* (Malibu, *BM*, forthcoming).

[138] See O. Rouault, "Terqa," in Weiss, "Archaeology in Syria" (1991) 727-729.

[139] A new Khana text, apparently contemporary with Tukulti-Ninurta I of Assyria (1244-1208 BCE), has been published by H.M. Kümmel: "Ein Kaufvertrag aus Ḫana mit mittelassyrischer *līmu*-Datierung," *ZA* 79 (1989) 191-200.

[140] However, see the contrary discussion in Buccellati, "Khana" (1987) 46-49.

sites of Terqa and Mari, but also at Tell Chagar Bazar.[141] Along with Sumerian and Akkadian, Hurrian literary productivity was also evident in Syria, even at Mari.[142] The independent Syrian literary contribution in this period appears to have been confined to ritual texts, primarily from Mari,[143] while the sole Sumerian literary text for all of Syria in this period is a previously unknown recension of the Sumerian King List, found at Tell Leilan.[144]

2.5 The Middle Syrian Period: The International Age (1600-1200 BCE) (Late Bronze Age)

The Hittite invasion of Babylon (c. 1595 BCE) changed the political climate of Syria. The region suffered domination from both Egypt and Anatolia (Hittites), endured a major Hurrian dynasty in the Khabur region (Mitanni), in addition to nomadic pressure and sedentarization from especially the Arameans (1600-1200 BCE).[145]

Arising out of the ruins of Babylon, the Hurrians (kingdom of Mitanni) became a major force in the Khabur region, as Syria was unified for the first time since Šamši-Adad I.[146] Tell Fakhariyah, near the headwaters of the Khabur, was probably a Hurrian capital of the Mitannian kingdom in this period.[147] Another important Mitanni center along the middle Euphrates was Tell Hadidi (ancient Azu), where a number of legal documents from this period were found,[148] as well as Taᵓidu, which may have been the ancient name of Tell Brak in this period.[149] Tell Hamidi also shows this evidence by the exposure of a Mitanni palace.[150]

Hittite presence is amply attested from the early 14th century BCE with the advent of the reign of Šuppiluliuma I, and his conquest of the primarily Syrian state of Mitanni.[151] The Syrian archives from both Ugarit and the recently excavated texts from Emar have shed

---

[141] As Hallo notes, "Syrian Contribution" 77.

[142] This was known as early as F. Thureau-Dangin, "Tablettes ḫourittes provenant de Mâri," *RA* 36 (1933) 1-28.

[143] Hallo, "Syrian Contribution" 80, and cf. A. Tsukimoto, *Untersuchungen zur Totenpflege (kispum) im alten Mesopotamien* (Kevelaer, 1985; *AOAT* 216).

[144] See C. Vincente, "Tell Leilan Recension of the Sumerian King List," *NABU* 1990/11 8-9.

[145] See H.S. Sader, *Les états araméens de Syrie depuis leur fondation jusqu'à leur transformation en provinces assyriennes* (Beirut, 1987).

[146] For a general survey of the Mitanni kingdom, see M. Drower, "Syria *c.* 1550-1400 B.C.," *CAH*[3] II/1 (1973) 417-436.

[147] C.W. McEwan et al., *Soundings at Tell Fakhariyah* (Chicago, 1958; *OIP* 79). For the internal organization of the Mitanni kingdom, see, for example, R. O'Callaghan, *Aram Naharaim: A Contribution to the History of Upper Mesopotamia in the Second Millennium B.C.* (Roma, 1948; *AnOr* 26) 51-92, and for Mitanni history, see Wilhelm, *Hurrians* (1989) 20-41.

[148] Dornemann, "Tell Hadidi" (1977) 144-149.

[149] D. Oates, "Tell Brak: The Mitanni Palace and Temple," in Eichler et al., *Tall al-Ḥamīdīya* 2 (1990) 156.

[150] M. Wäfler, "The Excavations at Tell Hamidi," in Eichler et al., *Tall al-Ḥamīdīya* 2 (1990) 219-228. Also see Eichler et al., *Tall al-Ḥamīdīya* 1 (1984).

[151] This is the subject of G. Beckman's article in this volume. For a general survey of Hittite involvement in Syria, see A. Goetze, "The Hittites and Syria (1300-1200 B.C.)," *CAH*[3] II/2 (1975) 252-273.

light on how the Hittites provided administrative rule in this area. These archives are especially important, since the primary Syrian centers in the Hittite period (e.g., Carchemish, Ḫalab [Aleppo], and Waššukkanni) have not revealed such documents. As Gary Beckman states, the Hittites used diverse tactics of rule for various parts of Syria, giving some autonomy to the previously existing governmental structures that they encountered.[152] The site of Carchemish was the seat of a secondary line of the Hittite royal house which directly administered the affairs of Syria. The Hittites also retained a ring of buffer kingdoms which included a smaller version of the kingdom of Mitanni, whose primary function was to defend against the Assyrian frontier.[153] Other buffer states included the kingdom of Aštata (including the city of Emar) to guard against a Babylonian threat (a number of sites in the surrounding area were evidently military stations and frontier posts[154]), Amurru in the west (to defend against Egyptian presence[155]), and Tell Atchana/Alalakh.[156] In fact, the Hittite state grew through this association of vassal states, rather than by intimate involvement in the affairs of Syria itself, which would have taken a great deal of manpower.[157] The vassal states had certain obligations to the Hittites (not unlike the Roman clients more than one millennium later[158]), including tribute and military assistance.[159] There was, however, no uniform system of government in Hittite-ruled Syria. The native authorities were allowed to conduct their own economic and internal political affairs, as long as tribute continued to arrive.[160]

The Hittites certainly were influential in the political and bureaucratic sphere in Syria in the last two centuries of this period. However, the channels of cultural influence were not one-sided. Syrian influence in Ḫatti is readily attested in many areas, including resettled Syrian colonists, imported royalty, political refugees, foreign diplomats, and skilled craftsmen.[161] Numerous Syrian personal names are also attested in Ḫatti,[162] in addition to Hurrian and Semitic words. In fact, Harry Hoffner has deduced a 'Hittite-Hurrian cultural symbiosis.'[163] Many foreign objects were introduced into Syria, especially

---

[152] G. Beckman, "Hittite Administration in Syria in the Light of the Texts from Ḫattuša, Ugarit, and Emar," p. 49.

[153] See A. Harrak, *Assyria and Hanigalbat* (Hildesheim, 1987).

[154] Beckman, "Hittite Administration" 44.

[155] See Klengel, *Geschichte Syriens* II (1969) 156-177.

[156] The Alalakh excavations have revealed numerous documents from this period. C.L. Woolley wrote the final report of the excavations at Alalakh: *Alalakh: An Account of the Excavations at Tell Atchana in the Hatay 1937-49* (Oxford, 1955), and his more popular account, *A Forgotten Kingdom* (1953). Much of Woolley's chronology has been reevaluated by M. Gates, "Alalakh Levels VI and V: A Chronological Reassessment," *SMS* 4 (1981) 11-50. The documents from Alalakh have been published in D.J. Wiseman, *The Alalakh Tablets* (London, 1953).

[157] Beckman, "Hittite Administration" 44-45.

[158] See E. Badian, *Foreign Clientelae (264-70 B.C.)* (Oxford, 1958).

[159] Beckman, "Hittite Administration" 45.

[160] Ibid., 49.

[161] Which is the subject of Hoffner's contribution to this volume, especially pp. 90-94.

[162] See E. Laroche, *Les noms des Hittites* (Paris, 1966).

[163] H. Hoffner, "Cultural Influence" 95.

innovations in weaponry.[164] The Hittite cuneiform script came from the east and was adapted to write this Indo-European language. This literary influence can especially be seen in their historiographic (the description of the king's campaigns) and religious literature.[165] The Hittite law codes, the Hurro-Hittite bilingual texts, and even the Hittite pantheon showed close connections with Syria. Many Hittite dynasts had Hurrian personal names. Hoffner concludes that few areas of Anatolian life remained impervious to Syrian cultural influences.[166]

One of these influential Syrian cities was Ugarit, a major trading post on the Mediterranean coast which was tributary to Ḫatti.[167] The art and architecture of this site is clearly different from that found in earlier Syrian excavations, providing evidence of an independent cultural tradition.[168] The documents from Ugarit have given the first attested picture of a Syrian center, showing that the scribes of Ugarit were multi-lingual, since texts in numerous languages and scripts were found. In terms of literature, scribal schools and learning were again paramount in Syria, particularly in its western portion.[169] The writing system at Ugarit featured an alphabetic cuneiform script.[170] The site also had a cuneiform scribal school.[171] This writing system, along with the Proto-Siniatic material, are the oldest known alphabetic scripts. Many literary texts found at Ugarit are completely unattested elsewhere.[172] As Hallo states, the extensive material from Ugarit is arguably derivative from Mesopotamia in great part, but adapted to the needs of the Syrian student population.[173] In sum, much of Syrian cuneiform literature in all periods was in fact derivative from Mesopotamia, but with many specific unique characteristics of its own.[174]

Although much of Syria was under political domination by Ḫatti in the latter part of this period (from the reign of Šuppiluliuma I), Syria still had many thriving centers other than Ugarit with independent cultural traditions. One of these centers was Emar. This site has become a 'second Ebla' in many respects because of its nearly 2000 tablets and fragments dating to the latter part of Middle Syrian period.[175] The variety of cuneiform

[164] Ibid., 97-98.

[165] The Kumarbi myth cycle, see ibid., 99, n. 61.

[166] Ibid., 106.

[167] See M. Liverani, *Storia di Ugarit nell'età degli archivi politici* (Roma, 1962; *SS* 6).

[168] The publications of the excavations at Ugarit are too numerous to recount in their entirety. C. Shaeffer, the primary excavator, published a number of preliminary reports in *Syria* (1929ff.) and *AAS* (presently *AAAS*) 1929ff. Final reports have been published in *Ugaritica* (Paris, 1939ff.).

[169] Hallo, "Syrian Contribution" 80.

[170] There are numerous works on Ugaritic literature, culture, and the alphabetic script, including various articles in *Ugarit Forschungen* 1ff. (Kevelaer, 1968ff.). For Ugaritic history, see Liverani, *Storia di Ugarit* (1962).

[171] J. Krecher, "Schreiberschulung in Ugarit: Die Tradition von Listen und sumerischen Texten," *UF* 1 (1969) 131-158.

[172] Hallo, "Syrian Contribution" 81-82.

[173] Ibid., 82.

[174] See the discussion, ibid., 87-88.

[175] See D. Arnaud for the Sumero-Akkadian texts: *Recherches au Pays d'Aštata: Emar VI.1-4. Les textes sumériens et accadiens* (Paris, 1985-87); "Les textes d'Emar et la chronologie de la fin du Bronze Récent," *Syria*

documentation at Emar includes Akkadian legal texts, letters, and ritual texts,[176] as well as some Hittite and Hurrian medical and divination texts. Daniel Fleming notes that over 400 ritual texts were discovered in a scribal center in Temple M_1 at Emar,[177] nearly half of which describe apparently indigenous Emarite religious practices not attested in archives in Anatolia or Mesopotamia.[178] Of course, there is evidence of Hittite presence at Emar, especially in regards to architecture.[179] But, as Fleming maintains, there was apparently no influx of Hittite population and the culture was not deeply affected by their political and bureaucratic presence.[180] Moreover, the Akkadian usage at Emar reflects many idioms not recognized in Mesopotamia proper.[181] Most likely, the Mesopotamian features were assimilated into the local traditions. The most unique of the Emar ritual texts are the festivals,[182] which expose local middle Euphrates religious practice. Emar thus reflected a local late second millennium BCE Syrian tradition, which, as Fleming notes, is more complex than just indigenous or foreign, but a mixture of the two.[183] The harvest of literary texts from Emar (omina, incantations, rituals, wisdom literature, etc.) is in fact richer than at Ugarit.[184] But clearly, many Mesopotamian texts were embellished with a local color.[185]

At the end of this period, much of eastern Syria came under control of Assyria and was given the name of Ḫanigalbat.[186] Numerous sites in Syria have produced textual information concerning the reigns of many of the middle Assyrian kings, especially Šalmaneser I (1273-1244 BCE). These sites include Tell Fray,[187] over 600 texts and

52 (1975) 89-92, and G. Bunnens, "Emar on the Euphrates in the 13th Century B.C.," *AbN* 27 (1989) 23-36. For the Hurrian texts, see E. Laroche, "Emar, étape entre Babylone et le Hatti," in Margueron, *Moyen Euphrate* (1980) 239-244. For the excavations at Emar, see J.-C. Margueron, "Les fouilles françaises de Meskéné-Émar (Syrie)," *CRAIBL* 1975 201-213; "Quatre campagnes de fouilles à Emar (1972-1974): un bilan provisoire," *Syria* 52 (1975) 53-85; "Rapport préliminaire sur les deux premières campagnes de fouilles à Meskéné-Emar (1972-1973)," *AAAS* 25 (1975) 73-86, and "Rapport préliminaire sur les 3ᵉ, 4ᵉ, 5ᵉ, et 6ᵉ campagnes de fouilles à Meskéné-Emar," *AAAS* 32 (1982) 233-249.

[176] D. Arnaud, "La bibliothèque d'un devin syrien à Meskéné-Emar (Syrie)," *CRAIBL* 1980 375-388.

[177] D. Fleming, "Rituals from Emar" 52-54.

[178] Ibid., 53.

[179] J.-C. Margueron, "Emar: Un exemple d'implantation hittite en terre syrienne," in idem, *Moyen Euphrate* (1980) 287-304.

[180] Fleming, "Rituals from Emar" 55.

[181] Ibid., 57.

[182] Ibid., 58.

[183] Ibid., 61.

[184] Hallo, "Syrian Contribution" 84.

[185] Ibid., 84.

[186] See E.F. Weidner, "Assyrien und Hanigalbat," *Ug* 6 (1969) 519-531, and Harrak, *Assyria and Hanigalbat* (1987).

[187] For the excavations at Tell Fray, see A. Bounni and P. Matthiae, "Tell Fray, ville frontière entre hittites et assyriens au XIIIᵉ siècle av. J.C.," *Archéologica* 140 (1980) 30-39, and P. Matthiae, "Ittiti ed Assiri a Tell Fray: Lo scavo di una città Medio-Siriana sull-Eufrate," *SMEA* 22 (1980) 35-51.

fragments from Tell Sheikh Hamad,[188] Tell Fakhariyah,[189] and Tell Amuda.[190] These exhibit a sophisticated Assyrian administrative presence in the area.

2.6 The Advent of the Neo-Syrian Period (1200-900 BCE) (Iron Age)

The end of the Bronze Age witnessed a Syria subjected to destruction and fragmentation. This continued for at least four centuries until the rise of imperial Assyria. However, the first millennium BCE also continued the tradition of close relations with Mesopotamia proper. Although much of Syria continued to be subject to Assyrian domination, it was successful in retaining its cultural autonomy. This can be seen, in part, in the discovery of a large life-size basalt statue at Tell Fakhariyah, reflecting the same tradition of Assyrian statues of this period. It is unique because of a bilingual inscription on the statue, two-thirds of which is in Akkadian (Assyrian dialect), and one-third in ancient Aramaic, making it the oldest attested Aramaic inscription known.[191] Further west, there was a group of Syro-Hittite kingdoms,[192] although Assyrian influence was also felt there, as shown by the excavations at Tell Ahmar[193] and Arslan Tash.[194]

3. Prospects

At present, there are over sixty ongoing research projects in Syria, many of which contain material remains from the periods discussed in this article.[195] There are a number of third millennium BCE period salvage operations in progress, including the Tishreen Dam Salvage Project in the northern Euphrates region south of Carchemish[196] and the salvage

[188] For the excavations at Tell Sheikh Hamad, see H. Kühne, "Vorläufiger Bericht über die erste Grabungskampagne auf dem Tall Šeḫ Ḫamad am Unteren Ḫabur," *Akkadica* 10 (1978) 16-23; "Tall Šēḫ Ḫamad/Dūr-Katlimmu, die Wiederentdeckung einer mittelassyrischen Stadt," *DamM* 1 (1983) 149-163; "Tell Šeḫ Ḫamad/Dur katlimmu: The Assyrian Provincial Capital in the Mohafazat Deir Az-Zor," *AAAS* 34 (1984) 160-179, and "Gedanken zur historischen und städtebaulichen Entwicklung der assyrischen Stadt Dūr-katlimmu," in Matthiae et al., *Bounni* (1990) 153-169.

[189] For the cuneiform texts at Tell Fakhariyah, see H.G. Güterbock, "The Cuneiform Tablets," in McEwan et al., *Tell Fakhariyah* (1958) 86-90, pls. 77-86.

[190] For the tablets reputed to have come from Tell Amuda, see P. Machinist, "Provincial Governance in Middle Assyria and Some New Texts from Yale," *Assur* 3/2 (1982) 67-76.

[191] A. Abou-Assaf et al., *La statue de Tell Fekherye et son inscription bilingue assyro-araméene* (Paris, 1982).

[192] See J.D. Hawkins, "The Neo-Hittite States in Syria and Anatolia," *CAH*^{2} III/1 (1982) 372-441.

[193] For Tell Ahmar, see F. Thureau-Dangin et al., *Til-Barsib* (Paris, 1936), and for more recent work see G. Bunnens, "Tell Ahmar on the Euphrates. A New Research Project of the University of Melbourne," *Akkadica* 63 (1989) 1-11, and idem, ed., *Tell Ahmar: 1988 Season* (Leiden, 1990; *AbN* Supplement 2).

[194] For Arslan Tash, see F. Thureau-Dangin et al., *Arslan-Tash* (Paris, 1931).

[195] See H. Weiss, "Archaeology in Syria," *AJA* 95 (1991) 683-740, and "Archaeology in Syria," *AJA* 97 (1993; forthcoming). Other publications which periodically include up-to-date summaries of excavations in Syria include *AfO*, *AAAS*, and *Syria*, in addition to the new publication *Orient Express, notes et nouvelles d'archéologie orientale* (Paris, 1991ff.).

[196] See T. McClellan and A. Porter, "Archaeological Surveys of the Tishreen Dam Flood Zone," *AAAS*

area in the middle Khabur region.[197] Among the previously mentioned sites that are continuing to be excavated are Ebla, Mari, Tell Mozan, Tell Hammam et-Turkman, Ugarit, Tell Barri, Tell Brak, Tell Chuera, and Tell Sheikh Hamad, in addition to many others. The rich archaeological harvests that are continuing in Syria will indeed expand the horizons of our understanding of the emergent field of ancient Syrian history.

(forthcoming), and T. McClellan et al., "The Tishreen Salvage Excavations, 1989," *AAAS* (forthcoming).

[197] Monchambert, "Prospection" (1984) 181-218.

THE DATE OF THE DESTRUCTION OF PALACE G AT EBLA[1]

Michael C. Astour

When one speaks of Ebla, one usually has in mind the flourishing period of its history which is covered by its rich cuneiform archives. The study of its numerous texts published or cited by now has allowed us to form an approximate but progressively clearer image of the geographical extent of Ebla's domination,[2] of its economy, and of the outlines of its internal history. One of several controversial problems in interpreting the written and material evidence of Ebla is the place of the age of archives within the absolute chronology of the ancient Near East. This is not a mere question of punctiliousness; without a convincing solution of the problem one cannot obtain a correct notion of Ebla's interrelation with the states of Mesopotamia, in the first place with the Sargonic empire.

The age of the Ebla archives—or, in archaeological terms, the Mardikh IIB1 period—is coterminous with the existence of the great royal palace G.[3] Its lower limit is the conflagration, total destruction, and abandonment of that palace. (This disaster saved for us the tablets stacked in the palace which would have otherwise been dumped at the next renovation or rebuilding of the edifice.) The tablets were written during the reigns of Igriš-Ḫalam, Irkab-Damu, and Išʾar-Damu and the administration of their seconds-in-command (to whom Archi gave the conventional title "vizier") Arennum, Ibrium, and Ibbi-Zikir.[4] These three reigns and tenures were not short ones, for they coincided with five, or at the least four and a half, reigns at Mari. Moreover, both the last king of Ebla and his "vizier" had, toward

[1] This paper is a preliminary version of section 7 of my "An Outline of the History of Ebla," the first part of which (sections 1-6) is to appear in *Eblaitica* 3 (1992) 3-82 and will be referred to hereinafter as Astour, "Outline".

[2] See Astour, "The Geographical and Political Structure of the Ebla Empire," in H. Waetzoldt and H. Hauptmann, eds., *Wirtschaft und Gesellschaft von Ebla* (Heidelberg, 1988; *HSAO* 2) 139-158. A revised map of Northern Syria and Osrhoene in the age of the Ebla archives will be presented in Part II of the study mentioned in the note above.

[3] P. Matthiae, *Ebla: An Empire Rediscovered* (Garden City, 1981) 53.

[4] The revised picture of Eblean kingship and "vizierate" at the time of the archives, mainly due to the analysis by A. Archi and F. Pomponio, is summarized, with pertaining references, in Astour, "Outline" 24-26.

the end of the period, adult sons who were groomed as their prospective successors. We are dealing, thus, with four generations, i.e., from eighty to a hundred years.[5]

Another determinant is the certitude that the tablets of Ebla formed a "living" archive and not a "dead" one.[6] There was no gap of any length between the time of the accumulation of the archival materials and the destruction of Palace G. Twenty-two large tablets, of the type of monthly reports, were found in the Court of Audiences upon charred remains of wooden tables on which they had been placed for drying prior to being transferred to one of the rooms of the palatial archives. They all come from the "vizierate" of Ibbi-Zikir and their prosopography is not different from that of analogous documents already stacked inside the palace. This has been rightly stressed by Matthiae and Archi.[7]

The Ebla texts have yielded no datable synchronisms with Mesopotamian rulers attested in other cuneiform sources. Of the six pre-Sargonic kings of Mari whose names appear on votive objects in local temples, only Iblul-Il is mentioned—prominently so—at Ebla.[8] But his chronological position is not known, and it is, on the contrary, the Ebla documentation which establishes his place in the sequence of seven Mariote kings, six of whom are not mentioned in the epigraphic material of their own city or anywhere else. Nevertheless, the correlation of those kings with the history of Ebla is important in a broader chronological context.[9]

---

[5] See the synchronistic table at the end of this paper.

[6] As noted by P.R.S. Moorey, "Abu Salabikh, Kish, Mari and Ebla: Mid-third Millennium Archaeological Interconnections," *AJA* 85 (1981) 448, with regard to the chronological correlation between Ebla and Mesopotamia, "the question to be answered is whether the Ebla archive was 'living' or 'dead'."

[7] P. Matthiae, "Carskij dvorec G v Èble i protosirijskie arxitekturnye tradicii" ("The Royal Palace G at Ebla and the Protosyrian Architectural Traditions"), in I.M. Diakonoff, ed., *Drevnjaja Èbla (Raskopki v Sirii) (Ancient Ebla [Excavations in Syria])* (Moscow, 1985) 39-40 (Note: This article is said to be the translation of Matthiae's paper at the symposium "La civiltà di Ebla: archeologia e filologia," Rome 1980. However, Matthiae's article under the same title, published in Italian in the first part of the proceedings of that symposium [P. Matthiae, "Il Palazzo Reale G di Ebla e la tradizione architettonica protosiriana," *SEb* 5 (1982) 75-92], differs considerably from the Russian text and does not contain the discussion of the tablets from the Court of Audiences and their importance for the chronology of the archive); A. Archi, "About the Organization of the Eblaite State," *SEb* 5 (1982) 204-205. Of the tablets from the Court of Audiences (L.2752), twenty-one have been published as *ARET* 8 (by E. Sollberger) and one as No. 4 of *ARET* 1 (by A. Archi).

[8] The names of five of these—Iku-Šamaš, Lamgi-Mari (or Iški-Mari), Iku-Šamagan, Asuka, and Iblul-Il—are inscribed on objects found in the temple of Ištar (A. Parrot, *Le temple d'Ishtar* [Paris, 1956; *MAM* 1] 68-70; F. Thureau-Dangin, "Inscriptions votives sur des statuettes votives de Ma'eri," *RA* 31 [1934] 137-144) and in the temples of Ištarat and Ninni-zaza (A. Parrot, *Les temples d'Ishtarat et de Ninni-zaza* [Paris, 1967; *MAM* 3], with a chapter on the inscriptions by G. Dossin, pp. 307-331; a new edition by M. Lambert, "Les inscriptions des temples d'Ishtarat et de Ninni-zaza," *RA* 64 [1970] 168-171). The name of the sixth king, Ikum-Mari, appears in an archaic inscription on a votive vessel published by M. Fales, "An Archaic Text from Mari," *MARI* 3 (1984) 269-270.

[9] We are not helped by the Sumerian King List (T. Jacobsen, *The Sumerian King List* [Chicago, 1939; *AS* 11]) which includes a Mari dynasty with six kings, differently placed in the WB and Su_1 versions and in a poor state of preservation. For an attempt to read there two Mariote royal names known from Ebla texts, see M.J. Geller, "The Lugal of Mari at Ebla and the Sumerian King List," *Eblaitica* 1 (1987) 141-145. According to a preliminary announcement by C. Vincente ("Tell Leilan Recension of the Sumerian King List," *NABU* 1990/11), an Old Babylonian recension of the Sumerian King List has been found at Tell Leilan and "it is the first text in which the names of the six Mari kings are legible." But these names have not been disclosed as of this writing. On the

The palace has, however, yielded two inscribed imported objects that can be dated more securely. One of them is represented by two fragments of a diorite lamp bearing the name of King Chephren (*Ḫ'fr'*) of the fourth dynasty, accompanied by his "Horus of Gold" name on one beak, his "Two Ladies" name on the other. The other object is the lid of an alabaster vessel with an inscription which includes the "Horus" name, the title "King of Upper and Lower Egypt," and the personal name of Pepi I of the sixth dynasty. Both items were found *in situ*, on the pavement of the inner court of the Administrative Quarters, in undisturbed layers of the debris of the burned palace.[10] What is their potential value for ascertaining the temporal parameter of Royal Palace G?

The late Ignace Gelb declared categorically: "The discovery of the inscription of Pepi I in the level in which the Ebla archive was found means nothing. It seems to me that archaeologists take too seriously the datings produced by philologists." Quoting some of the proposed dates for Pepi I, Sargon, and Naram-Sin, he found them "all open to question." Since the datings of both Pepi I and of Sargon and the Sargonic dynasty "may vary by at least as much as ±50 years...with that much leeway...Pepi I could be synchronous with the Ebla archive of the Pre-Sargonic period."[11] Indeed, it would be easy, but methodologically wrong, to pick out, from unconnected chronological systems based on differing premises, such dates that appear convenient for one's preferred synchronization. One has to be consistent and follow such chronologies for the countries of Western Asia and for Egypt that are compatible with each other and with data of astronomy and archaeology. I have explained elsewhere in detail why I consider that such systems are the so-called "low chronology" for Mesopotamia, Syria, and Anatolia, and the "Memphite chronology," based on the dates of heliacal risings of Sirius as observed from Memphis, for Egypt.[12]

---

relations between Mari and Ebla of the archives period see A. Archi, "I rapporti tra Ebla e Mari," *SEb* 4 (1981) 129-166; "Le synchronisme entre les rois de Mari et les rois d'Ebla au IIIe millénaire," *MARI* 4 (1985) 47-51; "Les rapports politiques et économiques entre Ebla et Mari," *MARI* 4 (1985) 63-83; on the kings of Mari involved in wars against Ebla, D.O. Edzard, "Neue Erwägungen zum Brief des Enna-Dagan von Mari (TM.75.G2367)," *SEb* 4 (1981) 89-97; on the peripeties of these wars, Astour, "Outline" 26-51. [This paper was finished before I had the opportunity to consult A. Archi, "Ebla: la formazione di uno Stato del III millennio a.C.," *La Parola del Passato* 46 (1991) 195-219, in which the synchronistic table (p. 198) includes an additional king of Mari mentioned at Ebla, Anubu, inserted between Iški-Mari and Saʾumu. This name, written *A-nu*-KA (presumably *-bu*$_{x}$), appears in TM.75.G.2367 obv.II.1, but was transliterated *sá-ù-mu* by G. Pettinato in his first publication of the text, "Bollettino militare della campagna di Ebla contro la città di Mari," *OA* 19 (1980) 238, and correctly, but with a wrong interpretation, in his second publication of it, in *Ebla: Nuovi orizzonti della storia* (Milano, 1986) 396. It was Amedeo Alberti, "AN.BU = *a-nu-bu*$_{x}$," *NABU* 1990/124, who first recognized it as the name of a Mariote king from the context in which it appears.]

[10] P. Matthiae, "Recherches archéologiques à Ébla, 1977: le quartier administratif du palais royal G," *CRAIBL* 1978 229-234; *Empire* (1981) 9; G. Scandone Matthiae, "Vasi iscritti di Chefren e Pepi I nel Palazzo Reale G di Ebla," *SEb* 1 (1979) 33-43; "I vasi egiziani in pietra dal Palazzo Reale G," *SEb* 4 (1981) 99-127; "Les Relations entre Ébla et l'Égypte au IIIème et au IIème Millénaire av. J.-Chr.," in Waetzoldt and Hauptmann, *Wirtschaft* (1988) 67-73. We are leaving aside the question whether the titles of Pepi I on the Tell Mardikh lid point to the making of the vase during the first thirty years of that king's reign, as Scandone Matthiae stated in 1979 (p. 40) (but no longer in 1988), for it could have been brought to Ebla years after it was made.

[11] I.J. Gelb, "Ebla and the Kish Civilization," in L. Cagni, ed., *La lingua di Ebla* (Napoli, 1981) 58-59.

[12] Astour, *Hittite History and Absolute Chronology of the Bronze Age* (Partille, 1989) 1-12. There are no Sothic

The reign of Chephren falls in the second third of the twenty-sixth century, and that of Pepi I was approximately between 2333 and 2283, while the ascent to power of Sargon, as obtained by dead reckoning from the last year of the Third Dynasty of Ur, would be 2267 or 2270.[13] Of the two datings provided by the Egyptian inscriptions found in Palace G, that of Chephren is important only as a testimony of some kind of link—probably indirect—between northern Syria and Egypt, which does not surprise us, for the long interrupted importation of lapis lazuli to Egypt is known to have resumed under the Fourth Dynasty.[14] But it cannot be used as a *terminus ante quem* for the construction of Palace G, as argued by Pettinato,[15] because that palace was preceded on the Acropolis by several phases of a palatial building which accommodated earlier kings of the same dynasty.[16] It was to one of the earlier structures that the diorite lamp was brought, and it was transferred to the new palace, as a valuable exotic artifact, along with other furnishings, when the royal family moved to its new residence.

Conversely, the alabaster lid with the names of Pepi I is an incontrovertible *terminus post quem* for the conflagration of Palace G. Its presence there totally refutes Pettinato's high dating for that event—2500 or, as he is willing to concede, 2400 at the latest.[17] But even if the lid

---

dates prior to the Twelfth Dynasty, but by using the available figures for earlier reigns and dynastic overlaps during the First Intermediate Period, and reckoning back from the start of the Twelfth Dynasty, it is possible to obtain fairly close dates for the Old Kingdom. See W.C. Hayes, "Chronology I. Egypt—to End of Twentieth Dynasty," *CAH*³ I/1 (1970) 173-193, whose Egyptian chronology is based upon "Memphite" reckoning and whose dates for Pepi I's reign are cited in the next paragraph.

[13] Cf. Astour, "Outline", 3 author's note.

[14] J. Payne, "Lapis Lazuli in Early Egypt," *Iraq* 30 (1968) 58-63. Lapis lazuli could reach Egypt only via Syria.

[15] Introduction to *MEE* 1:xxxvii-xxxviii.

[16] P. Matthiae, "Les dernières découvertes d'Ébla en 1983-1986," *CRAIBL* 1987 136-138; Astour, "Outline" 17.

[17] G. Pettinato, "Gli archivi reali di Tell Mardikh-Ebla," *RBI* 25 (1977) 33, repeated in his *Ebla: Un impero inciso nell'argilla* (Milano, 1979) 80-81 with the specification that "the Dynasty of Ebla was contemporaneous with the First Dynasty of Kiš (2600-2500 B.C.)" and the remark that in one Ebla text (TM.75.G.1435) "one finds a person with the singular name *me-sa-li-ma* which cannot fail to recall the homonymous king of Kiš." B. Kienast, "Der Feldzugsbericht des Ennadagān in literarhistorischer Sicht," *OA* 19 (1980) 247-248 misunderstood this remark in the sense that Pettinato had actually found at Ebla a mention of *Me-sa-li-ma lugal Kiš*ᵏⁱ "Mesalim, king of Kiš." However, A. Archi, "A Mythologem in Eblaitology: Mesilim of Kish at Ebla," *SEb* 4 (1981) 227-230 showed that the name in question was actually *Bar-za-ma-li*. In the passage cited in n. 15 above, Pettinato tried to remove the testimony of Pepi I's vase by the assumption that it may have somehow penetrated into the ruins of Palace G from a higher stratum, as, according to him, did the Middle Babylonian letter TM.76.G.412, which was allegedly found beneath the palace levels. But the debris levels in which the lid of Pepi I's vase was found were undisturbed, and as for the Middle Babylonian tablet, its publisher stated clearly that "it was found on the slopes of the Acropolis of Tell Mardikh, above the ruins of the Royal Palace G (Early Bronze IVA), among the debris of Middle Bronze levels," J.-R. Kupper, "Une tablette paléo-babylonienne de Mardikh III," *SEb* 2 (1980) 49. Pettinato repeated at length his argumentation for a higher chronology of Ebla in his *Orizzonti* (1986) 106-120 (including the alleged *Me-sa-li-ma*), but with the curious addition on p. 120: "If, instead, Ebla was destroyed later, around 2400, then it would be necessary to assume other Mesopotamian rulers as perpetrators of the destruction of Royal Palace G, for instance Eannatum of Lagaš who boasted of having conquered both Kiš and Mari, or else Lugalzagesi of Uruk who...had extended his dominion as far as the Mediterranean Sea." This is a very broad chronological margin. While Eannatum reigned, in terms of middle chronology, from 2454 to 2425, the beginning of Lugalzagesi's reign

in question had not been found, these dates for the end of the archives, and thus of the Mardikh IIB1 period, would still be untenable. Palaeographic reasons for attributing the Ebla tablets to the end of the Early Dynastic IIIB have already been presented by competent scholars.[18] To this should be added the following historical consideration. As mentioned above, Iblul-Il is the only pre-Sargonic king of Mari attested in local inscriptions whose name also appears in Ebla texts. This means, as correctly stated, that the other five kings of that group preceded him.[19] The votive inscription with the name of one of them, Lamgi-Mari, has been attributed by Thureau-Dangin to the time of Ur-Nanše, the founder of the First Dynasty of Lagaš,[20] and, insofar as I know, this attribution still stands.[21] This provides for a relatively close link with the history of Lagaš which is well known and serves as a chronological yardstick for the Early Dynastic III period.[22] It is agreed that the interval between the accession of Ur-Nanše and the destruction of Lagaš by Lugalzagesi amounted to ca. 150 years.[23] The reign of Lugalzagesi overlapped with the early reign of Sargon. On this basis, using the middle chronology followed by Pettinato and the date of 2334 accepted by him for the rise to power of Sargon,[24] one obtains 2494, or in round figures 2500, for the beginning of Ur-Nanše's rule. Now this is Pettinato's preferred date for the end of the Ebla archives. But Lamgi-Mari, if he was a contemporary of Ur-Nanše, belongs to the decades after 2500, and even if one admits that he was the latest of Iblul-Il's predecessors attested at Mari, he was still separated from him by two Mariote kings—Saʾumu and Ištup-Šar—and was followed by four other kings—Nizi, Enna-

---

took place a hundred years after the accession of Eannatum, almost fifty years after 2400. By his acceptance of Lugalzagesi as a possible contemporary of the last years of the Ebla archives, Pettinato (perhaps without giving much thought to it) tacitly agreed with the conclusion made by E. Sollberger, "Notes sur la paléographie des textes d'Ebla," *SEb* 5 (1982) 225 from his analysis of the Eblean script: "The period of Lugal-zage-si and of the first Sargonic rulers would provide a most plausible date for the Ebla archives," though only a few pages earlier, p. 115, he chided Matthiae for "blindly relying" on Sollberger in questions of palaeography.

[18] I.J. Gelb, "Thoughts about Ibla: A Preliminary Evaluation, March 1977," *SMS* 1/1 (1977) 5-9; "Kish" (1981) 57-58; "Mari and the Kish Civilization," in G.D. Young, ed., *Mari in Retrospect* (Winona Lake, 1992) 122 ("the Ebla archive is to be dated to the Pre-Sargonic period, with the proviso that 'Pre-Sargonic' extends in time to include the early years of Sargon"); Sollberger, "Paléographie" (1982) 221-228; D.O. Edzard, "Zur Syntax der Ebla-Texte," in P. Fronzaroli, ed., *Studies on the Language of Ebla* (Firenze, 1984; *QS* 13) 101 ("the writing system of Ebla from the 25th/24th century B.C. [middle chronology]"; the singular "century" points to a period of about a hundred years covering the latter part of the twenty-fifth century and the earlier part of the twenty-fourth century, ending thus shortly before the rise of Sargon); W. von Soden, "Ebla, die früheste Schriftkultur Syriens," in Waetzoldt and Hauptmann, *Wirtschaft* (1988) 325 ("the earlier date [of the destruction of Royal Palace G] about 2280 [low chronology] is also confirmed by the archaic aspect of the Ebla script").

[19] Archi, "Synchronisme" (1985) 49.

[20] Thureau-Dangin, "Statuettes" (1934) 140-142.

[21] Cf. E. Strommenger, "Das Menschenbild in der altmesopotamischen Rundplastik von Mesilim bis Hammurapi," *BagM* 1 (1960) 24, 27; A. Moortgat, *The Art of Ancient Mesopotamia* (London, 1969) 38, 64.

[22] The dates of the rulers of Lagaš followed here are those used in *IRSA*, but converted (unless stated otherwise) to low chronology by lowering them by 64 years.

[23] 152 years according to the dates in *IRSA*; 150 years according to the synchronistic chart in Strommenger, "Menschenbild" (1960), table 16, calibrated in years going upward from 0 (last year of Lugalzagesi).

[24] Pettinato, *Orizzonti* (1986) 56; on the previous page he cites the dates of the rulers of Lagaš, Eannatum and Enannatum I, which are also those in *IRSA*.

Dagan, Iku-(I)šar, and Ḫidar—as we know from Enna-Dagan's *aide-mémoire* on the wars between Mari and Ebla and from a great number of references in Ebla texts.[25] Ḫidar sat on the throne of Mari at the moment of the catastrophe of Royal Palace G. Assuming that the number of reigns from Lamgi-Mari to Ḫidar was eight and that the average length of a reign was twenty years, but allowing only five years for Nizi,[26] we reach the hypothetical but probable figure of ca. 145 years from Lamgi-Mari to the destruction of Royal Palace G, which happens to be very close to the duration of the contemporaneous First Dynasty of Lagaš. This pulls down the terminal year of Palace G well below not only Pettinato's preferred date of 2500 but also his lowest limit of 2400, even if one follows the middle chronology.

A very different dating for the destruction of Palace G and of Ebla was originally advanced by Matthiae who considered it "very probably the work of Naram-Sin of Akkad, around 2250 B.C."[27] As an archaeologist, Matthiae cited some ceramic and artistic evidence in support of his dating, but his principal reason was, of course, the seemingly plain assertion of Naram-Sin himself that, with the help of the gods, he had defeated Armanum and Ebla and captured Riš-Adad, king of Armanum.[28] This notwithstanding, other authors have indicated that such dating is excluded not only by the palaeography of the Ebla texts but also, and most importantly, by their contents.[29] They reflect a world which is sharply different from the era

---

[25] Edzard, "Erwägungen" (1981) 89-97; Archi, "Synchronisme" (1985) 47-51.

[26] As noted by Archi, "Synchronisme" (1985) 47, "NI-zi probably had a rather short reign, in any case much less long than that of Iblul-Il: the quantities of gold and silver attributed to him [as installment of the indemnity paid by Ebla to Mari] represent only 1/5 and 1/7 of those attributed to Iblul-Il."

[27] Matthiae, *Empire* (1981) 53 and elsewhere in the book, most categorically on pp. 9-10: "Any dating of the destruction to the Early Dynastic Period...any date that is of the pre-Sargonic age, is therefore [because of Pepi I's lid] excluded." Already in P. Matthiae, "Ebla in the Late Early Syrian Period: The Royal Palace and the State Archives," *BA* 39 (1976) 98 it is said: "It is likely that Naram-Sin of Akkad, who boasts in his triumphal inscriptions of the conquest of Armanum and Ebla...was responsible for the destruction of Building G."

[28] *UET* 1 275 = H. Hirsch, "Die Inschriften der Könige von Agade," *AfO* 20 (1963), text b 5 (Old Babylonian copy); translations: *IRSA* 107-108; B.R. Foster, "The Siege of Armanum," *JANES* 14 (1982) 27-36. I agree with Sollberger's opinion (*IRSA* 108 n. *e*): "There follows the description of a fortification which no longer belongs to the inscription," as against the hypothesis of F.R. Kraus, "Ein altakkadisches Festungsbild," *Iraq* 10 (1948) 81-92, followed and expanded by Foster, that *Si-ku-ma-núm*[ki] (quoted text V:15) is the copyist's mistake for **Ar-ma-núm*[ki] and that the measurements of the city's walls are those of Armanum captured by Naram-Sin. Indeed, (a) SI-KU does not resemble AR in either Sargonic or Old Babylonian script, (b) it is incredible that the scribe who had six times correctly copied the sign AR in the name *Armanum* should have grossly misunderstood it the seventh time, and (c) the description ends with the words (VI:18-19): "What is upon the side of the great statue of Sin-iribam," which means, *prima facie*, that the Old Babylonian scribe, after having copied the inscription on a statue of Naram-Sin, continued on the same tablet with a copy of the inscription on a statue of Sin-iribam, the tenth king of the Larsa Dynasty, and it is to him that the conquest of the otherwise unknown Sikumanum (or Sikumalum) should be attributed. Besides *UET* 1 275, a votive stone mace, dedicated by one of Naram-Sin's officials, extols the king as "the smiter of Armanum and Ebla and Elam" (M. Lambert, "Masses d'armes de pierre au nom de Naramsîn," *Or* 37 [1968] 85), and the title "smiter of Armanum and Ebla" appears in two short vase inscriptions (*SAKI* 166-167; cf. Hirsch, "Inschriften" [1963] 18 § 6).

[29] In the beginning of the decipherment of the Ebla tablets, when both their contents and the peculiarities of Eblaic spelling were yet insufficiently known, it was thought that Akkad (Agade) appears in them as *A*-EN-*ga-du*[ki], to be understood as *A-ga-du:*EN[ki] "Agade of the King," and Sargon, as *Ša-ri-gi-nu* (P. Matthiae, "Ébla à l'époque d'Akkad: archéologie et histoire," *CRAIBL* 1976 211; "Archives" [1976] 109; "Le palais royal protosyrien d'Ébla:

of Naram-Sin. There is not a hint of the Sargonic empire or even of Akkad itself. Ebla deals with the independent kingdoms of Mari, Kiš, and Nagar which, under Naram-Sin, were parts of his centralized domain.[30] Moreover—and this should be briefly discussed at this junction—Naram-Sin's Ebla, always mentioned together with Armanum, is in all likelihood not the north Syrian Ebla at all.[31] There also existed a Transtigridian city of that nature, attested (sometimes in composite or ethnic formations) from Old Akkadian to Neo-Assyrian times.[32] Indicative of its location are the Nippur geographical list, which places *Eb-la*[ki] among cities of

---

nouvelles recherches archéologiques à Tell Mardikh en 1976," *CRAIBL* 1977 168; *Empire* [1981] 166-168). A careful examination proved that the place name was actually *A-ru*$_{12}$*-ga-tù*[ki], borne by a town directly subordinated to Ebla, and that the personal name was *Ša-nam-gi-nu*. The two equations were withdrawn by Pettinato, *Impero* (1979) 80 and n. 24 on p. 124, and by Matthiae (after an attempt to defend them in "Tell Mardikh: The Archives and Palace," *Archaeology* 30 [1977] 253) in "Recherches 1977" (1978) 235 and in the preface (dated September 1979) to *Empire* (1981).

30 After the destruction of Mari by Sargon (which will be considered below), it was restored by one of his successors (perhaps Maništušu) and was administered by a succession of military governors (*šakkanakku*) appointed by the kings of Akkad and "not linked in any way to the rulers of Mari attested by the Ebla texts or by the royal statues found at Mari itself" (J.-M. Durand, "La situation historique des Šakkanakku: nouvelle approche," *MARI* 4 [1985], esp. pp. 154 and 158). One aspect of Naram-Sin's control of Mari was the appointment of two of his daughters to priestly offices there, as attested by inscribed bronzes uncovered at Mari (A. Parrot, *Mari: capitale fabuleuse* [Paris, 1974] 22, 90). Kiš, rebuilt by Sargon, became part of the Akkad Empire; the Old Akkadian texts found at Kiš and the nearby Umm el-Jir are written in standard Sargonic script and dialect (Gelb, "Kish" [1981] 67-68). The belief that Kiš continued to have its own kings during the reign of Sargon is an aberration based on the annotation in the Sumerian King List that Sargon, in his youth, served as a cupbearer of Ur-Zababa. That annotation was borrowed from one of the many legends about Sargon, and Ur-Zababa is clearly a mythical character, as shown by the reign of 400 years attributed to him; see the evaluation of another legend that brings together Ur-Zababa, Lugalzagesi, and Sargon by J.S. Cooper and W. Heimpel, "The Sumerian Sargon Legend," *JAOS* 103 (1983) 68-69, 74 as invented. As for Nagar, it appears (as NAGAR[ki]) in two administrative Sargonic tablets (*CT* 1 BU.91-5-9 588:obv.7 and 590:rev.2), and its name may be restored in the Sargonic tablet from Tell Brak, F.1153:2, originally published by C.J. Gadd, "Tablets from Chagar Bazar and Tell Brak, 1937-38" *Iraq* 7 (1940) pl. V and later, in a collated hand copy, by O. Loretz, *Texte aus Chagar Bazar und Tell Brak, Teil 1* (Kevelaer, 1969; *AOAT* 3/1) pl. XXXV No. 69. It lists corvée workers from a number of towns, all of which were located in the eastern part of the Khabur Triangle, close to Naram-Sin's palace at Tell Brak. The damaged second sign of the toponym, following the initial *na*, was read *ḫur* by K. Kessler, "Nilabšinu und der altorientalische Name des Tell Brak," *SMEA* 24 (1984) 22, thus yielding the name of the well-known city of Naḫur in the northwestern corner of the Khabur Triangle. It can, however, be restored, as easily, *gàr* (cf. *Na-gàr*[ki] in Ebla texts), which would fit the geographical context of the tablet even better.

31 I have already made brief statements to this effect, in another connection, in Astour, "Les Hourrites en Syrie du Nord: Rapport sommaire," *RHA* 36 (1978) 4 n. 28, and "Toponymic Parallels Between the Nuzi Area and Northern Syria, with an appendix: Nuzi Place Names in Egyptian Topographic Lists," *SCCNH* 1 (1981) 14 n. 19; 15 n. 21; 16.

32 The "canal of Ebla" in a Sargonic and two Ur III texts was located in the province of Umma (see Astour, "Outline" section 2). Sargonic references to the Transtigridian Ebla are: *Tu-tu šu Eb-la-ì-t[im]* in a text from the Diyala valley, *MAD* 1 52:II'-4'; *Dur-Eb-la*[ki] Nikol'skij *DV* 5 (1915) No. 10:3; *Maš-gan*-BÀD-*Eb-la HSS* 10 1 (geographical map from Gasur). Ur III references: see *RGTC* 2 35 s.v. *Dūr-Ebla*; add R.M. Sigrist, "Nouveaux noms géographiques de l'empire d'Ur III," *JCS* 31 (1979) 166 1. 18. It is generally assumed, following Meek, preface to *HSS* 10:xviii, that Dur-Ebla became Durubla in the Nuzi texts; a full list of its occurrences is given in the editorial addendum to A.R. Millard, "Strays from a 'Nuzi' Archive," *SCCNH* 1 (1981) 438 n. 5.

the Transtigris,[33] and the unmistakable contexts of its Middle and Neo-Assyrian appearances,[34] but especially a passage in the geographical treatise known as "The Empire of Sargon of Akkad," written in the Sargonid period of Assyria but reflecting ethnic and geographical conditions of the Old Babylonian age.[35] There, in the enumeration of Transtigridian countries, which follows from north to south, one finds, after Arrapḫa and Lulubu and before Akkad (here the Diyala valley) and Gutium, the entry "from Ebla to Bīt-Nanip is the land of the Armanians."[36]

We see here the same close connections between Armanum and Ebla as in Naram-Sin's inscriptions. Ebla is a border town of an entity named for its capital, Armanum. For Naram-Sin, Armanum is the more important of the two. It alone has a king, Riš-Adad, whose defeat and capture is Naram-Sin's main title to glory.[37] This is not the situation in northern Syria of the late third millennium, when Ebla dominated the region.[38] The Transtigridian Arman(um) is attested in other cuneiform sources. The Ur III mentions of corvée crews from Arman[39] only show that the place was, at that time, part of the directly administered territory of the kingdom (which excludes Syria), but its occurrences in late second millennium records allow for a more specific location. The city, called at that time Arman of Ugar-Sali, stood north of Mount Ebiḫ (Jebel Ḫamrin), south of the Little Zab, and west of Lubdi (near Ṭawuq) and the Radanu River (ᶜUẓaym and the middle of its headwater streams, Ṭawuq Çay).[40] It is no mere

---

[33] *MSL* XI:104, No. 272, preceded by Simurrum, Anšan, KAS$_4^{ki}$, and Ibratum, and followed by Diniktum, Neribtum, ABZU^{si}, Maḫili, Abarnium, and Laban-e.

[34] The LUGAL ^{uru}*Eb-li-ta-ia-e*, mentioned in *KAV* 107:8 in connection with ^{uru}*Ki-li-zi* (frequently cited in Middle Assyrian administrative texts, identical with Neo-Assyrian Kalzi,and located at Qaṣr Šemamuk west of Irbil, cf. *RGTC* 5 167), and the goddess ^{d}*Eb-la-i-tu*, III *R* 66:rev.d:20, are of course connected with the Transtigridian, and not with the Syrian, Ebla. The Neo-Assyrian deed of land sale, *AR* 145, deals with a lot between the roads to ^{uru}*Eb-li* and to ^{uru}*Su-mur-u-nu* (corresponding to ^{uru}*Ši-me-ru-un-ni* at Nuzi, L.R. Fisher, "Nuzi Geographical Names" [Ph.D. diss., Brandeis University, 1959] No. 539, and *Ši-me-er-ri-ni*^{ki} at Šušarra, *SH* 867:11 in J. Laessøe, *The Shemshāra Tablets* [København, 1959]), and near ^{uru}*Eb-'a-la* (corresponding to Ur III *šà-E-ba-al*^{ki}, *RGTC* 2 38).

[35] *KAV* 92, published and commented upon by E.F. Weidner, "Das Reich Sargons von Akkad," *AfO* 16 (1953) 1-24. A Neo-Babylonian copy of the same work, which continues the text of *KAV* 92 for seventeen more (mostly broken) lines but lacks its first twenty-two lines, was published, with a commentary upon the whole composition, by A.K. Grayson, "The Empire of Sargon of Akkad," *AfO* 25 (1974-77) 56-64.

[36] TA *Eb-lá* EN *É-Na-ni-ip* KUR *Ar-ma-ni-i*^{ki} (1. 13). Bīt-Nanip is otherwise unknown, but the onomastic element *nanip* is found in several Hurrian personal names, mainly at Nuzi (*NPN* 237-238).

[37] Riš-Adad may or may not have been the King of Ebla as well, but the rendering of *Ri-ID-*^{d}*Adad* LUGAL *Ar-ma-nim*^{ki} (*UET* 1:275 III:28-30) by "Rish$^{?}$-Adad, king of Armanum and Ebla" in the body itself of the translation (Foster, "Siege" [1982] 32) is unwarranted.

[38] Matthiaẹ, "Akkad" (1976) 212-213 and *Empire* (1981) 177 asserted that "it appears very probable that Armanum of the Akkadian inscriptions was Armi of the Eblaite inscriptions, and Armi, especially in the latest documents of Ibbi-Sipish [i.e., Ibbi-Zikir], appears clearly as the first city of the kingdom after Ebla." The Ebla texts disclose nothing of the sort. Armi was one of the sixty-odd vassal city-states of Ebla, among the twenty or so more prominent ones, but by no means outstanding in comparison with the rest.

[39] *RGTC* 2 15 (two mentions of erín-*Ar-ma-an*^{ki}).

[40] See the itinerary of Tiglath-Pileser III's expedition against Babylonia, E.F. Weidner, "Die Feldzüge und Bauten Tiglatpilesers I," *AfO* 18 (1958) 350-351, ll 37-39 (*ARI* II § 98), and the demarcation between Adad-Narari I of Assyria and Nazimurattaš of Babylonia in the Synchronistic History, A.K. Grayson, *Assyrian and Babylonian*

coincidence that Hildegard Lewy, proceeding form the topographic data of a local map excavated in Sargonic Gasur (later Nuzi), pinpointed the site of Maškan-Dūr-Ebla ("the settlement of the fortress of Ebla") right within the area of the latter Ugar-Sali district.[41]

It is true, of course, that Naram-Sin's quoted record couples the conquest of Armanum and Ebla with, the first time, "Amanum, the Cedar Mountain, and the Upper Sea," and, the second time, with "from the bank of the Euphrates to Ulisum," and then mentions again "Amanum, the Cedar Mountain." But this does not necessarily mean that all of these places belonged to the same region. The two sets of names are rather put in apposition, to demonstrate Naram-Sin's victories both in the East and the West. Concerning the latter, we see that Naram-Sin's goal was Mount Amanus with its cedar forests. To reach it, he must have crossed the Euphrates at its nearest spot.[42] Ulisum, the farthest point of his penetration, was located on the Gulf of Iskenderun, below the western slope of the Amanus.[43] These places are quite remote from the city of Ebla-Tell Mardikh.

Anyway, even without these historico-geographical considerations, the attribution of Ebla's destruction to Naram-Sin has by now faded. It is Sargon who is increasingly seen as its perpetrator,[44] and Matthiae, who originally preferred Naram-Sin, has concluded his

---

Chronicles (Locust Valley, 1975; *TCS* 5), Chronicle 21:I:24'-31'; *ARI* II § 520; cf. the commentary by Nashef, *RGTC* 5 218 (s.v. Pilasqi) and 270 (s.v. Ugār-Sallu), as well as the location of these places on his map ibid. The list of conquests of Šilḫak-Inšušnak, king of Elam, mentions the city ^{AŠ}*U-qa-ar-si-il-la-am-ni E-pe-eḫ* as the place where he had installed an administrator over a district which included several towns known from Nuzi texts and other sources relating to the area northwest of the Diyala (F.W. König, *Die elamischen Königsinschriften* [Graz, 1965; *AfO* Beiheft 16], text 54 § 37); the continuation of the list (§ 40) includes Arrapḫa and Nuza. The Elamite appelation proves that Ugar-Sali abutted on Mount Ebiḫ (Jebel Ḥamrin).

[41] H. Lewy, "A Contribution to the Historical Geography of the Nuzi Texts," *JAOS* 88 (1968) 159. In her topographic interpretation of the map *HSS* 10 1 she relied on the map of the German General Staff from the time of World War I. I checked her data on the British one-quarter inch map of Iraq, sheet No. 2A: Kirkuk.

[42] One may suppose that Naram-Sin's expedition to Syria originated—as did the one to the sources of the Tigris—at Tell Brak where Naram-Sin had built a palace as his headquarters for operations in the north.

[43] Ulisum is, of course, not Ullaza, a city known from Egyptian texts and Amarna letters to have been situated in the middle part of the Phoenician coast, as this had been suggested merely because of onomastic resemblance (S. Smith in *UET* 1 80; J. Bottéro, "Syria at the Time of the Kings of Agade," *CAH*^{3} I/2 [1971] 321-327). If Naram-Sin had proceeded that far south, he would not have failed to mention Mount Lebanon along with Mount Amanus. Ulisum should instead be identified with Uluzina in the Idrimi inscription of Alalakh, on the proposed location of which see Astour, "Tell Mardīḫ and Ebla," *UF* 3 (1971) 10-11.

[44] Gelb, "Kish" (1981) 58: "If there is any chance of connecting Ebla with the Sargonic Dynasty, then it is only with the early years of Sargon...;" Archi, "Synchronisme" (1985) 49-50 leans toward accepting Sargon as "the foreign element which provoked vast destructions like those that took place at Mari and Ebla. To be sure, one must take into account Naram-Sin's affirmation: 'no king among kings has overthrown Armanum and Ebla....' But this is not a definitive argument for excluding that Sargon, after Mari, did actually reach and conquer Ebla" (Note: That argument is eliminated if one recognizes that Naram-Sin dealt with a different Ebla); J.N. Postgate, "Abu Essalabikh and Tell Mardikh: Sumer and Ebla," *Sumer* 42 (1986) 68: "I would prefer to assign the destruction [of Ebla] to Naram-Sin's grandfather, Sargon," but he did not exclude other causes (see n. 70 below); von Soden, "Ebla" (1988) 325 on who had destroyed the Royal Palace G; Sargon or Naram-Sin: "I think with others that it could be only the former;" A. Westenholz, "Personal Names in Ebla and in Pre-Sargonic Babylonia," *ARES* 1 (1988) 99: "The date of the Ebla archive cannot as yet be fixed accurately, but everything points to the end of the Pre-Sargonic era and perhaps the beginning of Sargon's reign," but without ascribing to that king the destruction

detailed discussion of the problem with the statement: "actually the attribution of the destruction of Mardikh IIB1 to Sargon of Akkad is unanimously hinted at by all the data, as being the most probable, and the one which presents less difficulties."[45] However, difficulties, though fewer in number, do remain, and serious ones at that.

Sargon's inscription mentioning Ebla ensures that his expedition to the north came after his conquest of Sumer.[46] Then comes the statement: "Sargon the king, in Tuttul before Dagan he bowed down (and) prayed. The Upper Land he gave him: Mari, Yarmuti, Ebla as far as the Cedar Forest and the Silver Mountains." The enumeration follows the geography of the king's march.[47] At the time of the Ebla archives, both Mari and Ebla

---

of Ebla.

[45] P. Matthiae, "On the Economic Foundations of the Early Syrian Culture of Ebla," in Waetzoldt and Hauptmann, *Wirtschaft* (1988) 78. He reached this conclusion after holding for a while the position that either of the two kings could have destroyed Ebla of the Mardikh IIB1 period; see *I tesori di Ebla* (Bari, 1984) 36; "Ebla Recovered," in H. Weiss, ed., *Ebla to Damascus* (Washington, D.C., 1985) 137.

[46] Hirsch, "Inschriften" (1963) 37-39, text Sargon b 2 (Old Babylonian copy of a bilingual text which was originally inscribed on a statue of Sargon in Nippur). There also exists a badly damaged copy of the Akkadian version, ibid. pp. 49-50, text Sargon b 13. The inscription begins with the declaration that Sargon had fought thirty-four victorious battles and destroyed city walls all the way to the seacoast. This refers to his victories over Lugalzagesi, Ur, Umma, and Lagaš, and his reaching the Persian Gulf—successes described at greater length in some of his other inscriptions, e.g. Sargon b 1. An exact chronology of Sargon's expedition cannot be established. Relying in this respect on the much later Chronicle of Early Kings (L.W. King, *Chronicles Concerning Early Babylonian Kings* [London, 1907]; Grayson, *Chronicles* [1975], Chronicle 20; transl. by A.L. Oppenheim, *ANET* 266-267) which dates the conquest of "the land of the sunset" to Sargon's eleventh year, or on the related Omens Collection (in King, above) which adds an expedition to the same region in Sargon's third year, is unwarranted. A work which makes Naram-Sin Sargon's son and successor could not have used genuine historical material from the Sargonic period. Besides, Sargonic kings did not number their regnal years but named them for the principal event of the previous year.

[47] It is clear from the wording of the inscription that Tuttul (Du$_8$-du$_8$- ⌜li⌝ ^{ki}.a of the Sumerian version, *in Tu-tu-li*^{ki} of the Akkadian version) lay closer to Akkad than to Mari, for the conquest of Mari, Yarmuti, and Ebla is represented as the result of Sargon's prayer to Dagan at Tuttul and the god's granting to him these countries. It was therefore generally assumed that the Tuttul in question was the same as [*Tu*]-*ul-tu-ul*^{ki} (first sign restored from the occurrence of the toponym in another similar text), which the geographical list *KAV* 183 (*MSL* XI:35 l. 23) identifies with ^{uru}I-$^{i\text{-}tú}$ID, i.e. modern Hit on the right bank of the lower middle Euphrates. The identifications of *KAV* 183 are not always completely accurate, but at least the text equates localities that were close to each other. J.-R. Kupper, *ARM* 16/1 36, s.v. *Tuttul*, related some Mariote mentions of that place name not to the better known Tuttul at the confluence of the Balikh with the Euphrates but to a "town near Hīt, on the Euphrates" (where it is associated with Yabliya, Ḫarbe, Id, and Rapiqum). More recently, W. Mayer, "Grundzüge der Geschichte der Stadt Tuttul im 2. Jt. v. Chr.," *UF* 19 (1987) 121-160 and D. Charpin, "Tuttul et It d'après les archives de Mari," *NABU* 1989/16 denied the existence of the southern Tuttul. However, besides the plain sense of Sargon's quoted inscription and the awkwardness of taking out the Tuttul of the pertaining Mari texts from its geographical context, there are other proofs that there really was a Tuttul on the lower Middle Euphrates: (a) The letter *UCP* 9/4 29 from Sin-muballiṭ (who, as admitted by W. Mayer, above, could only be the Babylonian king, father of Ḫammurapi) states that its sender had repeatedly asked the ruler of Tuttul (*Du*$_8$*-du-li*^{ki}, 1. 5) for troops to his assistance; this can only refer to a state abutting on the kingdom of Babylon in its pre-Ḫammurapi borders and not to the distant Tuttul-on-the-Balikh which, by the way, did not even have a king after it was annexed by Yaḫdun-Lim of Mari, Sin-muballiṭ's contemporary. (b) In Naram-Sin's authentic inscription on the copper statue found at Bassekti (A.-H. Al-Fouadi, "Bassetki Statue with an Old Akkadian Royal Inscription of Narām-Sin of Agade (B.C. 2291-2255),"

controlled large territorial domains which may be called "empires," and both domains abutted on each other on the middle Euphrates.[48] There was no room between them for a third state. Hence Yarmuti, which by its association with Mari and Ebla was also a country, must have been located aside from the Euphrates route and in all likelihood corresponded to the Khabur Triangle, a thickly settled and wealthy region and an attractive prospect for tribute and loot.[49] This means that, after conquering Mari, Sargon's army marched up the Khabur, plundered the Triangle, then turned west by the great transversal road of North Mesopotamia into northernmost Syria up to the Amanus (the Cedar Forest) and the Taurus (the Silver Mountains)—an area which at that time was part of the Ebla Empire.[50] Did Sargon, on the return leg, make a detour in order to destroy the city of Ebla itself? Inscriptional and archaeological data speak against it.

What Sargon very certainly destroyed was Mari. An early Sargonic date formula, generally attributed to his reign, states mu *Ma-ri*[ki] ḫul-a "the year when Mari was

---

Sumer 32 [1976] 63-75; F. Reschid [Rashīd], "Preliminary Study of the Bassetki Statue," *Sumer* 32 [1976] Arabic 49-58) the group of gods invoked consists of Ištar in Eanna (Uruk), Enlil in Nippur, Dagan in Tuttul (*in Tu-tu-li*[ki]), Ninḫursag in Keš, Enki in Eridu, Sin in Ur, Šamaš in Sippar, and Nergal in Kutha. The southern Tuttul is perfectly in place among the cities of Sumer and Akkad, which cannot be said about its northern homonym. (c) Besides the already quoted *KAV* 183, the three other geographical lists in *MSL* XI which mention Tuttul (*Tu-ul-tu-ul*[ki], *Tu-túl*[ki]; see *MSL* XI, p. 37:24; p. 60:ii:47; p. 141:ii:20) group it with cities of Akkad and Sumer, each time in a different assortment, which excludes an error that was mechanically repeated. (d) More generally, these and all other geographical lists collected in *MSL* XI include only towns of Babylonia (Sumer and Akkad) and the Transtigris south of the Little Zab. Even Mari in these lists, to judge from its constant geographical association, is not the famous city on the Euphrates but the homonymous entity in the Transtigris of *KAV* 92:23 (see Weidner, "Sargon" [1953] 16) and the Nuzi texts (E.R. Lacheman, "Nuzi Geographical Names I," *BASOR* 78 [1940] 20; Fisher, "Names" [1959], No. 435). Therefore the Tuttul which is listed there can only be the southern Tuttul. (I am leaving aside, as having no relation to the present topic, the possible third Tuttul somewhere in the Transtigris, on which see Dossin as quoted by A. Pohl, "Personalnachrichten," *Or* 21 [1952] 500; A. Goetze, "Ḫulibar of Duddul," *JNES* 12 [1953] 114-123; and probably *Du*$_8$*-du*$_8$*-li*[ki] in *MSL* XI p. 60:i:20).

[48] Astour, "Structure" (1988) 146 n. 47; "Outline," end of section 5.

[49] Besides Sargon's inscription, a place name similar to Yarmuti is found only in the Amarna letters of Rib-Addi, king of Byblos, as [kur]*Ia-ri-mu-ta* (once [kur]*Ia-a*[*r-mu-ta*]), referring to a grain-producing country under Egyptian control, located south of Byblos, whence food supplies were brought by sea. Attempts to locate it anywhere in Syria or Palestine met insurmountable obstacles. (The É-*ìr-mu-ut*[ki] at Ebla, *ARET* 2 22:III:4-5, was not a country and not a city but a private land estate.) A correct solution was proposed by C. Niebuhr, "Das Land Jarimuta," *MVAG* 1 (1896) 208-212, who identified Yarimuta with the Delta of the Nile (this was accepted by, inter alia, W.F. Albright, "New Light on the History of Western Asia in the Second Millennium B.C. [I]," *BASOR* 77 [1940] 35). We are dealing here with a case of transference of place names found in archaic cuneiform sources to new territories, which already started in the Amarna Age. Rib-Addi was evidently well acquainted with the popular literature about Sargon; he addresses the pharaoh as *šar tamḫari* "King of Battle," the title of a novel about Sargon's exploits, and he is the only Amarna correspondent who called Nubia by the name *Meluḫḫa* (originally the Indus Basin), which appears, inter alia, in Sargon's own inscriptions. The Nile Delta and the Khabur Triangle resemble each other in several aspects: both are shaped as triangles with the apex in the south, both are intersected by streams, and both were known in antiquity as grain-producing areas.

[50] The eastern border of the Ebla Empire ran east of the Kulab-Balikh line, including Ḫarran; see Astour, "Structure" (1988) 145; A. Archi, "Ḫarran in the III Millennium B.C.," *UF* 20 (1988) 1-8.

destroyed."[51] Excavations have revealed that the pre-Sargonic palace, the temple areas, and probably the entire city were destroyed in a great conflagration, with evidence of preliminary acts of vandalism.[52] Directly under the destruction stratum lay tablets in a script similar to that of the Ebla texts but displaying some more recent traits.[53] Mari remained deserted for one or two generations and was restored as a city under governors appointed by Sargon's successors.[54] But in the Ebla tablets, found in the Court of Audiences and composed during the last month of the existence of Palace G,[55] business with Mari goes on as usual and its king Ḫidar is alive and well. For obvious geographical reasons, Sargon could not have destroyed Ebla before Mari, and the news of Mari's fall would have reached Ebla much faster than it would have taken Sargon's army on its long roundabout march. Hence the fire of Palace G occurred before Sargon's northern expedition and could not have been inflicted by him.

The same conclusion emerges from the fact that the relations of Ebla with Kiš also remained perfectly normal in the last month before the destruction of Palace G.[56] But it is

---

[51] *PBS* 13:27:IV:6-7; on its attribution to Sargon see Durand, "Šakkanakku" (1985) 158; D. Charpin, "Tablettes présargoniques de Mari," *MARI* 5 (1987) 96 and n. 46.

[52] A. Parrot, "Les fouilles de Mari: Huitème campagne (automne 1952)," *Syria* 30 (1953) 206; *Mari* (1974) 87-89 (cf. the remark by Archi, "Synchronisme" [1985] 49 n. 8); M. Lebeau, "Rapport préliminaire sur la séquence céramique du chantier B de Mari (IIIe millénaire)," *MARI* 4 (1985) 93-126; "Rapport préliminaire sur la céramique du Bronze Ancien IVa découverte au 'Palais Présargonique I' de Mari," *MARI* 4 (1985) 127-136.

[53] Charpin, "Tablettes" (1987) 65-127, particularly the comparative analysis of the script (pp. 94-96) and the sign list (pp. 126-127).

[54] Durand, "Šakkanakku" (1985) 147-172.

[55] See n. 7 above.

[56] On the relations between Ebla and Kiš see A. Archi, "Kiš nei testi di Ebla," *SEb* 4 (1981) 77-87; "More on Ebla and Kish, *Eblaitica* 1 (1987) 125-140. Even though Kiš appears in the Ebla texts in exactly the same writing (*Kiš*[ki], Labat sign 425) as in Sumerian and Akkadian texts, doubts about their identity were voiced by P. Michalowski, "Third Millennium Contacts: Observations on the Relationships Between Mari and Ebla," *JAOS* 105 (1985) 297-298 (but retracted by him in the same article, p. 298 n. 44) and E. Sollberger, *ARET* 8 46 s.v. *Kiš*[ki]. More recently, under the overconfident title "Exit Kiš from the horizons of Ebla," F. Pomponio, "Exit Kiš dagli orizzonti di Ebla," *Mesopotamia*[T] 25 (1990) 175-184 asserted that *Kiš* stood in the Ebla texts not for the famous Babylonian city but for some other place, which he located in the eastern part of the Khabur Triangle, north of Nagar (following Michalowski's abandoned assonance with *Ki-iš-ki-iš*, an obscure caravan stop mentioned in the Old Babylonian itinerary published by A. Goetze, "An Old Babylonian Itinerary," *JCS* 7 [1953] 51 11:2 and W.W. Hallo, "The Road to Emar," *JCS* 18 [1964] 63-21). Pomponio's reasons for this move were (a) association of Kiš with Nagar, (b) too great a distance between Ebla and Kiš, (c) similarity of personal names of Kišites in Ebla texts to those of Ebleans. However, Kiš is even more frequently associated with Mari, and once with Terqa. It is known from TM.75.G.2268 (quoted in Archi, "Rapports" [1985] 67) that, according to a convention with Mari, Eblean merchants could travel to Mari, and from Mari to Kiš, using deep-going boats (má-gur$_8$). This alone is enough to ascertain that Kiš was situated on the Euphrates downstream from Mari; besides, most of Ebla's transactions with Kiš were conducted through Mariote intermediaries. In addition to Kiš, relations with two other cities of the region later known as Akkad, Adab (UD.NUN[ki]) and Akšak (*Ak-sa-gú*[ki]), are attested at Ebla (Archi, "Rapports" [1985] 83). As for the distance, let us recall that Sumerians of the Late Uruk period reached Melitene and Egypt, and the means of transport did not deteriorate in the eight hundred or so years since then. The anthroponymic similarities between Ebla and the contemporaneous Kiš do not necessarily point to geographical proximity of the two (and how close is Ebla to Pomponio's Kiškiš?); Westenholz, "Personal Names" (1988) 100-101 saw it as an indication of "an

known from Sargon's own inscription that "he restored Kiš to its place and caused them to settle the city."[57] This has been confirmed by the excavations at Tell Ingharra (East Kiš).[58] The great Palace A of Kiš was destroyed by fire at the end of the Early Dynastic IIIb period and its site was used as a burial ground well into the Dynasty of Akkad. The post-restoration tablets of Kiš are written in standard Sargonic script.[59] The destruction is generally, and with great probability, ascribed to Lugalzagesi at a time prior to Sargon's accession.[60] This means that the conflagration of the Palace G at Ebla preceded not only the fall of Mari to Sargon but even that of Kiš to Lugalzagesi. This agrees well with the opinion that the palaeography of Ebla points to the time of Lugalzagesi and Urukagina. It should be noted that this chronological attribution is compatible with the *post quem* imposed by the jar lid of Pepi I only if the dates of Sargon's reign are defined in terms of the low chronology, i.e., 2270-2215. If one uses the commonly accepted middle chronology for Sargon (2334-2279), then the entire reign of Pepi I (2333-2283) would be comprised within the time limits of Sargon's reign, let alone if one chooses the now fashionable ultra-low dates for the Egyptian king.

But if not Naram-Sin and not Sargon, who then was the destroyer of Ebla's Phase IIB1? Lugalzagesi would fit chronologically, but his self-laudatory inscription says nothing about military campaigns in foreign countries,[61] and he could hardly have destroyed Ebla without first conquering Mari, where there are no traces of violence prior to Sargon. But must we necessarily look for a ferocious invader? And is it justified to equate the fire of Palace G with a catastrophe of the city as a whole? According to Matthiae, "after the savage destruction which put an end to the Mardikh IIB1 settlement our excavations have not turned up any evidence of interruption in the continuity of occupation.... The transition from Mardikh IIB1 to Mardikh IIB2 is marked by the destruction of the Palace but not by any real break of cultural development."[62] It looks very much as if Royal Palace G was

---

unbroken linguistic continuity from Ebla to Babylonia around 2400 B.C."

[57] Hirsch, "Inschriften" (1963) 36, text Sargon b 1, 27-34.

[58] P.R.S. Moorey, "A Re-Consideration of the Excavations on Tell Ingharra (West Kish), 1923-33," *Iraq* 28 (1966) 18-57; M.E.L. Mallowan, "The Early Dynastic Period in Mesopotamia," *CAH*³ I/2 (1971) 274-275.

[59] Gelb, "Kish" (1981) 67-68.

[60] The Sumerian King List, which stands on firmer historical ground when it reaches the Sargonic period, says that "Kiš was smitten with weapons, its kingship to Uruk was carried; in Uruk Lugalzagesi became king" etc. Cf. Jacobsen, *King List* (1939) 179: "Now the only one who could thus have destroyed Kish is obviously Lugal-zage-si...." Thus also H. Schmökel, *Geschichte des alten Vorderasien* (Leiden, 1957) 28; I. Diakonoff, *Obščestvennyj i gosudarstvennyj stroj drevnego Dvureč'ja: Šumer* [*Society and State in Ancient Mesopotamia: Sumer*] (Moscow, 1959) 206-210; P. Garelli, *Le Proche-Orient Asiatique* (Paris, 1969) 76.

[61] In his Nippur inscription (*SAKI* 154 II:4-11) Lugalzagesi states that "Enlil opened for him the road from the Lower Sea, up the Tigris and the Euphrates, to the Upper Sea." It means no more than what it says, *viz.*, that the great trade routes along the Tigris and the Euphrates were safe for travel by Lugalzagesi's envoys and merchants. To be sure, the inscription also says that the god "had rendered the lands (kur-kur) subject at his foot, and from the rising sun to the setting sun he had bound the neck (of all) to him." But the claim is very vague, with no specific geographical indications, unlike the practice of clearly naming the defeated cities or countries in the inscriptions of earlier rulers (Utuk of Kiš, Eannatum of Lagaš) or the immediately following Sargonic kings.

[62] Matthiae, *Empire* (1981) 105.

the only part of the city to have burned down. And not all fires that destroyed palaces and other public buildings have been set by enemy hands; some have been caused by nature or accident. Such a possibility has been envisaged for the Late Minoan palace of Cnossus.[63] The old temple at Delphi burned down, around 550 BCE, by accident. The temple of Artemis at Ephesus burned down, in 359 BCE, from an individual act of arson. The first state capitol of Missouri burned down in 1837; the second, struck by lightning, in 1911. The Winter Palace at St. Petersburg was almost entirely destroyed by fire in 1837, despite improved firefighting techniques and no lack of water from the Neva River. In the conditions of almost waterless Ebla, especially on a dry summer day, with a strong westerly wind blowing, a fire in the palace would be practically impossible to extinguish.

In Archi's words, "archaeological documentation shows that Palace G was destroyed, sacked, and burned.[64] But it does not look as though it was sacked before being burned. Plunderers would not have left behind twenty-two kilograms of unworked lapis lazuli.[65] If it paid to import this highly valued stone, through numerous intermediaries, from as far as Badakhshan, it was certainly worth the looters' while to move the lapis lazuli a few yards out of the doomed palace. There were also smaller quantities of carnelian, rock crystal, and obsidian.[66] Speaking about remains of figurines found in the palace, Matthiae stresses "the extremely precious nature of these images of gold, ivory, and hard stone."[67] Describing the miniature inlay plaques, some of them of lapis lazuli, with meticulously carved details of human and animal figures, he sees as "very probable that these images formed part of some precious fittings," and that "a number of remnants of gold foil...were certainly overlays for wooden furniture."[68] It is unlikely that such furnishings, fit for a king, would have been left by invaders in the palace prior to torching it.[69] It rather seems that the palace personnel, surprised by the raging fire, simply did not have the time to save all of its contents.[70]

We have, thus, arrived at the following time bracket for the destruction of Royal Palace G. It occurred prior not only to the destruction of Mari by Sargon but also to that of Kiš by Lugalzagesi. Since the last years of Lugalzagesi's twenty-five year reign overlapped with Sargon's first years, it was approximately comprised between 2290 and 2265. Assuming, with T. Jacobsen, that Lugalzagesi destroyed Kiš about the middle of his reign, we would

---

[63] R.W. Hutchinson, *Prehistoric Crete* (Harmondsworth, 1962) 300-302.

[64] Archi, "More Kish" (1987) 136.

[65] Matthiae, *Tesori* (1984) 47; F. Pinnock, "Observations on the Trade of Lapis Luzuli in the IIIrd Millennium B.C.," in Waetzoldt and Hauptmann, *Wirtschaft* (1988) 108.

[66] F. Pinnock, "About the Trade of Early Syrian Ebla," *MARI* 4 (1985) 87.

[67] Matthiae, *Empire* (1981) 80.

[68] Ibid.:1.c.

[69] Then there is the case of the numerous alabaster vases, imported from Egypt, which were left in the palace and were shattered not by vandal hands but by the weight of the collapsed roof.

[70] Insofar as I know, the only other author to envisage this possibility was Postgate, "Abu Essalabikh" (1986) 68, who continued his statement, quoted in n. 44 above, with the words: "and it is perfectly possible that the destruction of the palace was accidental, or perhaps more likely caused by a different enemy, closer to Ebla—there are several possible rivals." The considerations adduced above apply, however, to any enemy, close or remote.

tentatively place that event about 2280. This is the *terminus ante quem* for the end of the Mardikh IIB1 period. For palaeographic reasons, it is difficult to set the *terminus post quem* much before 2300. This date would leave ample time for the importation of the vase with Pepi I's cartouche to Ebla. The attribution of the Ebla archives to the late pre-Sargonic period has been envisaged by some students of Ebla, but only in general terms and without excluding the reign of Sargon. The present study, as its author wishes to believe, has eliminated the Sargonic option, narrowed down the end of the Ebla archives to within twenty years (2300-2280), and provided a more solid base for the pre-Sargonic dating.

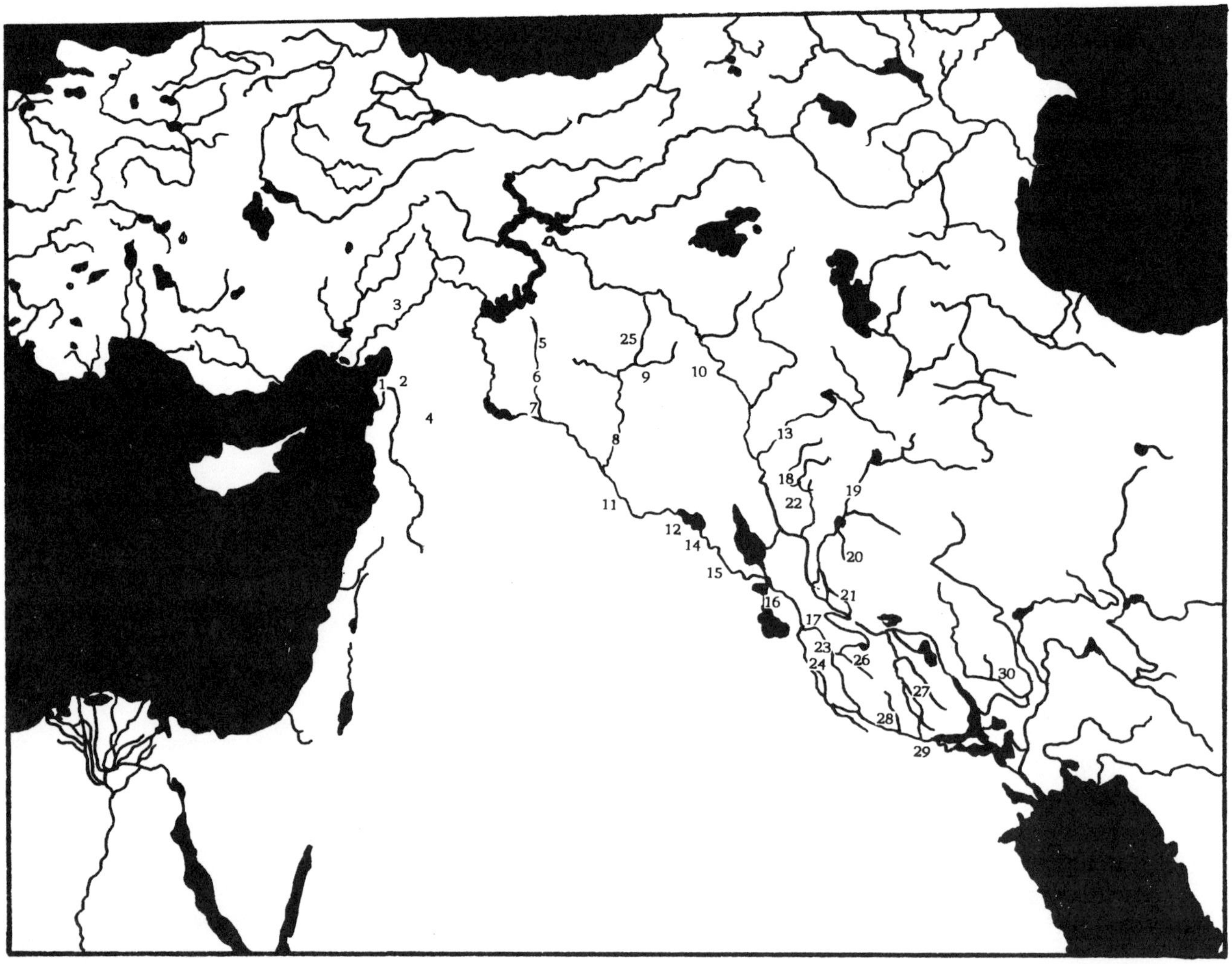

1 Ulisum
2 Amanus
3 Taurus Mountains
4 Ebla
5 Ḫarran
6 Balikh
7 Tuttul
8 Khabur
9 Nagar
10 Kiškiš
11 Mari
12 Yabliya
13 Little Zab
14 Ḫarbe
15 Itu
16 Rapiqum
17 Sippar
18 Arman Ebla
19 Turan (Diyala)
20 Ešnunna
21 Agade
22 Jebel Ḥamrin
23 Kutha
24 Kiš
25 Yarmuti
26 Nippur
27 Lagaš
28 Uruk
29 Ur
30 Elam

SYNCHRONISTIC TABLE

Years	LAGAŠ	MARI	EBLA Viziers/Kings	URUK/AKKAD	EGYPT	Years
2450						2450
2425	Ur-Nanše	Lamgi-Mari				2425
	2430-2401					
		Anubu	Išʾar-Malik			
2400	Akurgal	Saʾumu				2400
	2400-2391					
	Eannatum	Ištup-Šar	Kum-Damu			
2375	2390-2361					2375
		Iblul-Il	Adub-Damu			
2350	Enannatum I	Nizi				2350
	2360-2341	Enna-Dagan	Ar-ennum/			
	Entemenna		Igriš-Ḫalam			
2325	2341-2311					2325
	Enannatum II	Iku-Išar	Ibrium/		Pepi I	
	2310-2305		Irkab-Damu		2333-2283	
2300	Enentarzi 2304-2295		Ibbi-Zikir/	Lugalzagesi		2300
	Lugalanda 2294-2288	Ḫidar	Išʾar-Damu	ca. 2290-2265		
	Urukagina 2287-2278			Destruction of Kiš		
2275				ca. 2280		2275
		X				
		Destruction				
2250		of Mari		Sargon		2250
		ca. 2260		2270-2215		
2225						2225
				Rimuš		
				2214-2206		
2220				Maništušu		2220
				2205-2191		
2175				Naram-Sin		2175
				2190-2154		
2150						2150

HITTITE ADMINISTRATION IN SYRIA IN THE LIGHT OF THE TEXTS FROM ḪATTUŠA, UGARIT AND EMAR

Gary M. Beckman

Although the Hittite state of the Late Bronze Age always had its roots in central Anatolia,[1] it continually sought to expand its hegemony toward the southeast into Syria, where military campaigns would bring it booty in precious metals and other goods available at home only in limited quantities, and where domination would assure the constant flow of such wealth in the form of tribute and imposts on the active trade of this crossroads between Mesopotamia, Egypt, and the Aegean.

Already in the seventeenth century, the Hittite kings Ḫattušili I and his adopted son and successor Muršili I conquered much of this area, breaking the power of the "Great Kingdom" of Ḫalab and even reaching distant Babylon, where the dynasty of Ḫammurapi was brought to an end by Hittite attack. However, the Hittites were unable to consolidate their dominion over northern Syria and were soon forced back to the north by Hurrian princes, who were active even in eastern Anatolia.[2] Practically nothing can be said concerning Hittite administration of Syria in this period, known to Hittitologists as the Old Kingdom. During the following Middle Kingdom (late sixteenth-early fourteenth centuries), Hittite power was largely confined to Anatolia, while northern Syria came under the sway

---

[1] During the past quarter century research in Hittite studies has proceeded at such a pace that there currently exists no adequate monographic account of Anatolian history and culture of the second millennium. The most recent editions of the standard English-language histories, however, have been somewhat revised to take account of advances in knowledge. See O.R. Gurney, *The Hittites* (Harmondsworth, 1952; 2nd ed. 1954; repr. with revisions 1990); and J.G. Macqueen, *The Hittites and Their Contemporaries in Asia Minor* (London, 1975; 2nd ed. 1986). For a shorter, but more up-to-date, presentation, see H. Klengel, ed., *Kulturgeschichte des alten Vorderasien* (Berlin, 1989) 234-267. Numerous essays by experts on various aspects of the history and civilization of ancient Anatolia will appear in J.M. Sasson, ed., *Civilizations of the Ancient Near East* (New York: Scribners, 1993), and a useful and well-illustrated introduction to the field is to be found in a special issue of *BA* 52/2-3 (1989), edited by R.L. Gorney: *Reflections of a Late Bronze Age Empire: The Hittites*, which contains contributions by several scholars.

[2] S. de Martino, "I Hurriti nei testi dell'Antico Regno," *Seminari* [dello Istituto per gli studi micenei ed egeo-anatolici] anno 1990 (Roma, 1991) 71-83.

of the Hurrian state of Mitanni.[3] One of the Hittite rulers of this period, however, a certain Tudḫaliya, does seem to have reasserted Hittite claims over Ḫalab.[4] But his success was ephemeral.

Not so that of Šuppiluliuma I, founder of the Hittite Empire (or New Kingdom) in the first half of the fourteenth century. This greatest of Hittite monarchs destroyed the realm of Mitanni and absorbed the greater portion of its territories, extending Hittite dominion in Syria from the western reaches of the Khabur basin in the northeast to the upper end of the Beqᶜa valley in the south.[5] While his son and second successor Muršili II had to suppress a major uprising in this region,[6] and the later rulers Muwatalli II[7] and Tudḫaliya IV[8] confronted serious challenges from Egypt in the south and Assyria in the east, respectively, most of northern Syria remained securely in Hittite hands until the general collapse of the Late Bronze Age state system in the early twelfth century.[9]

Our primary sources for the history of the Hittite Empire in Syria are cuneiform tablets, chiefly from three sites: 1) the Hittite capital of Ḫattuša (Boghazköy) in central Turkey, where the central administrative archives of the Hittite imperial bureaucracy were uncovered; 2) the Syrian coastal emporium of Ugarit (Ras Shamra), where the archives of the local rulers include correspondence with the Hittite Great King and his representatives in Syria, as well as various edicts and day-to-day records involving the imperial administration; and 3) the outlying commercial town of Emar on the middle course of the Euphrates (present-day Meskeneh) and various settlements in its environs, from which many records of private individuals, as well as the technical library of a local priest, have been recovered.

While most of the relevant material from Ḫattuša and Ugarit has been published, and the epigrapher of the more recently-discovered Emar texts has made the Akkadian

---

[3] G. Wilhelm, *Grundzüge der Geschichte und Kultur der Hurriter* (Darmstadt, 1982) 23-58. This volume has been translated as *The Hurrians* (London, 1989).

[4] *KBo* 1.6 obv. 15-18 (*CTH* 75), edited by E.F. Weidner, *PDK* 82-83. See also O. Carruba, "Beiträge zur mittelhethitischen Geschichte I. *Die Tutḫalijas und die Arnuwandas*," *SMEA* 18 (1977) 137-174.

[5] The most important textual source for the military and diplomatic activities of Šuppiluliuma I is the account of his reign composed by his son (*CTH* 40). See the edition by H.G. Güterbock, "The Deeds of Suppiluliuma as Told by His Son, Mursili II," *JCS* 10 (1956) 41-68, 75-98, 107-130. An historical interpretation of the conqueror's Syrian campaign is presented by K.A. Kitchen, *Suppiluliuma and the Amarna Pharaohs* (Liverpool, 1962).

[6] The revolt of much of Syria in the ninth year of his reign is chronicled in his Annals (*CTH* 61), edited by A. Goetze, *Die Annalen des Muršilis* (Leipzig, 1933; *MVAG* 38/6. Repr. Darmstadt, 1967) 106-131.

[7] The confrontation with Egypt culminating in the famous battle of Kadesh is best known to us from Egyptian sources. For a thorough discussion see W.J. Murname, *The Road to Kadesh* (Chicago, 1985; *SAOC* 42; 2nd ed. 1990).

[8] Our understanding of the struggle between Ḫatti and Assyria in the late thirteenth century has become clearer due to the recent discovery at Ugarit of a letter with significant historical implications: S. Lackenbacher, "Nouveaux documents d'Ugarit. I.-Une lettre royale," *RA* 76 (1982) 141-156. For the historical interpretation of this text see I. Singer, "The Battle of Niḫriya and the End of the Hittite Empire," *ZA* 75 (1985) 100-123; and "Dating the End of the Hittite Empire," *Hethitica* 8 (1987) 413-421.

[9] H.A. Hoffner, "The Last Days of Ḫattuša," *Berytus* 39/40 (forthcoming), with full bibliography of the extensive secondary literature.

documents from the official excavations of that site available in timely fashion,[10] hundreds of tablets from this area are in private collections[11] or remain on the art market. As these texts gradually become known to scholarship,[12] our picture of life and society in Hittite Syria correspondingly becomes clearer.[13]

Four major deficits in our documentation must also be acknowledged: We do not have pertinent archives from the cities of Carchemish, Ḫalab, Ṣumur, or Waššukkanni. The first city, one of the most important in second millennium Syria, was long ago identified as Jerablus on the Euphrates, and was indeed partially excavated in the early years of this century, but no tablets from the second millennium were found, and its location on the sensitive Turkish-Syrian border has precluded further investigation.[14] Ancient Ḫalab lies inaccessible beneath the modern city of Aleppo.[15] Ṣumur, likely capital of Amurru, is probably Tell Kazel on the southern Syrian coast. Preliminary excavations there have turned up only a few suggestive indications of the presence of Hittite imperial government.[16] Finally, the location of Waššukkanni, chief city of Mitanni, is still one of the most hotly-debated questions in Ancient Near Eastern archaeology.[17]

Although other polities, such as Ḫalab, Mukiš, Niya-Nuḫašše,[18] Tunip[19] and Kinza, played a role in Hittite Syria, the most important dependencies were Carchemish, Ugarit, Mitanni, Aštata, and Amurru. Carchemish was the seat of a cadet line of the Hittite royal house, founded when Šuppiluliuma installed his son Piyaššili, who also bore the Hurrian name Šarri-Kušuḫ, as king of this city. Throughout the fourteenth and thirteenth centuries the king of Carchemish served as Hittite "viceroy" in Syria. In time of peace he was the

---

[10] D. Arnaud, *Recherches au Pays d'Aštata: Emar VI.1-4. Les textes sumériens et accadiens* (Paris, 1985-87).

[11] I am currently preparing an edition of more than 90 tablets from Emar and its environs in the collection of Jonathan Rosen of New York City (cited here as *RE*).

[12] See, for example, D. Arnaud, "La Syrie du moyen-Euphrate sous le protectorat hittite: l'administration d'après trois lettres inédites," *AuOr* 2 (1984) 179-188; "La Syrie du moyen-Euphrate sous le protectorat hittite: contrats de droit privé," *AuOr* 5 (1987) 211-241, and the Emar tablets in the Hirayama Collection, edited by A. Tsukimoto: "Akkadian Tablets in the Hirayama Collection (I)," *ASJ* 12 (1990) 177-259, and "Akkadian Tablets in the Hirayama Collection (II)," *ASJ* 13 (1991) 277-333.

[13] For the history of Hittite Syria in this period consult the relevant chapters of H. Klengel, *Geschichte Syriens im 2. Jahrtausend v. u. Z.* I-III (Berlin, 1965-70), and his supplemental "Neue Quellen zur Geschichte Nordsyriens im 2. Jahrtausend v. u. Z," *AoF* 2 (1975) 47-64. Although these works were written before the publication of the Emar tablets, Klengel has briefly discussed these latter sources in "Die Keilschrifttexte von Meskene und die Geschichte von Aštata/Emar," *OLZ* 83 (1988) 645-653. See also in general S.D. Waterhouse, "Syria in the Amarna Age: A Borderland between Conflicting Empires," (Ph.D. diss., University of Michigan, 1965).

[14] J.D. Hawkins, "Karkamiš," *RLA* 5 (1980) 426-446.

[15] H. Klengel, "Ḫalab," *RLA* 4 (1975) 50-53.

[16] M. Dunand et al., "Fouilles de Tell Kazel, Rapport préliminaire," *AAAS* 14 (1964) 3-14.

[17] See the literature listed by G.F. del Monte and J. Tischler, *Die Orts- und Gewässernamen der hethitischen Texte* (Wiesbaden, 1978; *RGTC* 6) 480; and also A. Dobel et al., "Neutron Activation Analysis and the Location of Waššukanni," *Or* 46 (1977) 375-382.

[18] M.C. Astour, "The Partition of the Confederacy of Mukiš-Nuḫašše-Nii by Šuppiluliuma," *Or* 38 (1969) 381-414.

[19] M.C. Astour, "Tunip-Hamath and Its Region: A Contribution to the Historical Geography of Central Syria," *Or* 46 (1977) 51-64.

chief political authority to the south of the Taurus mountains, and in time of war the highest military commander in the area. Remarkably, our sources reveal no friction between any of the kings of Carchemish and their cousins, the Hittite Great Kings.[20]

Ugarit was the major port and trading center of northern Syria, enjoying commercial connections with Mesopotamia and regions farther to the east, as well as with Egypt, the Aegean, Hittite-controlled Cilicia, and of course the Syro-Palestinian coast to the south. Her high tribute in gold, textiles, and fine wool was certainly of great importance to the Hittite economy, and her fleet of sea-going vessels was at the disposal of the imperial authorities for both military purposes and for the transshipment of foodstuffs in time of famine. In addition, of course, the incorporation of Ugarit into the Hittite system of states afforded Anatolian merchants better access to the international trade networks of the age.[21]

Mitanni, much of whose former territory was ceded by Šuppiluliuma to Carchemish, was allowed a continued existence as a buffer against newly-resurgent Assyria to the east. However, the Assyrians also had their own puppet Hurrian state, Ḫanigalbat, and it seems that the latter gradually expanded to the detriment of the Hittite vassal, until in the later thirteenth century Ḫatti and Assyria confronted one another directly not far to the east of Carchemish.[22]

The land of Aštata, of which Emar was one of the most important cities, constituted the frontier district against Babylonia to the southeast, from which direction no trouble is attested, as well as against the Assyrian realm to the northeast. From this quarter unpleasantness indeed emanated, as indicated by two Emar records which mention in passing the siege of the town by "the Hurrians,"[23] certainly a reference to the Assyrian pawn Ḫanigalbat. Several smaller archaeological sites around Meskeneh, such as Tell Faqʾous,[24] seem to have been military stations and frontier posts. The international character of life in this district is demonstrated by the presence in the archives of individual cuneiform tablets inscribed in a Babylonian[25] or an Assyrian hand,[26] as well as a number of texts composed in the Hittite and Hurrian languages.[27]

---

[20] See n. 14 above.

[21] M. Liverani, *Storia di Ugarit nell'età degli archivi politici* (Roma, 1962; *SS* 6).

[22] See n. 3 above and A. Harrak, *Assyria and Hanigalbat* (Hildesheim, 1987; *TSO* 4).

[23] *Hirayama* 7, 29-30: *inūma* erín.meš *Ḫurri* bàd ^{uru}*Emar*^{ki} *ilmi*, "when the Hurrian troops besieged the fortifications of Emar." Tsukimoto, "Hirayama I" (1990) 191-192, compares an excerpt from a copy of a dedicatory inscription, *Emar* VI, 42, 8-10: ^{m}*Pilsu*(!)-^{d}kur dumu ^{d}Iškur-*kabar* lugal ^{uru}*Emar* lugal erín.meš kur *Ḫurri* ^{uru}*Emar ilammin*, "Pilsu-Dagan, son of Ba'al-kabar (was) king of Emar. The king of the Hurrian troops and the city of Emar were(!) on bad terms." For the reading and interpretation of these lines, see J.-M. Durand's review of *Emar* VI, *RA* 83 (1989) 183-184. Both of these texts were composed under King Pilsu-Dagan, who as a contemporary of Ini-Teššup of Carchemish and Tudḫaliya IV of Ḫatti, ruled in the mid-thirteenth century.

[24] J.-C. Margueron, "Aux marches de l'empire hittite: une campaigne de fouille à Tel Faq'ous (Syrie), citadelle du pays d'Aštata," in M. Yon, ed., *La Syrie au Bronze Récent* (Paris, 1982) 47-66.

[25] *Emar* VI, 25-27.

[26] *RE* 19.

[27] This material has not yet been edited. See the preliminary discussion of a number of pieces by E. Laroche, "Documents hittites et hourrites," in D. Beyer, ed., *Meskéné-Emar: Dix ans de travaux 1972-1982* (Paris, 1982) 53-60.

The frontier of Hittite Syria over against Egyptian possessions in Syro-Palestine was guarded by Amurru,[28] and by the smaller state of Kinza, of which relatively little is known.[29] After the conclusion of the great peace treaty between the Ḫatti of Ḫattušili III and the Egypt of Ramses II in the mid-thirteenth century, Amurru served as the hub of diplomatic and trade contacts between the two great powers, and the local ruler was responsible for furthering the traffic in diplomats, sumptuous gifts, and brides.[30]

Given the slowness of communication in this age and the fact that all movement into or out of the core Hittite area was severely restricted during the winter months, the Hittite state throughout its history tended to grow by the association of vassal units rather than through their full political and economic integration into the central structure. In fact, the Hittites usually preferred to rule distant areas through the agency of members of the dynasties whom they had defeated.[31]

These kings assumed certain obligations toward Ḫatti and were bound by treaty to the person of the Hittite Great King. The primary duties imposed upon vassals in these treaties were the payment of tribute, the providing of military assistance when required, the renouncing of all independent foreign contacts, the extradition of fugitives from Ḫatti (of ordinary peasants and artisans as well as of disgruntled members of the ruling class), and the guarantee of the succession to the Hittite throne of the Great King's designated heir.[32]

This system was indeed employed in Hittite Syria, for most of whose states treaties are attested.[33] Should respect for the oaths upholding these agreements be insufficient to secure loyalty and obedience, the Hittites might resort to military action and the replacement of the recalcitrant vassal, should he indeed survive the war.[34] There might also be a punitive redrawing of borders upon the successful outcome of the campaign. Thus, during the initial establishment of Hittite rule, much of Mukiš was presented by Šuppiluliuma to Ugarit, which had had the good sense to pledge its allegiance to the conqueror earlier.[35] Conversely, when Ugarit herself later joined the Syrian rebellion against Muršili II, her southern dependencies of Siyannu and Ušnatu were removed from her jurisdiction and made directly subordinate to the king of Carchemish.[36] There can also be little doubt that the

---

[28] I. Singer, "A Concise History of Amurru," apud S. Izre'el, *Amurru Akkadian* (Atlanta, 1991) vol. 2, 135-195.

[29] Klengel, *Geschichte Syriens* II (1969) 156-177.

[30] See the thoughts of I. Singer, "A Hittite Hieroglyphic Seal Impression from Tel Aphek," *TA* 4 (1977) 178-190. As the southernmost major Hittite vassal, Amurru was certainly instrumental on the Hittite side of this exchange.

[31] On Hittite diplomatic practice in general see G. Kestemont, *Diplomatique et droit international en Asie occidentale (1600-1200 av. J.C.)* (Louvain-la-Neuve, 1974; *PIOL* 6).

[32] V. Korošec, *Hethitische Staatsverträge* (Leipzig, 1931).

[33] Actual treaty documents have been preserved in regard to Amurru (*CTH* 49, 62, 92, 105), Ḫalab (*CTH* 75), Carchemish (*CTH* 50, 122), Mitanni (*CTH* 51, 52), Nuḫašše (*CTH* 53), and Ugarit (*CTH* 46, 66). For other polities, such as Kinza and Aštata, a treaty relation is mentioned in other types of text.

[34] See, for example, T.R. Bryce, "Tette and the Rebellions in Nuhassi," *AnSt* 38 (1988) 21-28.

[35] See n. 18 above.

[36] M.C. Astour, "The Kingdom of Siyannu-Ušnatu," *UF* 11 (1979) 13-28.

function of the Hittite garrisons sometimes assigned to vassal kingdoms was as much to keep an eye on the activities of the local ruler as to protect his life.

But the Hittites preferred less coercive measures. The most important of these was the marriage alliance.[37] Such ties are known in respect to Mitanni, whose first vassal ruler Šattiwazza was married to a daughter of Šuppiluliuma I, as well as for Ugarit, whose final king ᶜAmmurapi married—and later divorced—Eḫli-Nikkalu, probably the daughter of Šuppiluliuma II.[38] But the most intricate marriage ties were with Amurru: its king Bentešina and his son Šaušgamuwa each married a daughter of the Hittite Great King Ḫattušili III, while the latter's son Nerikkaili was betrothed to a daughter of Bentešina, apparently the bridegroom's own niece. Political and familial relationships became yet more complicated in the next generation, when the daughter of Bentešina, and granddaughter of Ḫattušili III, became the wife of ᶜAmmistamru II of Ugarit. When as the result of some unexplained offence, the woman was divorced and her irate husband sought to punish her even more severely, the matter became an international incident, ultimately adjudicated by her brother Šaušgamuwa of Amurru, her cousin Tudḫaliya IV of Ḫatti, and her more distant cousin Ini-Teššup of Carchemish.[39]

But what of day-to-day administration? As mentioned earlier, although the Great King of Ḫattuša might on occasion intervene in Syrian affairs and could be appealed to in the final instance, the highest political and military authority in Hittite Syria was ordinarily the king of Carchemish.[40] His participation in judicial and economic affairs is manifest in documents from Ugarit and Emar. For example, the king of Carchemish whose activities are best known to us, Ini-Teššup, adjudicated disputes between Ugarit and Amurru on the one hand,[41] and between Ugarit and Siyannu-Ušnatu on the other.[42] He also concluded an agreement with ᶜAmmistamru II of Ugarit concerning compensation in the case of the murder of a merchant,[43] and arranged for the resurveying of the borders of Ugarit.[44] In at least two instances he received complaints concerning false imprisonment by high administrators of the port town.[45] Various documents from Ugarit and from Emar relating to private affairs—disputes at law, sales of real property, and testaments—are said to have been composed "in the presence of Ini-Teššup."[46] It is not clear whether this situation

---

[37] The Hittites also established such bonds with their equals, Egypt and Babylonia. See F. Pintore, *Il matrimonio interdinastico nel Vicino Oriente durante i secoli xv-xiii* (Roma, 1978) 33-78.

[38] M.C. Astour, "King Ammurapi and the Hittite Princess," *UF* 12 (1980) 103-108.

[39] See Singer, "Amurru" (1991) 174-175, with full bibliography on this matter.

[40] Consider the actions taken by Muršili II in *CTH* 63: H. Klengel, "Der Schiedsspruch des Muršili II. hinsichtlich Barga und seine Übereinkunft mit Duppi-Tešup von Amurru (KBo III 3)," *Or* 32 (1963) 32-55. It should be noted that the measures taken here are not to become final until the king of Carchemish has been consulted.

[41] *PRU* IV, 134ff.

[42] *PRU* IV, 161ff.

[43] *PRU* IV, 152ff.

[44] *PRU* IV, 188; cf. also *PRU* III, 6-7.

[45] *PRU* VI, 35-38.

[46] Ugarit: *PRU* IV, 165-169, 292-293. The first group of texts is made up of legal cases in which the King

involved the travel of the parties in these transactions to Carchemish, or whether the king rather made a periodic circuit of the area under his jurisdiction.[47]

Active throughout Hittite Syria were officials designated by the Sumerographic term dumu.lugal, literally "Son of the King"—the Hittite reading is uncertain. Although this turn of phrase may indicate that the higher echelons of the Hittite administration were generally occupied by persons of royal descent, it is quite clear that not all holders of this title were offspring of the reigning Great King.[48] Texts from Ḫattuša, Ugarit, and Emar demonstrate that the "Sons of the King" were very high ranking officials, often dispatched by the Hittite King to perform particular political or administrative tasks.[49] They do not seem to have been permanently posted to any single locality. Guy Bunnens has aptly compared them to the Carolingian *missi dominici*.[50]

At Ugarit we encounter "Sons of the King" redrawing the borders of the state,[51] arbitrating between the queen and a tax official,[52] and even ordering King ᶜIbiranu to make the required appearance before his sovereign, the Great King.[53] In the Emar documents the dumu.lugal are most often found as witnesses to various transactions in real estate[54] and slaves.[55] Their preeminence is signaled by their invariable position at the head of the list of witnesses.

In moving down the administrative hierarchy to more local officials, our sources are extensive enough to allow relatively detailed discussion only of the governments of Ugarit and of the region of Emar, that is, the Land of Aštata. Since the administration of Ugarit has already been extensively studied by others,[56] I will confine myself here to a few remarks concerning the governance of Aštata. This area was the province of an official designated

---

of Ugarit is one of the litigants, while the final, fragmentary, tablet deals with a dispute between two high officials. Emar: *Emar* VI, 18, 177, 202; *RE* 54, 55.

[47] In favor of the first alternative is Text B treated by A. Tsukimoto, "Sieben spätbronzezeitliche Urkunden aus Syrien," *ASJ* 10 (1988) 157-160, in which three persons agree to settle their affairs "upon our arrival in Carchemish" (rev. 6'-7': *nēnu ina* ᵘʳᵘ*Karkamiš ina kašādini*), but this may be atypical since those involved are all Hittite bureaucrats. In another text, however, persons who are certainly native Syrians include in a contract the following clause concerning a possible litigant: "let him (go) to the city of the king and swear" (*Hirayama* 5 [*ASJ* 12 (1990) 185-186], left edge 12-13: *ana* uru *šarri litmani*). This is more likely a reference to Carchemish than to either Emar or Ḫattuša.

[48] F. Imparati, "'Signori' e 'figli del re'," *Or* 44 (1975) 80-95.

[49] F. Pecchioli Daddi, *Mestieri, professioni e dignità nell'Anatolia ittita* (Roma, 1982) 503-512.

[50] "Emar on the Euphrates in the 13th Century B.C. Some Thoughts about Newly Published Cuneiform Texts," *AbN* 27 (1989) 27.

[51] *PRU* III, 6f.

[52] *PRU* IV, 189.

[53] *PRU* IV, 191.

[54] For example *Emar* VI, 182 and *Hirayama* 3.

[55] *Emar* VI, 211. Cf. D. Arnaud, "Humbles et superbes à Emar (Syrie) à la fin de l'âge du Bronze récent," in A. Caquot and M. Delcor, eds., *Mélanges bibliques et orientaux en l'honneur de M. Henri Cazelles* (Kevelaer, 1981; *AOAT* 212) 2-3.

[56] M. Heltzer, *The Internal Organization of the Kingdom of Ugarit* (Wiesbaden, 1982). See also his *The Rural Community in Ancient Ugarit* (Wiesbaden, 1976).

as the "Overseer of the Land," written sumerographically ugula.kalam.ma,[57] or on occasion simply ^{lú}ugula.[58] He was apparently responsible for the entire southeastern region of Hittite Syria and traveled about from town to town in the performance of his duties, to judge from correspondence recovered at Emar.[59] His attested activities include military intelligence,[60] administrative oversight,[61] and the witnessing of various legal transactions,[62] as well as (probably passive) participation in the local cult.[63] In witness lists he follows any "Son of the King" who might be present.

Native authority at Emar was held by the local king,[64] as well as by the collegium of city elders,[65] acting in most cases in conjunction with (the temple of$^{?}$) the god whose name is written with the Sumerogram ^{d}NIN.URTA.[66] These elders seized and resold the property of delinquent citizens[67] and guaranteed various other legal transactions.[68]

Lawsuits are attested before the local king,[69] before a group called "the great ones" (lú.meš gal),[70] who may be identical to the elders, and before a "Son of the King."[71] Most

---

[57] See Arnaud, "Administration" (1984) 182, n. 9, and Bunnens, "Emar" (1989) 25-26. This official appears in the following texts (in full writing): *Emar* VI, 90, 181, 252, 259, 262, 263, 289(?), 460, *RE* 56, and M. Fales, ed., *Prima dell'alfabeto* (Venezia, 1988; *Studi e documenti* 4) 203-204, No. 66.

[58] Arnaud, "Administration" (1984) 181-182, No. 1; and 186-187, No. 3.

[59] H.A. Hoffner has pointed out to me the great similarity between the duties of this official and those of the *BĒL MADGALTI*, "margrave, district governor," in Hittite Anatolia. On this latter official see the instructions text (*CTH* 261) edited by E. von Schuler, *Hethitische Dienstanweisungen* (Graz, 1957; *AfO* Beiheft 10) 36-59.

[60] *Emar* VI, 263.

[61] *Emar* VI, 262.

[62] *Emar* VI, 90, 181, 252, *RE* 56, and Fales, *Alfabeto* (1988) No. 66. Cf. also Arnaud, "Administration" (1984) 186-187, No. 3.

[63] *Emar* VI, 460.

[64] For the line of kings, see D. Arnaud, "Les textes d'Emar et la chronologie de la fin du Bronze Récent," *Syria* 52 (1975) 89-90.

[65] W.F. Leemans, "Aperçu sur les textes juridiques d'Emar," *JESHO* 31 (1988) 213-217.

[66] The identity of the West Semitic deity hidden behind this Sumerian writing is uncertain. It is remarkable that this ideogram is not employed as a theophoric element in any personal name from Emar and its environs known to me. Presumably one of the phonetically-written divine names is its equivalent, yet with the exceptions of Dagan and Ba^{c}al, who are not in question here, no single deity is so frequently attested in personal names as to correspond to the prominence displayed by ^{d}NIN.URTA in the contracts and thus in the life of the city of Emar.

[67] In many instances (e.g., *Emar* VI, 143-155), parcels of real property are sold by the "elders of the city of Emar" ($^{\text{lú.meš}}$*šībūt* ^{uru}*Emar*^{ki}) and the deity ^{d}NIN.URTA. Since there are far too many transactions of this type for them to represent a selling-off of temple property, and since no sales *to* ^{d}NIN.URTA are known, these actions must entail the disposal of some sort of delinquent property. On judicial matters at Emar in general see D. Arnaud, "Traditions urbaines et influences semi-nomades à Emar, à l'âge du bronze récent," in J.-Cl. Margueron, ed., *Le Moyen Euphrate* (Leiden, 1980) 245-264.

[68] The seal which D. Beyer, "Quelques vestiges de l'imagerie émariote du Bronze Moyen," *MARI* 6 (1990) 94, n. 7, has identified as that of ^{d}NIN.URTA (p. 95, No. 4; p. 96, No. 1) appears on the upper edge of many tablets from Emar, while the anepigraphic design which he recognizes as that of the dynastic seal (in four exemplars thus far known) is found even more frequently on the left edges of the tablets.

[69] *Emar* VI, 212, *RE* 21. Note that the local king also often heads the list of witnesses to sales of real property.

[70] *Emar* VI, 28, 252.

frequent by far, however, are cases brought to the attention of the king of Carchemish.[72] It is not possible to determine how a certain official came to be responsible for a given matter, or to follow any particular case through appeal from instance to instance. It is also puzzling why a particular type of transaction is sometimes carried out before the local king and his court, sometimes before a Hittite official, and sometimes before what is to all appearances a group of ordinary citizens.[73]

Finally, the Emar documents mention a fair number of other bureaucrats who, judging by their personal names, seem to be Syrian natives rather than Anatolian imperial officials. Among these are scribes[74] (including the "chief scribe"[75] and the "great scribe"[76]), the "mayor" (*ḫazannu*),[77] and the "lord of the storehouse."[78] Little can be gleaned from our sources concerning their duties and responsibilities.

In summary, the Hittites did not impose a uniform system of government upon all of their Syrian realm. Rather, they installed a thin layer of imperial bureaucracy over the societal structures which they found upon their conquest, structures which could differ greatly from one another. (The activities of the Emariote elders, for instance, do not seem to be paralleled at Ugarit.) This picture, by the way, is in harmony with what we know about Hittite rule in outlying regions of Anatolia as well.

In normal times, the Syrian locals directed their own economic and internal political affairs, while rendering unto the Hittite Great King his due in tribute and services. It seems that Hittite authorities were active as judges or witnesses under three sets of circumstances: First, when the rulers of local Syrian polities were themselves parties to a dispute, this would of course necessitate imperial adjudication, since their treaties with Ḫatti denied vassals recourse to military force among themselves. Secondly, if a native of sufficient wealth and prestige was unable to obtain satisfaction from the local authorities in some matter, he might turn to a "Son of the King," the king of Carchemish, or even the King of Ḫatti. Finally, a member of the local community might find it advantageous to put the prestige of the imperial service behind a legal settlement by arranging for the presence of a Hittite official at the head of his witnesses.

Further study of the ever-increasing number of published texts from the middle Euphrates region of this period, as well as their careful comparison with materials from Ugarit, will doubtlessly allow the refinement of the picture sketched here.

---

[71] A. Tsukimoto, "Eine neue Urkunde des *Tili-Šarruma*, Sohn des Königs von Karkamiš," *ASJ* 6 (1984) 65-74.

[72] *Emar* VI, 18, 19, 31, 177, 194, 201, 202, *RE* 54, 55, 85.

[73] For example, *Emar* VI, 130, 144, 148 (but note the presence of the *ḫazannu* in this document).

[74] Typical is the inclusion of "Baᶜal-malik, son of Imlik-Dagan, scribe," among the witnesses of *Emar* VI, 90. More than seventy-five occurrences of this title are to be found in the published Emar texts. It is, however, interesting to note that in the majority of recorded transactions, scribes do not sign their work, or at least do not append their professional designation to their names should they appear among the witnesses.

[75] *Emar* VI, 212. Note also the "overseer of scribes" in *Emar* VI, 315 (fragmentary).

[76] *Emar* VI, 201.

[77] *Emar* VI, 148, 149, 150, 157, 253, 254, *RE* 16, 24, 34, 39, etc.

[78] *Emar* VI, 186, 212.

THE RITUALS FROM EMAR: EVOLUTION OF AN INDIGENOUS TRADITION IN SECOND-MILLENNIUM SYRIA

Daniel E. Fleming

The ancient city of Emar on the great bend of the Euphrates River in Syria was excavated from 1972 to 1976 by a French team directed by Jean-Claude Margueron.[1] Excavations yielded 1-2000 cuneiform tablets and fragments, most written during the 13th century BCE. Excitement over the finds from nearby Ebla perhaps distracted attention from Emar, and although the Akkadian texts were published by Daniel Arnaud in 1985-1987, they are only beginning to receive the study they deserve.[2]

Emar constitutes a major new source for ancient Syria, from roughly the same time as Ugarit, about 125 miles further east.[3] My own involvement with Emar began with my dissertation study of the unique ritual texts, and these are my starting point for examining the mosaic of Emar culture.[4] The rituals display a native religious practice quite distinct

---

[1] Margueron has published several preliminary reports of his excavations, including: "Les fouilles françaises de Meskéné-Émar (Syrie)," *CRAIBL* 1975 201-213; "Quatre campagnes de fouilles à Emar (1972-1974): un bilan provisoire," *Syria* 52 (1975) 53-85; "Rapport préliminaire sur les deux premières campagnes de fouilles à Meskéné-Emar (1972-1973)," *AAAS* 25 (1975) 73-86; "Emar: un exemple d'implantation hittite en terre syrienne," in J.-C. Margueron, ed., *Le Moyen Euphrate: Zone de contacts et d'échanges* (Leiden, 1980) 285-312; "Rapport préliminaire sur les 3ᵉ, 4ᵉ, 5ᵉ, et 6ᵉ campagnes de fouilles à Meskéné-Emar," *AAAS* 32 (1982) 233-249.

[2] When a majority of the discovered tablets are broken as at Emar, precise numbers are difficult to give even where the catalogued texts have been published. Daniel Arnaud has published the Sumerian-Akkadian tablets as *Recherches au Pays d'Aštata: Emar VI.1-4. Les textes sumériens et accadiens* (Paris, 1985-87), and he lists in his catalogue (I, pp. 7-22) 1821 numbered tablets, which he gathers into 793 numbered texts. E. Laroche, "Emar, étape entre Babylone et le Hatti," in *Le Moyen Euphrate* (1980) 244, describes the Hurrian texts from Emar as a dozen large tablets and thousands of fragments.

[3] D. Arnaud, "Les textes d'Emar et la chronologie de la fin du Bronze Récent," *Syria* 52 (1975) 89-92, finds a *terminus ad quem* for the destruction of Late Bronze Emar in a contract dated to the second year of the Kassite king Melišiḫu (or Melišipak), or 1187 BCE. He sets the beginning of this Emar period at about 1310, comparing the reigns of Carchemish regents mentioned in the Emar texts and then the chronology for the Hittite king Muršili II. Laroche, "Emar" (1980) 239-240, discusses the campaign of Muršili II into this part of Syria, as told in his own annals.

[4] My doctoral dissertation (Harvard University PhD, 1990) is published in revised form as *The Installation of Baal's High Priestess at Emar: A Window on Ancient Syrian Religion* (Atlanta, 1992; *HSS* 42); cited hereinafter

from that known of its contemporary at Ugarit, but this native Emar practice itself shows a diverse heritage. Ancient Syria has long been viewed as a crossroads of cultures, influenced by the movement of trade and conquest across its territory from Egypt, Anatolia, and Mesopotamia, but Emar ritual allows discernment of separate developments within the sphere of what is properly Syrian culture.

This paper will introduce briefly the context of the Emar rituals and then discuss the evidence for non-Syrian and distinct Syrian features of the corpus.

THE EMAR TEXTS

When Margueron excavated the tell above the Euphrates River near the modern town of Meskeneh, he was looking for Middle Bronze Imar, known from the Mari texts as the point where trade with the west switched from the river to an overland route.[5] Instead he found only a Late Bronze II city built from scratch by the Hittites when they conquered the region in the late 14th century BCE, and destroyed utterly shortly after 1200, never to be rebuilt. The older city either was buried under the waters of the lake or lies deep below the tell layers manufactured in the massive Hittite project, now shorefront real estate on Lake Assad.[6] Late Bronze Emar served as an outpost at the southeastern edge of the Hittite empire, facing the declining kingdom of Mitanni and the rising power of Assyria.

The Emar texts are the product of the cuneiform scribes trained in the writing tradition of Mesopotamia and found across the ancient Near East in the second millennium. The texts from the excavations proper include:

1. Akkadian texts composed for the needs of life in Emar: contracts, wills, and other legal documents; letters; administrative lists, especially for temples; and texts for rituals and offerings;
2. Mesopotamian dictionary and literary texts, for scribal training;
3. a few Hittite letters, and a collection of Hurrian medical and divination texts, translated from the Akkadian Mesopotamian canon.[7]

---

as *Installation*.

[5] Margueron mentions this starting point for the search in "Fouilles" (1975) 202-203, and in "Implantation" (1980) 285-286. On Imar in the third and early second millennium, see A. Finet, "Le port d'Emar sur l'Euphrate, entre le royaume de Mari et le pays de Canaan," in E. Lipiński, ed., *The Land of Israel: Cross-roads of Civilizations* (Leuven, 1985) 27-38; A. Archi, "Imâr au IIIème millénaire d'après les archives d'Ebla," *MARI* 6 (1990) 21-38; J.-M. Durand, "La cité-état d'Imâr à l'époque des rois de Mari," *MARI* 6 (1990) 39-92.

[6] See Margueron, "Fouilles 1972-1974" (1975) 84-85, and "Implantation" (1980) 286. The Hittite builders constructed much of the tell from scratch, and Margueron does not believe such a project would have been undertaken to cover an existing city site. On the other hand, a tell of the size expected for the older Imar should not have been missed in the surveys preceding the filling of Lake Assad (personal communication, Mr. Hamido Hammade, the Aleppo National Museum).

[7] Only a few of these are available in translation by E. Laroche, "Documents hittites et hourrites," in D. Beyer, ed., *Meskéné-Emar: Dix ans de travaux 1972-1982* (Paris, 1982) 53-60. Laroche discusses the texts briefly in "Emar" (1980) 241-244.

The Akkadian texts are now available in transliteration and translation in volumes 3 and 4 of Arnaud's Emar editions, and the others are in various stages of publication.

Admitting partiality, the most remarkable, unique aspect of the Emar textual finds is the diviner's archive, which includes 400 of the more than 500 Akkadian texts composed for Emar use, along with the Mesopotamian scribal works and the Hurrian scholarly lore. These were found in one building, the "temple M_1," which appears to have been a scribal center under supervision of a man called "the diviner of the gods of Emar."[8] Among the diverse private and temple documents the real find was almost 200 texts and fragments for rituals composed at Emar.[9] They describe Emar practice and are not attested in the ritual corpora from Ḫatti (Hittite and Hurrian), Mesopotamia (Babylonian and Assyrian), and Ugarit.

The Emar ritual texts may be classified under four headings:[10]

1. "Festivals." The title is the Sumerian EZEN, the scribes' own designation for rites that include some of the most complex and interesting at Emar. These should represent deeply rooted native Syrian traditions.
2. Calendar ritual. These are set either as months in a year or days in a month. Arnaud suggests that they derive from Mesopotamian models, but they do not conform to known types.
3. Offering lists.
4. Rites for the gods of Ḫatti. These are definitely based on real Hittite ritual, though no exact equivalent has been found.[11]

Among the festivals, the following represent the major rites, and so the core of the Syrian ritual newly displayed at Emar:

1. The installation of the NIN.DINGIR (*Emar* VI, 369), the high priestess of the storm god's temple.[12] This covers nine days: selection, a separate "shaving

---

[8] The identification of the temple M_1 as "the diviner's archive" follows D. Arnaud (see "La bibliothèque d'un devin syrien à Meskéné-Emar (Syrie)," *CRAIBL* 1980 375-387) and derives from the prominence of a diviner's family in the legal documents found there (*Emar* VI, 199-226), along with the importance of scholarly and (Hurrian) omen works in the collection. Many contracts found in the temple M_1 refer to property held by the city god ^{d}NIN.URTA and the elders of Emar (e.g. *Emar* VI, 144-155), and based on these W.F. Leemans, "Aperçu sur les textes juridiques d'Emar," *JESHO* 31 (1988) 216, identifies the excavated building as the temple of ^{d}NIN.URTA. These contracts were likewise found in other buildings, however (e.g. *Emar* VI 1-4, 9), and I do not see a particular association of ^{d}NIN.URTA and the temple M_1.

[9] Arnaud lists the rituals as text numbers 369-535, and some of these involve multiple tablet fragments (not joined).

[10] See Fleming, *Installation*, 200-201.

[11] For recent discussion of the rites for the gods of Ḫatti, see E. Laroche, "Observations sur le rituel anatolien provenant de Meskéné-Emar," in F. Imparati, ed., *Studi di storia e di filologia anatolica dedicati a Giovanni Pugliese Carratelli* (Firenze, 1988) 111-117, and R. Lebrun, "Divinités louvites et hourrites des rituels anatoliens en langue akkadienne provenant de Meskéné," in *Hethitica* 9 (1988) 147-155.

[12] My dissertation and book focus on this festival, and the book offers a collated edition of the text and a full

day," and a seven-day "installation," offerings and feasting begun by enthronement and closed by the final move of the priestess into her temple residence.

2. The installation of the *maš'artu* (*Emar* VI, 370), priestess of Aštart of Battle; the title is unknown.[13] This covers eight days: an introductory day plus the same seven-day installation. In spite of the similar framework, the context of this initiation is quite distinct from the other.
3. The *zukru* festival (*Emar* VI, 373); the word could be related to Semitic roots for "male" or "remembering."[14] This festival operates on a seven-year cycle, with rites in the sixth year leading to the *zukru* itself, a seven or eight day sequence in the first month of the seventh year.
4. A set of *kissu* festivals (*Emar* VI, 385-388) associated with various deities, based outside Emar at a town called Šatappi.[15] The five *kissu* rituals are found in many copies in various combinations, and they are the most opaque of the festivals. The rites vary considerably, and the significance of the title remains uncertain.

Most of the calendar ritual is attested only in fragments, and the two fullest texts are a description of rites for various months in the year (*Emar* VI, 446) and a record of rites for the month of Abû (*Emar* VI, 452).[16] Neither covers systematically the months of the year or the days of the month, but each focuses on particular months or days that are deemed significant. The annual calendar text devotes more than half of its space to rites for the first month, so the new year.

THE DEVELOPMENT OF EMAR RITUAL TRADITIONS

Comparison of the Emar texts with the ritual traditions of Babylonia, Assyria, Ḫatti, and Ugarit shows that the Emar rites are not borrowed directly from any known ancient Near Eastern ritual.[17] Although the rituals are written in Akkadian, they are replete with uses not known in Mesopotamian texts and with many new words, mostly Semitic.[18] The pantheon for all but the rites for the Hittite gods is Syrian.[19] There is little question that

---

commentary. See also M. Dietrich, "Das Einsetzungsritual der Entu von Emar (Emar VI/3, 369)," *UF* 21 (1989) 47-100.

[13] On the *maš'artu* festival, see Fleming, *Installation* 209-211, 229.

[14] On the *zukru* festival, see Fleming, *Installation* 229-255. B. Lafont, "Le roi de Mari et les prophètes du dieu Adad," *RA* 78 (1984) 11, discusses the meaning of the word *zukrum* in a Mari letter from the west, the only other attestation of the term.

[15] On the *kissu* festivals, see Fleming, *Installation* 255-263.

[16] On the rites for the month of Abû, see Fleming, *Installation* 295-301.

[17] See Fleming, *Installation* 279-289.

[18] For example, in the above four festivals, three of the identifying terms fit this definition: the *maš'artu* (priestess), and the *zukru* and *kissu* festivals.

[19] The Emar ritual pantheon includes Dagan, the storm god (Baᶜal?), paired alternatively with Ḫebat and Aštart,

the Emar ritual corpus represents a native tradition, but this general observation requires qualification. It is possible to define further the particular Hittite and Mesopotamian influences, and the remaining Syrian foundation is not homogeneous.

1. The Hittite Contribution.

The excavated city of Emar was built by the Hittites, and the architecture of all but the four temples is distinctly Hittite.[20] The temples, however, share the Syrian character of the rituals. While the conquest by a foreign power surely produced major changes in Emar life, there was no major influx of Hittite population, and the fabric of Emar culture was not deeply affected. This is certainly true of the rituals, where the Hittite features can be fairly quickly identified.

The character of direct Hittite influence on rituals recorded at Emar is evident in the "rites for the gods of Ḫatti." Although the language of these texts shows many distinctive Emar features, and the materials offered are typical of Emar, the pantheon belongs wholly to the Hittite empire, and offering by breaking bread exemplifies a typically Hittite technique.[21] While the rest of the Emar rituals should be examined by trained Hittitologists, they appear to have very little in common with the abundant Hittite-Hurrian ritual tradition known from the capital at Boghazköy. In spite of this fact, the diviner-scribe who collected the rituals apparently had direct contact with Hittite scribes. His archive included a group of Mesopotamian omen and medical texts in Hurrian, with the character of Boghazköy.[22] The Emar festivals are the most deeply Syrian of the rituals, but the term EZEN which is used to categorize them may be inspired by the Hittite "festival" class.[23] Some of the Emar festivals are organized in two parts, the body of ritual activity followed by an administrative section. A Hittite model would include these two elements plus text for spoken liturgy.[24]

2. The Mesopotamian Contribution.

Mesopotamian influence on the Emar ritual texts is evident first of all in the language itself. They are written in Akkadian, not Hittite or Hurrian. Emar scribes had not

---

Ea, Išḫara, the moon god and the sun god, as well as the city god, whose identity is disguised by the Sumerian name ^{d}NIN.URTA, and the goddess similarly named ^{d}NIN.KUR. The Emar pantheon is discussed at length in various sections of Fleming, *Installation*.

[20] On the Hittite character of the palace and the many houses excavated at Meskeneh-Emar, see Margueron, "Implantation" (1980) 287-304.

[21] See Fleming, *Installation* 267 and n. 257.

[22] See Laroche, "Emar" (1980) 243-244. Laroche sees in the Emar omen texts evidence for Syrian mediation of the Mesopotamian omen tradition in Ḫatti. Whether or not the Hittite texts were transmitted via Syria, the Emar texts might more immediately reflect the reverse influence, from the Hittite capital.

[23] R. Lebrun, *Samuha: foyer religieux de l'empire hittite* (Louvain-la-Neuve, 1976; *PIOL* 11) 44-48, distinguishes the Hittite SISKUR, which are offerings or *ad hoc* magical ceremonies, from the EZEN, which are official ceremonies linked to the calendar.

[24] See I. Singer, *The Hittite KI.LAM Festival, I* (Wiesbaden, 1983; *SBT* 27) 52.

developed a system of writing their local dialect, and Akkadian was the language of everyday legal and economic affairs. The Sumero-Akkadian written language strongly colors the description of the rituals, all the more because the scribes show relatively little concern to preserve in the texts local names, titles, or words. There are few glosses, and Mesopotamian spellings appear to be used whenever possible. The Emar writers compose the ritual texts as if to make the Syrian content intelligible to Babylonian scribes.

Many deities in the pantheon especially are rendered with Sumerian cover-names, some of which are used with such consistency that a few of the most prominent Emar deities remain unidentifiable. For instance, Emar's city god is written ^{d}NIN.URTA, the heroic firstborn of the Sumerian pantheon head Enlil. In southern Mesopotamia Enlil ruled the gods from Nippur, where Ninurta played the role of city god, with particular authority in legal transactions. It seems that as Dagan was the pantheon head at Emar and in the middle Euphrates region of Syria, and his role gave him the place of Mesopotamian Enlil, Emar's city god was identified by the Nippur model. While a Syrian god certainly lies behind the Sumerian name, no persuasive equivalent has yet emerged.[25]

Sumerian logographic writings are also used frequently for many other nouns, so that the precise Syrian word and entity is camouflaged. Such Sumerian words have known Akkadian equivalents, but it is often doubtful whether that Akkadian represents the Syrian term in use behind the Sumerian. One example might be the term for "festival," EZEN, which the scribes use with certain Emar rites but which never appears with its Akkadian reading, *isinnu*.

The Sumerian ideographic spellings provided an easy way to give a Mesopotamian guise to Syrian reality, but the Akkadian language could serve the same purpose. The inhabitants of Emar would have spoken a West Semitic dialect quite unlike the East Semitic Akkadian, and by writing the rituals in good Akkadian the Emar scribes deepened the Mesopotamian color where possible.[26] Naturally the very framework of the descriptions bore this Mesopotamian hue through the Akkadian verbs, prepositions, and the like, but various nouns are given their Akkadian names, which would not equate to the local West Semitic word.[27] Every time this is done the person or thing so described is portrayed with an image to some degree foreign to its real nature.

By composing the texts for their rituals in Akkadian, with its combined Sumerian and Akkadian writing system, the Emar scribes force us to view their religious practices through Mesopotamian lenses, but they reveal at the same time the native content. The Akkadian is good but it is not right. This is especially evident in the verbs which carry the action of

[25] See Fleming, *Installation* 248-252, on ^{d}NIN.URTA at Emar, and P. Steinkeller, *Sale Documents of the Ur-III-Period* (Stuttgart, 1989) 73 and n. 209, on Ninurta at Nippur.

[26] The local dialect is shown to be Semitic in the many non-Akkadian words mentioned throughout the ritual texts, such as the priestess *maš᾿artu*, which should be an *m*-preformative noun derived from the root *š᾿r*. The West Semitic nature of the local language can be seen in personal names, whose verbal elements are frequently written with the prefix *ya-*.

[27] One example might be the festival *naptanu*-bread, whose name comes from the Mesopotamian term for regular ritual meals. The established place of the word in Mesopotamian ritual should indicate a distinct Akkadian origin.

the ritual. They are commonly used in idioms not properly Akkadian or to describe acts not known in Mesopotamian religion.[28] In spite of the wealth of Mesopotamian imagery, there is much less that may represent real Mesopotamian religious traditions. There are two principal candidates: the institution of the NIN.DINGIR-priestess, and ritual which follows the calendar.

The installation festival for the NIN.DINGIR of the storm god presents her as the human complement to the goddess Ḫebat, and thus a human consort to the god. Although the Emar institution shows significant differences from the much older Mesopotamian tradition,[29] the identification of the principal priestess in a temple as the wife of the god corresponds exactly to the Mesopotamian NIN.DINGIR or *entu*. Unless Syria independently developed this conception, and the Emar title is simply given to describe similar but unrelated priestesses, the Emar NIN.DINGIR should have roots in the Mesopotamian figure. The Emar festival and priestess, however, show little else that belongs demonstrably to the Mesopotamian tradition, and appear to have undergone centuries of adaptation to Syrian custom.

The calendar-based rites belong to a larger problem. Both Emar and Ugarit have ritual texts which record certain offerings or rites for various days within a given month.[30] At Emar these are supplemented by texts that describe rites for certain months within the year.[31] Certain Mesopotamian offering records move through different months and account for what was given at a single temple on every day of the month. The Syrian texts for days in a month seem to derive ultimately from this tradition, though neither the Ugaritic nor the Emar rituals have true Mesopotamian equivalents. In particular, they do not call for daily offerings for maintenance of a god's temple cult. As with the NIN.DINGIR, if the calendar rituals have Mesopotamian origins, they should be at some distance from the 13th century, allowing a long indigenous adaptation.

Therefore, the most likely Mesopotamian features of Emar ritual have lost the matrix of their foreign origins, unlike the "rites for the gods of Ḫatti," which display a Hittite pantheon and Hittite ritual technique. The one cultural transmission appears to be old and well-assimilated; the other, recent and unassimilated.

---

[28] Examples would include the verbs *qadāšu* (D) with gods as direct object, describing offering, *galābu* (D) for shaving a priestess (the NIN.DINGIR), and *malāku* (D) for "making rule" (putting in office) the NIN.DINGIR and *maš'artu* priestesses, without apparent relation to either counsel or kingship.

[29] For example, the residence of the priestess is the *bīt* NIN.DINGIR, not the *gipāru*, and the priestess is chosen by *purû* ("lot"?), apparently not by extispicy.

[30] The one Emar ritual that is clearly defined with reference to a month is *Emar* VI, 452, the rites for the month of Abû, though the fragments *Emar* VI, 453-459 and *Emar* VI, 463 involve rites for scattered days within various individual months. At Ugarit one good example is *KTU* 1.112, which has been discussed in two articles by G. del Olmo Lete, "Ritual regio ugarítico de evocación/adivinación (KTU 1.112)," *AuOr* 2 (1984) 197-206, and "The Cultic Literature of Ugarit: Hermeneutical Issues and Their Application to KTU 1.112," in K. Hecker and W. Sommerfeld, eds., *Keilschriftliche Literaturen: ausgewählte Vorträge der XXXII. Rencontre Assyriologique Internationale* (Berlin, 1986) 155-164.

[31] *Emar* VI, 446-451.

3. "Local" Emar Ritual.

The core of Emar ritual appears to have been the festivals, and these are the texts which portray the most deeply "local" religious practices of the city.[32] Nevertheless, each ritual type serves a different temple or city clientele, and mere superficial points of contact between them do not cover their essential diversity.[33] The combination of these into Emar's festival tradition seems to have occurred through two relatively recent developments: the introduction of a temple cult of Baᶜal and Aštart as a divine pair, and the resolution of the separate claims of Dagan and Baᶜal (or, the storm god) by making Baᶜal second in the pantheon, after Dagan.[34] While I do not present the following scheme of festival development as certain, these most "native" Emar rituals surely display a diversity of origin that demands to be located in the larger cultural interplay of ancient Syria.

The Installations:

The two installation festivals share several important traits and were treated by the Emar scribes as a pair. Both are constructed around a seven-day celebration called a *malluku*, or "putting-into-office." Baᶜal's NIN.DINGIR and Aštart's *mašʾartu* take part in each other's installations by receiving portions set on tables. The offering procedures for the two festivals are exactly alike, with animal slaughter followed by arrangement of meat portions and breads, pouring of wine, and then feasting by human celebrants. Each rite centers on the temple residence of the new priestess: "the house of the NIN.DINGIR" and "the house of the *mašʾartu*."[35] Furthermore, Baᶜal and Aštart appear to be the deities of a temple pair excavated at the highest point of the Emar tell,[36] at the city's western extreme, and Emar personal names show the particular popularity of the names Zū-Baᶜla and Zū-Aštarti, "Belonging-to-Baᶜal," and "Belonging-to-Aštart."[37] In 13th-century Emar, the installation festivals of the NIN.DINGIR and the *mašʾartu* belong to a linked cult for Baᶜal and Aštart.

In spite of this relationship, decisive differences between the two rites appear at a deeper level. Most important is the absence of Baᶜal and Aštart from each other's festivals. In the NIN.DINGIR installation the consort of Baᶜal is Ḫebat, not Aštart, and Aštart receives no mention in any context. Baᶜal is mentioned in the *mašʾartu* installation, but only as a recipient of offerings in a sequence that treats methodically a hierarchical Emar pantheon

[32] See Fleming, *Installation* 201.

[33] For example, the NIN.DINGIR belongs to the cult of the storm god ᵈIM/Baᶜal, the *mašʾartu* serves Aštart of Battle, and the *zukru* and the various *kissu* rites revolve principally around Dagan. See Fleming, *Installation* chapter IV.

[34] See Fleming, *Installation* 275-277.

[35] Ibid, 228-229.

[36] Ibid, 216-218; cf. Margueron, "Fouilles" (1975) 77; D. Arnaud, "Catalogue des textes cunéiformes trouvés au cours des trois premières campagnes à Meskéné Qadimé Ouest (Chantiers A, C, E, et trouvaille de surface)," *AAAS* 25 (1975) 92.

[37] These names are particularly concentrated in the texts found in the temples of Baᶜal and Aštart.

in which Baᶜal follows Dagan, who likewise has no active role in the festival.[38] Beyond the distinct treatments of the gods, the two festivals have very different foci. The *mašʾartu* installation's key events take place at night, and the principal players in that festival are the "men of battle." Originally, the *mašʾartu* installation seems to have belonged to the cult for "Aštart of Battle" alone, not Aštart paired with Baᶜal. She is an ancient West Semitic goddess whose presence in the region predates by far her pairing with the storm god.[39] The ritual for the storm god and Ḫebat, on the other hand, could have roots in their great cult center at Aleppo, which dominated the region from Emar west during the 18th-century Mari period.[40] Dagan, pantheon head of the middle Euphrates region, has no active part in the NIN.DINGIR installation, and his absence would be surprising in a truly local product.

The *zukru* Festival:

The *zukru* text includes a long list which establishes a hierarchy for making offerings to "all the gods of Emar," but if this list is set aside relatively few deities play an active role. The most important are Dagan and the city god ᵈNIN.URTA, whose statues are drawn in carts between stone stelae at a sacred site outside the city walls. These are two gods very much at home in Emar. Dagan is the regional chief, attested as such both up and downstream along the Euphrates, and regarded as the principal Emar god both in the offering hierarchies and by acclamation via divine names imbedded in personal names.[41] ᵈNIN.URTA, as mentioned previously, is identified with the city itself.

In contrast to both installations, then, the *zukru* festival appears to be truly local. The *zukru* celebrates the renewal of a seven-year cycle of time for the people of Emar, and its roots reach deeper than any city constructions to a shrine outside the walls. For this renewal of divine relations the festival brings out the regional pantheon head and the city god.

The *kissu* Festivals:

I can only mention the *kissu* festivals in passing, but these might also belong to a truly local middle Euphrates tradition. The festivals are a set based in a nearby smaller town called Šatappi. The pantheon suggested by assignment of *kissu* festivals to various deities includes Dagan, ᵈEREŠ.KI.GAL, Ea, Išḫara, and perhaps ᵈNIN.URTA. Baᶜal and Aštart have no place.[42]

---

[38] See *Emar* VI, 370:49, cf. 57, for mention of ᵈIM/Baᶜal.

[39] See Fleming, *Installation* 219-221.

[40] See H. Klengel, "Der Wettergott von Ḫalab," *JCS* 19 (1965) 87-88.

[41] On Dagan at Emar, see Fleming, *Installation* 240-248.

[42] Ibid, 255-263, on the *kissu*.

4. Emar Ritual and Inner-Syrian Development.

I have suggested that the association of Baᶜal and Aštart and the ordering of Dagan and Baᶜal were later developments in Emar religion, though both are properly Syrian. Baᶜal and Aštart are not so much a Syrian pair as a "West Syrian" or a Canaanite pair, really too western for Emar.[43] The excavator suggests that 13th-century Emar was built from scratch by the Hittite conquerors, and at least they manipulated the terrain on a massive scale. The dual temples for Baᶜal and Aštart at the western height might then represent an astute manipulation of local religious traditions as well by the new rulers, who would not impose their cults on the natives.[44] Under Ḫatti, Emar became the southeastern extreme of a Syrian administrative district reaching west to Ugarit and north, governed through a regent at Carchemish. Without introducing any foreign practices, they may have been at least catalysts for combining two native cults to produce a religious center that faced physically and figuratively west, away from the politically dangerous links with Mesopotamia.

The placement of Dagan and Baᶜal at the head of the pantheon likewise seems quite superficial in the Emar rituals. The two appear in the same festival texts only as part of a hierarchical pantheon in the *zukru* and *mašʾartu* rituals. This resolution to a tension between two powerful regional figures may have been more than an Emar adaptation. Baᶜal is made the rising young king below the father of the pantheon El at Ugarit, where he is also referred to as "Dagan's son."[45] The new evidence bears further analysis.

THE IMPORTANCE OF EMAR RITUAL

With the first decipherment of ancient Near Eastern texts, the great centers of Mesopotamia and Egypt naturally took prime place in the study of the region's cultures. Gradually the spaces have been filled in, especially the Hittite empire in second-millennium Asia Minor and then Hurrian influence across northern Mesopotamia and Syria for the same period. Ancient Syria has tended either to be defined as part of another region, especially Mesopotamia or Canaan, or to be regarded as a cultural crossroads, without a distinctly indigenous heritage. Emar belongs with Ebla at the core of new evidence that is providing a more nuanced picture of a diverse Syrian culture which both influenced and was influenced by its neighbors.

This emerging ancient Syrian culture is particularly evident in the realm of religion. Before Ebla and Emar, ancient Syrian religion was almost defined as "ancient Ugaritic religion," and the wealth of Ugaritic evidence is indeed marvellous: unique myths and tales

---

[43] Evidence comes principally from Ugarit, New Kingdom Egypt (from coastal Syrian influence?), and probably ᵈIM and ᵈIŠTAR in the Hittite myth with Elkuniršа and Ašertu.

[44] This explanation remains hypothetical. Nevertheless, construction of a new city by the Hittites may have produced a situation calling for new sacred sites as well, in contrast with the conservative norm. Presumably the Hittite planners would have influenced the layout of building sites, even if the temples followed local Syrian design. Among local possibilities, a Baᶜal-Aštart temple at the peak might have looked more attractive than, for instance, a sanctuary for the regional head Dagan.

[45] See N. Wyatt, "The Relationship of the Deities Dagan and Hadad," *UF* 12 (1980) 375-379.

which frame relations in and with the divine world, and a more limited collection of rituals expressing religious practice. Emar offers a balance and a complement to Ugarit. Emar has no myths, but the ritual texts far outnumber Ugarit's and offer a completely new perspective.[46] The festivals in particular are replete with previously unattested Semitic words, seeming to indicate a distinct inland Syrian West Semitic language. The core festivals are long and complex, each representing a different religious heritage at Emar and yielding a mine of information about pantheon, sacred sites and personnel, materials, utensils, and procedures for offering, processions, feasts, and the specific acts pertinent to the business of each event.

One of the most interesting aspects of Emar ritual is the relatively minor role played by the king, in contrast to the Ugaritic corpus and much recorded ancient Near Eastern ritual.[47] At Emar, the palace provides offering materials for some rites, and the king sometimes receives feast portions. Only one ritual fragment (*Emar* VI, 392) centers on the king, and none shows him actively involved, as in processions or offering. In the installation festival of the NIN.DINGIR, it is the elders of Emar who bow down before the new priestess at her enthronement and give her gifts, apparently representing the city government. Though the king is acknowledged with food portions, the NIN.DINGIR festival seems rooted in a society without kings. Emar had kings under Hittite rule, but the institution was either recent or always exercised a limited influence.[48] This is not the centralized society of the city-state and its palace government.

The Emar rituals offer an inland perspective on second-millennium Syrian religion and culture, distinct from both Ugarit and the great powers of Ḫatti and Mesopotamia. Within the diverse Emar ritual tradition it is possible to discern a clear recent Hittite element and a likely old Mesopotamian element, but beyond these there remain several separate Syrian strands. The Emar rituals should therefore not only give us one more information point for ancient Syria but also warn us to expect more complexity than the words "indigenous" and "foreign" can bear. The foreign is not the Hittite and the Mesopotamian, to be neatly removed to reveal below a homogeneous indigenous Emar religion or culture. Only some Syrian features displayed at Emar are truly local, while others appear to derive from nearby regions. Various elements flourished or faltered in the 13th century through foreign Hittite interests or simply through reoriented networks of trade and communication. Emar's indigenous religious traditions themselves thus evolved from diverse sources in the emerging mosaic of ancient Syrian culture.

---

[46] P. Xella, *I testi rituali di Ugarit - I* (Roma, 1981; *SS* 54), lists 83 texts and fragments in his study of Ugaritic ritual texts. Emar has at least twice this number.

[47] See Fleming, *Installation* 99-101, especially 100 n. 97.

[48] See Archi, "Imâr" (1990) 21-38, and Durand, "Imâr" (1990) 39-92, on the economic and political situation in Emar/Imar of third-millennium Ebla and early second-millennium Mari.

THE GEOGRAPHICAL HORIZONS OF EBLA

Cyrus H. Gordon

Such a straight-forward sounding topic as "The Geographic Horizons of the Ebla Archives" is in fact more vague than we would like. There is for example among the tablets of the Archives a gazetteer listing many place-names. The difficulty in using that text is that it is for the most part an edition of a geography textbook employed in at least one other cuneiform academy (Tell Abu Ṣalabikh). It has entries of strange as well as of familiar sites and the Ebla recension was studied as a general geography textbook at Ebla, and not exclusively as a list of places near, or of any special interest to, Ebla.[1]

Another difficulty lies in categorizing the documents, for some types of tablets deal with cosmography rather than geography, or, in any case with a world different from the one in which we live. For example, the magical texts deal with two deified rivers, called the ^{d}Baliḫā[2] which reflect Canaanite mythology. Thus, in Ugaritic literature El, the head of the pantheon, dwells at the source of The Two Rivers. Also in the incantations, *in a-ba-ri-iš ti-É/ha-ma-tim* "beyond the Ocean(s)" does not refer to a real place but rather to a mythological Transoceania. Pettinato[3] mentions two Ebla tablets that deal with the epic of "Gilgamesh and Aratta." Even if correct, this would not prove that Ebla had relations with Aratta in such a remote part of the Iranian plateau. The poetry of ancient epics is not the language of geographers.

Sum-ar-rúm "Sumer," mentioned in the Ebla archives,[4] is a real and important land known to the Eblaites, even though contacts between Sumer and Ebla were maintained through intermediaries—notably Mari.

The bulk of the Ebla archives are administrative and most of them deal with nearby sites. A frequent combination of geographical names is Saza and Ebla. Ebla is now called Tell Mardikh. Its high walls with four large gates enclosed an area containing an acropolis

---

[1] A. Archi, "Notes on Eblaite Geography [I]," *SEb* 2 (1980) 1-16; "Notes on Eblaite Geography II," *SEb* 4 (1981) 1-17.

[2] D.O. Edzard, *Hymnen, Beschwörungen und Verwandtes aus dem Archiv L.2769* (Roma, 1984; *ARET* 5) 50.

[3] *Catalogo dei testi cuneiformi di Tell Mardikh - Ebla* (Napoli, 1979; *MEE* 1) 198.

[4] Edzard, *Hymnen* (1984) 58. References to the geographical names are available in the indices to *MEE* 1 and all of the *ARET* volumes. For a convenient study of Eblaite toponymy see M.C. Astour, "Toponymy of Ebla and Ethnohistory of Northern Syria: A Preliminary Survey," *JAOS* 108 (1988) 545-555.

on which the royal palace containing the archives once stood. Ebla was the administrative and cultic center of the realm. Saza was within the protecting walls of Ebla, and served as the central store-house and treasury of the city-state.[5] Such places required maximum security and in ancient cities, they were often on the acropolis itself.

Ar-mi^{ki} is frequently mentioned and designates the largest city of the area; namely, Aleppo or the district in which Aleppo is situated. It was also called Armanum.[6]

Ì-mar^{ki} (Emar; now Tell Meskeneh), an important city on the bend in the Euphrates nearest Ebla, is commonly mentioned in the Ebla Archives.

As a commercial state, Ebla maintained close relations with active business communities such as Ḫarran. The place is situated between the Euphrates and the Balikh, and is still called Ḫarran. It was headed not by an EN like Ebla, but by a *ba-da-lum* "a merchant (prince)" reflecting the city's commercial role.[7] A comparable town headed by a *ba-da-lum* in the Ebla Archives is *Sa-nap-zu-gúm*^{ki} (which used to be read *Sa-nap-zu-lum*^{ki}).[8]

Tù-ne-íp is to be equated with Tunip of the Amarna Tablets. Tunip, Qatna and Hamath are situated in south inland-Syria.[9]

Hamath (Hebrew *Ḥămāt*), present day Hama, is still a large town on the Orontes. In the Ebla tablets it is variously written as *É/Ḥa-ma-tim*, *É/Ḥa-ma*, *É/Ḥa-ma-at* and *Ḫa-ma-du*.[10]

Ar-ga is spelled *Ar-qat* in the Amarna tablets; its gentilic occurs in the Old Testament *ha-ᶜarqī* "The Arqite."[11] It was situated closer to the Mediterranean shore.

Ù-ga-ru, *Ù-gú-ra-at* and *Ù-gú-ra-tum* are to be compared with the coastal city of Ugarit. *ugār-* is the Akk. word for "field" (< Sum. A-GÀR) and the name of the god of the field.

The mention of Ugarit in the Ebla Archives is not surprising. Ugarit, an important port only about fifty miles west of Ebla as the crow flies, was occupied during EB. The survival of old place-names is a phenomenon familiar to historical linguists. More interesting is that the name is Semitic, reflecting the Semitic character of the population in EB.

Eblaite references to places in the vicinity of Ugarit, and/or mentioned in the Ugaritic tablets, support the identification of Eblaite *Ugurat(um)* with Ugarit. Thus *Zi-a-nu* is probably the region of Siyannu just south of Ugarit. In the Ugaritic tablets, it appears

---

[5] Cf. L. Milano, *Testi amministrativi: Assegnazioni di prodotti alimentari (Archivio L.2712 - Parte I)* (Roma, 1990; *ARET* 9) 402-403.

[6] For the suggestion that Ḫalam, not Armi, was the Eblaite designation for Aleppo see W.G. Lambert, "Ḫalam, Il-Ḫalam and Aleppo," *MARI* 6 (1990) 641-643 and M. Bonechi, "Aleppo in età arcaica. A proposito di un'opera recente," *SEL* 7 (1990) 15-37.

[7] I.M. Diakonoff, "The Importance of Ebla for History and Linguistics," *Eblaitica* 2 (1990) 11-12.

[8] A. Archi and M.G. Biga, *Testi amministrativi di vario contenuto* (Roma, 1982; *ARET* 3) 330; and E. Sollberger, *Administrative Texts Chiefly Concerning Textiles (L.2752)* (Roma, 1986; *ARET* 8).

[9] Diakonoff, "Importance" (1990) 12.

[10] Archi and Biga, *Testi amministrativi* (1982) 316.

[11] Gordon, "Eblaite and Northwest Semitic," *Eblaitica* 2 (1990) 139.

sometimes as a part of the Ugaritic realm and sometimes as a separate vassal city-state within the Hittite alliance.

The god of death and catastrophe, Resheph, had a cultic center at a place called *Gú-nu*. In the alphabetic script of Ugarit he appears as *Ršp-Gn*; in the syllabic orthography of Ebla, as ^{d}*Ra-sa-ap-Gú-nu*^{ki}.

At Ugarit it is recorded that at *Lrgt* there was a shrine dedicated to *Yrḫ* "The Moon God" (*yrḫ lrgth* "Yariḫ at Largat"). Fales sensed that *Lgrt* is the same place as *La-ru*$_{12}$*-ga-du*^{ki} (var. *A-ru*$_{12}$*-ga-du*^{ki}) in the Ebla Archives.[12]

The important city of Carchemish at the bend in the Euphrates (now Jerablus in southern Turkey) is spelled *Gàr-ga-mi-iš* or *Gàr-ga-mi-su* at Ebla; and *[K]rgms* at Ugarit.

Kiš is not only mentioned at Ebla but there is evidence that Eblaite was also written there as a lingua franca. The late Edmond Sollberger[13] maintained that the Kiš, as well as the Carchemish of the Ebla tablets, may not be the famous ancient cities bearing those names but different homonymous places. It serves no useful purpose to call into question such obvious identifications. Yet when such skepticism is expressed by so reputable a scholar, it does add to the difficulties of defining the geographic horizons of Ebla. Sollberger goes on to insist that only nine geographical names can be identified with a fair degree of certainty: Ebla, Mari, *Ar-mi*, *Ḫa-ma-tù*, *Ḫa-ra-an*, *Ì-mar*, *Tù-ub*, *Tù-tù-lu* and *Ur-sá-um*. (No one is likely to contest those nine.)

Ma-rí on the Middle Euphrates is frequently mentioned at Ebla.[14] At Mari, texts in the Eblaite language have also been discovered. Indeed it has been correctly noted that if those early Mari texts had been found before the Ebla tablets, we would be calling the language "Mariote" instead of "Eblaite." Two Ebla texts refer to scribal students coming to Ebla from Mari.[15]

Letters and treaties exchanged between Mari and Ebla are normally found not in the sender's city but in the addressee's. It is reasonable to treat such documents linguistically as products of the place where they were written. However, this should not obscure the existence of a written lingua franca shared by both places. At Amarna, we note the differences typifying each dossier; from Byblos, Ḫattuša, Jerusalem, etc. But those differences do not negate the existence of the written lingua franca which we call Amarna Akkadian. By the same token, a British professor at Oxford University, corresponding with an American colleague at the University of Michigan, would normally follow British idiom and spelling, whereas he would receive the reply in what we may call standard American usage. All this does not change the fact that they are both employing the same English language, which also serves as the lingua franca for millions of Far Easterners, Hindus, Near Easterners, Africans, etc.

---

[12] "*(L)arugatu*^{ki} in a Ugaritic Text?" *SEb* 7 (1984) 83-85.

[13] *Textiles* (1986) 38. This suggestion has been revived recently by F. Pomponio, "Exit Kiš dagli orizzonti di Ebla," *Mesopotamia* 25 (1990) 175-184.

[14] A. Archi, "I rapporti tra Ebla e Mari," *SEb* 4 (1981) 129-166.

[15] Published as text numbers 47 and 50 in G. Pettinato, *Testi lessicali monolingui della Biblioteca L.2769* (Napoli, 1981; *MEE* 3). While not addressing the specific status of the DUB-SAR, the mobility of guildsmen in general is discussed by A. Archi, "Prices, Workers' Wages and Maintenance at Ebla," *AoF* 15 (1988) 28-29.

MAR-DU, pronounced "Amurru," means the West. The usual geographical location of Amurru is the Syrian steppe west of Mesopotamia. However, throughout ancient times different locations are called "Amurru." For example, Israel and Judah are sometimes called "The Land of the Amorite" in the Bible. But in the Amarna period, Amurru is a vassal city-state in the Hittite Empire near the Syro-Lebanese coast. Scholars speak of "Amorite" as though it were a specific language. The fact is that "Amurru" and "Amorite" are quite variable terms in the ancient sources themselves. As for its meaning in the Ebla Archives, we must pay attention to the contexts provided by the tablets themselves. In *ARET* 8, text 524:obv. vi:9-10, *Ì-mar*^{ki} (= Emar; = modern Tell Meskeneh) is located in Amurru, so that Amurru extended at least up to the Euphrates.

Du-ub^{ki} = Tu-ba, mentioned in tablets found in level VII of Alalakh.[16] Cf. O.T. *ᵓereṣ ṭôb* "the land of Ṭôb" (Judges 11:3, 5), and perhaps *ᵓîš ṭôb* "a man of Ṭôb" (II Samuel 10:6, 8).

Áš-da-du^{ki} is the same name as the toponym borne by the Philistine Pentapolis city Ashdod. At Ugarit it is written alphabetically *Aẓdd*. Again skeptics have doubted that we are dealing with what was later Philistine Ashdod. Against such skepticism is the mention of *É/ᶜa-qa-ru*$_{12}$*-nu* = *ᶜaqqarûn-* = Ekron: the name of another city in the Philistine Pentapolis. Hyperskepticism is no more scientific than uncritical acceptance.

Ga-sur$_{x}$ (written ḪI x MAŠ) in the Ebla Archives has been identified with Gasur (the pre-Hurrian name of Nuzi) near Kirkuk, in Assyria beyond the Tigris.[17] This is so distant from Ebla that it is important for our understanding of the geographical horizons of Ebla. The skeptics may conceivably be right in maintaining that the Gasur in the Ebla Archives is not the same place but only the same name as the Gasur east of the Tigris.

The city that Joshua attacked after Jericho is called *Hā-ᶜay*, which means "The Ruin." Phonetically, this could correspond exactly to the Eblaite geographical name *É-a-a* (var. *É-a*). Since the name is descriptive of the many ruins on which later settlements were built, it could have been appropriately applied to many sites within the same linguistic sphere. There is however a historical-linguistic argument against the identification. The definite article *ha(n)-* (as in *Hā-ᶜay*) was not widely used until the Iron Age (ca. 1200-); it occurs but sparsely in LB. This makes its occurrence in EB doubtful.

We have already referred to the deified pair of Balikh Rivers. River gods are well known in Greek and Roman antiquity. In the Semitic sphere they are also familiar. For example, in Hammurapi's Code the water ordeal consisted of throwing the litigant into the ^{d}ÍD "deified River" who tests and thus either condemns or vindicates the litigant. By the same token, in Ugaritic mythology the sea god Yamm is synonymously paralleled by *ṯpṭ nhr* "Judge River." The Balikh is still the name of a major tributary of the Euphrates, flowing into it from the northeast.

---

[16] P. Matthiae, "*DU-UB*^{ki} di Mardikh IIBI = *TU-BA*^{ki} di Alalakh VII," *SEb* 1 (1979) 115-118.

[17] Archi, "Rapporti" (1981); Pettinato, "Gasur nella documentazione epigrafica di Ebla," in M.A. Morrison and D.I. Owen, eds., *Studies on the Civilization and Culture of Nuzi and the Hurrians in Honor of Ernest R. Lacheman* (Winona Lake, 1981) 297-304. While the article by Pettinato does not prove that Eblaite Gasur is the Gasur in the vicinity of distant Kirkuk, it provides a valuable compendium of the Ebla texts relevant to Gasur.

The mention of the *Pu-ra-na-tim* [Purantim] "Euphrates" requires no comment because that great river was obviously within the geographical horizons of Ebla. It is to be distinguished from *bu-la-tim* [buʾlātim buʾrātim] "wells" in the bilingual *MEE* 4:336, #1343, where AB.A is translated both as *ti-É/ha-ma-tum* [tihāmatum] "ocean" and *bu-la-tum* [buʾrātum] "wells."[18]

Among the geographical names in the Ebla Archives are those that are descriptive of such common types of terrain or functions that they cannot be positively identified with the same geographical names found elsewhere. Thus, *Ma-ba-ra-at*^ki^, the variant of which, *Má-bar-du*^ki^ (with *má*) points to the normalization [Maᶜbartu] "Ford," and *Maš-bar-du* [Mašbartu] "Food Storage" (cf. Heb. *šeber* "grain"). This does not imply that such names must refer to places different from those bearing the same names in other sets of documents.[19]

Maš-a has to be compared with *Maššāʾ* in Proverbs 30:1; 31:1. The kings of Maššā are neither Judean nor Israelite. Their land is in a northern region within the orbit of Ebla.

É/ᶜA-ru$_{12}$*-gu* [ᶜArqu] is a geographical name borne by a city near the Syro-Lebanese coast. With the definite article it occurs in Genesis 10:17 as *haᶜarqî*; cf. *Sa-na-ru*$_{12}$*-gu* = *San* + *ᶜarq-*, with San (the moon god usually known as Sin).

Uš-du-mu^ki^ corresponds to the modern Arabic form for "Sodom" which is today called Usdum by the local Arabs.

The word for "city" may be applied to the metropolitan center of a region. In the Lachish tablets *ha-ᶜîrā* "(in)to the city" means "(in)to Jerusalem." Similarly, εἰς τῆν πόλιν "into the city" > Istanbul, which survives as the official designation of Constantinople. At Ebla, both Ālu (var. *É/ᶜA-lu*, *A-la*) "(The) City" and also Uru (var. *U*$_9$*-ru*$_{12}$, *U*$_9$*-ra*) "(The) City" designate The Metropolitan Center = Aleppo(?).

Ù-ti-gú (var. *Ù-ti-ig*) may anticipate a geographical name later applied by the Phoenicians to "Utica," their early colony in what is now Tunisia.

A hieroglyphic inscription of Pepi I on stone has been found in the Ebla level that contained the Archives. This indicates not only that the geographical horizons of Ebla include Egypt, but also that the Ebla Archives are to be dated after the accession of Pepi I; hence, not earlier than 2300.[20] Because the entire period of the Archives lasted only about half a century, we must reckon with the low chronology of Ebla in the 23rd century.

As an extensive commercial center, the city-state of Ebla had far-flung geographical horizons in every direction, via intermediaries. Most significantly, it spanned Egypt of the Pyramid Age and Mesopotamia of the dynasty of Sargon of Akkad. Syria was therefore not (as had been supposed) a backwash of pastoral Amorites but a great urban center with intellectual scribal academies that belonged to the same educational network as the cuneiform centers of Mesopotamia. The impressive EB cities of Syria-Palestine should have

---

[18] R.R. Stieglitz, "Ebla and the Gods of Canaan," *Eblaitica* 2 (1990) 88.

[19] In 1982-83 as I drove from Aleppo to Ugarit, I was impressed with the number of towns, villages, and districts still called by the names as recorded in the administrative tablets found in the capital city of Ugarit.

[20] G. Scandone-Matthiae, "Vasi inscritti di Chefren e Pepi I nel Palazzo Reale G di Ebla," *SEb* 1 (1979) 33-43 and "I vasi egiziani in pietra dal Palazzo Reale G," *SEb* 4 (1981) 99-127.

made this clear long ago, but it took the discoveries at Ebla by the Italian expedition under the direction of Paolo Matthiae to prove this to the academic community.

The city-state of Ebla controlled a commercial empire during the period of the Archives. Not only must regular empires be maintained by armed might, but also commercial empires. Ebla did have to defend its interests on the battlefield when diplomacy failed. That the city-state of Ebla endured for only half a century was due in great measure to its location. Aleppo was too close for the area to hold two great city-states simultaneously; and Aleppo enjoyed the better location. It is of interest to note that in MB, during the Mari Age prior to the conquests of Ḫammurapi, Aleppo with its vassals was the strongest power in southwestern Asia.

The Ebla tablets, constituting the most important epigraphical discovery made during the second half of the twentieth century, are the largest known archives anywhere in the world from EB.

THE SYRIAN CONTRIBUTION TO CUNEIFORM LITERATURE AND LEARNING

William W. Hallo[1]

It is now almost a century since the first cuneiform tablet was found in Syria. As Giorgio Buccellati put it in a recent issue of the *Bulletin of the American Schools of Oriental Research* devoted to "Ancient Syria",[2] "the first Khana tablet was published in 1897....it is also the first published cuneiform tablet found in Syria."[3] Since then, the steady rediscovery of cuneiform archives and libraries in Syria has proceeded without let-up. It is thus none too soon to sum up what a century of textual discoveries has contributed to our knowledge of the Syrian role in ancient Near Eastern culture. Other papers in this volume will do this on the basis of the relevant administrative and historical texts—or, as I prefer to call them, archives and monuments. I wish to turn, instead, to the literary or, better, the canonical texts as these were studied and transmitted in the scribal schools or employed in the cult. My object will be to address three related questions: To what extent was ancient Syria a cultural dependency of (lower) Mesopotamia? To what extent was it indebted to other cultural traditions or a participant in them? To what extent did it strike out on paths of its own?

In approaching my subject, I am going to impose some strict limits. It is obvious that cultural interconnections involve numerous components not to be dealt with here: language, law, the calendar, tribal institutions, kinship and kingship, to name only a few. In concentrating on literature to the exclusion of such other phenomena, there is no suggestion that it contains all the answers to the questions raised at the outset. Moreover, the literature here dealt with is the curriculum of the scribal schools or the agenda and dicenda of the cult. It includes a variety of genres not regarded as aesthetically satisfying according to modern notions of belles-lettres, while excluding many others whose function was monumental or archival. The cuneiform script to be considered here is that which originated in Mesopotamia, to the exclusion of the newer and vastly simpler cuneiform script invented in Syria and used primarily at Ugarit, let alone of the Aramaic and Hieroglyphic

---

[1] Presented, in part, to the Panel on "New Horizons in the Study of Ancient Syria: Syrian Influence in the Near East," Dennis Pardee, chair, American Historical Association, Chicago, December 30, 1991.

[2] "The Kingdom and Period of Khana," *BASOR* 270 (1988) 43.

[3] The reference is to F. Thureau-Dangin, "Tablettes chaldéennes inédites," *RA* 4 (1897) 69.

Hittite so prevalent in parts of Syria in the Iron Age. Nor will there be occasion to review the forerunners of Mesopotamian cuneiform as these have been identified in the system of clay counters and tokens which such Syrian sites as Habuba Kabira and Tell Kannas share with the rest of the Asiatic Near East in the Neolithic Period.[4] The texts in Hittite and Hurrian, although they are written in Mesopotamian cuneiform, will only be considered in passing. Finally, the texts from such places as Atchana-Alalakh and Sultan Tepe will be somewhat arbitrarily excluded, since they lie outside the borders of present-day Syria.

But even within these limits, recent discoveries and new studies of earlier ones make a first attempt at an assessment timely. This will be done here on a roughly chronological basis.

I. The Early Bronze Age (Proto-Syrian Period)

The age which witnessed the emergence of full writing also experienced the propagation of the new invention from its southern Mesopotamian base across most of the Near East. In some places, like Elam and Egypt, the new invention served as a stimulus to the development of indigenous scripts with little, or no, direct relationship to the writing system that ultimately became the cuneiform script. But in Syria, that script won early and wholesale adoption. The earliest and most striking illustration of this phenomenon is found at Tell Mardikh, some 55 km south-southwest of Aleppo. Here, the Italian expedition led by Paolo Matthiae since 1964 has uncovered the center of a thriving city-state known in antiquity as Ibla or Ebla. It flourished at the end of what, in Mesopotamian terms, was the Early Dynastic Period, and was destroyed at the end of this period or the beginning of the succeeding Sargonic Period. Whether it was razed by Sargon, the founder of the Sargonic dynasty, himself, or by another enemy, or by accident is hard to say.[5] In any case, the final conflagration that overtook the palace was so effective that it has preserved the clay tablets of the royal archives and library in better condition and larger numbers than any Mesopotamian site up to that time. The majority of these tablets constitute records of the state economy. There are also examples of other genres to be expected in a royal archive and library, such as letters and treaties. In theory these could constitute canonical texts from the curriculum of the scribal schools; in fact, the total absence of duplicates makes this quite unlikely and makes them far more likely candidates for the archival category. But a substantial number of tablets do represent genuine literary texts in the sense employed here, i.e., religious texts or school texts. How do these compare with the canonical texts of contemporary Mesopotamia?[6]

---

[4] A. Finet, ed., *"Lorsque la royauté descendit du ciel...": Les fouilles belges du Tell Kannâs sur l'Euphrate en Syrie* (Morlanwelz, Belgium, 1982) esp. pp. 98-101; D. Schmandt-Besserat, *Before Writing* (Austin, 1992) esp. vol. 1 88-91.

[5] M.C. Astour debates these questions elsewhere in this volume. The issue is largely moot in my chronological scheme, where much of Sargon's reign still falls into the Early Dynastic period, i.e., paradoxically, into "pre-Sargonic" times.

[6] For a thoughtful general introduction to the question see P. Michalowski, "Language, Literature, and Writing at Ebla" in L. Cagni, ed., *Ebla 1975-1985* (Napoli, 1987) 165-175. The article by B. Kienast and H. Waetzoldt,

To begin with the religious texts, the majority of these consist of incantations.[7] The seventeen tablets containing incantations can be divided into twenty-nine discrete compositions, of which seven recur on two separate tablets each.[8] Fourteen of the compositions are wholly in Sumerian, eight largely in Sumerian and partly in the Semitic language of Ebla (hereafter "Eblaite"), and six largely in the latter language.[9] One of the Sumerian compositions (Krebernik's No. 1) has a parallel among the "school-texts" from Šuruppak (Fara)[10] whose date may be a century or two earlier,[11] and another, as first noted by G. Pettinato[12] (Krebernik's No. 27) has one among the texts found at Lagaš (al-Hiba) in the season of 1970-71;[13] it probably dates from the time of Eannatum or Enannatum I, i.e., from the very same time as the Fara text, if I am right in assigning the Fara texts "to the time of Ur-Nanše or even a generation later."[14] It is not unreasonable to suppose that all the Sumerian incantations from Ebla have their roots in the Mesopotamian tradition. This seems true likewise of those Sumerian incantations which include an occasional "Semitic" word.[15] Nevertheless, they show some distinctive features. So for example the repeated subscript "spell of the goddess Nin-girim" (UD-du$_{11}$-ga ^{d}Nin-girim$_{x}$; phonetically: [NE-du-ga ne-gi-rí-má-(MA)]) does not recur in the parallel text from Lagaš nor in most of the incantations from Šuruppak,[16] or in Old Sumerian incantations generally.[17] In Mesopotamia, Nin-girim was, it is true, known as the goddess of incantations from at least Old Babylonian times on.[18] Her name, however, occurs in the body of incantations rather than in their subscript,[19] and this is true even when the entire formula

"Zwölf Jahre Ebla: Versuch einer Bestandsaufnahme," *Eblaitica* 2 (1990) 31-77, covers some of the same ground (see esp. pp. 66-74) but could not be incorporated here.

[7] Conveniently assembled by D.O. Edzard, *Hymnen, Beschwörungen und Verwandtes aus dem Archiv L. 2769* (Roma, 1984; *ARET* 5). Except for Edzard's Nos. 1-5, they were first published by G. Pettinato, "Le collezioni én-é-nu-ru di Ebla," *OA* 18 (1979) 329-351 and pls xxxvi-xlii; studied by M. Krebernik, *Die Beschwörungen aus Fara und Ebla* (Hildesheim, 1984; *TSO* 2).

[8] Edzard Nos. 1-5, 8-19.

[9] Edzard Nos. 1-5, 16. One text, No. 29 in Krebernik's enumeration, is of uncertain linguistic affiliation.

[10] A. Deimel, *Schultexte aus Fara* (Leipzig, 1923; *WVDOG* 43) No. 54 (VAT 12598) ix 1-9.

[11] Hallo, "The Date of the Fara Period: A Case Study in the Historiography of Early Mesopotamia," *Or* 42 (1973) 228-238.

[12] "én-é-nu-ru" (1979) 329-351 and pls. xxxvi-xlii, esp. p. 332 and n. 25.

[13] R.D. Biggs, *Inscriptions from Al-Hiba—Lagash: The First and Second Seasons* (Malibu, 1976; *BM* 3) No. 31.

[14] Hallo, "Fara" (1973) 235.

[15] Krebernik Nos. 21, 28, 30, 35, 37, 38.

[16] Krebernik Nos. 1, 2 and 3 and Deimel, *Schultexte* (1923) No. 54 only.

[17] According to Krebernik, *MDP* 14:91 is an Ur III incantation from Susa with the subscript SAR-du$_{11}$-ga ^{d}Nin-girima.

[18] R.D. Biggs, "The Abū Ṣalābīkh Tablets: A Preliminary Survey," *JCS* 20 (1966) 80f., n. 55, citing *CT* 44 30:25; idem, *ŠÀ.ZI.GA: Ancient Mesopotamian Potency Incantations* (Locust Valley, 1967; *TCS* 2) 43f.

[19] E.g. at Lagaš (above, note 13); in *YOS* 11:81:11; and in *PBS* 13:35 with duplicate *ISET* 1:217 No. 4176.

survives.[20] And while "spell" occurs in the subscript of one incantation (albeit in the spelling DU$_{11}$.UD),[21] it does not co-occur with the divine name there.

Turning next to the incantations written largely in Eblaite,[22] we find that these are entirely without parallel in the Mesopotamian tradition as so far attested. In the first place there *are* no incantations in other than Sumerian guise before Old Babylonian times in Mesopotamia, at which time they appear in a variety of languages, including Akkadian, "Subarian" (Hurrian) and Elamite.[23] In the second place, the Eblaite incantations are not recognizably related to any Sumerian ones, including those from Ebla itself. On the contrary, they feature proper names, both geographic and divine, which point to a native Syrian context. These include Baliḫ (^{d}Ba-li-ḫa-a), Adad (^{d}ʾÀ-da), Byblos (Gub-lu^{ki}), Kemosh (^{d}Kà-mi-iš), and the chariot or wagon[24] or yoke[25] (^{giš}uštil) of Adar-wa-An (^{d}A-dar-wa-an)[26] in Edzard No. 16 (= Krebernik No. 26 = Pettinato No. 12), and Baliḫ (^{d}Ba-li-ḫa) in Edzard No. 4. Pettinato is therefore justified in suggesting that at least the first of these incantations is an original Eblaite work.[27] W.G. Lambert refers to it similarly when he states "only one incantation out of a total of the twenty-four edited by M. Krebernik...was clearly composed in Syria, though not necessarily in Ebla."[28]

The remaining texts published by Edzard as "hymns, incantations and related" material include two which do not really belong there, No. 22, which he himself recognized as a lexical exercise, and No. 23, which M. Civil recognized as such; specifically it turns out to be a syllabically written equivalent to a unilingual Sumerian word list from Ebla.[29] The other texts include two in Sumerian and two in (Old) Akkadian.[30] The shorter of the Sumerian texts (Edzard Nos. 24-26) is one that has created quite a stir. The three duplicate

---

[20] P. Michalowski, "Carminative Magic: Towards an Understanding of Sumerian Poetics," *ZA* 71 (1981) 4 and 5, line 10.

[21] R. Jestin, *Tablettes Sumériennes de Šuruppak* (Paris, 1937) No. 170 = Deimel, *Schultexte* (1923) No. 54.

[22] Above, note 9. Cf. on some of these texts also V. Brugnatelli, "Sprachwissenschaftliche Überlegungen zu einem literarischen Text aus Ebla," in H. Waetzoldt and H. Hauptmann, eds., *Wirtschaft und Gesellschaft von Ebla* (Heidelberg, 1988; *HSAO* 2) 173-178.

[23] Cf. J. van Dijk, "Fremdsprachige Beschwörungstexte in der südmesopotamischen literarischen Überlieferung," in H.-J. Nissen and J. Renger, eds., *Mesopotamien und seine Nachbarn* (Berlin, 1982; *Berliner Beiträge zum Vorderen Orient* 1; *RAI* 25) 97-110; J. van Dijk, A. Goetze, and M.I. Hussey, *Early Mesopotamian Incantations and Rituals* (New Haven, 1985; *YOS* 11) 3f.

[24] Cf. F. Pomponio, "The Meaning of the Term uštil in the Ebla Documents," *ArOr* 51 (1983) 372-377.

[25] Krebernik, *Beschwörungen* (1984) 141f., who compares later ^{giš}šudul; cf. M. Civil, "Bilingualism in Logographically Written Languages: Sumerian in Ebla," in L. Cagni, ed., *Il bilinguismo a Ebla* (Napoli, 1984) 96.

[26] For compound divine names in West Semitic cf. e.g. Kothar-wa-Ḫasis in Ugaritic and Šagar-wa-Ištar at Deir Alla.

[27] "én-é-nu-ru" (1979) 336: "opera originale eblaita."

[28] "Notes on a Work of the Most Ancient Semitic Literature," *JCS* 41 (1989) 1.

[29] M. Civil, "Studies in Early Dynastic Lexicography II: 3. Word List D 50-57 (ARET 5 No. 23)," *ZA* 74 (1984) 161-163.

[30] As to the precise linguistic character of these two texts, see the admonitions of Michalowski, "Language" (1987) 171.

texts were originally published by Pettinato under the title of "The Lord of Heaven and Earth"[31] and figured in the debate between him and A. Archi as to the relevance of Ebla for biblical studies.[32] Edzard has, however, made a good case for the suggestion that the text is a school exercise of which only the first half has any pretensions to literary character, the second being simply a list of personal names, albeit conceivably names selected for beginning, like the first part, with the word for king or lord (lugal).[33] He suggests, with all due reserve, the following translation of the first part: "Lord, heaven (and) earth you do not... (or: do not...you). As on earth(?) you, like a father, do not let the orphan (fem.) have a life in interest (-debt)."[34]

The longer of the two Sumerian texts (Edzard Nos. 20f.) is again preserved in three duplicates, but only two of them are from Ebla. The third was identified by Pettinato among the texts from Abu Ṣalabikh,[35] and this fact already suggests, as in the case of the Sumerian incantations from Ebla, a Mesopotamian origin. The suggestion gains further support from the divine and geographical names in the text. The divine names include An and Enlil, Nanna and Utu, Inanna and Ama-ušumgal (in the Ebla exemplars: Ama-ušum); the last is a manifestation of Dumuzi to whom the entire text, to judge by its doxology, is dedicated. The geographical names include Uruk (in the Ebla exemplars: é-^{d}Inanna), Kulab[36] and Aratta, all well-known from Sumerian epic. Even though as yet imperfectly understood, the text represents one of the longest "epic" texts of Early Dynastic date, comparable in that respect to a tale of Lugalbanda known, so far, only from Abu Ṣalabikh.[37]

Of the Akkadian texts one is short and obscure (Edzard No. 7), the other (Edzard No. 6) long and, although not entirely preserved, to some extent intelligible, thanks to the recognition by M. Biga[38] and M. Civil[39] respectively that it duplicates two fragments of a text from Abu Ṣalabikh (*IAS* 326 [+?] 342) and the efforts of Edzard and Lambert to interpret it. Edzard called it a hymn to Šamaš, while Lambert prefers to see it as a myth about the same deity, and at the same time "a work of the most ancient Semitic literature."[40] In Lambert's opinion, its Mesopotamian affinities are evident and he is

---

[31] "Gli archivi reali di Tell Mardikh-Ebla: Riflessioni e prospettive," *RBI* 25 (1977) 231f.; *Ebla: Un impero inciso nell'argilla* (Milano, 1979) 278; "Ebla e la Bibbia," *OA* 19 (1980) 59-67; "Ebla and the Bible," *BA* 43 (1980) 209-213; *The Archives of Ebla: An Empire Inscribed in Clay* (Garden City, 1981) 259f.

[32] A. Archi, "The Epigraphic Evidence from Ebla and the Old Testament," *Biblica* 60 (1979) 556-566, esp. pp. 561f.

[33] For other Ebla lists of personal names beginning with lugal, cf. e.g. *MEE* 3:59 ii and 67 rev(?).

[34] "Herr, Himmel (und) Erde ...st du nicht (oder: Himmel (und) Erde ...en dich nicht). Wie auf der Erde (?) lässt du wie ein Vater die Waise ein Leben in Zins(schuld) nicht haben."

[35] *MEE* 1 (1979) 198 *sub* Nos. 2093f.; cf. R.D. Biggs, *Inscriptions from Tell Abū Ṣalābīkh* (Chicago, 1974; *OIP* 99) No. 278.

[36] Written Kul-UNU in *IAS* 278 iii 3, contrary to Edzard's note that Kulaba is lacking in this exemplar (*ARET* 5 p. 39).

[37] T. Jacobsen, "Lugalbanda and Ninsuna," *JCS* 41 (1989) 69-86.

[38] So according to Edzard, *ARET* 5 p. 30.

[39] "Studies II. 3" (1984) 163, n. 8.

[40] Lambert, "Notes" (1989) 1-33.

prepared to assign it a specifically south Mesopotamian origin, more particularly to Sippar, a city sacred to the sun-god. Like the great preceptive hymn to Šamaš,[41] it devotes a good deal of attention to the merchant, here called *garaš* as in the epic of "Enmerkar and the Lord of Aratta."[42] It represents the oldest literary work in Old Akkadian, and certainly the most sizeable one yet known in that language.[43] It is noteworthy that it was studied at Ebla, but it is presumably of Mesopotamian, not Syrian inspiration. The total harvest of original literary and liturgical works from Ebla is thus slim.

When we turn from these works to the scholastic tradition proper, however, the result is quite different. Lexical and mathematical texts played an essential part in the propagation of cuneiform writing since its invention before the end of the fourth millennium. Ebla proves no exception to this rule. The harvest of school texts strictly speaking is impressive both in the matter of lists shared with Mesopotamia and of those created locally for the specialized needs of the Eblaite scribes. Without here going into every last detail, suffice it to say that the former included representatives of all or nearly all of the standard lexical lists in use in Mesopotamia in the outgoing fourth and the entire third millennium, including lists of professions, geographical names, animals, fishes, birds, metals, and numbers.[44] A particularly intriguing example of a shared lexical tradition is represented by a list which combines personal names, professional names, and geographical names to create the effect of a cadastre; it is represented at Ebla and Abu Ṣalabikh,[45] and survived into Ur III times.[46] It lists the names and titles of the chief persons of some thirteen or more cities which, as far as they can be identified at all, are in or around Mesopotamia proper.[47]

But there is at least one lexical text, or rather family of lexical texts, that is an original creation of the Ebla scribes, and that has been suitably entitled the "Vocabulary of Ebla" by Pettinato. In its fullest form, it lists nearly 1500 Sumerian words and explains the

---

[41] Lambert, *Babylonian Wisdom Literature* (Oxford, 1960) 121-138.

[42] Cf. Hallo, "Trade and traders in the Ancient Near East: some new perspectives," in D. Charpin and F. Joannès, eds., *La circulation des biens, des personnes et des idées dans le Proche Orient ancien: Actes de la XXXVIIIe Rencontre Assyriologique Internationale* (Paris, 1992) 356 and at nn. 23-37.

[43] For other early literary texts in Akkadian, see Hallo and W.K. Simpson, *The Ancient Near East: A History* (New York, 1971) 62, n. 68, with the reservations of B.R. Foster, "Naram-Sin in Martu and Magan," *Annual Review of the Royal Inscriptions of Mesopotamia Project* 8 (1990) 44, n. 14; for the most extensive of these texts, see J. and A. Westenholz, "Help for Rejected Suitors: The Old Akkadian Love Incantation MAD V 8," *Or* 46 (1978) 198-219.

[44] H.-J. Nissen, "Bemerkungen zur Listenliteratur Vorderasiens im 3. Jahrtausend," in L. Cagni, ed., *La lingua di Ebla* (Napoli, 1981) 99-108. See especially the convenient summary on pp. 106f. Cf. also R.D. Biggs, "Ebla and Abu Salabikh: The Linguistic and Literary Aspects," ibid., 129-133; Michalowski, "Language" (1987) 170.

[45] See the edition by A. Archi, "La 'Lista di nomi e professioni' ad Ebla," *SEb* 4 (1981) 177-204. The incipit of the text is Lugal-men-nun according to the new fragments published by idem, "The 'Names and Professions List': more fragments from Ebla," *RA* 78 (1984) 171-174.

[46] F.M. Fales and Th.J.H. Krispijn, "An Early Ur III Copy of the Abū Ṣalābīkh 'Names and Professions' List," *JEOL* 26 (1979-80) 39-46 and pl. iii.

[47] According to my own reconstruction of the text, they are, in order: Sippar, Akšak, Badar or Matar, LAK 527, Adab, Uruk, ZA, Iškar, Durum, Aʾur or Awur, Urua, AB and x. For Matar see P. Steinkeller, "Seal of Išma-ilum, Son of the Governor of Matar," *VO* 6 (1986) 27-40.

majority of them by their Eblaite equivalents.[48] The text is preserved in a great number of duplicates,[49] reflecting its importance in the Eblaite scribal curriculum, and at the same time providing important variants. The same importance is attested by related vocabularies: a unilingual version (Sumerian only),[50] and "extract" tablets.[51]

A second possible candidate for an Eblaite origin is the so-called "Syllabary of Ebla" (*MEE* 3:51f.). According to Civil, this is "more precisely a sign list with sign names,"[52] but since it is in any case without Mesopotamian parallel, it may have been created for the specific needs of the scribes of Ebla. Indeed, it effectively provides a syllabic transcription for each logogram.

There are also a number of other unilingual lexical lists which have been claimed for Ebla.[53] Of these the first (*MEE* 3:55) was regarded by Pettinato as "lexical-historical" but by Sollberger[54] and Archi[55] as a simple archival text, not of a scholastic character.[56] The most extensive one (*MEE* 3:56) is the great geographical name list which Pettinato originally published as "the geographical atlas of the ancient Near East attested at Ebla and at Abu Ṣalabikh."[57] As this title indicates, the text had Mesopotamian duplicates, and in spite of some brave efforts to localize many of its place names in Syria and even Palestine,[58] the weight of opinion is in favor of a (north) Mesopotamian origin for most or all of this list.[59]

The shorter unilingual lexical texts can now also mostly be placed in the Mesopotamian tradition. *MEE* 3:61, for example, turns out to be the Eblaite translation of *MEE* 3:45+(!)46, which in turn has duplicates at Abu Ṣalabikh (*IAS* 33 and 37).[60] *MEE* 3:62 is

---

[48] G. Pettinato, "Il Vocabolario di Ebla," *MEE* 4 (1982) 115-343; "I vocabolari bilingui di Ebla," in Cagni, *Lingua* (1981) 241-277 and pls. 1f.

[49] These are edited separately by Pettinato as *MEE* 4:3-90, Texts 1-72.

[50] *MEE* 4:118-130; photo: P. Matthiae, *Ebla: An Empire Rediscovered* (Garden City, 1981) between pp. 112 and 113 (TM.75.G.2422). Cf. S.A. Picchioni, "Le liste monolingui sumeriche š è . b a r . k i n $_x$ di Ebla: Studio preliminare," in Cagni, *Ebla 1975-1985* (1987) 159-164.

[51] These are edited separately by Pettinato in *MEE* 4:91-113 as Texts 73-114, and on pp. 347-381 jointly. Cf. also *ARET* 5:22.

[52] "Bilingualism" (1984) 75-97, esp. pp. 77 and n. 4, 94-97. For a new edition see A. Archi, "The 'Sign-list' from Ebla," *Eblaitica* 1 (1987) 91-113.

[53] *MEE* 3 (1981) 217-254: II. *Testi lessicali eblaiti.*

[54] E. Sollberger, "Une tablette d'Ibla," *MARI* 6 (1990) 647f.

[55] *ARET* 7 (1988) No. 152.

[56] Cf. especially Archi, ibid. ad No. 151 = *MEE* 3:57.

[57] "L'Atlante Geografico del Vicino Oriente Antico attestato ad Ebla e ad Abū Ṣalābīkh (I)," *Or* 47 (1978) 50-73 and pls. vii-xii.

[58] Notably by W.H. Shea, "Two Palestinian Segments from the Eblaite Geographical Atlas," in C.L. Meyers and M. O'Connor, eds., *The Word of the Lord Shall Go Forth: Essays in Honor of David Noel Freedman* (Winona Lake, 1983) 589-612.

[59] See e.g., Michalowski, "Language" (1987) 169 and n. 15. A forthcoming study of the entire text by Douglas Frayne should clinch the matter: D.R. Frayne, *The Early Dynastic List of Geographical Names* (New Haven, 1992; *AOS*). According to F. Pomponio, "Notes on the Lexical Texts from Abū Ṣalābīkh and Ebla," *JNES* 42 (1983) 285-288, the correspondence between the Ebla and Abu Ṣalabikh versions is even closer than previously suggested.

[60] M. Civil, "The Early History of HAR-ra: The Ebla Link," in Cagni, *Ebla 1975-1985* (1987) 131-158, esp.

a syllabically written equivalent of "Animal List A" (*MEE* 3:12-17),[61] *MEE* 3:63 of "Wordlist D" (*MEE* 3:48f.),[62] and *MEE* 3:64 of the bird list (*MEE* 3:39).[63] All three of these lists have Mesopotamian antecedents going back to the earliest lexical texts from Uruk, as well as other ones at Fara and Abu Ṣalabikh, as seen by H. Nissen[64] and by Pettinato in his earliest edition of the bird list, which has meantime also been identified at Lagaš.[65] *MEE* 3:68 is duplicated by a newly published text from Abu Ṣalabikh[66] as seen by F. Pomponio,[67] while *MEE* 3:72 closely resembles one from Šuruppak (*TSŠ* 190) as seen by R. Englund.[68]

Finally, a word needs to be said about the mathematical texts from Ebla.[69] In the first place, there are the simple lists of numbers in certain lexical texts. One of these, the aforementioned "Wordlist D," begins with 15 numbers, written logographically in one exemplar (*MEE* 3:48f.) and syllabically in the other (*MEE* 3:63).[70] Another (*MEE* 3:54) lists the Sumerian numbers from one to ten in syllabic orthography, and therefore provides a precious clue to their (approximate) contemporaneous pronunciation, which is otherwise largely hidden from us behind logographic writing of the numerals in all but the later cuneiform texts from Mesopotamia itself.[71] Higher numbers occur in *MEE* 3:72 and *MEE* 4:78 (end).[72] In the second place there are genuine mathematical exercises (*MEE* 3:73f.).[73] Although without precise duplicates from Mesopotamia, the recognition by J. Friberg of comparable exercises from Šuruppak, and by M. Powell and A.A. Vaiman of other Early Dynastic mathematical texts provides "evidence for the possible derivation of these school texts from Sumer."[74]

---

pp. 140-158: Word List B 1-99.

[61] J. Krecher, "Eine unorthographische sumerische Wortliste aus Ebla," *OA* 22 (1983) 179-189.

[62] Th.J.H. Krispijn, "Die Identifikation zweier lexikalischen Texte aus Ebla: *MEE* III Nr. 62 und 63," *JEOL* 27 (1981-82) 47-59; M. Civil, "Studies on Early Dynastic Lexicography. I," *OA* 21 (1982) 1-26, esp. pp. 1-17.

[63] Civil, "Studies I" (1982) 17-26.

[64] "Listenliteratur" (1981) 106f. *sub* ÁB(Rinder), Mathematisch, and MUŠEN(Vögel) respectively.

[65] "Liste presargoniche di uccelli nella documentazione di Fara ed Ebla," *OA* 17 (1978) 165-178 and pls. xiv-xvi. The Lagaš duplicate was first called to his attention by Biggs and incorporated in the edition in *MEE* 3:109-120.

[66] R.D. Biggs and J.N. Postgate, "Inscriptions from Abu Salabikh, 1975," *Iraq* 40 (1978) 101-117 and pls. xiv-xvi, esp. pp. 108 and 112 (*IAS* 523).

[67] "Lexical Texts" (1983) 285-290, esp. pp. 288f.

[68] Apud J. Friberg, "Mathematik," *RLA* 7 (1990) 538.

[69] See in general Michalowski, "Language" (1987) 169f. and 175 with notes 16f. and addendum.

[70] Krispijn, "Identifikation " (1983) 55f.; Civil, "Studies I" (1982) 1-8.

[71] D.O. Edzard, "Sumerisch 1 bis 10 in Ebla," *SEb* 3 (1980) 121-127 and fig. 26; G. Pettinato, "La pronuncia sumerica dei numeri da 1 a 10 in un testo lessicale di Ebla," *AION* 41 (1981) 141-143 and pl. 1. The earliest lexical list with syllabic pronunciation of these numbers is Middle Assyrian; see *MSL* XIV (1979) 252f.

[72] Cf. above, note 69.

[73] For *MEE* 3:74, see V. Brugnatelli, "Per un'interpretazione di TM.75.G.1392," *OA* 21 (1982) 31f; A. Archi, "Tables de comptes eblaïtes," *RA* 83 (1989) 1-6, who adds another example of the genre.

[74] See above, note 69.

Summing up the Early Bronze Age evidence from Ebla, we can say that Syria was dependent on Mesopotamia for much of its literary and scholarly output, but capable of building on the base so derived to serve its own particular needs.

II. The Middle Bronze Age (Old Syrian Period)

The Middle Bronze Age was the heyday of the scribal schools in Mesopotamia proper. The great schools of Ur and Nippur were, if not actually founded by King Šulgi of Ur in the 21st century, certainly the objects of his patronage.[75] Other schools were established on their model, and used their curriculum, wherever cuneiform learning penetrated. The reigns of Ḫammurapi and Samsuiluna of Babylon in the eighteenth century marked the floruit of their efforts. And at this same time, Syria too indulged in a flurry of scribal activity, as is clear from the archives of sites such as Terqa, Chagar Bazar, and above all Mari. Such activity presupposes scribal schools attached to their courts, and indeed Mari has revealed the existence of what, for a long time, was regarded as a classroom—the only one ever discovered intact. More recently, the interpretation of this room full of different sized benches in parallel rows with the biggest bench in front has had to be reviewed and revised, and there is now a disposition to regard contemporary Nippur as providing a more likely schoolroom.[76] More importantly, there is a startling dearth of "school texts" or literary texts of any kind—far fewer than a tenth of the contemporaneous archival texts as would be expected on the analogy of the Mesopotamian situation or even the earlier one at Ebla in Syria itself. Perhaps we are dealing with the accidents of discovery, and the libraries or real school rooms are still waiting to be unearthed.[77] In fact, Lambert has recently published a god list from the house of Asqudum at Mari,[78] and J.-M. Durand has promised a separate publication of the lexical texts found in this house and in the palace.[79] But it remains a fact that the sole Sumerian literary text yet found for this period in all of Syria is a copy of the Sumerian King List from Tell Leilan signalled by Claudine Vincente.[80] It probably dates from the middle of the 18th century (ca. 1775-1725 B.C.E.) and includes, among other things, "the names of the six Mari dynasty kings," hitherto largely broken in the surviving manuscripts. Whether the new recension will confirm the restoration of the hitherto missing portions of the dynasty as proposed on the basis of evidence from

[75] See most recently Hallo, "Nippur Originals," in H. Behrens et al., eds., *DUMU-E$_2$-DUB-BA-A: Studies in Honor of Åke W. Sjöberg* (Philadelphia, 1989) 237-247, esp. p. 237 and n. 9.

[76] E.C. Stone, *Nippur Neighborhoods* (Chicago, 1987; *SAOC* 44) 56f., cited by S.A. Meier, "Women and Communication in the Ancient Near East," *JAOS* 111 (1991) 542 n. 12 end.

[77] Cf. e.g. J. Krecher, "Schreiberschulung in Ugarit: Die Tradition von Listen und sumerischen Texten," *UF* 1 (1969) 130: "Nicht alle Fundstätte von Texten in babylonischer Keilschrift haben auch Schülertexte erbracht. So fehlen sie bis jetzt m.W. unter anderem in Kültepe und in Mari...Für Mari...dürften die Zufälligkeiten der Fundumstände massgeblich sein."

[78] "A list of Gods' Names found at Mari," in J.-M. Durand and J.-R. Kupper, eds., *Miscellanea Babylonica: Mélanges offerts à Maurice Birot* (Paris, 1985) 181-190; cf. J. Oelsner, "Zu einer Schülertafel aus Mari," *NABU* 1989/33.

[79] Apud Lambert, "Gods' Names," (1985) 181, n. 2.

[80] "Tell Leilan Recension of the Sumerian King List," *NABU* 1990/11.

Ebla,[81] Emar,[82] or Mari itself[83] only the full publication by Vincente will be able to reveal.[84]

In spite of this, there is ample indication that the knowledge of Sumerian was not by any means lost to mind in the Syria of the Middle Bronze period. It was occasionally used in monumental inscriptions of both the neo-Sumerian[85] and the Old Babylonian periods,[86] and frequently in the archival texts at least of the earlier period.[87] It survived in the schools of the Late Bronze Period. And, perhaps most tellingly, there are several Sumerian lamentations and other compositions cited by incipit in the great Ritual to Ištar recovered from Old Babylonian Mari.[88] The fact that they are cited in syllabic transcription implies on the one hand a degree of unfamiliarity with Sumerian, at least in its normal logographic orthography, but on the other that the texts were presumably to be recited in the original Sumerian.

The situation is a little more promising in Akkadian, but before we turn to that we need to note the significant presence of still another language in the literary productivity of the time, namely Hurrian. The Hurrians were at home in Syria at least from the Late Sargonic period on, and by Old Babylonian times were a considerable factor in the population of Mari, as shown, particularly on the basis of personal names, by Jack Sasson.[89] It thus should not come as a total surprise that a corpus of Hurrian incantations was identified among the Mari texts as long ago as 1939 by Thureau-Dangin.[90] One of Thureau-Dangin's texts has since then been joined to another published by E. Laroche,[91] and the combined text turns out to be a prayer or letter mentioning Zimri-Lim of Mari.[92] Hurrian incantations have meantime been identified in Mesopotamia as well,[93] but there

---

[81] M.J. Geller, "The Lugal of Mari at Ebla and the Sumerian King List," *Eblaitica* 1 (1987) 141-145; cf. A. Alberti, "AN.BU = *a-nu-bu*$_x$," *NABU* 1990/124.

[82] See below, note 143.

[83] H. Lewy, "The Chronology of the Mari Texts," in J.-R. Kupper, ed., *XV*^{e} *Rencontre Assyriologique Internationale: La Civilisation de Mari* (Liège, 1967) 13-28.

[84] Among the Brockman tablets at the University of Haifa is a duplicate of the Sumerian King List that joins P_3, but it does not preserve any part of the dynasty of Mari, according to information kindly supplied by Jacob Klein (letter of 10-6-91).

[85] E.g. the inscription of Taram-Uram daughter of Apilkin and bride or daughter-in-law of Ur-Nammu of Ur: M. Civil, "On Some Texts Mentioning Ur-Namma," *Or* 54 (1985) 41 vii; cf. *IRSA* IIIE1a and Hallo, *RLA* 4 (1972) 13f. *sub* Ḫabil-kīn.

[86] E.g. the seals of Iṣi-Dagan, Tura-Dagan and Yaggid-Lim (*IRSA* IVF). But the inscriptions may also have been intended to be read off in Akkadian.

[87] For texts of the period of the "šakkanakku's," see I.J. Gelb, "On the Recently Published Economic Texts from Mari," *RA* 50 (1956) 1-10; H. Limet, *Textes administratifs de l'époque des šakkanakku* (Paris, 1976; *ARM* 19).

[88] J. Krecher, *Sumerische Kultlyrik* (Wiesbaden, 1966) 34.

[89] J.M. Sasson, "Ḫurrians and Ḫurrian Names in the Mari Texts," *UF* 6 (1974) 353-400.

[90] "Tablettes ḫurrites provenant de Mâri," *RA* 36 (1939) 1-28.

[91] "Fragment hourrite provenant de Mâri," *RA* 51 (1957) 104-106.

[92] M. Salvini, "Un texte hourrite nommant Zimrilim," *RA* 82 (1988) 59-69.

[93] Cf. above, note 23.

is no reason to insist on their priority; in this case it may well be that the genre was at home in Syria and borrowed thence into Mesopotamia.

The Akkadian literary texts from Mari belong chiefly to the religious realm. Marguerite Rutten has published a group of more than thirty liver models for use in divination.[94] They are inscribed in Old Akkadian, but since all are of similar date, and two of them mention Išbi-Irra, the first king of Isin (ca. 2017-1985 B.C.E.), they cannot be earlier than his reign.[95] The Ritual to Ištar was already mentioned; it was published by Georges Dossin,[96] and has a parallel of sorts in the Old Babylonian cult at Larsa, at least as far as the clergy and the structure of the ritual day are concerned.[97] Another ritual text was published by Maurice Birot and described by him as possibly a liturgical calendar extending over one or more months and reflecting the cultic practice of Mari.[98] The prominence it accords to the rites for Sargon and Naram-Sin, the deceased kings of the Sargonic dynasty, indicate, however, that it belongs ultimately in the Mesopotamian tradition.[99]

Perhaps the most interesting literary text from Mari yet to see the light of day is a version of the historiographic text describing the great revolt against Naram-Sin of Akkad. The text, of which only some twenty lines are preserved, was first signalled and copied by Dossin, who recognized it as a duplicate of an Old Babylonian text of unknown provenience published long before by Alfred Boissier, but it was not published until Edmond Sollberger discovered a further Old Babylonian duplicate in the British Museum.[100] The Mari exemplar appears to be a school exercise with extracts of a prototype of the Boissier text and of other texts.[101] Here, too, the Mari tradition follows, by and large, that of the Mesopotamian canon. An interesting peculiarity of the Mari exemplar is, however, its consistent use of syllabic spellings to represent the geographical and divine names written logographically in the corresponding portion of the Boissier text.

Before we leave the Middle Bronze Age entirely, we may make brief mention of the texts recovered at Terqa and dated to the Late Old Babylonian period, i.e., to the "dark age" when the Kingdom of Khana, based in Terqa, ruled the Middle Euphrates region and provided one of the few documented dynasties contemporary with the successors of

---

[94] "Trente-deux modèles de foies en argile inscrits provenant de Tell-Hariri (Mari)," *RA* 35 (1938) 36-70.

[95] Gelb, "Economic Texts" (1956) 1-10, esp. pp. 2f.

[96] "Un rituel du culte d'Ištar provenant de Mari," *RA* 35 (1938) 1-13.

[97] E.C. Kingsbury, "A Seven Day Ritual in the Old Babylonian Cult at Larsa," *HUCA* 34 (1963) 1-34, esp. p. 3 and n. 12.

[98] "Fragment de rituel de Mari relatif au *kispum*," in B. Alster, ed., *Death in Mesopotamia: Papers read at the XXVIe Rencontre assyriologique internationale* (Copenhagen, 1980) 139-150, esp. p. 145.

[99] Hallo, "Royal Ancestor Worship in the Biblical World," in M. Fishbane and E. Tov, eds., *Shaarey Talmon: Studies in the Bible, Qumran, and the Ancient Near East Presented to Shemaryahu Talmon* (Winona Lake, 1992) 381-401, esp. p. 391 and n. 67 and p. 394 and n. 88.

[100] A.K. Grayson and E. Sollberger, "L'insurrection générale contre Narām-Suen," *RA* 70 (1976) 103-128; see p. 113 for the copy and p. 114 for the photograph.

[101] Ibid., 104.

Ḫammurapi at Babylon (ca. 1750-1550 B.C.E.).[102] Most of these texts are archival in character, but mention may be made here of one mathematical text of a particularly simple variety (probably a multiplication table for 15),[103] and one small monumental text, a bead[104] which, according to Claus Wilcke, was dedicated by Kudur-mabuk, son of Šimti-šilḫak, the father of kings Warad-Sin and Rim-Sin of Larsa (ca. 1834-1763 B.C.E.).[105] Summing up the evidence for the Middle Bronze (Old Syrian) period, the Syrian contribution to cuneiform literature and learning was largely limited to some ritual texts which reflected the particular nature of the cult at Mari.[106]

III. Late Bronze Age (Middle Syrian Period)

This was the heyday of scribal schools and schooling in Syria and all of the "western periphery" of Mesopotamia. During this period, and particularly in the Amarna age, Akkadian became the lingua franca of international communication for diplomatic and commercial purposes. To this end, scribal schools appeared throughout the area, including Amarna itself, in Egypt,[107] as well as Hazor, Megiddo, Taanach, Shechem, Aphek and Gezer in Israel,[108] Kumidi in Lebanon,[109] and Ḫattuša in Anatolia.[110] It is a fact that wherever in the western periphery cuneiform texts of the Late Bronze Age have turned up at all, they have included scholastic texts; the only exception to this rule thus far is Hebron.[111] This shows that it was deemed necessary to instruct local scribes in Mesopotamian traditions of learning, including the heritage of Sumerian language and literature.

---

[102] Hallo and Simpson, *Ancient Near East* (1971) 102f.

[103] O. Rouault, *Terqa Final Reports No. 1: L'Archive de Puzurum* (Malibu, 1984; *BM* 16) 60 No 57.

[104] Ibid., p. 61 No. 58.

[105] Wilcke, "Kudurmabuk in Terqa," in Ö. Tunca, ed., *De la Babylonie à la Syrie, en passant par Mari: Mélanges offerts à Monsieur J.-R. Kupper* (Liège, 1990) 179-181.

[106] On this cult, see especially A. Tsukimoto, *Untersuchungen zur Totenpflege (kispum) im alten Mesopotamien* (Kevelaer, 1985; *AOAT* 216).

[107] P. Artzi, "Observations on the 'Library' of the Amarna Archives," in K.R. Veenhof, ed., *Cuneiform Archives and Libraries: Papers read at the 30e Rencontre Assyriologique Internationale* (Istanbul, 1985) 210-212; "Studies in the Library of the Amarna Archive," in J. Klein and A. Skaist, eds., *Bar-Ilan Studies in Assyriology dedicated to Pinḥas Artzi* (Ramat-Gan, 1990) 139-156.

[108] Cf. A. Demsky, "The Education of Canaanite Scribes in the Mesopotamian Cuneiform Tradition," in Klein and Skaist, *Artzi* (1990) 157-170; previously H. Tadmor, "A Lexicographical Text from Hazor," *IEJ* 27 (1977) 101f., nn. 23-25; Hallo, "The Expansion of Cuneiform Literature," *PAAJR* 46-47 (1980) 307-322, esp. p. 312. The Hazor texts may be somewhat earlier than the rest.

[109] R. Hachmann, *Bericht über die Ergebnisse der Ausgrabungen in Kāmid el-Lōz in den Jahren 1968 bis 1970* (Bonn, 1980; *Saarbrücker Beiträge zur Altertumskunde* 22), *Bericht über die Ergebnisse der Ausgrabungen in Kāmid el-Lōz in den Jahren 1971 bis 1974* (Bonn, 1982; *Saarbrücker Beiträge zur Altertumskunde* 32), and article "Kumidi (Tell Kāmid al-Lōz)," *RLA* 6 (1980-83) 330-334, for general summaries. D.O. Edzard, "Ein neues Tontafelfragment (Nr. 7) aus Kāmid al-Lōz," *ZA* 70 (1980) 52-54 may be a school text; note the sequences ab-í[b], la-l[í], ma-me-m[u?], su-šú(?)-še, ru-ri.

[110] Cf. e.g. G. Beckman, "Mesopotamians and Mesopotamian Learning at Ḫattuša," *JCS* 35 (1983) 97-114.

[111] M. Anbar and N. Na'aman, "An Account Tablet of Sheep from Ancient Hebron," *TA* 13-14 (1986-87) 3-12.

Sumerian texts were often given not only in the traditional logographic orthography standardized at Nippur, but in a phonetic transcription intended to help the local students to pronounce the long-lost language, thus carrying on a practice already noted at Ebla and intermittently in the Middle Bronze Age texts from Mari. The scholastic texts were also routinely translated into the more familiar Akkadian. And in addition, some schools provided translations into the local vernacular(s), or created new compositions in their own language that imitated or reflected the traditional Sumero-Akkadian texts.

The outstanding illustration of all these rules for this period is Ugarit. Ugarit, the great seaport on the north Syrian coast opposite Cyprus, lay at the crossroads of many cultural influences: Egyptian, Aegean, Anatolian, Canaanite and Mesopotamian. It developed its own proto-alphabetic script which in no more than thirty simplified cuneiform characters was able to render the West Semitic and Hurrian languages that were its native speech. But it also maintained a full-scale scribal school on the Mesopotamian pattern, where the complicated Mesopotamian cuneiform was mastered by the traditional techniques of learning, first Sumerian, then Akkadian, and finally translating both, where necessary, into the local idioms. Only the products of this traditional learning will be reviewed here, and even that only in outline.

An early survey of the lexical (and Sumerian) texts from Ugarit was provided by Joachim Krecher in 1969.[112] According to his survey, the following lexical texts are represented at Ugarit: the primers tu-ta-ti and "Silbenalphabet A"; the Syllabary A, including examples with archaic signs and other with translations into Akkadian, Hurrian and Ugaritic; forerunners to the vocabularies A-Tablet and Diri; a grammatical paradigm (*OBGT* XIV); forerunners to the "encyclopedic" texts ḪAR-ra and lú=ša; lists of personal names and divine names, and mathematical texts.[113] As Krecher notes, the peculiarities of the Ugaritic versions of the lexical (and literary) texts may go back to the influence of the Hittite scribes from whom some of the texts were clearly derived, or possibly both Ugaritic and Hittite scribes drew on some third and as yet unknown but at any rate extra-Mesopotamian tradition.[114] In some cases the Ugaritic exemplars may actually represent imports from Ḫattuša.[115]

The connected literary texts which followed the study of the lexical texts in the traditional scribal curriculum are best represented at Ugarit by the great libraries (or archives) of Rapᵓanu and other "men of letters," and were published by Jean Nougayrol in 1968.[116] We can only highlight here those texts which have particularly received attention in the secondary literature, among them both such as are shared with Mesopotamia (and/or Ḫatti) and others which are, so far, unique to Ugarit.[117] Among the former are the series Si-du (Nos. 164-166) of which more later,[118] "Scribal Letter B 20," (No. 15)[119] and the

[112] "Schreiberschulung" (1969) 131-158.

[113] Ibid., 134-141.

[114] Ibid., 143.

[115] So for example below, note 119.

[116] *Ug* 5 (Paris, 1968) 1-446: "Textes suméro-accadiens des archives et bibliothèques privées d'Ugarit."

[117] Cf. also e.g. note 137 below.

[118] See below, notes 145-147.

"Message of Lu-dingira to his Mother" (No. 169).[120] The latter are, so far, more numerous, though the possibility must always be kept in mind that Mesopotamian prototypes may yet turn up or be identified among already known texts. In one case an alleged example of "Syrian wisdom literature" known also from Emar[121] has been reclaimed for Mesopotamia by the recognition of its incipit in an Old Babylonian catalogue text,[122] even though not a single Mesopotamian exemplar has yet turned up (No. 163).[123]

The literary texts, then, that are for now unique to Ugarit include a medical ritual (No. 16), a collection of incantations (No. 17), a variation on the theme of the "just sufferer" (No. 162),[124] and one on the Deluge as incorporated in the Epic of Atra-ḫasis (No. 167); the last is considered to be "a good Babylonian work of literature, not a Syrian composition" by W.G. Lambert and A.R. Millard.[125] Little can be said about the fragment which Nougayrol connected to Gilgamesh (No. 168) but von Soden held to have nothing to do with that epic.[126] Summing up the extensive material from Ugarit, it is arguably derivative from Mesopotamia in great part, either directly or via Ḫattuša. But there is no question that, especially in its orthography and its translation into the local language(s), it was adapted to the needs of the Syrian student population.

IV. The Iron Age (Late Syrian Period)

After 1200 B.C.E. Syria increasingly turned to the newly emerging "alphabetic" scripts (Aramaic and Hieroglyphic Hittite) and away from the older and more cumbersome Mesopotamian cuneiform. But one site that straddled the transition from Bronze to Iron Age harbored a last floruit of cuneiform literature and that is Emar. Although its destruction is virtually contemporaneous with that of Ugarit, its evidence will be used here, somewhat arbitrarily, as representative of the next age.

---

[119] Nouygarol No. 15; according to P. Michalowski, "On the Early History of the Ershahunga Prayer," *JCS* 39 (1987) 38, n. 6, the Ugarit exemplar represents an import from Ḫattuša.

[120] M. Civil, "The 'Message of Lú-dingir-ra to his Mother' and a Group of Akkado-Hittite 'Proverbs'," *JNES* 23 (1964) 1-11; cf. J.S. Cooper, "New Cuneiform Parallels to the Song of Songs," *JBL* 90 (1971) 157-162.

[121] See below, note 158.

[122] M.E. Cohen, "Literary Texts from the Andrews University Archaeological Museum," *RA* 70 (1976) 131 No. 15, according to M. Civil, "The Texts from Meskene-Emar," *AuOr* 7 (1989) 7 ad No. 778.

[123] For these "Instructions of Šube-awilim" and their possible connections to Mesopotamian wisdom texts, see for now Hallo, [review of Alster, *Instructions of Suruppak* (1974) and *Studies in Sumerian Proverbs* (1975)], *JNES* 37 (1978) 271f. See now the new treatment by M. Dietrich, "Der Dialog zwischen Šūpē-amēli und seinem 'Vater': die Tradition babylonischer Weisheitsgesprüche im Westen," *UF* 23 (1991) 33-68.

[124] Cf. most recently G.L. Mattingly, "The Pious Sufferer: Mesopotamia's Traditional Theodicy and Job's Counselors," in Hallo et al., eds., *The Bible in the Light of Cuneiform Literature: Scripture in Context* III (Lewiston, 1990; *Ancient Near Eastern Texts and Studies* 8) 305-348, esp. pp. 324f.

[125] *Atra-ḫasīs: The Babylonian Story of the Flood* (Oxford, 1969) 131-133, esp. p. 131; cf. R. Borger, "Sur le récit du Déluge RS 22421," *RA* 64 (1970) 189.

[126] "Bemerkungen zu einigen literarischen Texten in akkadischer Sprache aus Ugarit," *UF* 1 (1969) 189-195, esp. p. 195.

Emar lay on the Euphrates at the point where that river turns southeast toward Babylonia, and therefore became the logical transshipment point where overland traffic from the west took ship for the south.[127] Following Daniel Arnaud, its final fall is generally dated to the second year of Melišiḫu (or Melišipak) of the Kassite Dynasty of Babylonia, for a text bearing that date was found among a lot of seven tablets which appear to have been dispersed at the instant of the destruction, i.e., in 1187 B.C.E.[128] That date may serve as the *terminus post quem non*, both for the numerous tablets that have appeared as the result of illicit digs at the site,[129] and the truly massive numbers recovered by the official French excavations. With one exception,[130] it is only the latter that include canonical texts, both lexical and literary, and Arnaud has earned the gratitude of all Assyriologists by publishing them with utmost despatch and without waiting to reconstruct final editions by himself.[131] As a result, a number of such editions have been contributed by others, and the significance of the entire find has rapidly become clear.[132] While the Hurrian (and Hittite) texts of Emar still await publication,[133] it is thus already possible to give an overview of the canonical material in Sumerian and Akkadian.[134]

Turning first to the lexical texts, these resemble closely the finds from Ugarit—not surprisingly, since they are only a few decades later—but also, to some extent, the earlier recensions from Nuzi.[135] Thus we again meet "Silbenalphabet A" ("Syllabic Vocabulary A"); the Syllabary A ("Vocabulary S(a)"), including examples with archaic signs; forerunners

---

[127] Hallo, "The Road to Emar," *JCS* 18 (1964) 57-88, esp. p. 81.

[128] D. Arnaud, "Les textes d'Emar et la chronologie de la fin du Bronze Récent," *Syria* 52 (1975) 87-92, esp. pp. 88f.

[129] E.g., M. Sigrist, "Miscellanea," *JCS* 34 (1982) 242-252; J. Huehnergard, "Five Tablets from the Vicinity of Emar," *RA* 77 (1983) 11-43; J.-W. Meyer and G. Wilhelm, "Eine spätbronzezeitliche Keilschrifturkunde aus Syrien," *DamM* 1 (1983) 249-261; A. Tsukimoto, "Eine neue Urkunde des *Tili-Šarruma*, Sohn des Königs von Karkamiš," *ASJ* 6 (1984) 65-74; "Sieben spätbronzezeitliche Urkunden aus Syrien," *ASJ* 10 (1988) 153-189; "Akkadian Tablets in the Hirayama Collection (I)," *ASJ* 12 (1990) 177-259; G. Beckman, "Three Tablets from the Vicinity of Emar," *JCS* 40 (1988) 61-68; D. Arnaud, "La Syrie du moyen-Euphrate sous le protectorat hittite: contrats de droit privé," *AuOr* 5 (1987) 211-241.

[130] K. Watanabe, "Freiburger Vorläufer zu ḪAR-ra = *ḫubullu* XI und XII," *ASJ* 9 (1987) 277-291. For the structure of ḪAR-ra in OB and MB texts, see Hallo, "Notes from the Babylonian Collection, II: Old Babylonian HAR-ra," *JCS* 34 (1982) 81-93, esp. p. 87; for the structure of ḪAR-ra at Emar in particular, see M. Civil, "Meskene-Emar" (1989) 11-20.

[131] *Recherches au Pays d'Aštata: Emar VI. 1-4. Les textes sumériens et accadiens* (Paris, 1985-87).

[132] See especially Civil, "Meskene-Emar" (1989), devoted to the canonical texts, and M. Dietrich, "Die akkadischen Texte der Archive und Bibliotheken von Emar," *UF* 22 (1990) 25-48, devoted to all the Akkadian texts.

[133] E. Laroche and M. Salvini, *Recherches au Pays d'Aštata: Emar VII. Les textes hourrites* (Paris, forthcoming). Cf. meantime Laroche, "Observations sur le rituel anatolien provenant de Meskéné-Emar," in F. Imparati, ed., *Studi di storia e di filologia anatolica dedicati a Giovanni Pugliese Carratelli* (Firenze, 1988) 111-117 and "Documents hittites et hourites" in D. Beyer, ed., *Meskéné-Emar: Dix ans de travaux 1972-1982* (Paris, 1982) 53-60.

[134] See in detail P.Y. Hoskisson, "Emar as an Empirical Model of the Transmission of Canon," in K.L. Younger, Jr. et al., eds., *The Biblical Canon in Comparative Perspective: Scripture in Context* IV (Lewiston, forthcoming; *Ancient Near Eastern Texts and Studies* 11) 21-31.

[135] Civil, "[Note]," *RA* 81 (1987) 187-188.

to Diri;[136] forerunners to ḪAR-ra and lú=ša, and lists of divine names. In addition there are exemplars of Izi, Níg-ga and Sag B. Of the school texts from Ugarit, only tu-ta-ti, the A-tablet, grammatical paradigms, personal name lists and mathematical texts are so far missing at Emar.[137]

The harvest of connected literary texts is, on the other hand, much richer than at Ugarit. It includes omens, incantations, rituals and wisdom texts, among other genres. The mantic category is represented by astrology, extispicy, physiognomic omens, teratoscopy and medical omens. The related category of hemerologies and menologies includes almanacs and the series *iqqur ippuš*, among others. The incantations include the series "Evil Spirits" (udug-ḫul) and "Headache" (sag-gig) as well as others. The rituals are probably Mesopotamian but remain to be identified. None of these purely religious and cultic texts are known at Ugarit.

When we turn from them to the literary texts of a more properly belletristic variety, we find many correspondences to Ugarit. But we also encounter an interesting new phenomenon: the tendency to embellish traditional Mesopotamian texts with a bit of "local color." This is most apparent in the text which Arnaud, with apologies to François Villon, has entitled "La Ballade des héros du temps jadis" (No. 767).[138] This remarkable text is, in effect, a drinking song with the theme of "carpe diem." To press its point, it invokes the names of long-dead kings and heroes, including Alulu the first antediluvian, Ziusudra the flood-hero, Etana, effectively the first postdiluvian king, and Gilgamesh, Enkidu, and Huwawa. As shown by Wilcke in his convenient edition,[139] the Emar exemplar is duplicated by exemplars from Ugarit and Late Old Babylonian Sippar, hence may be called a traditional Mesopotamian text. But the Emar recension characteristically adds to the list of ancient worthies two names, Bazi and Zizi, which are not found in the other recensions. In the "Ḫamazi Letter," the archives of Ebla have preserved the copy of a diplomatic letter addressed by the vizier (*abarakku*) of the royal palace to the ambassador (sukkal-du_8) of the king of Ḫamazi, and his name is Zizi.[140] But the only early king of Ḫamazi known to the Mesopotamian historiographic tradition is Ḫataniš of the Sumerian King List.[141] Hence the new names must represent "local heroes" of comparable antiquity. But although Emar itself had independent kings with names like EN.ZI-Da-mu in the time of the Ebla texts, it

---

[136] Civil, "Meskene-Emar" (1989) 20 includes here No. 563, which Arnaud had assigned to Ea, a text otherwise unknown in the periphery.

[137] Cf. also above, note 117.

[138] See already his remarks in "Les textes suméro-accadiens: un florilège," in Beyer, *Meskéné-Emar* (1982) 51.

[139] "Die Sumerische Königsliste und erzählte Vergangenheit," in J. von Ungern-Sternberg and H. Reinau, eds., *Vergangenheit in Mündlicher Überlieferung* (Stuttgart, 1988; *Colloquium Rauricum* 1) 113-140, esp. pp. 137-139 and foldout.

[140] G. Pettinato, "Archivi" (1977) 225-243, esp. 238-242; idem, *Archives* (1981) 97f. The designation goes back to Gelb, "Ebla and the Kish Civilization," in Cagni, *Lingua* (1981) 12.

[141] For this name see T. Jacobsen, *The Sumerian King List* (Chicago, 1939; *AS* 11) 98f.; van Dijk, Goetze and Hussey, *Incantations* (1985) 11; Hallo, "Texts, Statues and The Cult of the Divine King," *SVT* 40 (1988) 55; idem, "Ancestor Worship" (1992) 390.

was under foreign sovereignty for most of its history,[142] and one should look elsewhere in its vicinity for the more likely home of Bazi and Zizi; whether it turns out to be Mari only time will tell.[143]

In its Sippar recensions, the text formed part of a miscellaneous collection of three or four separate compositions, as Bendt Alster has shown in his latest edition.[144] The collection began with the blessing of a king and a (separate?) poem about Abi-ešuḫ of Babylon (1711-1684 B.C.E.), continued with the poem "Nothing at all is valid but life is sweet" (níg-nam nu-kal zi ku_7-ku_7-da) and concluded with our drinking song. By neo-Assyrian times, however, our text had become the concluding work in a much larger collection of some 35 wisdom compositions called the "Series of Si-du,"[145] as we now know from a neo-Assyrian table of contents of this series recently published by Irving Finkel.[146] This series was duly entered in the catalogue of the royal library of Assurbanipal, and in other literary catalogues of the time, and its author was dated to the time of Išbi-Irra of Isin (ca. 2017-1985 B.C.E.) by a Seleucid period roster of sages[147] which also gave him the Akkadian name of Enlil-ibni. Thus the Emar scribes were not reluctant to tamper with a text that stood in the millennial tradition of Mesopotamian literature.

A similar observation can be made with regard to a second wisdom composition known as "Enlil and Namzitarra" and hitherto attested only in unilingual Sumerian exemplars of Old Babylonian date.[148] As Civil has noted, five Emar fragments join to make up one bilingual Sumero-Akkadian version of this poem,[149] but with many transpositions of lines and other changes from the original. The most startling change is the expansion of line 20 which in the Old Babylonian recension read simply: "The (appointed-/terminal) days of the human being are approaching;" in the Emar recension this becomes a six-line disquisition on human frailty, translated by Jacob Klein thus: "The days of the human being are approaching; Day to day they verily decrease, Month after month they

---

142 A. Archi, "Imâr au IIIème millénaire d'après les archives d'Ebla," *MARI* 6 (1990) 21-38; E. Laroche, "Emar, étape entre Babylone et le Hatti," in J.-C. Margueron, ed., *Le Moyen Euphrate* (Leiden, 1980) 237-239.

143 See above, note 82.

144 "The Sumerian Poem of Early Rulers and Related Poems," *OLP* 21 (1990) 5-25. Cf. idem, "Väterliche Weisheit in Mesopotamien," in A. Assmann, ed., *Weisheit: Beiträge zur Archäologie der literarischen Kommunikation* III (München, 1991) 103-115, esp. pp. 110f.

145 For this personal name see Hallo, "Fara" (1973) 232 and n. 26. At Ebla, the name (or word?) is equated with *di-mu-mu* = lament?; cf. Vocabolario di Ebla 1116 (*MEE* 4 [1982] 320) and Pettinato, "én-é-nu-ru" (1979) 115. It recurs there (and in a duplicate from Abu Ṣalabikh) also in a unilingual lexical text (*MEE* 3:68; cf. above, note 66), and in an archival text where a sheep is sacrificed for the laments for the dead kings: 1 udu íb-tag si-dù si-dù en-en (Pettinato, "én-é-nu-ru" [1979] 131).

146 "On the Series of Sidu," *ZA* 76 (1986) 250-253. Our incipit occurs here as the last of 35 entries. Cf. previously W.G. Lambert, "A Late Assyrian Catalogue of Literary and Scholarly Texts," in B. Eichler, ed., *Kramer Anniversary Volume* (Kevelaer, 1976; *AOAT* 25) 315f. The series is also listed in the "Assyrian Library Records;" cf. S. Parpola, "Assyrian Library Records," *JNES* 42 (1983) 12:7'.

147 See the references in Finkel, "Sidu" (1986) 250.

148 M. Civil, "Enlil and Namzitarra," *AfO* 25 (1974-77) 65-71; cf. H. Vanstiphout, "Some Notes on 'Enlil and Namzitarra'," *RA* 74 (1980) 67-71; B. Alster, "A duplicate to 'Enlil and Namzitarra'," *NABU* 1990/102.

149 "Meskene-Emar" (1989) 7 *ad* Nos. 771-774 and 592.

verily decrease, Year after year they verily decrease! One hundred twenty years (are) the years of mankind—verily it is their bane;[150] (This is so) from the day that humanity exists until today!"[151] The life-span of 120 years is of course well known from the Hebrew Bible (Gen. 6:3) and quite different from the ideal life-spans of other Near Eastern traditions;[152] whether the Emar formulation is the source of the biblical concept or rather part of a wide-spread "West Semitic" one remains for now an open question.

The other literary texts from Emar can be dealt with more briefly. Two fragments (Nos. 783f.) reproduce the Akkadian debate of "The Tamarisk and the Palm"; they belong to a single tablet as Wilcke has shown in his edition[153] and constitute a valuable centerpiece between the Old Babylonian and the Middle Assyrian and neo-Assyrian recensions previously known of this composition. Two other fragments about a fowler (bilingual; Nos. 768f.) are reminiscent of the Sumerian ditty about "The Fowler and his Wife," though they do not actually reproduce any of the latter's lines.[154] A bilingual blessing for an unnamed king (No. 775) has a duplicate in syllabic Sumerian from Ugarit,[155] but belongs in a Sumerian tradition of royal blessings beginning "Oh my king, may you live (forever)" as attested already by four such prayers for Sin-iddinam of Larsa (ca. 1849-1843 B.C.E.)[156] and by the millennial use of this phrase as a royal acclamation.[157] For the alleged example of "Syrian wisdom" of a certain Šube-awilim (Nos. 778-780) we have already noted a corresponding entry in a Mesopotamian catalogue in connection with the Ugarit exemplar.[158] There are also two excerpts from the Gilgamesh Epic, corresponding to the fourth and sixth tablets (chapters) of the later canonical recension (Nos. 781f.).[159]

Finally we need to consider the Akkadian ritual texts of Emar. Whether these were at home in the school or the cult is not clear; like the purely literary texts, they were found in Temple 1 of excavation-area M. M. Dietrich straddles the question neatly by assigning

---

[150] Sum. níg-gig, Akkadian *ikkibu*; for this concept in earlier Sumerian texts see J. Klein, "The 'Bane' of Humanity: A Lifespan of One Hundred Twenty Years," *ASJ* 12 (1990) 64f., n. 15; Hallo, "Biblical Abominations and Sumerian Taboos," *JQR* 76 (1985) 21-40.

[151] "Bane" (1990) 57-70.

[152] Ibid.; cf. A. Malamat, "Longevity: Biblical Concepts and Some Ancient Near Eastern Parallels," in *Vorträge gehalten auf der 28. Rencontre Assyriologique Internationale in Wien* (Horn, 1982; *AfO* Beiheft 19) 215-224.

[153] "Die Emar-Version von 'Dattelpalme und Tamariske'—ein Rekonstruktionsversuch," *ZA* 79 (1989) 161-190.

[154] B. Alster, "Paradoxical Proverbs and Satire in Sumerian Literature," *JCS* 27 (1975) 214f.; F. Rochberg-Halton and P. Zimansky, "The University of Iowa Cuneiform Texts," *JCS* 31 (1979) 143:18.

[155] D. Arnaud, "Les textes cunéiformes suméro-accadiens des campagnes 1979-1980 à Ras Shamra-Ougarit," *Syria* 59 (1982) 209-216, reproduced in *Emar* VI/4:374-376.

[156] Hallo, "New Texts from the Reign of Sin-iddinam," *JCS* 21 (1967) 95-99, esp. p. 96 *sub* Sin-iddinam C.

[157] Hallo, "The Death of Kings: Traditional Historiography in Contextual Perspective," in M. Cogan and I. Eph'al, eds., *Ah, Assyria...: Studies in Assyrian History and Ancient Near Eastern Historiography Presented to Hayim Tadmor* (Jerusalem, 1991; *SH* 33) 149 and nn. 8-10, with previous literature.

[158] See above, notes 121-123. Neither Arnaud nor Civil remarked on the parallel from Ugarit. But cf. now B. Alster, "The Instructions of Urninurta and Related Compositions," *Or* 60 (1991) 145, n. 13.

[159] On these see C. Wilcke, *NABU* 1991/5.

them to the "cultic library" ("Kultbibliothek")[160] but they may safely be classed among the canonical texts for at least two reasons. First, they typically occur in two or more duplicates which, in spite of considerable variations among each other, ultimately reflect a single cultic tradition, if not a uniform underlying text,[161] and, second, they routinely employ the present-future tense; they are thus to be considered prescriptive rituals, not descriptive rituals or accounts.[162] There are many of these prescriptive rituals at Emar (Nos. 369-535), but we will confine ourselves here to one in particular which has attracted attention ever since the preliminary announcement of its identification by Arnaud.[163] This is the ritual for the installation of a high-priestess (*entu*) and it is remarkable for at least two features: it takes place over a seven-day period[164] and it involves some kind of sacred marriage between the priestess and the god. In the latter respect it thus echoes a Mesopotamian cultic tradition while in effect turning it on its head. For in the Sumerian sacred marriage, it was the male partner that was avowedly mortal (the king), while the female partner, whoever may have played her role,[165] represented the deity. A full edition of the text has now been provided by Dietrich.[166]

Summing up the situation for all the periods surveyed, it can be said in a general way that the cuneiform literature of Syria was in very large part derivative from Mesopotamia. Nevertheless, it made certain distinctive contributions, of which five may be singled out as characteristic of several or even all periods: (1) The lexical texts with which the scribal school curriculum began were adjusted to the needs of Syrian scribes either by supplementing them with translations into the local vernacular(s) or by creating whole new vocabularies in the style of the traditional Mesopotamian prototypes. (2) Both lexical texts and connected literary texts served to maintain some knowledge of Sumerian, but there was a degree of reliance on syllabically written Sumerian unknown in main-dialect texts from Mesopotamia proper. (3) Beyond lexical texts, the scribal curriculum emphasized wisdom texts which tended to form the intermediate stage of instruction in Mesopotamia, and rarely went on to the other genres of the more advanced curriculum. (4) The traditional texts were sometimes embellished with touches of local color, but truly original texts were largely confined to rituals at home in Syria and differing widely from corresponding Mesopotamian

---

160 "Die akkadischen Texte der Archive und Bibliotheken von Emar," *UF* 22 (1990) 41-43.

161 On this question see in detail M. Dietrich, "Das Einsetzungsritual der Entu von Emar (Emar VI/3, 369)," *UF* 21 (1989) 48-76.

162 For the distinction see most recently B.A. Levine, "The Descriptive Ritual Texts from Ugarit: Some Formal and Functional Features of the *Genre*," in Meyers and O'Connor, *Freedman* (1983) 467-475 and literature cited there, to which add A.F. Rainey, "The Order of Sacrifices in Old Testament Ritual Texts," *Biblica* 51 (1970) 485-498; R.M. Sigrist, "Offrandes dans le temple de Nusku à Nippur," *JCS* 29 (1977) 169-183.

163 "Religion assyro-babylonienne," *Annuaire de l'École pratique des Hautes Études* (*Ve Section*) 84 (1976-77) 223f.

164 See the summary by Dietrich, "Archive" (1990) 41-43; for the significance of this "week," see already Hallo, "New Moons and Sabbaths," *HUCA* 48 (1977) 1-18, esp. p. 17 n. 83.

165 On this question see most recently Hallo, "The Birth of Kings," in J.H. Marks and R.M. Good, eds., *Love and Death in the Ancient Near East: Essays in Honor of Marvin H. Pope* (Guilford, 1987) 45-52, esp. p. 51.

166 "Einsetzungsritual" (1989) 47-100. Cf. also the reedition of the text by Daniel Fleming in *The Installation of Baal's High Priestess at Emar* (Atlanta, 1992; *HSS* 42).

rituals. (5) Except in the Ebla corpus, all the Syrian libraries and archives provided significant numbers of Hurrian texts written in Mesopotamian cuneiform. These texts may yet prove to be the single most significant original contribution of Syria to cuneiform literature and learning.

SYRIAN CULTURAL INFLUENCE IN ḪATTI

Harry A. Hoffner, Jr.

Throughout the 400-year history of the Hittite kingdom the influence of Syria on the cities of the Anatolian plateau was strong and varied. This influence was particularly marked during the so-called New Kingdom, the period after the Syrian conquests of the emperor Šuppiluliuma I. After Šuppiluliuma replaced the earlier Mitannian rule over the native kingdoms of North Syria with Hittite overlordship and installed Hittite princes as founders of new ruling dynasties in Carchemish and Aleppo, the channels for cultural intercommunication were wide open and constantly active.

Channels of Cultural Influence

If we are to speak of such intercommunication, we should identify the possible channels. In antiquity only written documents allowed direct transmission of ideas and cultural values across great distances, apart from people who traveled. Usually ideas went where people did.

Captives

Although there is no evidence for massive movements of people from Syria into Asia Minor during the Hittite period, we know from the texts of groups of captives who were brought back to the Hittite homeland by Hittite armies. These were designated by the Sumerogram NAM.RA which covered the native Hittite word *arnuwalaš* meaning "persons subject to periodic resettlement."[1] Among the translations which have been tried are "colonists" and "civilian captives." What is meant is captives who can be settled as a group in areas needing population and agricultural exploitation.[2]

---

[1] S. Alp, "Die Soziale Klasse der NAM.RA-Leute und ihre hethitische Bezeichnung," *JKF* 1 (1950) 113-135; J. Friedrich and A. Kammenhuber, *Hethitisches Wörterbuch*[2] (Heidelberg, 1975-84) sub *arnuwala-*.

[2] E. von Schuler, *Hethitische Dienstanweisungen für höhere Hof- und Staatsbeamte* (Graz, 1957; *AfO* Beiheft 10) 48; J. Puhvel, *Hittite Etymological Dictionary* (Berlin, 1984ff) vol. 1, 166f., 186.

Imported wives and princesses

If such captives represent group transfers at the lowest rung of society, there were also individual transfers at the highest level. Hittite kings and queens regularly brought foreign women into the court as wives. Šuppiluliuma I's last wife was from Babylonia.[3] Ḫattušili III's queen Puduḫepa boasted in a letter to the Egyptian pharaoh Ramses II that she had brought high-bred young women from Babylonia and Amurru to be brides of her sons.[4]

Political refugees of high birth

Sanctuary was also given to persons of royal descent who had been driven from their own countries. A good example of this is Bentešina of Amurru, who succeeded his father Duppi-Teššup at the end of the reign of Muršili II, surrendered to an Egyptian invasion and severed ties with Ḫatti prior to the Battle of Kadesh, at the command of Muwatalli II was replaced on the throne of Amurru by Šapili, entered Ḫatti as a political refugee from Amurru, spent thirty years in Ḫatti mostly under the custody of prince Ḫattušili in Ḫakmiš, and was installed again on the throne of Amurru as an old man thirty years later by King Ḫattušili III.[5] The long and not unpleasant stay in Ḫatti as a guest of Ḫattušili left a deep impression upon Bentešina which affected the Kingdom of Amurru after Bentešina's return.[6]

"Privileged foreigners"

This still does not exhaust the possibilities. Diplomats, merchants and skilled craftsmen constituted what can be called the class of "privileged foreigners." For members of this broader class Hittite scribes used the Akkadian term *ubārum*.[7] This Akkadian term was used as a logogram. Unfortunately, we do not yet know its Hittite equivalent.

The privileges enjoyed by this class were not rights exceeding those possessed by natives, but a sub-set of the rights of free (i.e., upper class) natives.

---

[3] J. Danmanville, "Anatolie hittite," in P. Grimal, ed., *L'histoire mondiale de la femme* (Paris, 1965) vol. 1, 248-266; S.R. Bin-Nun, *The Tawananna in the Hittite Kingdom* (Heidelberg, 1975; *TH* 5); R. Lebrun, "Considérations sur la femme dans la société hittite," *Hethitica* 3 (1979) 109-125; A. Archi, "Le testimonianze oracolari per la regina Tawannanna," *SMEA* 22 (1980) 19-29; H.A. Hoffner, "A Prayer of Muršili II about his Stepmother," *JAOS* 103 (1983) 187-192.

[4] *KUB* 21.38 i 47ff.; W. Helck, "Urḫi-Tešup in Ägypten," *JCS* 17 (1963) 87-97; R. Stefanini, "Una lettera della Regina Puduhepa al Re di Alasija (KUB XXI 38)," *Atti e memorie dell'Accademia Toscana di Scienze e Lettere "La Colombaria"* 29 (1964) 1-69; H. Otten, *Puduḫepa: Eine hethitische Königin in ihren Textzeugnissen* (Mainz, 1975).

[5] A. Goetze, "The Hittites and Syria (1300-1200 B.C.)," *CAH*³ II/2 254-259.

[6] I. Singer, "A Concise History of Amurru," apud S. Izre'el, *Amurru Akkadian* (Atlanta, 1991) vol. 2, 135-196.

[7] The corresponding term in biblical Hebrew is *gēr*, in classical Greek *metoikos* or *paroikos*. Cf. E. von Schuler, "Hethitische Kultbräuche in dem Brief eines ugaritischen Gesandten," *RHA* 21 (1963) 43-46; A. Süel, "In den Urkunden von Boğazköy verwendete Wort ᴸᵁ́*UBĀRU*," *Anadolu* 20 (1976-77) 131-140.

One of the most important privileges sought by new residents was the legal right to acquire land. That this privilege was not readily accorded can be seen from the edict of Ḫattušili III[8] concerning the merchants from the Cilician city of Ura who were doing business in the tributary state of Ugarit on the Mediterranean coast.[9]

As a courtesy to royal wives from foreign lands the kings often constructed small temples or chapels for the worship of the principal deities of their homelands. We are not well-informed about the nationalities of foreign wives of Hittite kings. But we do know of one woman from Babylonia who is only referred to in the texts as "Tawannanna" (a title borne by Hittite queens).[10] Her native Babylonian name is not preserved. As the last queen of Šuppiluliuma I, who survived him and remained the Tawannanna during the first years of his son and successor, she exercised considerable influence and power in the Hittite capital. Because some of her official acts seemed improper and threatening to her step-son Muršili II, she was eventually brought to trial and removed from her position.[11] The exact nature of the charges brought against her is unclear. But at least one of them seems to relate to the diversion of royal and temple funds and the improper introduction of cultic customs from her homeland.

Although there were abuses of the privilege of free worship by foreigners, this does not obscure the fact that certain privileged foreigners (*ubārum*) were allowed access to the Hittite temples themselves for purposes of worship.[12] But any foreigner attempting to enter a Hittite temple without proof of this privileged status would be put to death.[13]

Diplomatic corps

Each kingdom in the ancient Near East had its permanent resident diplomatic corps in the capital city of other powerful neighbor kingdoms. There is no Hittite term or logogram known to me which can properly be translated as "ambassador" unless it be the Akkadian *mār šipri* "messenger, envoy."[14] But persons who served a similar function in ancient Ḫatti certainly existed.

---

[8] *CTH* 93; *PRU* IV 103ff.; *CAH*³ II/2 140.

[9] C.H. Gordon, "Abraham and the Merchants of Ura," *JNES* 17 (1958) 28-31; E. Laroche, "Études sur les hiéroglyphes hittites [III]," *Syria* 35 (1958) 252-283; H.A. Hoffner, "A Hittite Text in Epic Style about Merchants," *JCS* 22 (1968) 34-45.

[10] Bin-Nun, *Tawananna* (1975); Archi, "Testimonianze" (1980) 19-29; O.R. Gurney, *The Hittites*² (Harmondsworth, 1954; revised and reprinted 1990) 53f.

[11] Hoffner, "Stepmother" (1983) 187-190.

[12] E.H. Sturtevant and G. Bechtel, *A Hittite Chrestomathy* (Philadelphia, 1935) 150-153; §§5-6. Sturtevant's translation "good citizen" should be corrected to "privileged foreigner" or "foreigner in good standing (with the crown)." The contrast in §6 is between a "privileged foreigner" (Akkadian *ubārum*) and an ordinary "foreigner" (Hittite *araḫzenaš*) without such special rights.

[13] *KUB* 13.4 ii 10-11, ed. Sturtevant and Bechtel, *Chrestomathy* (1935) 152f.

[14] On the ancient Near Eastern messengers cf. S.A. Meier, *The Messenger in the Ancient Semitic World* (Atlanta, 1988; *HSM* 45).

Merchants

Trade between the Anatolian plateau and the lands to the East and South had been flourishing for centuries before the rise of the Hittite state. That it continued under the patronage of the Hittite rulers is certain.[15]

But unlike the archives of the Assyrian merchants from the previous period, the archives of the Hittite kings did not contain business documents. We are, therefore, much less well informed about the state of trade—both domestic and international—during the Hittite period.

In spite of this glaring gap, we are not totally uninformed about merchants in the texts.[16] The Hittite laws, first put into writing during the early Old Kingdom (c. 1600 B.C.), cover cases of homicide perpetrated against Hittite merchants in foreign lands.[17] This must have been a constant problem which always raised the delicate question of jurisdiction: whose law covered such cases, the merchant's home country or the country in which he was temporarily residing? And how were the dead man's heirs to be compensated across national boundaries?

Information about foreign merchants in Ḫatti is lacking. Already in 1959, 12 years prior to its publication in *KBo* 18.88, Otten noted the mention of merchants in a small fragment from a New Hittite letter, which in the immediate context also mentions the land of Canaan (*Kinaḫḫa*).[18] In a deposition text dating to the later New Kingdom we learn the name of a merchant who "fenced" stolen silver from a Hittite bureaucrat.[19] But his name, Karpani, seems to be local Anatolian, borne also by a man who lived during the reign of Arnuwanda I in the early New Kingdom.[20] Another deposition text mentions a merchant by the name of Šaḫli.[21] But nothing in either his name or the context indicates he is a foreigner.

---

[15] Hoffner, "Merchants" (1968) 34-45; L.L. Orlin, *Assyrian Colonies in Cappadocia* (The Hague, 1970); H. Klengel, "Handel und Kaufleute im hethitischen Reich," *AoF* 6 (1979) 69-80; C. Watkins, "NAM.RA GUD UDU in Hittite: Indo-European poetic language and the folk taxonomy of wealth," in E. Neu and W. Meid, eds., *Hethitisch und Indogermanisch: Vergleichende Studien zur historischen Grammatik und zur dialektgeographischen Stellung der indogermanischen Sprachgruppe Altkleinasiens* (Innsbruck, 1979) 269-288; A. Archi, "Anatolia in the Second Millennium B.C.," in idem, ed., *Circulation of Goods in Non-Palatial Context in the Ancient Near East* (Roma, 1984) 195-206.

[16] H. Otten, "Zur Kontinuität eines altanatolischen Kultes," *ZA* 53 (1959) 182f.; Hoffner, "Merchants" (1968) 34-45; Klengel, "Handel" (1979) 69-80.

[17] Law § 5.

[18] Otten, "Kontinuität" (1959) 182 n. 46.

[19] R. Werner, *Hethitische Gerichtsprotokolle* (Wiesbaden, 1967; *SBT* 4) 30f.

[20] Werner, *Gerichtsprotokolle* (1967) 2; E. Laroche, *Les noms des Hittites* (Paris, 1966) 88 no. 528. In a broken context of another deposition the name Tiqqa-UR.MAḪ occurs in the line following the word "merchant" and a few lines later the expression "man from Ura" (Werner, *Gerichtsprotokolle* [1967] 38f. = *KUB* 13.34 + i 23-24, 27), but without a full context there is nothing to guarantee that this was the merchant's name.

[21] Werner, *Gerichtsprotokolle* (1967) 38f = *KUB* 13.34 + i 13-14.

Skilled craftsmen

Men whom Homer called the *dēmioergoi* "masters of a craft which benefits the public" who were in demand everywhere because of their skills,[22] are in fact the subject of regulations in the Hittite treaties. Although it was standard procedure for the Hittites not to return persons who fled from their vassal states, King Muršili II wrote the following exception into a treaty with Targasnalli of Ḫapalla: "If a farmer, or a weaver, a carpenter or a leather worker, or any kind of craftsman (Akkad. *bēl qāti*)...flees from your land and comes into the land of Ḫatti, I (the Hittite king) will seize him and restore him to you."[23] In a letter to Kadašman-Enlil of Babylon, Ḫattušili III swore that he had never tried to detain Babylonian physicians, incantation priests or other experts who had been sent to Ḫatti for temporary service.[24] Such was the importance of each country's limited supply of skilled craftsmen.

But what evidence do we have of foreign, and for our subject most importantly, Syrian craftsmen in Ḫatti? The mere presence of foreign commodities might only indicate trade or the payment of tribute, not necessarily the presence on Hittite soil of foreign artisans. Fortunately the texts provide us with clear evidence for some types of foreign artisans.

Although there were many persons in the Hittite court who are styled "physician" ([LÚ]A.ZU), and the texts mention both an "overseer of the physicians" and a "chief physician," in cases of serious illness Hittite royalty seems to have set great store by foreign medical experts.[25] On several occasions physicians were brought from Babylonia or Egypt. In a shelf list of the library on the acropolis one entry briefly summarizes the contents of a tablet containing a ritual authored by a woman named Azzari, who is called "a Hurrian female physician."[26] The fact that her procedure is more magical than practical therapeutic tells us something about the nature of "Hurrian" physicians.

There was also demand for makers of fine garments. A garment often mentioned in rituals and religious contexts as well as listed in inventories[27] is the "Hurrian garment/shirt" (Sum. TÚG.GÚ.È.A [Akk. *naḫlaptu*] *ḪURRI*). We can safely claim that some of these were made on Hittite soil. For a Middle Hittite (early 14th century) land grant text[28] mentions "the household of Mr. Muliyaziti, a maker of Hurrian shirts." But in a fragmentary context

---

[22] *Odyssey* xvii 383-386: "Who of himself ever seeks out and bids a stranger from abroad, unless he be one of those who are masters of some public craft (*dēmieorgoi*): a prophet, or a healer of ills, or a builder, or a divine minstrel who gives delight with his song? For these men are welcome all over the boundless earth."

[23] Targ. (*KBo* 5.4) obv. 39-40 (§7). J. Friedrich, *Staatsverträge des Hatti-Reiches in hethitischer Sprache, 1. Teil* (Leipzig, 1926; *MVAG* 31) 58f.

[24] G. Beckman, "Mesopotamians and Mesopotamian Learning at Ḫattuša," *JCS* 35 (1983) 108f.

[25] H.G. Güterbock, "Hittite Medicine," *Bulletin of the History of Medicine* 36 (1962) 109-113; E. Edel, *Ägyptische Ärtzte und ägyptische Medizin am hethitischen Königshof* (Opladen, 1976); G. Beckman, "Medizin. B. Bei den Hethitern," *RLA* 7 (1990) 629-631.

[26] MUNUS A.ZU *ḫurlaš KUB* 30.42 i 8. Cf. also MUNUS ŠU.GI [URU]*ḫurlaš* (*IBoT* 2.116:4 [*CTH* 490.2]).

[27] *KBo* 18.175 i 3 (*CTH* 241); *KBo* 18.181 obv. 2-4, 8, 21-29 (*CTH* 243); *KUB* 42.106 obv.? 4, 8.

[28] *KBo* 5.7 rev. 3 (*CTH* 223).

of at least one text thought to be a receipt of materials the Hurrian shirt is mentioned only one line away from the city name Ugarit.[29] The item is firmly attested in the Middle Hittite period by an inventory text from Maşat.[30] Here, interestingly enough, it appears in immediate context with "47 garments from the Hurrian land" (line 4). That it was a fine garment is indicated by the fact that in a vow text the Hittite queen promises to have one made for a deity.[31] In several texts such a Hurrian shirt is described as KÙ.GI GAR.RA "trimmed with gold."[32]

Personal Names

Sometimes the presence of persons from foreign lands can be detected through their personal names. And although Hittite scribes might assume a Babylonian *nom de plume* for reasons of prestige, Beckman has made a convincing case that the Babylonian name borne by Anu-šar-ilani, the ancestor of a long line of Hittite scribes, is a genuine indicator that he came to Ḫattuša from Mesopotamia and exemplifies the personal channel of transmission of both Mesopotamian scribal art and Mesopotamian literature.[33]

Beckman also has compiled a list of ten distinct individuals or groups of Assyrians and eight Babylonians known to have resided at least temporarily in Ḫatti.[34] Five (possibly six) were ambassadors to the courts of Ḫattušili III and Tudḫaliya IV. One became queen. Three Babylonians were *āšipus*. One Babylonian and two Assyrians were scribes.

In his standard collection of Hittite personal names, Emmanuel Laroche collected a number of names which contain Syrian city names.[35] The following are Aleppo names: Ḫalpaziti, Ḫalpamuwa, Ḫalparunta, Ḫalpašulupi, Ḫalpaḫi. Also attested are the cities of Ḫaššu(m), (Ḫaššuili, Ḫaššiuman) and Ḫarran (Ḫaranamuwa).

The following brief prosopographic research is of interest in evaluating the significance of the Aleppo names. Muršili II's oldest son, who died before he could become emperor, was named Ḫalpašulupi, and he was certainly not born in Aleppo. One of the Hittite princes holding a very high administrative position in Ḫattuša who was one of those who sealed as witnesses the great treaty between Tudḫaliya IV and Kurunta of Tarḫuntašša was a Ḫalpaziti. Another Ḫalpaziti was a *bārû* seer-exorcist appearing in a court deposition.[36] One of the Hittite officials at Maşat-Tapikka who was in charge of distributing grain bore the name Ḫalpaili "he of Aleppo." These names rather than indicating that their bearers were born in the named locality probably indicated some more

---

[29] *KUB* 42.84:23-24 (*CTH* 247).

[30] S. Alp, *Hethitische Keilschrifttafeln aus Maşat-Höyük* (Ankara, 1991) text no. 108 rev. 2.

[31] *KUB* 15.23:10-11 (*CTH* 584).

[32] *KUB* 34.45 + *KBo* 16.63 i 7, 10 = Werner, *Gerichtsprotokolle* (1967) 50f.; *KUB* 42.67:9 (*CTH* 250).

[33] Cf. comments in Beckman, "Mesopotamians" (1983) 104.

[34] Beckman, "Mesopotamians" (1983) 108. We must now add the Babylonian name *Mār-ešrē* (sometimes written DUMU.20.KAM) borne by an official at Maşat, if it is not a *nom de plume*.

[35] Laroche, *Noms* (1966) 273f.

[36] Werner, *Gerichtsprotokolle* (1967) 34-37 = *KUB* 13.33 iv 1.

distant family tie. It is not likely, however, that they indicate no connection at all with the named region.

The only Dagan name in the Hittite archives is that of Nur-Dagan ("light of Dagan"), the king of Purušḫanda in the *King of Battle* epic, which is of course irrelevant to our search for people living in Anatolia during the Hittite Old and New Kingdom epochs. There is Iršappa, whose Hurrian name contains the Syro-Palestinian deity Resheph.

Names containing Hurrian deities (Teššup, Ḫebat, etc.) are no indicator of a Syrian nationality, since during the New Kingdom such names were routinely given to children in Ḫatti itself.

Areas of Culture Affected

Among the areas of culture affected by influences from Syria, the first to be considered will be language.

Words in the Hittite language

In the age of the Hittite kings the languages of North Syria were Hurrian and West Semitic. It is not difficult to find Hurrian words in Hittite religious, magic, or divination contexts. Such was the Hurrian-Hittite cultural symbiosis during the New Kingdom, that Hittite religion was in large measure simply Hurrian religion in Hittite language. Containers used in magic and cult, such as censers (Hurrian *aḫrušḫi)*, carry Hurrian names. Hurrian nouns designating the goals of certain ritual actions (*keldiya* "for well-being") abound in Hurrian-influenced ritual texts. The rituals themselves bear Hurrian names, such as SISKUR *itgaḫiyaš* or SISKUR *itkalziyaš* "ritual for the washing/purifying of the mouth."[37] Inasmuch as the Hurrians entered Ḫatti from Syria this abundance of Hurrian linguistic material bears powerful testimony to the indebtedness of Hittite culture to Syria.

In 1963 Chaim Rabin claimed 22 words known from Hittite texts are found in the Hebrew Bible.[38] Not all of his examples will convince others. But it is interesting to note how many of the more plausible ones fall within the military, diplomatic and bureaucratic areas. Terms in these areas are very likely to spread across national and geographic barriers through trade and diplomacy.

Among them he listed (1) in the architectural sphere: *ḫila-* "court", *gurta-* "fortress",

[37] *CTH* 777.

[38] C. Rabin, "Hittite Words in Hebrew," *Or* 32 (1963) 113-139.

(2) among textiles and garments: *argaman* "purple > tribute,"[39] *kariulli-* "a female garment covering head and body, hood" and *maššiya-* "shawl", (3) tools, weapons and armaments: *kubaḫi-* "headdress, helmet," *kullupi-* "hatchet, mattock," *lappiya-* "glowing thing, torch(?)," (4) relating to the technology of pottery and glass making: *zapzigi-* "glass, glaze," and (5) agricultural terms, like Luwian *tuwarša-* "vine" and Hittite *wiyana-* "wine". The translations are those of Rabin and were based upon translations suggested by J. Friedrich in his *Hethitisches Wörterbuch* in 1952. Several are now clearly inaccurate, some were questionable even at the time Rabin wrote. And even if we accept the entire list, we must ask: Are these "Hittite" words or culture words, what in German are called *Kulturwörter* and *Wanderwörter*? Did both the ancient Hittites and the Israelites of biblical times inherit them from some older, third source? It would seem to me that both *tuwarša-* "vine" and *wiyana-* "wine" belong in this category.

So while this list—and really, it could be extended with some imagination—does demonstrate the international character of the vocabulary (particularly the repertoire of nouns) of ancient Near Eastern languages, it certainly does not show direct influence from Ḫatti on Israel or vice versa.

Yet in spite of my skepticism I must stress that some of these connections are persuasive. The term *zapzigi* "glass, glaze" occurs also in Ugaritic, which provides a helpful link both geographically and chronologically between Late Bronze Age Anatolia and Iron Age Palestine. The Hittite word for "tribute" (*argaman*), so very important in the political and administrative spheres, is curious. On the one hand the scribes knew and used the Akkadian term *mandattu* as a logogram. Yet the term they used in their own speech, though it also was a borrowed term, was not borrowed from Akkadian *mandattu* but from West Semitic *argaman*, which in Akkadian only has the alleged meaning "tribute" in texts from the Hittite capital itself. Elsewhere it only means red-purple wool sometimes used as a tribute. While the Hittite noun *kubaḫi-* denotes a headwear for males, it is not specifically a helmet, as is the biblical Hebrew word *kobaᶜ*. Yet the fact that the same Hebrew word is written with either *q* or *k* suggests already that this is a non-Semitic word whose velar stop did not find a consistent spelling in the Canaanite writing system.[40]

---

[39] On the Hittite word *argama(n)-* see especially the helpful remarks of A. Goetze, [review of J. Friedrich, *Hethitisches Wörterbuch*], *JCS* 22 (1968) 18. Other bibliography is Rabin, "Hebrew" (1963) 113-139; E. Neu, *Der Anitta-Text* (Wiesbaden, 1974; *SBT* 18) 123; M. Poetto, [review of J. Tischler, *Hethitisches Etymologisches Glossar* (1977)], *Paideia* 32 (1977) 317, N. Oettinger, "Die *n*-Stämme des Hethitischen und ihre indogermanischen Ausgangspunkte," *Zeitschrift für vergleichende Sprachforschung* 94 (1980) 60f.; idem, [review of J. Tischler, *Hethitisches Etymologisches Glossar* (1977)], *ZDMG* 130 (1980) 592; H. Otten, "Bemerkungen zum Hethitischen Wörterbuch II," *ZA* 71 (1981) 138f. The word has, of course, been treated in the dictionaries: Friedrich and Kammenhuber, *Wörterbuch*[2] (1975-84) 302-304; Puhvel, *Dictionary* (1984ff.) vol. 1 143-146.

[40] H.A. Hoffner, "Some Contributions of Hittitology to Old Testament Study," *Tyndale Bulletin* 20 (1969) 27-55.

Objects introduced from Syria as plunder, tribute or trade

We have already identified military campaigns and international trade as major channels of transmission for cultural influences. What objects can be specifically identified as being brought to Ḫatti from Syria or Upper Mesopotamia?

Occasionally the eastern reaches of Syria are called "Hurri lands," and the Mediterranean littoral could be referred to as "the Cedar Lands." But the Hittites did not have a geographical term which comprehended Syria and only Syria, such as West Semitic *Aram* or Egyptian *Retenu*. So in order to identify imported goods as to their points of origin we must either look for specific geographical terms such as Carchemish, Aleppo, Mukiš, Nuḫašše, or we must be satisfied with the more general designation "Hurrian". For although admittedly the Hittite royal family was of an ethnically Hurrian background, when objects are called "Hurrian" or territories are called "Hurrian", nine times out of ten they are Syro-Mesopotamian. It was, after all, from Syria that the Hurrians entered Asia Minor.

Judging from records found at Ugarit, the annual tribute sent to Ḫattuša consisted principally of gold, vessels of gold and silver, pieces of clothing, and quantities of red and blue purple wool for the king, queen, crown prince, and a few high officials.[41]

This picture is confirmed from inventory texts found at Ḫattuša,[42] which include numerous items marked with the Akkadogram *mandattu* "tribute". These lists include gold, silver, and copper,[43] garments, wool, but also specific items made from metal (horses' bits, axeheads) and beautiful chests inlaid with ivory having legs made to resemble lions' paws.

In the Old Hittite text describing the siege of Uršu, Hittite troops besieging the city employ something called a "Hurrian battering ram."[44] The choice of this particular type could have been influenced by local availability, since Uršu was after all in North Syria. But it is probable that the Hittite armies did not travel without battering rams.

There was apparently a difference in the quivers of Hittite and foreign manufacture. In one inventory three juxtaposed entries read: "three leather Hittite-style quivers with 930 arrows; four leather Hurrian-style quivers with 127 arrows; four leather Kashkaean-style quivers with 87 arrows."[45]

Hittite inventory texts record the presence of axes sent to Ḫatti as tribute (*mandattu*).[46] Also found there are metal bits for horses,[47] metal agricultural implements

---

[41] M.C. Astour, "Ugarit and the Great Powers," in G.D. Young, ed., *Ugarit in Retrospect* (Winona Lake, 1981), esp. p. 20f.

[42] Comprehensive editions in S. Košak, *Hittite inventory texts* (*CTH 241-250*) (Heidelberg, 1982; *TH* 10); J. Siegelová, *Hethitische Verwaltungspraxis im Lichte der Wirtschafts- und Inventardokumente* (Praha, 1986).

[43] x minas of gold *mandattu KBo* 18.153 (*CTH* 242); x minas URUDU *mandattu KBo* 18.164 i 5; x bars (PAD) of silver *mandattu KBo* 18.156:3-5.

[44] H.G. Güterbock, "Die historische Tradition und ihre literarische Gestaltung bei Babyloniern und Hethitern bis 1200 (2. Teil)," *ZA* 44 (1936) 114ff.; H.A. Hoffner, "Histories and Historians of the Ancient Near East: The Hittites," *Or* 49 (1980) 299f.

[45] *KUB* 42.81:7-8 (*CTH* 242). Cf. also Ebony of Hurri: *IBoT* 1.31 (A. Goetze, "The Inventory IBoT I 31," *JCS* 10 [1956] 32-38) obv. 5; 4 ^{GIŠ}BAR.KÍN KÙ.GI *ḫurluš KUB* 42.81:11 (*CTH* 242).

[46] ^{URUDU}*PAŠU* GAL *MAND[ATTU] KUB* 42.29 ii 11, (10) ^{URUDU}*ḪAṢṢINNU MANDATU KUB* 42.29. obv.? ii 13.

such as sickles,[48] and metal household objects[49] and jewels.[50] One inventory text records an ivory decorated table described as "Hurrian".[51] Another entry records a table from Aleppo.[52] Another, a large box with feet in the shape of a lion's, the product of Amurru.[53] Garments, wool, and sheepskins[54] also came in from Syria either as items of tribute or trade. There were, of course, also statues of Syrian deities brought as booty to Ḫattuša, for example the "gods of Ḫaššuwa" and the "gods of Ḫaḫḫum" brought back by Ḫattušili I.[55] There must have been cult images for the "gods of Ḫaššuwa" (flanked by Ulma and Ḫatra) which appear in a listing of "gods of this and that city" receiving offerings in the *ANTAḪŠUM* fest.[56]

Literature

The very writing system by which we know so much about Hittite history and culture is itself an importation which at least proximally came from Syria. It is not completely clear where the Hittites first learned Mesopotamian cuneiform writing. Some, such as Gamkrelidze,[57] have proposed a Syrian center. Recently, in a still unpublished paper read in Istanbul, K. Hecker has argued that a form of cuneiform which is rare among the Old Assyrian tablets and is quite similar to the Hittite type, was the source, and that the Hittites could have learned it in the heart of Anatolia itself.

So far as Syrian influence on Hittite literature goes, it begins already in the earliest period. Some of the texts which are the oldest palaeographically are those fragments which describe the military activities of Syrian generals in the days of the earliest Hittite kings and slightly before.[58] Also from the Old Hittite period, although in a much later copy,[59] comes a fascinating text which has been dubbed "The Cannibal Tale" because of the prominence

---

[47] x-number *TAPAL* [URUDU]*šurziya KUB* 42.28 obv. right column 5, 6.

[48] 100 [URUDU]KIN GAL *KBo* 7.24 ii 6.

[49] 12[URUDU]*ANG/KURINU MAND[ATTU] KUB* 42.28 obv. rt. 14. The reading of *ang/kurinu* as Akkadian (i.e., *ANG/KURINU*) follows Siegelová, *Verwaltungspraxis* (1986) 68f.

[50] In a list of metals and jewels [...*Š*]*UL-MAN* [URU]*Ugarit KUB* 26.66 iv 5 (*CTH* 242).

[51] Siegelová, *Verwaltungspraxis* (1986) 490-492.

[52] [GIŠ]BANŠUR [URU]*ḪALAB KUB* 59.56 obv. 8 (purification ritual).

[53] (A box) with feet of a lion IGI.DU$_8$.A *ŠA* KUR [URU]*AMURRI IBoT* 1.31 obv. 2 confirmed by *KUB* 42.65 rev? 6-7 (*CTH* 247.4); cf. also 1 [GI]PISAN SA$_5$ GAL GÌR UR.MAḪ *MANDAT* [URU]*Ankuwa IBoT* 1.31 obv. 12 (Goetze, "Inventory" [1956] 32ff.); cf. also one small red [GIŠ]*tuppaš KUB* 42.18:13 with *KUB* 42.20:4 (*CTH* 241.6), [GIŠ]PISAN GIŠ TUR SA$_5$, *KUB* 42.22 right col. 7-8 (*CTH* 241.12).

[54] NBC 3842 obv. 1-5 (J.J. Finkelstein, "A Hittite *mandattu*-Text," *JCS* 10 [1956] 101-105).

[55] These are described in the annals text as: DUMU.MUNUS [d]*Allatum* [d]*Ḫebat* 3 ALAN KÙ.BABBAR 2 ALAN KÙ.GI. (*KBo* 10.1 obv. 43f = *KBo* 10.2 ii 36ff [*CTH* 4]). Cf. also booty and gods of Ḫaḫḫu brought home by Ḫattušili I: *KBo* 10.2 iii 14.

[56] *KBo* 4.13 + *KUB* 10.82 i 44 (*CTH* 625).

[57] T.V. Gamkrelidze, "The Akkado-Hittite Syllabary and the Problem of the Origin of the Hittite Script," *ArOr* 29 (1961) 406-418; cf. also Beckman, "Mesopotamians" (1983) 100.

[58] These texts mention Yarim-Lim (*CTH* 14) and Zukraši (*CTH* 15).

[59] The New Hittite scribe has even misread the old ligature [d]EN in the name [m]DUMU.[d]EN.LÍL as MAḪ.

in the story of alleged cannibalism practiced in a North Syrian locale.[60]

Not as early as the Old Hittite quasi-historical traditions from Syria, but much more influential on Hittite culture, is the Kumarbi cycle of myths.[61] Although fragments of Hurrian copies of some of the stories exist at Boghazköy, we owe our knowledge of the cycle to Hittite translations.

This grand epic cycle celebrated nothing less than the entire course of divine kingship from the beginning down to the present. The debt of the Hurrians to Mesopotamian myths is apparent everywhere, and nowhere more strikingly than in the names of the first kings of the gods: Alalu and Anu. But the principal focus of the narrative is clearly on the two figures who follow: the grain-god Kumarbi and the storm-god Teššup. Although Teššup early displaced Kumarbi as king of the gods, the latter repeatedly plots to overthrow his successor by means of various monsters whom Kumarbi begets through various "female" beings. In its Hittite adaptation the cycle consisted of at least the following units: the Song of Kumarbi, the Song of the God LAMMA, the Song of Silver, the Song of Ḫedammu, and the Song of Ullikummi. All but the first are named after the monster or hero whom Kumarbi raises up to overthrow Teššup. But in each case he fails.

One myth in the Hittite repertoire concerns West Semitic or "Canaanite" deities.[62] Since nowhere in the large amount of preserved text does a single Hurrian word occur, it may belong to that corpus of Mesopotamian literary material which came to Ḫatti from Syria without Hurrian intermediacy.[63] The tale is of special interest for several reasons. First, to date it is unknown from Syria itself. No Semitic original of this story exists. Second, even though the Hurrian and Hittite adaptor-translators have obviously made changes, there remain unmistakable traces of its original Semitic modes of expression, including the well-known *parallelismus membrorum*.[64]

Law

The external impetus for drawing up a corpus of Hittite laws in cuneiform undoubtedly came from the introduction of the Syro-Mesopotamian writing system and the scribal training which accompanied it. Perhaps this subject should rather appear under "Literature", since it was more the idea of writing out their laws which came as a foreign influence. The laws themselves are quite different in content and indeed in the concept of

---

[60] Edited first by Güterbock, "Tradition" (1936) 104f. More recently treated by A. Kempinski, "Die hethitischen und akkadischen Dokumente aus Boğazköy," in idem, ed., *Syrien und Palästina (Kanaan) in der letzten Phase der Mittelbronze IIB-Zeit (1650-1570 v. Chr.)* (Wiesbaden, 1983) 41-43.

[61] The literature on the Kumarbi myths is vast. The most recent translations together with complete bibliographies of anterior literature are H.A. Hoffner, *Hittite Myths* (Atlanta, 1990) 38-61 and F. Pecchioli Daddi and A. Polvani, *La mitologia ittita* (Brescia, 1990).

[62] H. Otten, "Ein kanaanäischer Mythus aus Boğazköy," *MIO* 1 (1953) 125-150; H.A. Hoffner, "The Elkunirsa Myth Reconsidered," *RHA* 23 (1965) 5-16; Hoffner, *Myths* (1990) 69f.

[63] Beckman, "Mesopotamians" (1983) 103 includes hymns and lexical lists in this category. We can add not only the Ašertu myth but also Signalement Lyrique (*CTH* 315), copies of which were found at Ugarit with a Hittite version, but no Hurrian one.

[64] Hoffner, "Elkunirsa" (1965) 5-16.

compensation as opposed to retribution.

Like Mesopotamian law "codes", the Hittite is a collection of cases described in the traditional format "If someone does this or that" followed by the required disposition. In the Mesopotamian collection the disposition is often a payment of some kind, but also frequently a form of retribution or punishment involving bodily injury or even death. Such dispositions are much rarer in the Hittite corpus, where the focus is almost entirely on the practical compensation of the victim or his heirs.

Ḫattušili I, the first king to rule from the capital city of Ḫattuša, conducted the first Hittite raids into North Syria. He left behind a narrative record of these raids in a bilingual Akkadian-Hittite text first discovered in 1958. Among the Syrian urban centers which he attacked was Ḫaḫḫu(m). After overcoming the military resistance, the Hittite king claims to have liberated its population. The terms which he used are especially interesting. In the Akkadian version he wrote: *i-na ša-pal ša-me-e* AMA.AR.GI-*šu-nu aš-tá-kán* "under heaven I effected their liberation."[65] The Hittite version reads instead: *na-aš-kán ša-aḫ-ḫu-un lu-uz-zi-it a-ra-wa-aḫ-ḫu-un* "I freed them from taxation and forced labor."[66] The Akkadian reading of the Sumerian logogram AMA.AR.GI used here would have been *andurāru*, the Biblical Hebrew reflex of which is *d^erōr*. Without delving into the complexities of the Mesopotamian and Israelite institutions respectively, it was at least clear that both concern periodic remissions of financial obligations, whether public or private. But in 1958 when this Ḫattušili I text was first published it was somewhat of a mystery what a Hittite king was doing instituting a debt release.

The Hittite version's equivalent of *andurāru* was the exemption from *šaḫḫan* and *luzzi*, two forms of public indebtedness, which we usually translate as "taxes" and "public labor", respectively. In the Hittite laws the obligation to pay *šaḫḫan* is binding on property holders, unless that property was given to them by the king. But in some cases the populace of entire cities was exempted.

In Law §54 it is a group of cities in North Syria which are exempted: Tamalki, Ḫatra, Tašḫiniya, Zalpa and Ḫemuwa. Many of these same cities appear in the section of Ḫattušili I's military annals which deals with the North Syrian campaigning.

Furthermore, why did Ḫattušili I use the specific technical term AMA.AR.GI in the Akkadian version of his annals, unless he had become familiar with the institution during his Syrian campaigns?

New light has been shed on this question by the Hurro-Hittite bilingual texts found in 1983 and published in hand copies during 1991. In these texts the Hurrian god Teššup, whose home city Kummiya was located in North Syria, is depicted as having once become destitute and was rescued by the generosity of the other gods. He therefore instituted the practice of a general debt release and required rulers who worshiped him to perform it regularly.[67]

---

[65] *KBo* 10.1 rev. 13-14.

[66] *KBo* 10.2 iii 18-19. Cf. *luzzi-* bilingual sect. and b 1' b'.

[67] H. Otten, "Blick in die altorientalische Geisteswelt: Neufund einer hethitischen Tempelbibliothek," *Jahrbuch der Akademie der Wissenschaften in Göttingen* (Göttingen, 1984) 50-60; idem, "Die Tontafelfunde aus Haus 16," *Archäologischer Anzeiger* (1984) 372-375; E. Neu, "Neue Wege im Hurritischen," *Akten des XXIII. Deutschen*

These texts date from the early part of the Hittite empire (c. 1500-1400 B.C.), the period during which a new ruling family of Hurrian origin had assumed the Hittite throne. There is as yet no evidence, however, that these kings who worshiped Teššup as the chief deity of their pantheon, under the influence of the traditions represented in these texts, introduced into Ḫatti the practice of a periodic general debt release.

Religion

But the Hittites imported more than luxury items and foodstuffs from their neighbors to the southeast. It has long been seen that the pantheon of Ḫatti, which during the Old Kingdom showed no significant Hurrian or Syrian elements, took on a pronounced Hurrian character during the New Kingdom.

Pantheon. Nowhere is this more evident than in the imperial shrine at Yazilikaya, where the gods and goddesses of Ḫatti are shown in two processions converging at a central focal point at the back of the outdoor sanctuary. Heading the procession of gods is Teššup, heading the goddesses is his consort Ḫebat. Each deity in the procession bears a hieroglyphic name, and it is now known that each of these is Hurrian. By a process of syncretism the Hittites merged their old gods with their new ones.

In addition to the Hurrian gods who came to the Hittites from an earlier home in Syria there are Semitic deities who appear rarely. Among these are El (Elkuniršа), Asherah, and Baᶜal and ᶜAnat-Astarte.

While it is true that these deities are principally known to us at Boghazköy from the above-mentioned Ašertu Myth, the myth has an accompanying description of a ritual to purify and restore Baᶜal. This too could have been merely foreign literature in translation, but I am inclined to think that there was at least a limited "cult" of Baᶜal at Boghazköy, if only for the benefit of the Syrian diplomats.

A cult inventory[68] mentions images of the "gods of Išuwa" and thus affords us a tantalizing glimpse at the distinctive pantheon of that region. The text reads: "two statues: one wooden statue of a standing male (representing the god) ᵈAMAR.UTU; one wooden statue of a seated female (representing the goddess) *I-i-ya-aš*[...]." The god's name is written ideographically with the Sumerian name for Marduk, and only the beginning of the goddess' name is preserved.

Orientalistentages (Stuttgart, 1989; *ZDMG* Supplement 7) 293-303; idem, *Das Hurritische: Eine altorientalische Sprache in neuem Licht* (Mainz, 1988); idem, "Varia Hurritica. Sprachliche Beobachtungen an der hurritisch-hethitischen Bilingue aus Ḫattuša," in E. Neu and C. Rüster, eds., *Documentum Asiae minoris antiquae: Festschrift für Heinrich Otten* (Wiesbaden, 1988) 235-254; H. Otten, "Ebla in der hurritisch-hethitischen Bilingue aus Boğazköy," in H. Waetzoldt and H. Hauptmann, eds., *Wirtschaft und Gesellschaft von Ebla* (Heidelberg, 1988; *HSAO* 2) 291-292.

[68] *KUB* 38.10 iii 12-13 (*CTH* 510). On this text genre see C. Carter, "Hittite Cult Inventories" (Ph.D. diss., University of Chicago, 1962).

Cult. The people of the ancient Near East were generally careful to worship deities according to the modes to which they were believed to be accustomed. This naturally meant that, when the worship of a foreign deity was instituted, priests from that deity's homeland were brought in to advise. The result of this was a cult which differed in many respects from that of other "native" deities.

In the case of the Hittites and their neighboring Syrian states we can see this operating in both directions. The cults of Syrian deities (many of them Hurrian) at Ḫattuša can be seen to differ from those of native Anatolian deities. On the other hand, at Meskeneh-Emar there exist Akkadian texts from the period of the Hittite hegemony which describe and prescribe "the rites of the gods of the land of Ḫatti."[69] Any reader of these texts from Emar who is familiar with the festival texts from Ḫattuša can easily reconstruct in his mind the wording of the Hittite-language models from which these were translated.

Cult of Ḫalab.[70] The cult statue of the Stormgod of Aleppo was carried off from Aleppo to Ḫattuša by Ḫattušili I.[71] By the time of Šuppiluliuma I this deity had a fixed place in the list of "Hittite" deities invoked in state treaties.[72] In the technology of the snake oracles one location is named "Stormgod of Aleppo."[73] Texts about this deity's cult were gathered by Laroche[74] and a full edition of them made by Klengel.[75] Texts reveal that the cult of the Aleppo triad was carried out in a temple in Ḫattuša itself.[76] An exorcist-priest ([LÚ]ḪAL) from Aleppo by the name of Eḫal-Teššup is mentioned in several tablet catalogs.[77] Eḫal-Teššup's specialty is described thus: "If someone's manservants and maidservants cannot get along, or if a man and a woman (his wife) cannot get along, or if a man and a woman see evil dreams." In the texts which describe the cult of Teššup and Ḫebat of Aleppo carried out in various Anatolian cities, a group called "palace men of Aleppo" LÚ.MEŠ É.GAL [URU]*ḪALAB* take part.[78] In one text the cult of the Stormgod of Aleppo in a given region of Anatolia observed 13 festivals in the course of each year.[79] On the 29th day of the *ANTAḪŠUM* festival for the god Ea (*KBo* 11.45 v 16 [*CTH* 616.3]) a prominent officiant is the priest of the Stormgod of Aleppo.

---

[69] *parṣī ša ilānī māt Ḫatti ME* 110:1.

[70] H. Klengel, "Der Wettergott von Ḫalab," *JCS* 19 (1965) 87-93; V. Souček and J. Siegelová, "Der Kult des Wettergottes von Ḫalap in Ḫatti," *ArOr* 42 (1974) 39-52; G.F. del Monte and J. Tischler, *Die Orts- und Gewässernamen der hethitischen Texte* (Wiesbaden, 1978; *RGTC* 6) 72f.

[71] *KBo* 10.1 obv. 38 = 10.2 ii (26).

[72] *CTH* 42 Huqq. *KBo* 5.3 + i 42, J. Friedrich, *Staatsverträge des Ḫatti-Reiches in hethitischer Sprache, 2. Teil* (Leipzig, 1930; *MVAG* 34) 110f. §7; later cf. *KUB* 21.1 + iv 4 (*CTH* 76) Friedrich, *Staatsverträge* (1930) 78f.; H. Otten, *Die Bronzetafel aus Boğazköy: Ein Staatsvertrag Tutḫalijas IV* (Wiesbaden, 1988; *SBT* Beiheft 1).

[73] *IBoT* 1.33:22, 43, 44 (*CTH* 575) E. Laroche, "Lécanomancie hittite," *RA* 52 (1958) 150-162.

[74] Under the entry *CTH* 698 (cults of Teššup and Ḫebat of Aleppo).

[75] Klengel, "Wettergott" (1965) 87-93. Cf. also Souček and Siegelová, "Wettergottes" (1974) 39-52.

[76] *KUB* 5.3 iii 102; *KUB* 55.5 iv 8-9; del Monte and Tischler, *Gewässernamen* (1978) 73.

[77] *KUB* 30.51 + ii 14 (*CTH* 277.4); *KUB* 30.56 iii 10 (*CTH* 279.1); *CTH* 180ff.

[78] *KUB* 27.15 iv 12, 17 (*CTH* 698C); *KBo* 14.142 iii 16, 19 (*CTH* 698.1A).

[79] *KBo* 26.156 rev. 2 (*CTH* 698.1F).

Cult of IŠTAR of Nineveh. Another cult which was introduced through Syria into Ḫatti was that of Ištar of Nineveh.

CTH 716 in i 23ff.[80] summons *IŠTAR* from Nineveh itself and from a large number of cities in Upper Mesopotamia, Syria and the Levant, including Mitanni, Alše, Tunip, Ugarit, Alalakh, Canaan (Kinaḫḫa), Sidon, Tyre (Zunzurḫa), Nuḫašše, and ᶜAmqa.

In other evocation texts (*CTH* 483 i 52ff.) the gods as a group are recalled from various places in the orbit of the Hittite world: Mitanni, Kadesh, Tunip, Ugarit, Zinzira, Dunanapa, Idarukatta, Gatanna, Alalakh, Canaan, Amurru, Sidon, Zunzurḫa, Nuḫašše, Ugulzit, Arrapḫa, etc.

Cult practices of Aštata (Meskeneh). A text describing hepatoscopic oracle inquiry informs us that a certain deity must be worshiped "in the manner of Aštata"[81] and that two festivals of Aštata must be performed (lines 21, 27). In order to fulfill this a priest was supposed to be brought to Ḫattuša from Aštata (i 38-43). We learn further that in fact several specialists were brought from Aštata and gave instructions to the Hittite priests as to how rites were to be performed in the manner of Aštata (i 44f.). With the publication of the cult texts from Meskeneh-Emar we are now in a better position to see what that manner was.

Specific religious practices. We would all like to be able to pinpoint specific religious practices which entered Ḫatti from Syria. But identifying these is extremely difficult. Having issued that warning, let me mention a few possibilities. I consider them possible because of their relative rare occurrence in the huge mass of Hittite religious texts and because they are mentioned in the Hebrew Bible as characteristically "Canaanite".

One of the oldest descriptions of Canaanite ecstatic prophecy is to be found in the tale of the travels of the Egyptian Wen-Amon in Palestine.[82] A young man standing near Wen-Amon was seized by his god, thrashed about wildly, and began to speak the words of the god to those assembled there. The incident occurred while Wen-Amon was in the Canaanite city of Byblos. Now ecstatic prophets are found the world over. Ecstasy is merely a mental state appropriate for the reception of a divine revelation. Hebrew prophets likewise went into ecstatic trances, as did prophets associated with the Greek oracle at Delphi. It is therefore not impossible that this phenomenon was already known to the Hittites on Anatolian soil. But this is so rarely mentioned in Hittite texts, that when it does occur and then somewhat late (in the period after Šuppiluliuma I), one is inclined to view it as due to foreign influence. In Palestine frenzied dancing was sometimes accompanied by self-mutilation, i.e., the prophets or priests cut themselves. This too seems now to be attested in a Hittite ritual text from the late period.[83]

---

[80] J. Friedrich, *Aus dem hethitischen Schrifttum, 2. Heft: Religiöse Texte* (Leipzig, 1925; *Der Alte Orient* 25/2) 20ff.

[81] *KUB* 5.6 + 18.54 i 17ff. (*CTH* 570), F. Sommer, *Die Aḫḫijavā-Urkunden* (München, 1932) 275f.

[82] *ANET* 26b.

[83] A man described as a "physician" (ᴸᵁ́A.ZU) plays a *ḫuḫupal* instrument while singing to the gods in the language of the land of Ištanuwa. When he has circled the fireplace three times, singing and playing the *ḫuḫupal*, he takes two copper lances or pins, pierces himself (*nu=za=kan ḫatta*), and places them back before the deity.

As in Mesopotamia proper,[84] but as opposed to Syro-Palestine, the blood of the sacrificial animal was of no particular value in the Anatolian Hittite ritual of sacrifice to the deity. The exceptions to this picture occur in Hittite texts describing the Hurrian-influenced cult from Kizzuwatna, which bordered directly on Syria.[85] It would appear that the limited use of the blood in sacrifice and the employment of the smoke of the sacrifice first was introduced to the Hittites from Syria by the intermediacy of the Hurrians of Kizzuwatna.

Syrian Influence as Seen Over Time

Having surveyed the various forms which cultural influences from the east and southeast took, let us view them from a diachronic point of view. What kinds of Syro-Mesopotamian influences entered Ḫatti during the various epochs of her history?

Old Kingdom

Already during the Old Kingdom the practice existed of bringing home to the palace and temples valuables from conquered cities. These foreign art works served as inspiration for local innovations. Along with this plunder often came captives who possessed useful skills: scribes, exorcists and diviners, metalsmiths, horse-trainers, and others.

From our point of view as students of the texts the most important importation of this epoch was the cuneiform writing system and the entire way of thinking and expressing oneself which went with it.

Also with the Mesopotamian scholastic tradition which the Hittite scribes learned went the forms of expressing, if not promulgating, law. To this we owe the Old Hittite drafting of the Hittite laws, which continued to be copied and revised down to the opening years of the 12th century.

From their Syro-Mesopotamian teachers of cuneiform the Hittite scholars also learned to draw up descriptions of the king's campaigns. From this came the first abbreviated attempts to write annals in the Old Kingdom. From the fact that the earliest attempt at annals, that of Ḫattušili I, was written in both an Akkadian and a Hittite version we can see that the impetus came from an Akkadian source. The full flower of this annalistic writing only appeared centuries later in the reign of King Muršili II.

Then he again picks up the *ḫuḫupal* and dances in front of the offering table. Picking up the pins again he pierces those sitting before him and the man whom he is treating medically. *KUB* 41.15:6-13 + *KUB* 53.15 i! 16-23. Another example, which however mentions no dancing, is in the Hattian cult text *KBo* 27.55 right col. 4-9 restored from *KUB* 1.14 ii 7-14: *zilipuriyatalla*—men come in and strike themselves six times. One of them pricks himself in the arm, another pricks himself in the leg. Then their overseer recites in Hattian. If these two passages reflect the same cultic practice, since Luwian-speaking Ištanuwa was in the south or east (del Monte and Tischler, *Gewässernamen* [1978] 152), while Hattic-speaking areas were in the center or north, it might suggest that this was not a practice due to foreign influences but was at home in Anatolia since before the Hittite kingdom.

[84] A. Oppenheim, *Ancient Mesopotamia* (Chicago, 1964; revised edition 1977) 192 with notes 17 and 18 on p. 365.

[85] A. Goetze, *Kleinasien*[2] (München, 1957) 164 notes the use of blood and the burning of sacrifices without noting that this practice was limited to the Hurrian-influenced cult.

Early New Kingdom (= "Middle Hittite")

With the change of dynasties which signaled the end of the Old Kingdom there appeared a line of kings and queens with Hurrian personal names, although the kings also took traditional Hittite "throne names."

The earliest Hittite royal prayer we have dates from the reign of King Arnuwanda I and his Queen Ašmunikal. Another formal literary prayer is attributed to a prince by the name of Kantuzzili who lived during the Early New Kingdom. These prayers established a literary form for such prayers which was followed during the reigns of the kings Muršili II, Muwatalli II and Ḫattušili III. It has been shown that a formative influence for these earliest Hittite royal prayers was the Syro-Mesopotamian literary tradition.[86] Many of the *topoi* of the prayers are lifted literally out of the Akkadian hymns.

During the 15th and early 14th centuries the first Hurrian texts were written in Ḫatti. Many are unilingual, but fortunately for us some were provided with a Hittite translation. Among these Hurro-Hittite bilingual texts are the first myths involving deities who were to become the reigning deities in the Hittite pantheon: Teššup, Ḫebat, Šarruma, Šaušga, and others.[87]

For this reason, although we have as yet no copies of any of them earlier than the last half of the 14th century, I am inclined to place the translation of the great Hurrian mythological cycle of Kumarbi into Hittite during this "Middle Hittite" period.

The Hittite manual for the training of chariot horses composed by the Hurrian expert Kikkuli has been known since the beginnings of Hittitology in the 1920s and 1930s. The first attempt to study it was made by the decipherer of Hittite, B. Hrozny, in 1931.[88] Also of great interest has been the appearance in this treatise of Indo-Aryan terms. Along with Kikkuli's treatise there exist two other treatises without the Indo-Aryan words and with no obvious clues as to a foreign origin. These are (1) the so-called "Second Training Regimen," a treatise with a ritual introduction (*CTH* 285: Hipp. heth 148-169 "TrAn II") and (2) the so-called "Third Training Regimen" (*CTH* 286: Hipp. heth 170-225 "TrAn III").

These treatises, which used to be dated to the period after Šuppiluliuma I's Syrian conquests, are now dated by the most reliable authorities to the century preceding his reign.[89]

---

[86] H.G. Güterbock, "The Composition of Hittite Prayers to the Sun," *JAOS* 78 (1958) 237-245; idem, "Some Aspects of Hittite Prayers," in T.T. Segerstedt, ed., *The Frontiers of Human Knowledge* (Uppsala, 1978) 125-139; idem, "Hymnen und Gebete," in W. Röllig, ed., *Altorientalische Literaturen* (Wiesbaden, 1978; *Neues Handbuch der Literatur-Wissenschaft* 1) 211-253; idem, "Randbemerkungen zu einigen hethitischen Gesetzen," *WO* 11 (1980) 89-92; idem, "A Hurro-Hittite Hymn to Ishtar," *JAOS* 103 (1983) 155-164.

[87] Otten, "Tempelbibliothek" (1984); idem, "Tontafelfunde" (1984); Neu, "Varia" (1988); idem, "Das Hurritische" (1988); Otten, "Ebla" (1988); Neu, "Neue Wege" (1989).

[88] B. Hrozný, "L'entraînement des chevaux chez les anciens Indo-Européens d'après un texte mîtannien-hittite provenant du 14e siècle av. J.-C.," *ArOr* 3 (1931) 438-441; H.A. Potratz, *Das Pferd in der Frühzeit* (Rostock, 1938); A. Kammenhuber, *Hippologia Hethitica* (Wiesbaden, 1961).

[89] E. Neu, "Zur Datierung der Hethitischen Pferdetexte," in H.A. Hoffner and G.M. Beckman, eds., *Kaniššuwar: A Tribute to Hans G. Güterbock* (Chicago, 1986; *AS* 23) 151-163.

Later New Kingdom

With the Syrian campaigns and conquests of Šuppiluliuma I in the early part of the 14th century there appear the first treaties between the Hittites and their Syrian tributary states. These were all executed in both Akkadian and Hittite copies. This period also saw the beginning of regular annual tribute payments from Syria to Ḫatti. This period between Šuppiluliuma I and II also witnessed the temporary residence in Ḫatti of Syrian ambassadors and even Syrian royalty in exile in the person of Bentešina of Amurru.

Although a few divination texts written in the ductus typical for the Old Kingdom have been published, those particular types of oracle which show the heaviest indebtedness to the Syro-Mesopotamian cuneiform tradition first appear during the New Kingdom. The technical terminology of these texts is almost entirely Hurrian, although prototypes exist in Syria and Mesopotamia written in Akkadian. Of these the vast majority exist in copies from the end of the 13th and the beginning of the 12th century.

Also during the latter part of the New Kingdom the process of syncretizing the older Hittite and the newer Hurrian pantheons reached its completion and was dramatically embodied in the outdoor rock sanctuary of Yazilikaya. This sanctuary was Tudḫaliya IV's masterwork, even though we also owe to this great king the entire design and building of the Upper City with its scores of small temples and its intricately designed processional way.

Conclusion

What can we say in conclusion? Most areas of the life of the Capital City were touched by cultural influences from the east and southeast: fashions of dress and food, the administration of law, religious expression, literature, modes of ascertaining the divine will and formulating of military strategy, training of the chariot corps, weaponry and military tactics.

Some areas show that influence in its most concentrated form: scribal practices, oracular inquiry, military training and equipment, public worship. Others were affected only moderately.

The sustained contact with Syria during the New Kingdom through military campaigning, diplomatic exchanges, trade, and above all through the permanent establishment of branches of the old royal family in the kingships of strategically placed urban centers such as Carchemish and Aleppo, kept the flow of ideas and fashions particularly vigorous. That there were cultural influences which flowed in the other direction, i.e., from Anatolia toward Syria, we have not discussed here. But it is certain that these too existed.

The Hittite court may have regarded these Syrian kingdoms somewhat patronizingly as their own "daughter" cultures, extensions of the Great Hittite Culture with its center in Ḫattuša. But in every age where colonialism is operative, the parent culture often learns significantly more from its children than it is aware. It is very likely that in such a short survey as this I have seriously underestimated the true impact of Syro-Mesopotamian civilization upon Ḫatti. But we have at least drawn the main lines. Using this overview, it is possible for interested persons to explore individual topics on their own.

SYRIANS IN SUMERIAN SOURCES FROM THE UR III PERIOD

David I. Owen

Table of Contents

Introduction 108

Historical Overview 109

Syrian Cities and Their Representatives 114

Catalogue of Cities and Personal Names 117

Index of Syrian Personal Names 136

Concordance of Quoted Texts 137

Concordance of Texts by Date 140

Transliterated Sources 141

Index of Personal Names 157

Index of Professions, Titles, Etc. 166

Index of Geographical Names and Gentilics 171

Copy and Comments to Wabash 1 by G.D. Young 176

Introduction

The following publication corrects, revises and brings up-to-date (July 1992) the data published as Appendixes I-II in Owen and Veenker, "MeGum, the First Ur III Ensi of Ebla."[1] Although new inscriptional material has not been substantial since its publication, I have considered it sufficient enough to warrant this revision in conjunction with the publication of the 1991 American Historical Association meeting's Syrian Session.[2] In addition, fully revised transliterations of most of the relevant text sources have been included. Every attempt has been made to include all sources, published and unpublished, known to me at this time.[3] Used in conjunction with the constantly increasing body of archaeological evidence, it should expedite future work on Syria in the third millennium. The geographical area covered in this article excludes the Khabur region which warrants a study of its own.[4]

---

[1] In L. Cagni, ed., *Ebla 1975-1985* (Napoli, 1987) 276-286. No attempt has been made here to list exhaustively names that have occurred without the presence of a geographical designation. All citations are from economic texts only. References to votive inscriptions from Mari and to later Old Babylonian sources have been collected by I.J. Gelb in "Mari and the Kish Civilization," in G.D. Young, ed., *Mari in Retrospect* (Winona Lake, 1992) 121-202 and J.-M. Durand in "La situation historique des Šakkanakku: nouvelle approche," *MARI* 4 (1985) 147-172.

It is also important to note that the actual number of appearances of the Syrians cited in the listing below can be reduced when one considers that two or more texts record the same visit and expenditure(s)/offering(s) reflecting different stages in the recording of individual transactions. A glance at the concordance of dated texts included below reveals how these texts are grouped. Note also that the clustering of references might indicate some special event that took place during a particular month or year or, more basic, that our archival documentation, mostly from clandestine sources, is not evenly represented.

[2] Due to a conflicting commitment, I was unable to attend the meeting after initially agreeing to participate. I would like to thank Professor Mark W. Chavalas for his kind invitation to present a paper at the meeting and for his willingness to accept this much expanded contribution to the symposium proceedings. I would also like to thank Professor Piotr Steinkeller for commenting on certain texts, the co-editor, Dr. John L. Hayes for his meticulous reading of the manuscript and Mr. James H. Platt, managing editor of Undena Publications, for his careful oversight of the publication process. Needless to add, none is responsible for any errors of commission or omission that might be found herein.

[3] Line numbers in references follow the transliterations published below unless otherwise indicated. It should be noted that the sources collected here do not, with a few exceptions, include texts in which individuals, otherwise known from specific cities, occur without geographical qualification.

[4] H. Weiss, "Tell Leilan and Shubat Enlil," *MARI* 4 (1985) 269-270, implies that such a study is warranted now in view of the growing archaeological evidence for the region, especially from sites such as Tell Leilan. The discovery and rapid publication of two tablets found *in situ* in Old Akkadian levels at Tell Mozan (=? Urkiš) (L. Milano, "Mozan 2: The Epigraphic Finds of the Sixth Season," *SMS* 5/1 [1991] 1-34 and previously G. Buccellati and M. Kelly-Buccellati, *Mozan 1* [Malibu, 1988; *BM* 20] 31-38) have revealed that the area of the Upper Khabur region had already a significant Hurrian component. The clarification of the settlement history of sites in the area will ultimately effect our understanding of the Ur III control or lack thereof in the area. The presence of written evidence, meager as it is at present, allows us to be optimistic about future discoveries in third millennium levels. [According to G. Buccellati (personal communication) new Old Akkadian tablets were found in the 1992 season at Tell Mozan.]

Historical Overview[5]

The discovery of the pre-Sargonic royal archives in Palace G at Ebla[6] has pushed the recorded history of Syria back into the first half of the third millennium BCE. One of the more curious aspects of the discovery of these archives at Ebla is the near total absence of references to commercial or diplomatic contact between Ebla and other Syrian cities with the Sumerian cities of contemporary, Early Dynastic III, southern Mesopotamia. While the absence may be due simply to the nature of the archive, it also may indicate a true reflection of limited contact, the result of an existing political situation that, only now, is becoming clearer. One perhaps may obtain some insight into the later Ur III historical situation as reflected in a much larger and more diverse collection of sources. As already described in the article cited above,[7] there is surprisingly little evidence for intense contact—military, commercial or political—between Sumer and Syria throughout the entire century of the Ur III dynasty. The overwhelming interest of the Ur III kings appears to have been the areas to the north, northeast and southeast of Sumer which were the focus of their frequent military campaigns, dynastic marriages, and religious, diplomatic and commercial exchanges. Indeed, the evidence accumulated below in the form of seventy-seven texts demonstrates how few these contacts with Syria were when considered against the availability of the tens of thousands of archival records.

---

[5] For a valuable, general survey of written sources relating to Syria during the Ur III period see J. Bottéro, "Syria During the Third Dynasty of Ur," *CAH*[3] I/2 (1971) 559-566; for Ebla in particular, see now A. Archi, "Ebla: la formazione di uno stato del III millennio a.C.," *La Parola del Passato* 46 (1991) 195-219. Although now much outdated by the numerous archaeological discoveries of the past two decades in Syria, the various chapters in *CAH*[3] I/2 (1971) dedicated to Syria in the third millennium B.C. still retain their usefulness. For more recent archaeological surveys, see H. Weiss, ed., *Ebla to Damascus: Art and Archaeology of Ancient Syria* (Washington, 1985); P. Matthiae, *Ebla: An Empire Rediscovered* (Garden City, 1981) and, with revisions, idem, *Ebla: Un impero ritrovato* (Torino, 1989); also now S. Mazzoni, "Ebla e la formazione della cultura urbana in Siria," and P. Matthiae, "Architettura e urbanistica di Ebla paleosiriana," *La Parola del Passato* 46 (1991) 163-194 and 304-371, respectively.

[6] The general consensus now is that the date of the Royal Archive from Palace G is pre-Sargonic, coming to a close at the latest during the first decade of Sargon's rule, the date Matthiae favors. However, there remain cogent arguments for an earlier dating. See the latest statements on the subject by P. Matthiae, "On the Economic Foundations of the Early Syrian Culture of Ebla," in H. Waetzoldt and H. Hauptmann, eds., *Wirtschaft und Gesellschaft von Ebla* (Heidelberg, 1988; *HSAO* 2) 75-80, "The Destruction of ⟨the⟩ Ebla Royal Palace; Interconnections between Syria, Mesopotamia and Egypt in the Late EB IVA," in P. Åström, ed., *High, Middle or Low?* (Gothenburg, 1989) 163-169 and his most recent views in "Nouvelles fouilles à Ébla en 1987-1989," *CRAIBL* 1990 384-431, especially p. 389 n. 11 and idem, "Architettura" (1991) 304-371, especially pp. 304-308. M. Astour believes that Palace G was destroyed not by invasion but by a natural catastrophe, probably during the reign of Lugalzagesi. See his contribution, "The Date of the Destruction of Palace G at Ebla," in this volume. A. Archi also appears to date the archive to the reign of Lugalzagesi to judge from his recently published "Formazione" (1991) 195-219, especially the chronological chart on p. 198. The internal chronology of the archive has now been greatly clarified in the recent studies of M.G. Biga and F. Pomponio, "Critères de rédaction comptable et chronologie relative des textes d'Ebla," *MARI* 7 (1992) 1-22 and "Elements for a Chronological Division of the Administrative Documentation of Ebla," *JCS* 42 (1990) 179-201.

[7] Owen and Veenker, "MeGum," esp. pp. 263-275.

The apparently peaceful frontier with Syria along the upper Euphrates valley, at least until the Mardu incursions in the reign of Šu-Suen, when contrasted with the Zagros and Elamite areas, suggests a situation which is, as yet, poorly understood. It is likely that Mari stood as a buffer state between Syria and Sumer although the influence of the Ur III state in Syria is in evidence from the beginning of the dynasty.[8] Early in the dynasty, there was a marriage between Ur-Nammu's son and a princess, the daughter of Apil-kîn, king of Mari, which may have resulted in an agreement over spheres of influence. This is, perhaps, reflected in the orientation of the Ur III archival and later historical sources. It may not be fortuitous that twenty-four "ambassadors" from Mari are recorded in the archival records, more than from any other Syrian city, followed by only seven from Ebla and six from Uršu.[9] Gelb's description of the situation of Mari,

> The continued dependence of the governor-generals of Mari is witnessed by Ur III administrative texts which show that the governor-generals of Mari fully participated in the economic and religious life of Babylonia. At the same time, their independence is manifested in their votive inscriptions which, contrary to tradition, never refer to their Babylonian overlords.[10]

appears to be an accurate assessment. The situation in the pre-Sargonic period may not have been much different. Mari was probably the southern buffer to Eblaite contacts with Sumer and perhaps acted as the intermediary for commercial,[11] cultural, religious and diplomatic

---

[8] The traces of a rebuilt structure at Tell Brak overlaying the destroyed fortress of Naram-Sin have been excavated along with a tablet and a clay bulla originally reported by C. Gadd ("Tablets from Chagar Bazar and Tall Brak, 1937-38," *Iraq* 7 [1940] 61) and M. Mallowan ("Excavations at Brak and Chagar Bazar," *Iraq* 9 [1947] 69) to contain Ur-Nammu's name (e.g. D.O. Edzard, in J. Bottéro et al., *The Near East: The Early Civilizations* [New York, 1967] 145-146). Edzard, however, does go on to note that "Anything north of Assur and Mari was probably too far removed from the centers of [Ur III] administration to be controlled in any effective way" (ibid., 146). See Weiss, "Tell Leilan" (1985) 270 n. 5 (with bibliography), and I.L. Finkel, "Inscriptions from Tell Brak 1984," *Iraq* 47 (1985) 200-201, for the clarification and correction concerning the alleged Ur-Nammu inscriptions from Tell Brak.

[9] See the listings below. The total for Mari may be reduced somewhat if certain names are, in fact, spelling variants of one another. Matthiae's suggestion that "political power in the area shifted to the city of Urshu" in Syria at this time (in Weiss, *Ebla to Damascus* [1985] 137) is not substantiated by the evidence, archaeological or epigraphical. Until the site of Uršu is found and excavated, the point will remain moot. See already Owen and Veenker, "MeGum" 274 n. 39.

[10] Gelb, "Mari" (1922) 162.

[11] F. Pinnock remarks that "Mari was the 'port of trade' where Ebla sent the materials it controlled, and which later on were envoyed to Mesopotamia. At the same time, the city on the middle Euphrates was also the market where Ebla could obtain—and in amazingly large amounts—semi-precious stones, shells, and other commodities coming from Mesopotamia or Iran," in "About the Trade of Early Syrian Ebla," *MARI* 4 (1985) 92 and again in "The Lapis Lazuli Trade in the Third Millennium B.C. and the Evidence from the Royal Palace G of Ebla," in M. Kelly-Buccellati, ed., *Insight Through Images: Studies in Honor of Edith Porada* (Malibu, 1986; *BM* 21) 221-228, where she states (p. 222), "On the basis of the materials found so far, it could be proposed that Mari acted as a mediator, and sent the lapis lazuli to the Syrian coast, whence it reached Egypt." See also idem, "The Lapis Lazuli in the Royal Palace of Ebla," in *Studies in the History and Archaeology of Palestine* 2 (Aleppo, 1987) 65-71. Most recently, Pinnock expanded upon this theme in her "Considerazioni sul sistema commerciale di Ebla protosiriana

activities.[12] If the hypothetical role of Kiš[13] is eliminated from consideration,[14] then Mari was the most likely intermediary between Syria and Sumer for both the pre-Sargonic[15] and Ur III periods. Indeed, Pomponio's conclusions for the Ebla period that,

> *...il monopolio dei rapporti tra Mesopotamia e Siria può esser stato tenuto saldamente da Mari*, and further, *Dobbiamo concluderne che la porta di communicazione tre la Mesopotamia e la Siria, quale è tradizionalmente considerata Mari, al tempo degli Archivi reali sembra sia rimasta accuratamente sbarrata,*[16]

may be valid equally for the Ur III period, albeit with seemingly less friction between the parties involved.

As noted above, the documentation for relationships between Syria and Sumer for the Ur III period is very scarce. No site in Syria, including Mari and Ebla, has produced yet any significant written documentation for the Ur III period. Not only is the epigraphic

---

(c. 2350-2300 A.C.)," *La Parola del Passato* 46 (1991) 270-284. See also now the remarks of M.C. Astour, "An Outline of the History of Ebla (Part 1)" *Eblaitica* 3 (1992) 3-82 where he writes (p. 59) "If any city emerges from the Eblean documentation as a commercial city *par excellence*, it is certainly Mari."

[12] See in particular, P. Michalowski, "Third Millennium Contacts: Observations on the Relationships between Mari and Ebla," *JAOS* 105 (1985) 293-302, A. Archi, "Les rapports politiques et économiques entre Ebla et Mari," *MARI* 4 (1985) 63-83, idem, "Formazione" (1991) 195-219 and, most recently, Astour, "Outline" (1992) 3-82.

[13] Gelb's elaborate hypothesis of a "Kiš Civilization" ("Thoughts about Ibla: A Preliminary Evaluation, March 1977," *SMS* 1/1 [1977] 130; "Ebla and the Kish Civilization," in L. Cagni, ed., *La lingua di Ebla* [Napoli, 1981] 9-73; and "Mari" [1992] 121-202), at least insofar as the role of Kiš in the Ebla texts is concerned, had already been questioned by Michalowski as early as 1983 and has been challenged again by Pomponio with more evidence. See the following note.

[14] Already in a 1983 lecture, Michalowski ("Contacts" [1985] 293-302, esp. pp. 297-298) signaled the problems of associating Kiš in the Ebla texts with the Babylonian Kiš. This has now been taken up anew in the recent analysis of the data by F. Pomponio in his "Exit Kiš dagli orizzonti di Ebla," *Mesopotamia*[T] 25 (1990) 175-184. According to Pomponio, Kiš in the Ebla documentation refers to a city by that name in the Khabur valley, east of the river and north of Nagar and not to its homonymous central Mesopotamian counterpart which may have been meant only with respect to the home town of the "professor of mathematics" who taught at Ebla. The location of Nagar, according to the evidence from newly published Mari texts, is either Tell Brak in the region to the south of Tell Barri, or possibly Tell Aswad. For a comprehensive discussion with previous bibliography see D. Charpin, "A Contribution to the Geography and History of the Kingdom of Kaḫat," in S. Eichler et al., eds., *Tall al-Ḥamīdīya* 2 (Freiburg, 1990) 68-69 and n. 7 and p. 78, n. 42. However, one significant problem with Pomponio's location of Kiš near Nagar is the personal name component associated with Kiš in the Ebla sources. As noted by M. Bonechi, "..., gli elementi nunu e Su'en caratterizzano la «regione onomastica babilonese», centrata su Kiš. Come già notato, è soli il comune denominatore semitico a unirla alle regioni onomastiche siriane" ("Onomastica dei testi di Ebla: nomi propi come fossili-guida?," *SEL* 8 [1991] 77, §15.) The personal names appear to be quite different in form from those of allegedly nearby Nagar. P. Steinkeller will address this subject in a forthcoming publication (personal communication). On the general relations between Ebla and Nagar, see now Astour, "Outline" (1992) 63-65.

[15] Astour, "Outline" (1992) 60 states, "Thus the prevailing pattern of trade between Ebla and Mari consisted in Mariote merchants being active all over the territory of Ebla, while the government of Mari severely limited the activities of Ebleans in the areas under its own control."

[16] "Exit" (1990) 184.

evidence lacking from excavated sites, but the published stratigraphy and associated materials from the equivalent Ur III period are conspicuously absent even from sites in Syria which have been excavated for decades. This is a curious anomaly when one considers the not infrequent references to Syrian cities, their rulers and their ambassadors that are documented below and which imply that these city-states were powerful enough to warrant such contacts. However, this condition is not unique to the Ur III period and appears to be characteristic of much of the third millennium. The Ebla documentation indicates a similar historical situation in the pre-Sargonic period. For the Sargonic period, Sargon and Naram-Sin's claims of conquest notwithstanding, there is little evidence in either the archaeological or the written record for direct and substantial relationships between the two areas.[17] One might consider the possibility that contacts throughout this long period had always been somewhat indirect and via an intermediary power such as Mari. Presumably when Mari was seized by Sargon's army, its commercial and political control over its former holdings also fell under Sargon's sway. But the mechanics of the control as well as the extent are not known. The fact that Naram-Sin, as recorded in an Old Babylonian copy of an earlier historical inscription,[18] had to subdue once again Armanum and Ebla and the Cedar Mountains, suggests that the control was not very effectual.[19] Indeed, his successor Šarkališarri had to campaign again in the region of Mt. Basar where he claimed to have subdued the Mardu. Surprisingly, after the fall of the Sargonic Empire to the Quti, Gudea could still boast of his ability to import precious metal and other luxuries from Syria[20] suggesting that the trade connections, perhaps via unknown intermediaries such as the resurgent city of Mari.[21] Certainly, by the time Ur-Nammu had established himself in Ur, Mari had once again assumed its former status as the intermediary political and economic power between Syria and Mesopotamia.

Among the major, excavated, third millennium sites in Syria, none has revealed any significant material evidence for a wealthy or powerful occupation level during the Ur III period or what would be classified as Early Bronze IV.[22] Indeed, the lack of chronological

---

[17] See J. Bottéro, "Syria at the Time of the Kings of Agade," *CAH*^{3} I/2 (1971) 321-327 and M.S. Drower, "Syria Before 2200 B.C.," *CAH*^{3} I/2 (1971) 315-321, 328-343. The evidence from glyptics, wall decorations such as the Mari plaques, architecture and the like, provides indications primarily of economic relations mostly with or via Mari. Pinnock's remarks quoted above in note 11 with respect to the pre-Sargonic age would be equally valid for the later Sargonic and Ur III periods.

[18] Quoted by Bottéro, "Syria" (1971) 325.

[19] The cautionary remarks of Michalowski, "We indeed put too much emphasis on the raids which Sargon and Naram-Sin effected in the north and north-west of Mesopotamia" ("Contacts" [1985] 301) are worth noting in this context.

[20] C.J. Gadd, "The Dynasty of Agade and the Gutian Invasion," *CAH*^{3} I/2 (1971) 460.

[21] Other possible routes to Syria might have been used as they were likely used earlier. Note the interesting observation of Bonechi concerning the Ebla period; "Poiché le communicazioni commerciali fra la valle del Ḫabur e l'alto Eufrate (fra Imar e Karkamiš), attraverso la regione di Tell Khuera e Ḫarran, sono sempre state agevoli, *Mari non deve essere stata l'unico tramite fra la bassa Mesopotamia e quell'area che diventerà lo Yamḫad*" [emphasis mine] ("Onomastica" [1991] 76 n. 107).

[22] See the somewhat dated but still useful survey of K. Kenyon, "Syria: The Sites," *CAH*^{3} I/2 (1971) 583-594 and the important studies of S. Mazzoni, "Elements of the Ceramic Culture of Early Syrian Ebla in Comparison

precision in the excavation reports, due primarily to the lack of inscriptional evidence, does not allow for a critical appraisal of the historical relationships between Syria and Sumer other than suggestions of cultural and economic contacts via overland trade as evidenced from the material culture. The Ur III kings did not record any military campaign into the area of Syria[23] and nothing in the archival records indicates major economic relationships. The later historical tradition does not alter this impression.

It would seem that the city-states of Syria never presented Sumer with any unified military threat[24] and this appears to be valid also for the second and first millennia. Until the Mardu incursions during the reign of Šu-Suen, seemingly all major military efforts by the Sumerians were directed towards the Zagros and Elamite regions. For whatever reasons, the northwestern frontier remained relatively peaceful and secure. It would seem that the Mardu incursions were as great a threat to the Syrian city-states as they were to the Sumerian state and that they represented a totally new factor for which the Sumerians simply were not prepared. As was suggested elsewhere,[25] the Syrian city-states may have, in fact, been destroyed or otherwise reduced already in the cataclysms, natural or man-made, that brought the third millennium to an end in that area.[26] If so, the collapse of any central control

---

with Syro-Palestinian EB IV," *BASOR* 257 (1985) 1-18 and "Formazione" (1991) 163-194. These articles deal also with sites on the Syro-Canaanite axis as well as the Syro-Mesopotamian one.

[23] P. Michalowski, "Likewise, not a single military campaign is known to have been directed towards Syria in the [Ur III] period," in his "Foreign Tribute to Sumer during the Ur III Period," *ZA* 68 (1978) 45 and Owen and Veenker, "MeGum" 266 n. 20.

[24] This does not mean that localized military operations did not take place. Note the references to nam-ra-ak kur-mar-tu in the Drehem texts which indicate that there were, in fact, some police actions that took place in the Syrian area although their importance was not significant enough to warrant year name designations. See, for example, the text to be published by M. Sigrist, *Toronto* 639 (ROM 910×209.593) dated probably to Šulgi's 46th year which records booty from both the Mardu-region and the city of Urbilum: (1) 4 gu$_4$ ba-da-du lú-S[U] (2) 2 sila$_4$ ad-da-tur (3) 3 máš 1 ^{mí}ešgar (4) du$_{11}$-ga-[z]i-d[a] (5) 2 máš šar-ru-um-ì-lí (6) 1 sila$_4$ i$^{!}$(TUR)-ti-é-a (7) 181 maš-dù a-mur-é-a (8) 10 dúsu-níta (9) 1 dúsu-níta-mu-1 (10) 11 dúsu-mí (11) 1 dúsu-mí-mu-1 (12) 3 gukkal-giš-dù (13) 5 gukkal 32 U$_8$+ḪÚL (14) nam-ra-ak kur-mar-tu (15) gìri šu-ì-lí nu-bànda (16) ugula ^{d}en-líl (17) [x] gu$_4$ 3 áb (18) šà-gu$_4$ lá-ìa nam-ra-ak / ur-bí-lum^{ki} (19) kìšib ki-iz-zi lú-ḫa-ar-me-me-ta / ba-ra-su (20) gìri is-ga-ga maš-en-kak / lú-ì-lí-am-ra^{ki}-ka (21) 25 u$_8$ 6 sila$_4$-ga (22) 11 udu 6 [x]-ga (23) 67 ùz 31[+?] ^{mí}ešgar (24) 18 ^{mí}ešgar-ga 26 máš-gal (25) 23 máš 23 máš-ga (26) udu-mu$_7$-mu$_7$ (27) ki lú-sukkal-an-dùl-ta (28) gìri lugal-dal[la] (29) 2 sila$_4$ šeš-da-[da] (30) 1 sila$_4$ lugal-dingir-[ra] (31) 2 amar-az [šu$^{?}$-^{d}suen$^{?}$] (32) DOUBLE LINE (33) mu-DU [lugal$^{?}$] (34) mu ki-[maš^{ki} ḫu-mur-ti]/^{ki} [ba-ḫul] (35-side) u$_4$-20-kam.

[25] Owen and Veenker, "MeGum" 275 n. 41.

[26] According to P. Matthiae, "...comparative evidence from other [other than Ebla, ed.] contemporary centers of the Syrian area, all of which from the Amuq to Hama show the same destruction, indicates that the catastrophe which overwhelmed the Late Protosyrian culture must in any case be dated in the various Upper Syrian cities which were affected by it between 2050 and 1950 B.C. Between these upper and lower limits, some years may be found to separate the various destructions from one another. What is certain is that in the decades around 2000 B.C. the centres (sic!) of the Protosyrian culture were involved in a disastrous crisis which devastated the whole area, putting an end to its development with fire." (*Empire* [1981] 111). Furthermore, note also the more recent opinion of S. Mazzoni, "It is still to be demonstrated that the end of the EB IVB in Syria is a sudden and general phenomenon occurring contemporaneously at all sites, as a result of violent destructions rather than a slow general decay. I would suggest, on the contrary, that what we have to deal with is an economic and environmental phenomenon that gave rise to socioeconomic complications." ("Elements" [1985] 16 n. 11).

along the upper Euphrates valley may have allowed for the eruption of an uncontrolled movement of tribal elements manifested in the Mardu incursions as indicated in the year names[27] and in the later collection of inscriptions of Šu-Suen. The near total cessation of references to Syria and Syrians other than Mardu after Šu-Suen's sixth year could merely be the result of the random nature of archival finds, but it could also be a true reflection of the collapse of the Syrian city-states as well as the disruptions which reached as far as southern Canaan and the borders of Egypt.[28]

Syrian Cities and Their Representatives in Ur III Archival Sources[29]

Nature of the Sources

Perhaps the most significant change in our understanding of Syria in the third millennium has been with respect to our view of its ethnic makeup in that period. As recently as 1971 it could still be written that,

> ...we can regard it as almost certain that among the whole population of ancient Syria the Semites were the latest comers. It has long been observed that most of the old place-names in the country cannot be explained as Semitic, but belong to one or several unknown linguistic complexes.[30]

Evidence for a widespread, natural disaster consisting of desertification and large scale desertion has been suggested in a paper given in Heidelberg at the XXXIXe Rencontre Assyriologique Internationale (1992) by H. Weiss, M.-A. Courty and L. Senior, "Subir, Sìla-Bowls and Collapse: Tell Leilan Data for Late Third Millennium Mesopotamian History." In this study, they presented recently excavated evidence from Tell Leilan which strongly indicates what they designate the Khabur Hiatus 1 (2200-1900) during which Tell Leilan and many other sites in the Khabur Plains area were abandoned. No significant archaeological evidence from Tell Leilan and other Khabur Plains sites appears to exist for the Ur III period, indicating that the Khabur Plains were mostly abandoned. They further suggest a correlation between this natural disaster, probably a prolonged drought, and the movements of the Amorites and others along with other disruptions which engulfed the Aegean and much of Syro-Canaan during this same time span. I am grateful to Prof. Weiss for making available an advance copy of this paper.

[27] It is possible to see in the name for the fourth year of Šu-Suen, mu [d]šu-[d]suen lugal-uri$_5$[ki]-ma-ke$_4$ bàd-mar-tu *mu-ri-iq-ti-id-ni-im* mu-dù, "the year Šu-Suen, the king of Ur, built the Mardu-wall (called) 'the Tidnim-barrier,' a relatively secure date for the neutralization or destruction of the major Syrian cities which, as I have signaled above, may have preceded the Mardu movements. Such movements likely followed upon a breakdown of urban control of the countryside in the Syrian area. Similar views have been suggested before by M. Liverani, in "I tell pre-classici," *Missione Archeologica Italiana in Siria, Rapporto preliminare della Campagna 1964* [Roma, 1965] 124 and again by W.G. Dever, "New Vistas on the EB IV ('MB I') Horizon in Syria-Palestine," *BASOR* 237 (1980) 35-64, esp. p. 58.

[28] "Disruptive elements thus appear in Syria and Palestine in the last third of the third millennium B.C., just as they do in Egypt and Mesopotamia," Kenyon, "Sites" (1971) 592-593. See also the forthcoming paper by H. Weiss et al. cited in n. 26 above.

[29] This collection does not include any of the numerous names designated mar-tu, only names associated with specific cities within the Syrian orbit.

[30] Bottéro, "Syria" (1971) 566 following upon the ideas earlier expressed by I.J. Gelb, A. Goetze and others. See now also the remarks of Bonechi, "Onomastica" (1991) 74.

The massive amount of new data on both personal[31] and place names[32] provided by the Ebla texts has shown that this assessment is certainly not valid for the third millennium and probably also for the earlier periods.[33] Most likely the dominant population of Syria was Semitic as were the names of most of the cities, towns and villages. The rich vocabulary of Eblaite, much of which is unknown from later Semitic dialects, demonstrates quite clearly that many archaic and unclassified place and personal names indeed may be purely Semitic even though they elude current interpretation.[34] A study of Ur III Semitic personal names from Syria other than those designated Mardu,[35] suggests that the linguistic makeup of Syria during the Ur III dynasty[36] had not changed significantly since the pre-Sargonic, Ebla period.[37]

---

[31] See the seminal work by A. Archi, ed., *Eblaite Personal Names and Semitic Name-giving* (Roma, 1988; *ARES* 1) and the recent observations of Astour, "Outline" (1992) 5-8.

[32] See now the remarks of Astour, "Outline" (1992) 8-10.

[33] The tablet published by A. Archi, *ARET* 7 150 (TM.75.G.2628) has shown that the Semitic dynasty of Ebla goes back well into the first half of the third millennium. See the commentary on this text by idem, "Die ersten zehn Könige von Ebla," *ZA* 76 (1986) 213-217 and idem, "Cult of the Ancestors and Tutelary God at Ebla," in Y.L. Arbeitman, ed., *Fucus: A Semitic/Afrasian Gathering in Remembrance of Albert Ehrman* (Amsterdam, 1988) 103-112. See now also the extensive discussion by Astour, "Outline" (1992) 19-26.

[34] See the detailed remarks of M.C. Astour, "Some Recent Works on Ancient Syria and the Sea People," *JAOS* 92 (1972) 447-459, esp. 447-452 where he advocated the dominant Semitic character of the Syrian population and place names before the discovery of the Ebla archive and idem, "Continuité et changement dans la toponymie de la Syrie du Nord," in T. Fahd, org., *La Toponymie Antique* (Leiden, 1977) 117-141. Note also the observations of P. Fronzaroli, "West Semitic Toponomy in Northern Syria in the Third Millennium B.C.," *JSS* 22 (1977) 145-166 which reflected the first results of the study of the Ebla texts but which did not take into account the earlier observations of Astour. Nevertheless, we should not discount the presence of a substantial non-Semitic population as well. Note the recent observations of Bonechi, "Onomastica" (1991) 74, where he writes, "..., le affinità ora proposte fra certi NP di Armi e di DUlu potrebbero essere spiegate con il persistere di tradizioni onomastiche diverse da qualle semitiche sulla costa siriana per influenza cilicia."

[35] One the reading and meaning of the term Mardu/Martu, see now Astour, "Outline" (1992) 55-56 and n. 336.

[36] There are numerous names in the Ur III sources which end in *-an*, *-um*, or *-anum* but whose etymologies have hitherto defied interpretation. However, comparison with the published Ebla corpus of personal names has revealed striking similarities with many of those names and suggests that the Ebla "dialect" continued, at least in the form of personal names, into the Ur III period. This conclusion was already anticipated on the basis of our interpretation of the Yibbiṭ-Lim inscription in Owen and Veenker, "MeGum" 273 and presented in more detail in my paper, "On the Survival of Eblaite: Observations on Semitic Personal Names from the End of the Third Millennium," delivered at the Ninth Annual David Rose Conference on the Ebla Archives, New York University, November 10, 1991, and with extensive revisions, at the Altorientalisches Seminar, Freie Universität Berlin, March 10, 1992 and the Università di Roma "La Sapienza," April 13, 1992. I hope to publish the results shortly.

[37] M. Bonechi's recent study, "Onomastica" (1991) 59-79 has revealed both the richness and complexity of personal names in a regional context. Following particularly upon the earlier work of A. Archi, he has combined the careful isolation of groups of PNs associated with particular cities and towns, and combined the results with the data resulting from the studies of the regionalization of ceramics producing a model for the future study of onomastics. At the same time he has been able to demonstrate that PNs often reflect naming patterns which are restricted to defined geographical areas that appear to sometimes coincide with ceramic zones established through archaeological research. Unfortunately, for the Ur III period, the PNs associated with Syrian cities are too few in number while the Mardu names are rarely associated with a specific geographical area or individual cities and towns to warrant any regionalization study in association with ceramic regionalization such as noted by Mazzoni,

Virtually all contemporary sources from the Ur III Dynasty are in the form of archival and votive inscriptions. Later Old Babylonian copies of historical inscriptions and the corpus of literary letters from the scribal academies fill out the general historical picture. The emphasis in this study is on the archival records since the votive,[38] historical,[39] and literary sources[40] have been collected and studied. Although there has been a number of small additions and corrections to the record over the past few years,[41] the overall picture of the Ur III period has not been altered significantly.

The overall majority of references to Syrian cities, Syrians and to Mardu/Amorites derives from the texts from Puzriš-Dagan (Drehem) which come from clandestine excavations with no records whatsoever of their archaeological contexts.[42] Fortunately, most tablets are dated and are well preserved. The texts generally record the deliveries of animals—sheep, goats and cattle—to and from Syrians and others, for a variety of purposes—food, cultic and donations. None of the sources indicates any unusual number of animals nor do they record any other items other than livestock which might be characterized as gift-exchanges. The uniformity of the record suggests that the Puzriš-Dagan archives did not record what must have been important gift-exchanges from the city-state rulers of Syria and from Elam, whose ambassadors are found often in the same archival records.[43] If Mari acted as a buffer state between Syria and Ur, then no indications in our sources suggest the purpose of the visits of "ambassadors" from as far away as Gubla on the Mediterranean coast. Any fuller understanding of the relationship between the Ur III state and the cities of Syria must, for the time being, await the discovery of additional archives.

"Elements" (1985) 1-18.

[38] See above, note 1.

[39] M. Civil, "Šū-Sîn's Historical Inscriptions: Collection B," *JCS* 21 (1967) 24-38 and C. Wilcke, "Drei Phasen des Niedergangs des Reiches von Ur III," *ZA* 60 (1970) 54-69.

[40] P. Michalowski, "The Royal Correspondence of Ur" (Ph.D. diss., Yale University, 1976).

[41] See, for example, C. Wilcke, "Zur Rekonstruktion der Šū-Sîn Inschriften-Sammlung B," *NABU* 1990/33.

[42] For the first time we have now a complete reference guide to all the published Ur III archival texts compiled by M. Sigrist and T. Gomi, *The Comprehensive Catalogue of Ur III Tablets* (Bethesda, 1992). This listing provides dates and origin for every published tablet, organized chronologically and including the cities of origin when known.

[43] Particularly, but not exclusively, from Marḫaši. See P. Steinkeller, "The Question of Marḫaši: A Contribution to the Historical Geography of Iran in the Third Millennium B.C.," *ZA* 72 (1982) 237-265 and the comprehensive survey of both the epigraphical and archaeological evidence for Elam in E. Carter and M.W. Stolper, *Elam: Surveys of Political History and Archaeology* (Berkeley, 1984). A still puzzling question is why, if Marḫaši is to be located in eastern Iran, do its ambassadors inevitably appear together with those from Syria. This suggests to me that the earlier location of Marḫaši in northwestern Iran better suits the Ur III evidence from Drehem. This anomaly in the data was not addressed in the study of Steinkeller. See already my remarks in Owen and Veenker, "MeGum" 270 n. 25.

Catalogue of Cities and Personal Names

1. ABARNIUM[44]

[...g]izi

Amar-Suena 6/iv/1
[...g]i-zi lú-kin-gi$_4$-a énsi-a-ba-ar-ni-um^{ki} (Fish, *CST* 468:rev. 3, collated by Gomi, *MVN* 12, p. 114 with copy of traces of the PN on plate cvi.)

2. EBLA[45]

Ezun-^{d}Dagan (=? Izzin-^{d}Dagan)[46]

Šu-Sin 3/iii/6
e-zu-un-^{d}da-gan lú-eb-la^{ki} (Owen, Anonymous 1:13)

[Gura'a][47]

Ili-^{d}Dagan

---

[44] Abarnium has been associated by I.J. Gelb ("Studies in the Topography of Western Asia," *AJSL* 55 [1938] 66-67) with Classical (Cappadocian) Abarne, modern Çermük in Turkey, halfway between Malatya and Amida (Edzard and Farber, *RGTC* 2 [1974] 1 s.v. with bibliography). It would thus be among the cities furthest to the northwest mentioned in the Ur III texts. Unfortunately, no additional citations to either the ensi or the city have appeared since they first were published by Fish. Its appearance as Abarnum, the last in a series of Syrian cities listed in an apparently northwesterly orientation (from the viewpoint of Sumer) in Šu-Suen's historical inscriptions (Civil, "Šū-Sîn" [1967] 37-38), supports such an assessment.

[45] This listing supersedes that of G. Pettinato in his preprint to the never published Matthiae et al., *MAIS* 4 (1972) 31-34 and his "Ibla (Ebla). A. Philologisch," *RLA* 5 (1976-1980) 10. Pettinato then published an updated version in *Ebla: Nuovi orizzonti della storia* (Milano, 1986) 386-388 based on my compilation but curiously omitted the same list in his unrevised and abridged translation to this book, *Ebla: A New Look at History* (Baltimore, 1991).

[46] On the alternation of vowels in Syrian personal names, see the remarks in Owen and Veenker, "MeGum" 271 n. 29 and compare below the name Ami/ur-Šulgi.

[47] Pomponio, in his recent article, "Exit Kiš" (1990) 175-184, mistakenly adds in his note 28 the name of Gura'a to those originating from Ebla in the Ur III period. He bases this on two texts, E. Weidner, "Assyriologische Studien," *RSO* 9 (1921-23) 472 P370:2 and E. Sollberger, *MVN* 5 (1978) 111:16, both of which are included under my listing of individuals from Uršu. I believe both Weidner's text and Sollberger's, which was not published in copy, should be read gu-ra-a lú-ur$^!$-šu$^{!ki}$ in keeping with virtually all the other citations as already noted by Edzard and Farber, *RGTC* 2 (1974) 39. See my note, "Exit Gura'a from Ebla!," in *NABU* 1992/3 for more detailed comments.

Šulgi 44/iii/18
ì-lí-^{d}da-gan lú-kin-gi$_{4}$-a-lú-eb-la^{ki} (Sigrist, *Toronto* 287:11-12 [= ROM 925.62.275:11-12])[48]

[Amar-Suena(?) ?/?]/7
ì-lí-^{d}da-gan lú-eb-la^{ki} (Dhorme, "Tablettes de Dréhem à Jérusalem," *RA* 9 [1912] 56 SA 239)

Amar-Suena 1/ii/26
ì-lí-^{d}da-gan lú-eb-la^{ki} (Young, Wabash 1:5)[49]

Amar-Suena 1/iii/4
ì-lí-^{d}da-gan lú-eb$^{!}$-la$^{!ki}$ (Çığ, et al., *PDT* 1 594:16, collated by Picchioni, "Miscellanea neo-sumerica, II," *OA* 14 [1975] 166 and Gomi [unpublished])

Amar-Suena 2/iii/13
ì-lí-^{d}da-gan lú-eb-la^{ki} (Owen, *MVN* 15 360:4 [Birmingham (Alabama) Art Museum 56. 86.1:4] = Dhorme, *RA* 9 [1912] 59 SA 79:4)

Amar-Suena 2/iii/20
ì-lí-^{d}da-gan lú-eb-la^{ki} (Goetze, "Four Ur Dynasty Tablets Mentioning Foreigners," *JCS* 7 [1953] 104 St. Louis City Art Museum 61:27, 2)

Amar-Suena 2/vi/3
ì-lí-^{d}da-gan lú-eb-la^{ki} (Fish, *CST* 254:1, copy of obverse also published in *BJRL* 8 [1924] 110, no. 507, collated by Gomi, *MVN* 12, p. 105)

Amar-Suena 2/vi/4
ì-lí-^{d}da-gan lú-eb-la^{ki} (Legrain, *TRU* 305:10)

Amar-Suena 2/vi/8
ì-lí-^{d}da-gan lú-eb-la^{ki} (Arnaud, Laval 2544:12 [= AO 26098:12] quoted in Pettinato, *RLA* 5 [1976-1980] 10a)

Amar-Suena 2/vii/21
ì-lí-^{d}da-/gan lú-eb-la^{ki} (Owen, "Some New Evidence on Yaḫmadiu = Aḫlamû," in M. Cohen, D. Snell, and D.B. Weisberg, eds., *The Temple and the Book: Ancient Near Eastern Studies in Honor of William W. Hallo* (Bethesda, 1993), in press, Anonymous 3:9)

---

48 M. Sigrist, *Ur III Texts in the Royal Ontario Museum, Toronto*, in preparation, courtesy of the author.

49 The indication in Owen and Veenker, "MeGum" 289 n. 54, that this text was to be published by Young in *Mari in Retrospect*, was premature. The text did not appear in that volume but Professor G.D. Young has kindly consented to publish his copy and comments on the text below, p. 174.

Amar-Suena 2/viii/-
ì-lí-^{d}da-gan lú-eb-la^{ki} (Goetze, *JCS* 7 [1953] 105 NCBT 1593:5)

Amar-Suena 3/iv/14
ì-lí-^{d}da-gan lú-eb-la^{ki} (courtesy Hallo, NCBT 1669:4)

Amar-Suena [6]/iv/1$^{!}$
ì-lí-^{d}da-gan lú-eb-la^{ki} (Fish, *CST* 468:6, collated by Gomi, *MVN* 12, p. 114)

Amar-Suena 6/iv/4
ì-lí-^{d}da-gan lú-eb-la^{ki} (Goetze, *JCS* 7 [1953] 104 Smith College 473:10)

Amar-Suena 6/iv/5
ì-lí-^{d}da-gan lú-eb-la^{ki} (Sigrist, Owen, Young, *MVN* 13 635:5 [= FLP 277])

Amar-Suena 6/iv/6
ì-lí-^{d}da-gan lú-eb-la^{ki} (Legrain, *TRU* 344:16)

Amar-Suena 6/iv/23
ì-lí-^{d}da-gan lú-eb-la^{ki} (Gomi and Hirose, *Hirose* 231:5)

Amar-Suena 6/iv/26
ì-lí-^{d}da-gan lú-e[b-l]a[^{k}]^{i} (Owen, *MVN* 11 146:11 [= HSM 911.3.31:11])

Izzin-^{d}Dagan (=? Ezun-^{d}Dagan)

[Šu-Sin 6/viii/?]
i-zi-in-^{d}da-gan...kur-bi-la-ak...lú-eb-[la]^{ki}[-me$^{?}$-šè$^{?}$] (Goetze, *JCS* 7 [1953] 107 Kenrick Theological Seminary 72:iii:10-12 = Jean, *ŠA* LXXI:85:iii:10-12)

Šu-Sin 6/viii/14
i-zi-in-^{d}da-gan...kur-bi-la-ak...lú-eb-la^{ki}-me-šè (Buccellati, *Amorites*, plate x, no. 21:9-12 [= A.29365:9-12])

Šu-Sin 6/⟨viii⟩/20
i-zi-in-^{d}da-gan...kur-bi-la-ak...lú-eb-la^{ki}-me-šè (Buccellati, *Amorites*, plate xi-xii, no. 21:27-29 [= A.2970:27-29])

Kurb-ilak

[Šu-Sin 6/viii/?]
i-zi-in-^{d}da-gan...kur-bi-la-ak...lú-eb-[la]^{ki}[-me$^{?}$-šè$^{?}$] (Goetze, *JCS* 7 [1953] 107 Kenrick Theological Seminary 72:iii:10-12 = Jean, *ŠA* LXXI:85:iii:10-12)

Šu-Sin 6/viii/14
i-zi-in-^{d}da-gan...kur-bi-la-ak...lú-eb-la^{ki}-me-šè (Buccellati, *Amorites*, plate x, no. 21:9-12 [= A.29365:9-12])

Šu-Sin 6/⟨viii⟩/20
i-zi-in-^{d}da-gan...kur-bi-la-ak...lú-eb-la^{ki}-me-šè (Buccellati, *Amorites*, plate xi-xii, no. 21:27-29 [= A.2970:27-29])

MeGum[50]

Amar-Suena 7/v/21
me-GU-um énsi-eb-la^{ki} (Owen and Veenker, Trout 1:15)

Meme-šura

(no date)
me-me-šu-ra lú-eb-la^{ki} (Contenau, *UDU* 27:1-3)

[Nur-ili][51]

---

[50] To the data collected in Owen and Veenker, "MeGum" 229 n. 23 for the epithet, *meKim eblaim*, on the Yibbiṭ-Lim statue inscription from Ebla can now be added the (re)discovery of the same epithet, *meKim eblaim* (*me-KI-im eb-lá-*[*im*]) qualifying the Old Assyrian personal name, Ibdamu/Ebdamu (*ib-da-mu*) written in mirror writing on a seal, J. Lewy, *TCL* 21, plate ccxxxi, no. 14, as collated, deciphered and reported by K. Veenhof *apud* K. Nashef, *Die Orts- und Gewässernamen der altassyrischen Zeit* (Wiesbaden, 1991; *RGTC* 4) 38 and further, in a personal communication with me (5 June 1992) where he indicated that B. Teissier will publish a note on the seal impression. The tablet on which the seal was impressed, J. Lewy, *TCL* 21, plate cciv, no. 247B, adds nothing about Ibdamu and the seal itself may have been used by another person. The use of antique seals, especially in the Ur III style, is well known at Kaniš. The name on the seal, Ibdamu, is known, at least once, from the Pre-Sargonic Ebla onomastica. See Biga and Milano, *ARET* 4 17 obv. I:2, *ib-da-mu*, who interpret the name as Ib-Damu. Unfortunately, this new reference does not enhance our understanding of the epithet although it could lend more support for a twentieth century dating for the Yibbiṭ-Lim statue as advocated by P. Matthiae and I.J. Gelb.

[51] Šulgi 43/v/-. Kìšib nu-úr-ì-lí lú$^{!}$-dur$^{?}$-eb-la^{ki} (Keiser and Kang, *BIN* 3 491:32 and Edzard and Farber, *RGTC* 2 35, s.v.). The suggestion of Pettinato, *MAIS* 4 33 n. 74, idem, *RLA* 5 10b, to read dam$^{!}$-gàr$^{!}$-Ebla is not substantiated after collation by B. Foster and G. Beckman (letter of 1.10.86), nor is the reading in Owen and Veenker, "MeGum" 217 where it was suggested it be read as lú-gú$^{!}$-eb-la^{ki} and associated with Sumer. Kang's reading is substantiated in Pettinato and Waetzoldt, *MVN* 1 (1974) 113:12 (AS 8/viii/17) where I read nu-úr-ì-lí lú-BÀD-eb-la^{ki}. Note that this text also includes the names of two other "easterners," ḫu-un-ki-ib-ri lú-ul-li^{ki} (*MVN* 15 113:6), a city now known to have been the seat of an ensi (mu-gu-ud énsi-ul-li^{ki}, NBC 9998:6, courtesy of M. Sigrist and W.W. Hallo) and ḫé-ti dumu ra-ši (*MVN* 15 113:9). Nur-ili should not be associated with Syrian Ebla but with Dur-Ebla in the vicinity of Nuzi. See now also Astour, "Outline" (1992) 12 n. 51.

Zurim[52]

Šulgi 46/?/?
zu$^!$-ri-im lú-kin-gi$_4$-a-lú-eb-la^{ki} (Luckenbill, "A Messenger from Ibla," *AJSL* 39 [1922] 65-66. The reading Suri-Adad for this name in *RLA* 5 10a is unlikely.)

Šulgi 46/iii/1
gún lú-eb-la^{ki} gìri zu-rí-im lú-na (Pohl, *TMH NF* 1/2 313:3-4)

Šulgi 46/vi/28
zu-ri-im lú-kin-gi$_4$-a lú-eb-la^{ki} (Gomi, "Administrative Texts of the Third Dynasty of Ur," *Orient* 16 [1980] 40, no. 7 Liverpool Merseyside County Museums 51-63-51 = Fish, "Some Place Names and Their Contexts," *MCS* 7 [1957] 19-20 Liverpool 51.63.51:rev. 4. The reading Suri-Adad for this name in *RLA* 5 10a is unlikely.)

Amar-Suena 7/v/21
(tentative, depending on restoration of name) z[u$^?$-ri$^?$-im$^?$] lú-kin-gi$_4$-a me-GU-um énsi eb-la^{ki} (Owen and Veenker, Trout 1:14)[53]

lu-Ebla^{ki}

No Date (Lagaš)
lú-eb-la^{ki} (Pettinato, *MVN* 6 100:5 [= *ITT* 4 7101:5])

No Date (Lagaš)
lú-eb-[la^{ki}] (Pettinato, *MVN* 6 110:rev. 5 [= *ITT* 7111:rev. 5])

No Date (Lagaš)
lú-eb-la^{ki} (Pettinato, *MVN* 6 247:7 [= *ITT* 4 7253:7])

Šulgi 46/iii/1 (Drehem)
gún lú-eb-la^{ki} (Pohl, *TMH NF* 1/2 313:3)

Šulgi 47/ix/9 (Drehem)
lú-eb-la^{ki} (Sigrist, *AUCT* 1 494:7)

---

[52] See now the remarks on Zurim by P. Steinkeller, "The Container *kabkūru*," *NABU* 1991/4. He does not cite our more complete listing of references in Owen and Veenker, "MeGum" 278-279.

[53] The reconstruction is based on very slight traces of what appears to be either a ZU or perhaps a SU at the very beginning of the break (see photo, Owen and Veenker, "MeGum," Plate I, opposite p. 292). It would be unusual for Zurim to reappear as an ambassador after such a long absence and then only this one time. But he may have been a long-lived ambassador at the court at Ebla and our documentation is simply inadequate. Nevertheless, the very few traces on the tablet make this restoration very tentative indeed. In any case, no other ambassador is known for this year. I would suggest further that the lú-eb-la^{ki} for whom Zurim was a messenger was MeGum himself.

3. GUBLA

Ibati

Amar-Suena 4/v/6!
i-ba-ti lú-kin-gi$_4$-a-ib-da-ti énsi-gu$_5$-ub-la^{ki} (Schneider, *AnOr* 7 [1932] 99:24-25, collated with comments by Cagni, "Miscellanea neo-sumerica, IX," *OA* 22 [1982] 90-91; see below for revised transliteration.)

Amar-Suena 4/v/9
i-ba-ti lú-kin-gi$_4$-a-ib-da-ti énsi-gu$_5$-ub-la^{ki} (Sollberger, "Byblos sous les rois d'Ur," *AfO* 19 [1959-60] 120 = idem, *MVN* 5 111:21; see below for revised transliteration.)

Ibdati

Amar-Suena 4/v/6!
ib-da-ti énsi-gu$_5$-ub-la^{ki} (Schneider, *AnOr* 7 [1932] 99:24-25, collated with comments by Cagni, *OA* 22 [1983] 90-91; see below for revised transliteration.)

Amar-Suena 4/v/9
ib-da-ti énsi-gu$_5$-ub-la^{ki} (Sollberger, *AfO* 19 [1959-60] 120 = idem, *MVN* 5 111:21; see below for revised transliteration.)

4. IA'MADIUM (YAḪMADU)[54]

Dulqanum

Amar-Suena 2/vii/21
du-ul-qá-/nu-um lú-ìa-a-ma-dì-um^{ki} (Owen, "Yaḫmadiu" [1993], in press, Anonymous 3:11)

Amar-Suena 2/viii/-
dú-ul-qá-núm mar-tu ìa-a-ma-dì (Goetze, *JCS* 7 [1953] 105 NCBT 1593:8-9 [collated])

Ia'madu

Šu-Suen 1/vi/24
ìa-a-ma-dú (Owen, Newell 1978, collated [without GN])

[54] On this GN, see the comments of C. Wilcke, "Šu-Sin" (1990) 25-26 and Owen, "Yaḫmadiu" (1993).

Ipiq-re'u

[Šu-Sin 6/viii/? (date restored from Buccellati, *Amorites* plate xi-xii, no. 22)]
i-pí-iq-re-e-ú mar-tu ìa-ma-d[ì-um$^{?ki?}$] (Goetze, *JCS* 7 [1953] 107 Kenrick Theological Seminary 72:iii:14-15 = Jean, *ŠA* LXXI:85:iii:14-15)

Šu-Sin 6/viii/14
i-pí-iq-re-e-ú mar-tu ìa-a-ma-dì-um (Buccellati, *Amorites*, plate x, no. 21:17 [= A.29365:17])

Šu-Sin 6/⟨viii⟩/20
i-pí-iq-re-e-ú mar-tu ìa-a-ma-dì[-um$^{?ki?}$] (Buccellati, *Amorites*, plate xi, no. 21:ii.31 [= A.2970:ii.31])

lu-Ia'madium(?)

Šulgi 46/viii/3
lú-kin-gi$_4$-a-/lú-ìa-ma$^{!?}$(⌜AB⌝)-dì-um (Gomi, *Orient* 16 [1980] 42, no. 10:3 Liverpool Merseyside County Museums 51-63-122:4)

5. MARI[55]

'à-um (Ḥayyum)[56]

[Amar-Suena 4]/iii/7
'à-um lú-ma-rí^{ki} (Owen, *MVN* 3 384:11 [= FLP 1383:11])

Amar-Suena 4/iii/22
'à-um lú-ma-rí^{ki} (Hallo, *TLB* 3 24:3 = Weidner, *RSO* 9 [1921-23] 474 P370:3)

Amar-Suena 4/v/6$^{!}$ (so Cagni, collation)
'à-um$^{!}$ lú-ma-rí^{ki} (Schneider, *AnOr* 7 [1932] 99:18, collated by Cagni who read líl-la in *OA* 22 [1983] 91. However, this reading is unlikely in view of parallel texts, and

---

[55] A list of Mari Ur III names appears in Durand's "Šakkanakku" (1985) 170 and in Gelb's "Mari" (1992) especially pp. 151-160. However, our list here adds a name and corrects others listed by Durand. We do not include the name Išbi-Erra since it is known only from Old Babylonian sources (for which see Edzard and Farber, *RGTC* 2 [1974] 129) nor do we list the names of the governors-general (*šakkanakku*) who may be dated to the Ur III period. References to the latter have been collected by Durand and Gelb in the articles cited immediately above.

[56] On the proposed reading Ḥayyum, see E. Arcari, "Remarks on AnOr 7,99 and Parallel Texts," *Or* 53 (1984) 442-443 now followed for additional reasons by C.H. Gordon, "Eblaitica," *Eblaitica* 1 (1987) 19-20. The same interpretation seems to be implied by Durand who reads the name as 'à-um in "Šakkanakku" (1985) 170. The name has been read also as líl-lá and as É.MES. See the comments of Gelb, "Mari" (1992) 161, where the reading É.MES is retained.

another collation is warranted; see below for revised transliteration. See also E. Arcari, *Or* 53 [1984] 443.)

Amar-Suena 4/v/19
'à-um lú-ma-rí^{ki} (Sollberger, *AfO* 19 [1959-60] 120:17 = idem, *MVN* 5 111:17; see below for revised transliteration.)

Šu-Sin 2/iv/6
'à-um lú-ma-rí^{ki} (Oppenheim, *AOS* 32 R 11:2 = Sauren, *PIOL* 19 274:2)

Šu-Sin 2/vi/30
'à-um lú-ma-rí^{ki} (Keiser and Kang, *BIN* 3 221:34)

Abu-ṭab

Amar-Suena 7/v/21
[a-b]u-DU$_{10}$ lú-ma-rí^{ki} (Owen and Veenker, "MeGum," p. 267 Trout 1:7)

Šu-Suen 1/iii/7
a-bu-DU$_{10}$ lú-ma-rí^{ki} (de Genouillac, *TrD* 18:5)

Šu-Sin 1/iv/1
a-bu-DU$_{10}$ lú-ma-rí^{ki} (Sigrist, *AUCT* 3 294:25 [= AUAM 73.1044:25])

Šu-Sin 1/iv/18
a-bu-DU$_{10}$ lú-ma-rí^{ki} (Çığ, et al. *PDT* 1 567:6)

Šu-Sin 1/vi/21
a-bu-DU$_{10}$ lú-ma-rí^{ki} (Watson, *Birmingham* 1 95:1-2)

[Šu-Sin 6/viii/?]
a-bu-DU$_{10}$ lú-ma-r[í^{ki}] (Goetze, *JCS* 7 [1953] 107 Kenrick Theological Seminary 72 iii 2)

Šu-Sin 6/viii/14
a-bu-DU$_{10}$ lú-ma-rí^{ki} (Buccellati, *Amorites*, Plate x, 21:15 [= A.29365:15])

Šu-Sin 6/⟨viii⟩/20
a-bu-DU$_{10}$ lú-ma-rí^{ki} (Buccellati, *Amorites*, Plate xi-xii, 21:19 [= A.2970:19])

Adatum

Šulgi 45/x/6
a-da-tum lú-ma-r[í$^{?ki}$] (Owen, A.3188:3, name quoted by Gelb, "Mari" [1992] 160)

Amir-^{d}Šulgi (=? Amur-^{d}Šulgi)[57]

Šulgi 47/viii/28
a-mi-ir-^{d}šul-gi lú-ma-rí^{ki} (Owen, *MVN* 15 189:14 [= Kelsey 89125:14])

Šulgi 47/x/16
a$^{!}$-mi$^{!}$-ir-^{d}šu[l-gi]...^{d}šul-gi-pa-lí-il lú-ma-rí^{ki}-me (Fish, *CST* 190:2-5, collated with corrections by Gomi, *MVN* 12, p. 103 with partial copy on Plate cv. The reading here is based on Owen, *MVN* 15 189:14 [= Kelsey 89125:14])

Šulgi 48/ix/9
a-mi-ir-^{d}šul-gi...^{d}š[ul-gi-pa-lí-il]...aq-ba-ìa...ì-lí-iš-ti-kál lú-ma-rí^{ki}-me (Schneider, *Or*SP 18 [1925] 17:22-32)

Amur-^{d}Šulgi (=? Amir-^{d}Šulgi)[58]

Amar-Suena 4/vii/1
a-mur-^{d}šul-gi (Sigrist, apud Spar, *CTMMA* 1 17:75 [without GN])

Amar-Suena 8/viii/11
a-mur-^{d}šul-gi...^{d}šul-gi-pa-lí-il...aq$^{!}$-ba-ìa lú-ma-rí$^{\langle ki \rangle}$-me (King, *CT* 32 [1912], Plate 23 104458:rev. 1-5)

Aqbaya

Šulgi 46/viii/3
aq-ba-ìa (Gomi, *Orient* 16 [1980] 42 no. 10:4)

Šulgi 48/ix/9
...aq-ba-ìa...ì-lí-iš-ti-kál lú-ma-rí^{ki}-me (Schneider, *Or*SP 18 [1925] 17:28-32)

Amar-Suena 2/viii/6
aq-ba-ìa lú-ma-rí^{ki} (Watson, *Birmingham* 1 77:6-7)

Amar-Suena 4/i/6
aq-ba-ìa (de Genouillac, *TCL* 2 5508:iii:9)

---

[57] While it is likely that MUR is to be read *mir*$_{x}$ in this name, a not unusual factor given the variability of the vowels in CVC signs, it should be noted that there is a clear chronological separation between the sources for the syllabic spellings that occur in the reign of Šulgi and the exclusive writing with MUR, which occurs in the later reign of Amar-Suen.

[58] See the preceding note.

Amar-Suena 4/vii/1
aq-ba-ìa (Sigrist, apud Spar, *CTMMA* 1 17:79 [without GN])

Amar-Suena 5/iv/19
aq-ba-ìa (Owen, *MVN* 11 152:6 [HSM 911.3.48:6])

Amar-Suena 6/-/-
aq$^{!}$-ba$^{!}$-ìa lú-ma-rí^{ki} (Cagni and Pettinato, *MVN* 4 71:37)[59]

Amar-Suena 8/viii/11
a-mur-^{d}šul-gi...^{d}šul-gi-pa-lí-il...aq$^{!}$-ba-ìa lú-ma-rí$^{\langle ki \rangle}$-me (King, *CT* 32 [1912], Plate 23 104458:rev. 1-5)

Amar-Suena 8/xii/29
^{d}šul-gi-pa-lí-il...aq-ba-ìa...^{d}šul-gi-ì-lí (Nies, *UDT* 92:30-32 [without GN])

[Girisaga][60]

Idin-aka

Amar-Suena 6/iv/4
i-din-AK lú-ma-rí^{ki} (Goetze, *JCS* 7 [1953], 104a Smith College 473:14. Goetze read i-mur-AG. We follow Edzard and Farber, *RGTC* 2 [1974] 129.)

Ili-dan

Date unknown
ì-lí-dan (Gelb, "Mari" [1992] 161 Dawson 9)

---

[59] Reading follows the convincing suggestion of C. Wilcke, "Anmerkungen zum 'Konjugationspräfix' /i/- und zur These vom 'silbischen Charakter der sumerischen Morpheme' anhand neusumerischer Verbalformen beginnend mit ì-íb-, ì-im- und ì-in-," *ZA* 78 (1988) 26 n. 93 and idem "Genealogical and Geographical Thought in the Sumerian King List," in H. Behrens, D. Loding, and M.T. Roth, eds., *DUMU-E$_2$-DUB-BA-A: Studies in Honor of Åke W. Sjöberg* (Philadelphia, 1989) 560 n. 20. If the name is to be read as copied, ⌈gìri$^{?}$-sa$_6$$^{?}$-ga⌉, then it would represent a new ambassador from Mari, bearing an unlikely Sumerian name. Collation of the text is required.

[60] This name should be deleted from the list of Mari names. See preceding note.

Iliš-tikal[61]

Šulgi 48/ix/9
...^{d}š[ul-gi-pa-lí-il]...aq-ba-ìa...ì-lí-iš-ti-kál lú-ma-rí^{ki}-me (Schneider, *Or*SP 18 [1925] 17:22-32)

Amar-Suena 2/xi/-
ì-lí-iš-ti-kál (courtesy Hallo, YBC 3635:iv [without GN])[62]

Ilum-abi

Šulgi 46/iv/25
ì-lum-a-bi$^{!}$ lú-ma-rí^{ki} (Fish, *CST* 107:5, collated and corrected by Gomi, *MVN* 12, p. 98. Change readings in Edzard and Farber, *RGTC* 2 [1974] 129 and Gelb, *MAD* 3 where they read ilum-a-ḫi based on Fish's *ṭab*[DU$_{10}$].)

Išme-^{d}Dagan

Amar-Suena 1/ii/26
iš-me-^{d}da-gan lú-ma-rí^{ki} (courtesy Young, Wabash 1:8)

Amar-Suena 1/iii/4
iš-me-^{d}da-gan lú-ma-rí^{ki} (Çığ, et al., *PDT* 1 594:12)

[It]rak-ili

Šulgi 47/iv/25
[it]-ra-ak-DINGIR lú-ma-rí^{ki} (Çığ, et al., *PDT* 1 161:rev. 1, collated and corrected by Picchioni, *OA* 14 [1978] 156. Change reading in Edzard and Farber, *RGTC* 2 [1974] 129.)

Kapanum

Amar-Suena 4/i/6
kà-pá-núm u$_4$-da-tuš lú-ma-rí^{ki} (de Genouillac, *TCL* 5 6063:x:33')

---

[61] The interpretation of this name is uncertain. See following note. It has been overlooked hitherto as a Mariote. As has been pointed out in my review of *RGTC* 2 (*JCS* 33 [1981] 266), much more care is required in the checking of the contexts of texts with the pattern lú-GN-me. This name was not noted in that review and has been missed by most everyone else. However, Gelb included him in his list of Mariotes compiled in "Mari" (1992) 161.

[62] YBC 3635 is a twelve column summary of royal deliveries. Compare the Mardu name, Iliš-Baba (Owen, review of *RGTC* 2, *JCS* 33 [1981] 256) and similarly constructed Amorite names listed by Gelb, *Computer-aided Analysis of Amorite* (Chicago, 1980; *AS* 21) 594, nos. 2733-2738. See also the remarks on Old Babylonian names with iliš (*ili* + adverbial *-iš*) by M. Stol, "Old Babylonian Personal Names," *SEL* 8 (1991) 195-196.

Laqip(um)

Amar-Suena 8/[i]v/[ ]
la-qì-pu-um lú-ma-rí^{ki} (Molina, MM 1103:5)

Amar-Suena 8/iv/[ ]
la-qì-pu-um lú-ma-rí^{ki} (Çığ, et al., *PDT* 1 180:2)

Amar-Suena 8/v/15
la-qì-ip lú-ma-rí^{ki} (Sigrist, *TPTS* 1 73:4)

Amar-Suena 8/v/28
la-qì-pu-um lú-ma-rí^{ki} (Owen, *MVN* 15 204:13 [= Kelsey Museum 89234:13])

Puzur-^{d}Adad

Amar-Suena 8/viii/-
puzur$_4$-^{d}adad lú-kin-gi$_4$-a-lú-má$^!$-ri$^!$-ke$_4$$^{[k]i}$ (Myhrman, *BE* 3 46:6)

Puzur-Mama

[Amar-Suena ?/?]/7
puzur$_4$-ma-ma lú-ma-rí^{ki} (Dhorme, *RA* 9 [1912] 56 SA 239)

Amar-Suena 2/iii/13
puzur$_4$-ma-ma lú-ma-rí^{ki} (Dhorme, *RA* 9 [1912] 59 SA 79:2 = Owen, *MVN* 15 360:2 [= Birmingham (Alabama) Art Museum 56.86.1:2])

Amar-Suena 2/iii/20
puzur$_4$-ma-ma lú-ma-rí^{ki} (Goetze, *JCS* 7 [1953] 104 St. Louis City Art Museum 61:27,1)

Amar-Suena 2/vi/3
puzur$_4$-ma-ma lú-ma-rí^{ki} (Fish, *CST* 254:5)

Amar-Suena 2/vi/4
puzur$_4$-ma-ma lú-ma-ri^{ki} (Legrain, *TRU* 305:8)

Amar-Suena 2/vi/8
puzur$_4$-ma-ma lú-ma-rí^{ki} (Arnaud, Laval 2544 = AO 26098:14, quoted in Pettinato, *RLA* 5 [1976-1980] 10a)

Amar-Suena 2/vii/21
puzur$_4$-ma/-ma lú-ma-rí^{ki} (Owen, "Yaḫmadiu" [1993], in press, Anonymous 3:10)

Amar-Suena 2/viii/-
puzur$_4$-ma-ma lú-ma-rí^{ki} (Goetze, *JCS* 7 [1953] 105 NCBT 1593:2)

Amar-Suena 3/iv/14
puzur$_4$-ma-ma lú-ma-rí^{ki} (courtesy Hallo, NCBT 1669:2)

Šeda-kuku

Amar-Suena 4/vii/1
še-da-ku-ku lú-ma-rí^{ki} (Sigrist, apud Spar, *CTMMA* 1 17:92)[63]

Šu-^{d}Dagan

Amar-Suena 5/x/18
šu-^{d}da-gan lú-ma-rí^{ki} (Jean, *ŠA* VI:2)

Šu-^{d}Išḫara

Amar-Suena [6]/iv/1 (so collation, Gomi)
šu-^{d}iš-ḫa-ra lú-ma-rí^{ki} (Fish, *CST* 468:8, collated by Gomi, *MVN* 12, p. 114)

Amar-Suena 6/iv/4
šu-^{d}iš-ḫa-ra lú-ma-rí^{ki} (Goetze, *JCS* 7 [1953] 104 Smith College 473:12)

Amar-Suena 6/iv/5
šu-^{d}iš-ḫa-ra lú-ma-rí^{ki} (Sigrist, Owen and Young, *MVN* 13 635:8 [= FLP 277:8])

Amar-Suena 6/iv/6
šu-^{d}ḫa:iš-ra lú-ma-rí^{ki} (Legrain, *TRU* 344:20)

Amar-Suena 6/iv/23
šu-^{d}iš-ḫa-ra lú-ma-rí^{ki} (Gomi and Hirose, *Hirose* 231:8)

Amar-Suena 6/iv/26
šu-^{d}iš-ḫa-ra lú-ma-rí^{ki} (Owen, *MVN* 11 146:14 [= HSM 911.3.31:14])

^{d}Šulgi-ili(?)

Šulgi 47/x/16

[63] Šeda-kuku is otherwise known to have been from Maḫ(i)li (Edzard and Farber, *RGTC* 2 [1974] 115 s.v.) and his identification in this text as being from Mari may be a scribal error. See now the comments of R. Zadok, "Elamite Onomastics," *SEL* 8 (1991) 238.

$^{d!}$š[ul$^{?}$-gi$^{?}$-ì$^{?}$-lí$^{?}$]...^{d}šul-gi-pa-lí-il lú-ma-rí^{ki}-me (Fish, *CST* 190, collated with corrections by Gomi, *MVN* 12, p. 103)

Amar-Suena 4/vii/1
^{d}šul-gi-ì-lí (Sigrist, apud Spar, *CTMMA* 1 17:73 [without GN])

Amar-Suena 8/xii/29
^{d}šul-gi-pa-lí-il...aq-ba-ìa...^{d}šul-gi-ì-lí (Nies, *UDT* 92:30-32 [without GN])

^{d}Šulgi-palil

Šulgi 47/viii/28
^{d}šul-gi-pa-lí-il lú-ma-rí^{ki} (Owen, *MVN* 15 189:17 [= Kelsey Museum 89125:17])

Šulgi 47/x/16
$^{d!}$š[ul$^{?}$-gi$^{?}$-ì$^{?}$-lí$^{?}$]...^{d}šul-gi-pa-lí-il lú-ma-rí^{ki}-me (Fish, *CST* 190:4-5, collated with corrections by Gomi, *MVN* 12, p. 103)

Šulgi 48/ix/9
...^{d}š[ul-gi-pa-lí-il]...aq-ba-ìa...ì-lí-iš-ti-kál lú-ma-rí^{ki}-me (Schneider, *Or*SP 18 [1925] 17:22-32)

Amar-Suena 4/vii/1
^{d}šul-gi-pa-lí-il (Sigrist, apud Spar, *CTMMA* 1 17:77)

[Amar-Suena 8$^{?}$/?/?]
^{d}šul-gi-pa-lí-il (Yıldız and Gomi, *PDT* 2 959:vi,7)

Amar-Suena 8/viii/11
...^{d}šul-gi-pa-lí-il...aq$^{!}$-ba-ìa lú-ma-rí$^{(ki)}$-me (King, *CT* 32 [1912], Plate 23 104458:rev. 3-5)

Amar-Suena 8/xii/29
^{d}šul-gi-pa-lí-il...aq-ba-ìa...^{d}šul-gi-ì-lí (Nies, *UDT* 92:30-32 [without GN])

[Amar-Suena 8/?/1-30]
^{d}šul-gi-pa-lí-il lú-ma-rí^{ki} (Yıldız and Gomi, *PDT* 2 959:vi: rev. 7)

Šu-Mama

Amar-Suen 2/xi/15
šu-ma-ma lú-ma-rí^{ki} (Archi and Pomponio, *TCND* 232:9)

Turam-^{d}Dagan

Amar-Suena 3/i/3
tù{-a}-ra-am-^{d}da-gan lú-ma-rí$^{!ki}$ (Jones and Snyder, *SET* 59:11)

[x-G]I$^{?}$-ŠI$^{?}$

[Ibbi-Sin(?) ?]/i/19[64]
[x-G]I$^{?}$-ŠI? lú-ma-rí^{ki} (Sigrist, *AUCT* 3 480:37 [= AUAM 73 1323]. Originally read by Owen, review of *RGTC* 2, *JCS* 33 [1981] 259 as ig-gi-lim and quoted by J.-M. Durand, "Šakkanakku" [1985] 170, the reading cannot be confirmed. The tablet was collated by B. Shea, letter of 25.ii.86, and again by Owen, 8.iii.86. The damaged tablet does not retain the remains of the signs as copied by Sigrist and quoted in *JCS* 33 [1981] 259. The ŠI does not have a clear vertical as copied by Sigrist and which appears in the published copy. Thus the PN must remain, for the time being, obscure.)

lu-Mari^{ki}

[Date Broken]
lú-ma-rí^{ki}-me (Oppenheim, *AOS* 32 C 1:iii:10 = Sauren, *PIOL* 19 373:iii:10)

Šulgi 43/i/-
lú-ma-rí^{ki} (courtesy Sigrist, *Toronto* 279 [ROM 925.62.267])

Šulgi 45/viii/30
kaš$_{4}$ lú-ma-rí^{ki} (Snell and Lager, *YOS* 18 12:28)

Šulgi 46/?/?
lú-ma-rí^{ki}-me (Chiera, *Princeton Catalogue* Ex 250)

Šulgi 46/viii/3
lú-kin-gi$_{4}$-a-lú-ma-rí^{ki} (Gomi, *Orient* 16 [1980] 42, no. 10:4 Liverpool Merseyside County Museums 51-63-122:4)

Šulgi 46/ix/- (Lagaš)
sipa-lú-ma-rí^{ki} (Nies, *UDT* 29:7)

Šulgi 47/ix/9 (Drehem)

---

[64] The reconstructed date to the reign of Ibbi-Sin is based on the seal inscription of the scribe, Ur-Enlila, son of Lugal-ura. A scribe by this name is known from a single seal from Ibbi-Sin 2 (Çığ, et al., *PDT* 1 310) although the seal is not of the same type. A date during the reign of Šu-Suen probably is excluded on the basis of the offering to ^{d}šu-^{d}suen. Offerings are made to deified kings usually, but not exclusively, after their deaths (see S. Greengus, "Bridewealth in Sumerian Sources," *HUCA* 61 [1991] 38 n. 56 with bibliography). Prosopographical considerations based on the careers of Atu, Bazaza and Nanna-kam would allow for dates during the reign of Šu-Suen as well.

lú-ma-rí^{ki} (Sigrist, *AUCT* 1 494:5)

Šulgi 47/vii/17 (Drehem)
kaš$_4$-lú-ma-rí^{ki} (Snell and Lager, *YOS* 18 12:28)

Amar-Suena 8/viii/- (Nippur)
lú-ma-ri-ke$_4$-ne (Myhrman, *BE* 3 46:5)

Šu-Sin 8/i-xii/- (Lagaš)
lú-^{giš}tukul-ma-rí^{ki} (Virolleaud, *TEL* 46:iii:3)

6. MUKIŠ[65]

Gababa

Amar-Suena 9/xi/3
ga-ba-ba lú-mu-ki-iš^{ki} (Owen, A.2852, transliteration below)[66]

Amar-Suen 9/xi/4
ga-ba-ba lú-mu-ki-iš^{ki} (Archi and Pomponio, *TCND* 260:7 = Boson, *TCSD* 203:7)

7. TERQA[67]

éren-Terqa^{ki}

[Date Broken]
éren-te-er-qà^{ki} (de Genouillac, *TrD*, 54:i:3)

---

[65] Neither Mukiš nor Gababa, the man of Mukiš, was listed in Owen and Veenker, "MeGum," passim.

[66] A.2852, cited by Gelb in "Topography" (1938) 82, has remained unpublished (see also Edzard and Farber, *RGTC* 2 [1974] 133-134). See my review of Archi and Pomponio, *TCND*, in *OLZ* 82 (1992) for comments to this text.

[67] Steinkeller (letter of 21.ii.92) pointed out to me me that this Terqa probably is not the Syrian city but a Terqa in the Diyala region as already concluded by R.M. Whiting, "Tiš-atal of Nineveh and Babati, Uncle of Šu-Sin," *JCS* 28 (1976) 180-181 and n. 20-21. Whiting convincingly equated the Terqa of our text with *ter-qa-an šá pa-an qù-ti* of *KAV* 183:14 located in the vicinity of Assyrian Ḫarḫar (= Ur III Karaḫar) as against the original association with the homonymous city at Tell Ashara on the Euphrates near Mari (Gelb, "Topography" [1938] 84-85 and Edzard and Farber, *RGTC* 2 [1974], p. 192). If this is the case, then these references and the associated texts included below, should be deleted from this compilation.

8. TUTTUL[68]

^{d}Dagan-abu

Amar-Suena 4/v/6$^{!}$
^{d}da-gan-a-bu lú-kin-gi$_{4}$-a ìa-ši-li-im énsi-tu-tu-la^{ki} (Schneider, *AnOr* 7 [1932] 99:18,[69] collated by Cagni, *OA* 22 [1983] 91; revised transliteration below.)

Amar-Suena 4/v/9
^{d}da-gan-a-bu lú-kin-gi$_{4}$-a ìa-ši-lim énsi-tu-tu-la^{ki} (Sollberger, *AfO* 19 [1959-60] 120 = idem, *MVN* 5 111:18; revised transliteration below.)

Iaši-Lim

Amar-Suena 4/v/6$^{!}$ (so Cagni, collation)
ìa-ši-li-im énsi-tu-tu-la^{ki} (Schneider, *AnOr* 7 [1932] 99:18, collated by Cagni, *OA* 22 [1983] 91; revised transliteration below.)

Puzur-Dagan

Amar-Suena 7/v/21
puzur$_{4}$-^{d}da-gan lú-tu-tu-ul^{ki} (Owen and Veenker, "MeGum," p. 267 Trout 1:11 with comments on p. 268)

9. URŠU

Budur

Amar-Suena 1/ii/26
bu-du-úr lú-ur-šu^{ki} (courtesy Young, Wabash 1:6)

Amar-Suena 1/iii/4
bu-du-úr lú-ur-šu^{ki} (Çığ, et al., *PDT* 1 594:14)

Dasalibri

Šu-Sin 2/iv/6
da-sal-ib-ri lú-ur-šu$^{ki!}$ (Oppenheim, *AOS* 32 R 11:4 = Sauren, *PIOL* 19 274:4)

---

[68] Tuttul is much better attested in the Ebla sources as collected by A. Archi, "Tuttul-sur-Baliḫ à l'âge d'Ebla," in Ö. Tunca, ed., *De la Babylonie à la Syrie, en passant par Mari: Mélanges offerts à Monsieur J.-R. Kupper* (Liège, 1990) 197-207.

[69] Following the line numbers of our transliteration below.

Šu-Sin 2/vi/30
da-sal-ib-ri lú-ur-šu^{ki} (Keiser and Kang, *BIN* 3 221:35)

Gura'a[70]

[Amar-Suena 4]/iii/7
gu-ra-a lú-ur-šu^{ki} (Owen, *MVN* 3 384:10 [= FLP 1383:10]. On p. 27 under catalogue description of 384:10, erroneously read as tibir-ra-a.)

Amar-Suena 4/iii/12
gu-ra-a lú-ur-šu^{ki} (Hallo, *TLB* 3 24:2 = Weidner, *RSO* 9 [1921-23] 474 P370:2)

Amar-Suena 4/v/6$^{!}$ (so Cagni, collation)
gu-r[a]$^{!}$-a lú-ur-[šu^{k}]^{i} (Schneider, *AnOr* 7 [1932] 99:17, cited by Goetze, *JCS* 7 [1953] 103 note 4 as gu-la-a and erroneously restored by Sollberger, *AfO* 19 [1959-60] 121 as a man from Ebla. See the collation and comments of Cagni, *OA* 22 [1983] 90-91 and Arcari, *Or* 53 [1984] 442-443. Revised transliterations below.)

Amar-Suena 4/v/9
gu-ra-a lú-ur$^{!}$-šu$^{!ki}$ (Sollberger, *AfO* 19 [1959-60] 120 = idem, *MVN* 5 111:16; revised transliteration below.)

[Er]ištiar

Amar-Suena 7/v/21
[e$^{?}$-r]i-iš-ti-ar lú-ur-šu^{ki} (Owen and Veenker, "MeGum," p. 267 Trout 1:9 with comments on p. 268)

Kurb-ilak[71]

(no date)
kur-bi-la-ak lú-ur-šu^{ki} (Contenau, *UDU* 27:1-3)

Nana'u

Amar-Suena 1/iii/4
na-[na$^{?}$-ù$^{?}$] ⌜lú-kin⌝-gi$_{4}$-/a ⌜lú⌝-[ur$^{?}$-šu$^{?ki}$] (Çığ, et al., *PDT* 1 594:20)

---

[70] See note 46 above.

[71] If the copy is accurate and not to be read eb$^{!}$-la$^{!ki}$, then Kurb-ilak would be the only "ambassador" known to have come from two Syrian cities, Ebla and Uršu. This may be another case of mis-writing by either the original scribe or the modern copyist as occured with Gura'a, originally thought to have come from both Ebla and Uršu but known now to have been only from Uršu.

Amar-Suena 2/iii/13
na-na-ù lú-ur-šu^{ki} (Dhorme, *RA* 9 [1912] 59 SA 79:4 = Owen, *MVN* 15 360:4 [= Birmingham (Alabama) Art Museum 56.86.1:4])

Amar-Suena 2/iii/20
na-na-ù lú-ur-šu^{ki} (Goetze, *JCS* 7 [1953] 104 St. Louis City Art Museum 61:27, 3)

Amar-Suena 3/iv/14
na-na-⌈ù⌉ lú-[ur]-šu^{ki} (courtesy Hallo, NCBT 1669:6)

lu-Uršu^{ki}

Šulgi 31/vii/9
lú-ur-šu^{ki} (Nesbit, III:2)

Šulgi 47/ix/9
lú-ur-šu^{ki} (Sigrist, *AUCT* 1 494:6)

Index of Syrian Personal Names

’à-um (see Ḥayyum)
Abu-ṭab (Mari: AS 7-SS 6)
Adatum (Mari: date unknown)
Amir-^{d}Šulgi (Mari: Š 47-48)
Amur-^{d}Šulgi (Mari: AS 8)
Aqbaya (Mari: Š 48-AS 8)
Budur (Uršu: AS 1)
^{d}Dagan-abu (Tuttul: AS 4)
Dasalibri (Ursu: ŠS 2)
Dulqanum (Yaḫmadu: AS 2)
[Er]ištiar (Uršu: AS 7)
Ezun-^{d}Dagan (Ebla: ŠS 3)
Gababa (Mukiš: AS 9)
Gura’a (Uršu: AS 4)
Ḥayyum [’à-um] (Mari: AS 4-ŠS 2)
Iaši-Lim (Tuttul: AS 4)
Ibati (Gubla: AS 4)
Ibdati (Gubla: AS 4)
Idin-aka (Mari: AS 4)
Igriš-Ḫepa (Ebla: ?)
Ili-^{d}Dagan (Ebla: Š 44-AS 6)
Ili-dan (Mari: ?)
Iliš-tikal (Mari: Š 48)
Ilum-abi (Mari: Š 46)
Išme-^{d}Dagan (Mari: AS 1)
Itrak-ili (Mari: Š 47)
Izzin-^{d}Dagan (Ebla: ŠS 6)
Kapanum (Mari: AS 4)
Kurb-ilak (Ebla: ŠS 6)
Kurb-ilak (Uršu(?): ?)
Laqip(um) (Mari: AS 8)
MeGum (Ebla: AS 7)
Meme-šura (Ebla: ?)
Nana’u (Uršu: AS 1-3)
Nur-ili (Gu-Ebla: Š 43)
Puzur-^{d}Adad (Mari: AS 8)
Puzur-^{d}Dagan (Tuttul: AS 7)
Puzur-Mama (Mari: AS 2-4)
Šeda-kuku (Mari(?): AS 4)
Šu-^{d}Dagan (Mari: ?)
Šu-^{d}Išḫara (Mari: AS 6)
^{d}Šulgi-ili (Mari(?): Š 47-AS 8)
^{d}Šulgi-palil (Mari: Š 47-AS 8)
Šu-Mama (Mari: AS 2)
Turam-^{d}Dagan (Mari: AS 3)
Zurim (Ebla: Š 46-AS 7?)
[x-x-g]i-zi (Abarnium: AS 4)
[x-G]I$^{?}$-ŠI$^{?}$ (Mari: IS 2?)

Concordance of Quoted Texts[72]

5. A.2970, collated = Buccellati, *Amorites*, plates xi-xii, no. 22
4. A.29365 = Buccellati, *Amorites*, plate x, no. 21
3. AO.26358 = Arnaud [= Laval 2544]
1. Archi and Pomponio, *TCND* 260 = Boson, *TCSD* 203
2. Archi and Pomponio, *TCND* 232
3. Arnaud, AO.26358 [= Laval 2544]
62. AUAM 73.1044 = Sigrist, *AUCT* 3 294
63. AUAM 73.1323 = Sigrist, *AUCT* 3 480
61. AUAM 73.1362 = Sigrist, *AUCT* 1 494
52. Birmingham (Alabama) Art Museum 56.86.1 = Dhorme, *RA* 9 (1912) 59 SA 79 = Owen, *MVN* 15 360
1. Boson, *TCSD* 203 = Archi and Pomponio, *TCND* 260
4. Buccellati, *Amorites*, plate x, no. 21 [= A.29365]
5. Buccellati, *Amorites*, plates xi-xii, no. 22 [= A.2970, collated]
6. Cagni and Pettinato, *MVN* 4 71
7. Chiera, *Princeton Catalogue* Ex 250
8. Çığ, et al., *PDT* 1 161, collated by Picchioni, *OA* 14 (1975) 156 and Gomi (unpublished)
9. Çığ, et al., *PDT* 1 180, collated by Gomi (unpublished)
10. Çığ, et al., *PDT* 1 567, collated by Picchioni, *OA* 14 (1975) 166 and Gomi (unpublished)
11. Çığ, et al., *PDT* 1 594, collated by Picchioni, *OA* 14 (1975) 166 and Gomi (unpublished)
12. Contenau, *UDU* 27
13. Dhorme, *RA* 9 (1912) 56 SA 239
53. Dhorme, *RA* 9 (1912) 59 SA 79= Owen, *MVN* 15 360 [= Birmingham (Alabama) Art Museum 56.86.1]
14. Fish, *CST* 107
15. Fish, *CST* 190, collated with corrections by Gomi, *MVN* 12, p. 103
16. Fish, *CST* 254 copy of obverse also published in *BJRL* 8 (1924) 110, no. 507, collated by Gomi, *MVN* 12, p. 105
17. Fish, *CST* 468, collated by Gomi, *MVN* 12, p. 114 with copy of traces on plate cvi
26. Fish, *MCS* 7 (1957) 9-20 Liverpool 51-63-51 = Gomi, *Orient* 16 (1980) 40, no. 7 Liverpool Merseyside County Museums 51-63-51
67. FLP 277 = Sigrist, Owen and Young, *MVN* 13 635
48. FLP 1383 = Owen, *MVN* 3 384
18. *Gelb, "Mari and the Kish Civilization," p. 161, Dawson 9 (unpublished)
19. *de Genouillac, *TCL* 5 6063
20. de Genouillac, *TrD* 18
21. de Genouillac, *TrD* 54
22. Goetze, *JCS* 7 (1953) 104 Smith College 473
23. Goetze, *JCS* 7 (1953) 104 St. Louis City Art Museum 61:27

[72] The presence of an * before an entry indicates the text is not included among the transliterations. Bolded numbers indicate primary entry.

24. Goetze, *JCS* 7 (1953) 105 NCBT (collated)
25. Goetze, *JCS* 7 (1953) 106 Kenrick 72 = Jean, *ŠA* LXXI:85
26. Gomi, *Orient* 16 (1980) 40, no. 7 Liverpool Merseyside County Museums 51-63-51 = Fish, *MCS* 7 (1957) 9-20 Liverpool 51-63-51
27. Gomi, *Orient* 16 (1980) 42, no. 10 Liverpool Merseyside County Museums 51-63-122
28. Gomi and Hirose, *Hirose* 231
29. Hallo, NCBT 1669
30. Hallo, *TLB* 3 (1963-73) 24 = Weidner, *RSO* 9 (1921-23) 472 P370
49. HSM 911.3.31 = Owen, *MVN* 11 146
50. HSM 911.3.48 = Owen, *MVN* 11 152
55. *ITT* 4 7101 = Pettinato, *MVN* 6 100
56. **ITT* 4 7111 = Pettinato, *MVN* 6 100
57. **ITT* 4 7253 = Pettinato, *MVN* 6 247
31. Jean, *ŠA* VI:2
25. Jean, *ŠA* LXXI:85 = Goetze, *JCS* 7 (1953) 106 Kenrick 72
32. Jones and Snyder, *SET* 59
33. Keiser and Kang, *BIN* 3 221
51. Kelsey Museum 89125 = Owen, *MVN* 15 189
52. Kelsey Museum 89234 = Owen, *MVN* 15 204
34. King, *CT* 32 (1912), Plate 23 BM 104458
35. Legrain, *TRU* 305
36. Legrain, *TRU* 344
26. Liverpool Merseyside County Museums 51-63-51 = Fish, *MCS* 7 (1957) 9-20 Liverpool 51-63-51 = Gomi, *Orient* 16 (1980) 40, no. 7
27. Liverpool Merseyside County Museums 51-63-122 = Gomi, *Orient* 16 (1980) 42, no. 10
37. Luckenbill, *AJSL* 39 (1922) 65-66
77. Molina, MM 1103
38. Myhrman, *BE* 3 46 [= CBS 10230]
39. Nesbit, iii
29. NCBT 1669
54. NCBT 1978
40. Nies, *UDT* 29
41. Nies, *UDT* 92
42. *Oppenheim, *AOS* 32 C 1 = Sauren, *PIOL* 19 373
43. Oppenheim, *AOS* 32 R 11 = Sauren, *PIOL* 19 274
44. Owen, A.2852
45. Owen, A.3188
46. Owen, Anonymous 1
47. Owen, *Hallo AV*, Anonymous 3
48. Owen, *MVN* 3 384 [= FLP 1383]
49. Owen, *MVN* 11 146 [= HSM 91.3. 31]
50. Owen, *MVN* 11 152 [= HSM 911.3. 48]
51. Owen, *MVN* 15 189 [= Kelsey Museum 89125]
52. Owen, *MVN* 15 204 [= Kelsey Museum 89234]
53. Owen, *MVN* 15 360 [= Birmingham (Alabama) Art Museum 56.86.1 = Dhorme, *RA* 9 (1912) 59 SA 79]
54. Owen, Newell 1978
55. Owen and Veenker, "MeGum," p. 267 Trout 1
56. Pettinato, *MVN* 6 100 [= *ITT* 4 7101]
57. *Pettinato, *MVN* 6 110 [= *ITT* 4 7111]
58. *Pettinato, *MVN* 6 247 [= *ITT* 4 7253]
59. Pohl, *TMH NF* 1/2 313
65. PTS 312 = Sigrist, *TPTS* 1 73

66. ROM 925×62.267 = Sigrist, *Toronto* 279
67. ROM 925×62.275 = Sigrist, *Toronto* 287
ROM 910×209.593 = Sigrist, *Toronto* 639: **Note 24**
42. *Sauren, *PIOL* 19 373 = Oppenheim, *AOS* 32 C 1
43. Sauren, *PIOL* 19 274 = Oppenheim, *AOS* 32 R 11
60. Schneider, *AnOr* 7 (1932) 99; collated and transliterated by L. Cagni, *OA* 22 (1983) 90-91
61. Schneider, *Or*SP 18 (1925) 17
62. Sigrist, *AUCT* 1 494 [= AUAM 73. 362]
63. Sigrist, *AUCT* 3 294 [= AUAM 73.1044]
64. Sigrist, *AUCT* 3 480 [= AUAM 73.1323]
65. Sigrist, *TPTS* 1 73 [= PTS 312]
66. Sigrist, *Toronto* 279 [= ROM 925× 62.267]
67. Sigrist, *Toronto* 287 [= ROM 925× 62.275]
Sigrist, *Toronto* 639 [= ROM 910× 209.593]: **Note 24**
68. Sigrist, Owen and Young, *MVN* 13 635 [= FLP 277]
69. Sigrist, apud Spar, *Metropolitan* 1 17
70. Sollberger, *AfO* 19 (1959-60) 120-121 Pinches Manuscript 82 = idem, *MVN* 5 (1978) 11170.
Sollberger, *MVN* 5 (1978) 111 = idem, *AfO* 19 (1959-60) 120-121 Pinches Manuscript 82
71. *Virolleaud, *TEL* 46
72. Watson, *Birmingham* 1 77
73. Watson, *Birmingham* 1 95
30. Weidner, *RSO* 9 (1921-23) 472 P370 = Hallo, *TLB* 3 (1963-73) 24
74. *YBC 3635
75. *Yıldız and Gomi, *PDT* 2 959
76. Young, Wabash 1
77. Molina, MM 1103 (unpublished)

Concordance of Texts by Date[73]

Š 31/vii//9	Text 39.
Š 43/i/-	Text 66.
Š 44/iii/18	Text 67.
Š 45/x/6	Text 45.
Š 46/?/?	Text 7.
Š 46/?/?	Text 37.
Š 46/-/20	Note 24.
Š 46/iii/1	Text 59.
Š 46/iv/6	Text 36.
Š 46/iv/25	Text 14.
Š 46/vi/28	Text 26.
Š 46/viii/3	Text 27.
Š 46/ix/-	Text 40.
Š 47/iv/25	Text 8.
Š 47/viii/28	Text 51.
Š 47/x/16	Text 15.
Š 48/ix/9	Text 61.
AS 1/ii/26	Text 76.
AS 1/iii/4	Text 11.
AS 2/iii/13	Text 53.
AS 2/iii/20	Text 23.
AS 2/vi/3	Text 16.
AS 2/vi/4	Text 35.
AS 2/vi/8	Text 3.
AS 2/vii/6	Text 72.
AS 2/vii/21	Text 47.
AS 2/viii/-	Text 24.
AS 2/xi/-	Text 74.
AS 2/xi/15	Text 2.
AS 3/i/3	Text 32.
AS 3/iv/9	Text 29.
AS 4/i/6	Text 19.
[AS 4]/iii/7	Text 48.
AS 4/iii/22	Text 30.
AS 4/v/6	Text 60.
AS 4/v/9	Text 70.
AS 4/vii/1	Text 69.
AS 5/iv/19	Text 50.
AS 5/x/18	Text 31.
AS 6/-/-	Text 6.
AS [6]/iv/1!	Text 17.
AS 6/iv/1	Text 22.
AS 6/iv/5	Text 68.
AS 6/iv/23	Text 28.
AS 6/iv/26	Text 49.
AS 7/v/21	Text 55.
[AS 8?/?/?]	Text 75.
AS 8/iv/[?]	Text 9.
AS 8/[i]v/[?]	Text 77.
AS 8/v/15	Text 65.
AS 8/v/28	Text 52.
AS 8/viii/-	Text 38.
AS 8/viii/11	Text 34.
AS 8/xii/29	Text 41.
AS 9/xi/3	Text 44.
AS 9/xi/4	Text 1.
ŠS 1/iii/17	Text 20.
ŠS 1/iv/1	Text 63.
ŠS 1/iv/9	Text 62.
ŠS 1/iv/18	Text 10.
ŠS 1/vi/21	Text 73.
ŠS 1/vi/24	Text 54.
ŠS 2/iv/6	Text 43.
ŠS 2/vi/30	Text 33.
ŠS 3/iii/6	Text 46.
ŠS 6/?/?	Text 25.
ŠS 6/viii/14	Text 4.
ŠS 6/⟨viii⟩/20	Text 5.
ŠS 8/i-xii/-	Text 71.
[IS(?) 1(?)]/i/19	Text 64.

Dates Lost or Lacking

Texts 12, 13, 18, 21, 42, 56, 57, 58

[73] I would like to thank my Cornell University graduate students, Scott Noegel and Richard Wright, for their help in preparing the chronological concordance of tablets and the indexes of personal, geographical and professional names.

Transliterated Sources[74]

1. Archi and Pomponio, *TCND* 260 = Boson, *TCSD* 203 (AS 9/xi/4)
(1) 2 [udu]-niga (2) ^{d}inanna-unug^{ki}-šè (3) ^{d}en-líl-á-maḫ sagi / maškim (4) 1 udu-niga (5) ki-ri-ib-ul-me / lú-si-mu-ru-um^{ki} (6) gìri ḫu-zi-ri sukkal (7) 1 udu-niga **ga-ba-ba lú-/mu-ki-iš^{ki}** (8) gìri kir-ba-tal sukkal (9) árad-mu maškim (10) iti u$_4$-4 ba-zal (11) ki sú-ba-ga-ta ba-zi (12) gìri ad-da-kal-la dub-sar (13) iti ezem-me-ki-gál (14) mu en-^{d}nanna-kar-/z[i-da] ba-ḫun (15) 4 udu

2. Archi and Pomponio, *TCND* 232 (AS 2/xi/15)
(1) [1 u]du-niga-sig$_5$ (2) ^{mí}ešgar-niga-sig$_5$ (3) 6 udu-niga (4) 7 máš-gal-niga (5) kak-gu-lá-šè (6) ur-ni$_9$-gar maškim (7) 5 udu-niga (8) 5 máš-gal-niga (9) **šu-ma-ma lú-ma-rí^{ki}** (10) 1 udu-niga (11) ra-ši lú-⌜zi-/da-núm^{ki}⌝ (12) árad-mu maškim (13) 2 sila$_4$-ga šà é-gal-šè (14) lú-an-dùl rá-gaba / maškim (15) iti u$_4$-15 ba-zal (16) ki ^{d}šul-gi-a-a-mu-/ta ba-zi (17) iti ezem-me-ki-gál (18) mu ^{d}amar-^{d}suen lugal-e / [u]r-bí-lum^{ki} mu-ḫul (19-side) 28

3. Arnaud, AO.26358[75] [= Laval 2544] (AS 2/vi/8)
(1) 1 udu-niga (2) 1 máš-gal-niga (3) mu mar-tu maš-maš-tilmun$^{\langle ki\rangle}$-/ta e-ra-ne-šè (4) 4 udu (5) 1 u$_8$ (6) 4 máš-gal (7) šu-gíd mu àga-ús-e-ne-šè (8) é-muḫaldim-šè (9) 1 udu-niga (10) ra-ši lú-zi-da-núm^{ki} (11, rev.) 1 udu-niga (12) **ì-lí-^{d}da-gan / lú-eb-la^{ki}** (13) 1 máš-gal-niga (14) **puzur$_4$-ma-ma lú-ma-rí^{ki}** (15) lugal-má-gur$_8$-re maškim (16) iti u$_4$-8 ba-zal (17) ki lú-dingir-ra-ta (18) ba-zi (19) iti á-ki-ti (20) mu ^{d}amar-^{d}suen lugal-/e$^{!}$ ur-bí-lum^{ki} mu-ḫul (21-side) 14

4. Buccellati, *Amorites*, plate x, no. 21 [= A.29365] (ŠS 6/viii/14)
(1) [^{mí}eš]gar-niga 3-kam-ús (2) 1 udu-niga 4-kam-ús (3) 1 ^{mí}ešgar-niga 4-kam-ús (4) sískur-^{d}inanna-šà-é-gal (5) ^{d}nanna-palil sagi maškim (6) a-ge$_6$-ba-a (7) 5 udu-niga-gu$_4$-e-ús-sa (8) 5 máš-gal-niga-gu$_4$-e-ús-sa (9) **i-zi-in-^{d}da-gan** (10) 3 udu-niga-gu$_4$-e-ús-sa (11) **kur-bi-la-ak** (12) **lú-eb-la^{ki}-me-šè** (13) 5 udu-niga-gu$_4$-e-ús-sa (14) 5 máš-gal-niga-gu$_4$-e-ús-sa (15) **a-bu-DU$_{10}$ lú-ma-rí^{ki}** (16) 5 udu-niga-gu$_4$-e-ús-sa (17) **i-pí-iq-re-e-ú mar-tu ìa-a-ma-dì-um** (18) uru-ne-ne-šè gin-né (19) má-a ba-ne-gub (20) 3 udu-niga-gu$_4$-e-ús-sa (21) 2 máš-gal-niga-gu$_4$-e-ús-sa (22) ìa-ù-ša dumu me-ša-[nu-n]u lú-simaški(SU) (23) gìri ur-sukkal sukkal (24) árad-mu maškim (25) 2 udu-niga-sig$_5$-ús (26) 8 udu-niga 3-kam-ús (27) a-bí-sí-im-ti (28) tu-ra-am-^{d}da-gan maškim (29) á-ba-te-na (30) ud-14-kam (31) ki [a]-ba-^{d}en-líl-gin$_7$-ta (32) [ba]-zì (33) [šà]

---

[74] The following transliterations incorporate all collations known to me along with reconstructions based on parallel texts. They are reproduced from an electronic corpus of Ur III texts, primarily from Puzriš-Dagan (Drehem), being created by me at Cornell University. Many of these texts have never appeared in transliteration and it is hoped that by providing a corpus in this way the data can be more widely utilized. Presenting these texts in camera-ready copy should reduce typographical errors to a minimum. Collection numbers have often been included since certain texts have been quoted in earlier publications by these numbers. The concordance should facilitate cross references. **Bolded** names are those included above in the catalogue of Syrian names. Comments to these texts have been kept to a minimum.

[75] From a transliteration kindly provided by D. Arnaud and quoted by permisson of Mrs. B. Andrée-Salvini, Musée du Louvre.

nibru[ki] (34) gìri lú-[d]nin-šubur dub-sar (35) iti ezem-[d]šu-[d]suen (36) mu [d]šu-[d]suen lugal-urí[ki]-ma-ke$_4$ (37) na-rú-a-maḫ (38) [d]en-líl (39) [d]nin-líl (40) [mu]-ne-dù (41) 46

5. Buccellati, *Amorites*, plates xi-xii, no. 22 [= A.2970, collated] (ŠS 6/⟨viii⟩/20)
(I.) (1) [1 gú [giš]ma]-nu/ [.... sìla] kaš-sig$_5$ 4 sìla/ zì-gu-ta (2) 10 guruš 2 sìla kaš 2 sìla zì-ta (3) lú-SU[ki]-me-šè (4) 1 guruš 6 sìla kaš-sig$_5$ 4 sìla zì-gu (5) lú-ša-ri-it-ḫi[!ki] (6) 2 guruš 2 sìla kaš 2 sìla zì-ta (7) lú-ḫur-ti[ki]-me-šè (8) 10 sa gi (9) kaš$_4$-me-šè šà en-nu-gá (10) gìri be-lí-šar (11) ki na-wi-ir-ilum (12) 0.1.0. kaš-sig$_5$ (13) 0.2.0. kaš-gin (14) 0.1.0. zì-gu-sig$_5$ (15) [0.0.]5. sìla zì-še sa (16) 20! sa gi (17) 1 gú [giš]ma-nu (18) pá-na-na lú-mar-ḫa-ši[ki] (19) 1 guruš 0.0.1. kaš-sig$_5$ 0.0.1. zì-/gu (20) 2 guruš 0.0.1. kaš-sig$_5$ 5 sìla zì-/gu-ta (21) [sukkal]-eme-bal ki lú-mar-/ḫa-ši[ki] gub-ba-me-šè (22) 0.0.2. kaš-sig$_5$ 0.0.1. zì-gu-sig$_5$ (23) 10 sa gi (24) a-ri-du-bu-uk (25) dumu-ni 5 sìla kaš-sig$_5$/ 5 sìla zì-gu-ta/ 1 guruš 2 sìla kaš 2 sìla zì-ta (26) [x] guruš 2 sìla zì (27) [....] 1 sìla kaš (28) [....] zì (29) [....] (II.) (1) l[ú-ḫu-....] (2) 2 guruš [4 sìla zì-ta] (3) lú-MÙŠ.E[RIN.KI-šè] (4) 0.0.2. kaš-sig$_5$ [0.0.1 zì-gu-sig$_5$] (5) 3 sa [gi] (6) ḫu-un-zi-[ib-tum] (7) 0.0.1. kaš 0.0.1. zì 2 [sìla zì-gu] (8) šu-ab-ba mar-[tu] (9) 5 sìla kaš 5 sìla [zì-gu?] (10) ša-pu-núm SAG.[X] (11) 0.0.2. kaš-sig$_5$ 0.0.1. zì-gu-[sig$_5$[?]] (12) 5 sa gi (13) guruš ad-da (14) 5 lú-ús-sa-ni-me (15) 62 sìla kaš 2 sìla zì-ta (16) 0.0.2. kaš-sig$_5$ 0.0.2. kaš-gin (17) 0.0.1. zì-gu-sig$_5$ (18) 10 sa gi (19) **a-bu-DU$_{10}$ lú-ma-rí[ki]** (20) 2 ab-ba 0.0.1. kaš 5 sìla zì 1 [...] (21) 15 lú-ús-sa-ni 2 sìla-[ta] (22) 0.0.2. kaš-sig$_5$ 0.0.2. kaš-g[in] (23) 0.0.1. zì-gu-sig$_5$ (24) 10 sa-gi (25) **i-zi-in-[d]da-[gan]** (26) 0.0.1. kaš-sig$_5$ 5 sa-gi (27) **kur-bi-la-ak** (28) 15 guruš 2 sìla kaš 2 sìla zì-[ta] (29) **lú-eb-la[ki]-me-šè** (30) 0.0.2. kaš-sig$_5$ 5 sa gi (31) **i-pí-iq-re-e-ú mar-tu / ìa-a-ma-dì-[um[?]]** (32) 4 sìla zì lú-ús-sa-ni-[me-šè] (33) 4 sìla zì kí-ba-a-[tal] [lú-ur/]-bí-[lum[ki]-šè] (34) 4 sìla zì si-mu lú-[....] (35) 0.0.1. kaš-sig$_5$ 5 sìla zì-[gu?] (36) 10 sa [gi] (III.) (1) é-gi$_4$-a [....] (2) 4 guruš 2! [zì?-ta] (3) 10 géme 1 sìla kaš 1 sìla [zì?-ta] (4) lú-ús-sa-ni-me-[šè] (5) 0.0.2. kaš-sig$_5$ 0.0.2. kaš-gin (6) 0.0.1. zì-gu-sig$_5$ (7) 10 sa gi (8) ni-im-sí lú-ìa-ab-ra-at[ki] (9) 7 lú-ús-sa-ni 2 sìla kaš-ta (10) šu-a-gi-na (11) 0.0.3. zì i-za lú-[i]b-ni-[d]šu-[d]suen (12) 6 lú-ús-sa-ni 0.0.2. zì-ta (13) 0.0.3. zì ḫu-uz-taḫ lú-ḫu-na-t[al] (14) 6 lú-ús-sa-ni 0.0.2. zì-ta (15) 0.0.2. ḪAR-ti lú-ši-ik-ri-[i]š[[ki]] (16) 6 lú-ús-sa-ni 0.0.2. zì-ta (17) 0.0.3. zì ga[?]-ba[?]-a (18) 0.0.2. šar-ri-a (19) 0.0.3. ú-NE-nu-um (20) 0.0.3. ša-lim-be-lí (21) 0.0.2. pu-ú-la (22) 20 guruš 0.0.2. zì-ta (23) lú-a-la[ki]-me-šè (24) 0.0.2. zì i-na-LUM (25) 0.0.2. DU$_{10}$-bi-tum (26) 12 guruš 0.0.1.5 sìla zì-ta (27) lú-šu-ru-uš-kí-in (28) 0.0.2. zì lú-dam-a-ḫu-a (29) 8 lú-ús-sa-[ni 0.0.2.? z]ì-ta (30) 0.0.3. zì a-rí-ip[?][-....] (31) 19 guruš 0.0.2. zì-[ta] (32) lú-ur-bí-[lum[ki]-me-šè] (33) [....] (IV.) (1) [....] (2) [....] (0) BLANK SPACE (3) šu+nígin 0.4.4.3 sìla kaš-sig$_5$ (4) šu+nígin 1.1.[3?].1 sìla kaš-gin ⟨gur⟩ (5) šu+nígin 0.1.1.5 sìla zì-gu-sig$_5$ (6) šu+nígin 0.0.5.8 sìla zì-gu-gin (7) šu+nígin 10?.3.0.9 sìla zì-še ⟨gur⟩ (8) šu+nígin 0.0.5. zì-še sa (9) še-bi 13.4.3.3 ½ sìla gur (10) šu+nígin 104 sa gi (11) šu+nígin 1 gú [giš]ma-nu (12) u$_4$-20-kam (13) gìri lú-[d]en-líl-lá (14) mu [d]šu-[d]suen lugal-e / na-rú-a-maḫ-[d]en-[líl-/[d]n]in-líl-ra mu-[na-dù]

6. Cagni and Pettinato, *MVN* 4 71 (AS 6/-/-)
(1) ⌜10,800⌝ sa gi (2) 60 gu-kilib pa-TAR [giš]ásal (3) kìšib sukkal-maḫ (4) 5400 sa gi (5) [kì]šib ib-ni-ilum sukkal (6) [x] sa gi (7) [kìšib] šu-eš$_4$-tár šagina-gú-du$_8$-a[⟨ki⟩]-ka (8) [x] sa gi ur-[d]šul-gi-ra / šagina šu ba-ti (9) kìšib bí-ša-za-núm eger-a-na (10) 900 sa gi šu-ì-lí sukkal šu ba-ti (11) 300 sa gi kìšib lú-ša-lim ḫa-za-núm gar-ša-na[ki]-ka (12) gìri šu-ì-lí sukkal-lugal (13) 1800 sa gi ṣi-il-be-lí sukkal šu ba-ti (14) 600 sa gi ilum-ba-ni dub-sar-kaš$_4$ (15) gìri [d]utu-mu sukkal

(16) 120 sa gi 2 gu-kilib pa-TAR ^{giš}ásal (17) kìšib a-ḫu-ni sukkal (18) 1040 sa gi é-é-duru$_5$-lugal-šè (19) kìšib kù-^{d}nanna sukkal (20) 50 sa gi ur-šar-ru-gin$_7$ sukkal šu ba-[ti] (21) gìri lú-^{d}da-ni sukkal (22) 120 gu-kilib ^{giš}ma-nu (23) 120 gu-kilib pa-TAR ^{giš}ásal (24) kìšib ur-^{d}nanše lú-énsi[-ka] (25) 1485 sa gi na-[....] / sukkal [šu ba-ti] (26) 18,000 sa gi [..../....] (27) gìri a-ḫu-ni [sukkal] (28) 2400 sa gi ur-^{d}[.... sukkal šu ba-ti] (29) 3600 $^{(dug)}$sìla-bur-zi (30) DOUBLE LINE (31) šu+nígin 3600 $^{(dug)}$sìla-bur-zi (32) šu+nígin 108,055 sa gi (33) šu+ nígin 120 gu-kilib ^{giš}ma-nu (34) šu+nígin 182 gu-kilib pa-TAR ^{giš}ásal (35) mu en-unu$_6$-gal-an-na en-^{d}inanna ba-ḫun (36) 5400 sa gi šu-ku$_8$-[bu]-um šu [ba]-ti (37) 2400 sa gi šu-^{d}suen sukkal šu ba-ti (38) 5400 sa gi **aq$^!$-ba$^!$-ìa lú-ma-rí^{ki}** (39) šu+nígin 13,200 sa gi (40) mu ^{d}amar-^{d}suen lugal-e ša-aš-ru-um^{ki} mu-/ḫul (41) DOUBLE LINE (42) [36]00 $^{(dug)}$sìla-bur-zi (43) [x+]20,095 sa gi (44) [šu+nígin] 120 gu-kilib ^{giš}ma-nu (45) šu+nígin 182 gu-kilib ^{giš}ásal (46) gi-á-diri$^!$ mu-2-kam (47) ki énsi-umma^{ki}-ta

7. Chiera, *Princeton Collection* Ex 250, from a summary of Chiera (Š 46/?/?)
še gur; **lú-ma-rí^{ki}-me**; (seal) lú-igi-ma / dub-sar

8. Çığ, et al., *PDT* 1 161, collated by Picchioni, *OA* 14 (1975) 156 and Gomi [unpublished] (Š 47/iv/25)
(1) 8 udu-niga 2 sila$_4$ (2) ur-mes sagi (3) 2 u$_8$-niga (4) 1 sila$_4$ (5) lugal-nir-gál (6) 1 sila$_4$ ur-^{d}tílla (7) 1 sila$_4$-niga (8) 2 máš en-^{d}inanna (9) 1 udu-giš-dù 1 u$_8$ (10) **[it-r]a-ak-ì-lí lú-/ma-rí^{ki}** (11) 1 sila$_4$ zabar-dab$_5$ (12) 1 ^{mí}ešgar-niga kur-gìri-ni-šè (13) mu-DU na-sa$_6$ ì-dab$_5$ (14) iti ki-síg-^{d}nin-a-zu (15) mu ús-sa ki-maš^{ki} ba-ḫul (16-side) u$_4$-25-kam

9. Çığ, et al., *PDT* 1 180, collated by Gomi [unpublished] (AS 8/iv/[x])
(1) 1 máš-gal-niga (2) **la-qì-pu-um lú-ma-rí^{ki}** (3) gìri šu-ab-ba sukkal (4) ilum-dan maškim (5) iti u$_4$-[x] ba-zal (6) ki a-ḫu-we-er-ta (7) ba-zi (8) iti ki-síg-^{d}nin-a-zu (9) mu en-nun-e ^{d}amar-^{d}suen ki-ág-en-eridu^{ki} ba-ḫun (10-side) 1 (seal) ad-da[-....] / dub-sar / [....][76]

10. Çığ, et al., *PDT* 1 567, collated by Picchioni, *OA* 14 [1975] 166 and Gomi [unpublished] (ŠS 1/iv/18)
(1) 1 udu-niga (2) tap$_x$(MAN)-pá-an-da-ra-aḫ lú-si-/mu-ru-um^{ki} (3) gìri èr-ra-a sukkal (4) šà nibru^{ki} (5) 1 udu-niga (6) **a-bu-DU$_{10}$ lú-ma-rí^{ki}** (7) gìri ì-lí-be-lí sukkal (8) árad-mu maškim (9) iti u$_4$-18 ba-zal (10) ki zu-ba-ga-ta (11) ba-zi (12) gìri ad-da-kal-la dub-sar (13) iti ki-síg-^{d}nin-a-zu (14) mu ^{d}šu-^{d}suen lugal (15-side) 2 udu (seal) ad-da-kal-la / dub-sar / dumu nì-érim-e-du$_{10}^?$

11. Çığ, et al., *PDT* 1 594, collated by Picchioni, *OA* 14 [1975] 166 and Gomi [unpublished] (AS 1/iii/4)
(1) 1 gu$_4$ (2) 3 udu-niga (3) 2 máš-gal-niga (4) a-rá-1-kam (5) 3 udu-niga (6) 2 máš-gal-niga (7) a-rá-2-kam (8) 1 udu-niga a-rá-3-kam (9) é-muḫaldim-šè (10) mu kaš$_4$-ke$_4^?$-ne-šè (11) 1

---

[76] The reading of the seal is based on Gomi's collation and is the same as on Hallo, *TLB* 3 33 and Keiser and Kang, *BIN* 3 402. This is confirmed on the unpublished MM 54 (No. 77, below) which contains the same seal impression.

u$_8$-niga (12) **iš-me-^{d}da-gan lú-ma-rí^{ki}** (13) 1 udu-niga (14) **bu-du-úr lú-ur-šu^{ki}** (15) 1 máš-gal-niga (16) **ì-lí-^{d}da-gan lú-eb$^{!}$-la$^{!ki}$** (17) 1 máš-gal-niga (18) a-an-[....] (19) 1 [máš$^{?}$-gal$^{?}$]-niga (20) **na-[na$^{?}$-ù$^{?}$] ⌜lú-kin⌝-gi$_4$-/a ⌜lú⌝-[ur$^{?}$-šu$^{?ki}$]** (21) 1 udu-niga (22) ama-úg-ga (23) gìri lugal-inim-gi-na sukkal (24) 1 udu-niga 1 máš-gal-niga (25) lú-kin-gi$_4$-a ḫu-un-ti-pá lú-du$_8$-du$_8$-lí^{ki} (26) gìri šu-^{d}adad sipa-gú-gur$_5$ (27) é-a-ne-ne-šè (28) árad-mu maškim (29) šà nibru^{ki} (30) iti u$_4$-4 ba-zal (31) ki lú-dingir-ra-ta ba-zi (32) iti u$_5$-bí-kú (33) mu ^{d}amar-^{d}suen lugal

12. Contenau, *UDU* 27 (no date)
(1) 0.0.4. kaš-sig$_5$ (2) 0.1.5. kaš-gin (3) **me-me-šu-ra lú-/eb-la^{ki}** (4) 0.0.4. kaš-sig$_5$ (5) 0.1.5. kaš-gin (6) **kur-bi-la-ak / lú-ur-šu^{ki}** (7) 0.0.2. kaš-sig$_5$ lú-ki-maš^{ki} (8) 0.5.0. lú-ús-ra-ni / 2 sìla-ta (9) kìšib ù-ma-ni (19) šà-bala

13. Dhorme, *RA* 9 (1912) 56 SA 239 [fragment, no copy][77] (date lost)
udu-niga; sískur-^{d}suen; **puzur$_4$-ma-ma lú-ma-rí^{ki}**; **ì-lí-^{d}da-gan lú-eb-la^{ki}**; ni-la-lum; u$_4$-7

14. Fish, *CST* 107, collated and corrected by Gomi, *MVN* 12, p. 98 (Š 46/iv/25)
(1) 1 gu$_4$ (2) 2 áb (3) gu$_4$-giš-1-šè (4) larsa(UD.UNU)^{ki}-šè (5) gìri **ì-lum-a-bi$^{!}$ (6) lú-ma-rí^{ki}** (7) [iti] u$_4$-25 ba-zal (7) ki lú-dingir-ra-ta (8) na-sa$_6$ ì-dab$_5$ (9) iti ki-síg-^{d}nin-a-zu (10) mu ḫu$^{!}$-ur$_5$-ti^{ki} ba-ḫul

15. Fish, *CST* 190, collated with corrections by Gomi, *MVN* 12, p. 103 (Š 47/x/16)
(1) 2 udu-niga (2) 2 áb-máḫ **$^{d!}$š[ul$^{?}$-gi$^{?}$-ì$^{?}$-lí$^{?}$]**[78] (3) 1 udu-[ni]ga (4) **^{d}šul-gi-pa-lí-il** (5) **lú-ma-rí^{ki}-me** (6) é-a-ne-ne-šè (7) gìri ba-a-a sukkal (8) árad-mu maškim (9) šà unug^{ki}-ga (10) u$_4$-16 ba-zal (11) zi-ga ki lú-dingir-ra (12) iti ezem-an-na (13) mu ús-sa ki-maš^{ki} ba-ḫul

16. Fish, *CST* 254 copy of obverse also published in *BJRL* 8 (1924) 110, no. 507, collated by Gomi, *MVN* 12, p. 105 (AS 2/vi/3)
(1) 1 udu-niga é-muḫaldim-šè (2) mu mar-tu maš-maš-/tilmun$^{\langle ki \rangle}$-ta e-ra-ne⟨-šè⟩ (3) 1 udu-niga (4) ra-ši lú-zi-da-núm^{ki} (5) 1 udu-niga (6) **puzur$_4$-ma-ma lú-ma-/rí^{ki}** (7) 1 udu-niga (8) **ì-lí-^{d}da-gan lú-eb-la^{ki}** (9) gìri lugal-inim-gi-na sukkal (10) lugal-má-gur$_8$-re maškim (11) iti u$_4$-3 ba-zal (12) ki lú-dingir-ra-ta ba-zi (13) iti á-ki-ti (14) mu ^{d}amar-^{d}suen lugal / ur-bí-lum^{ki} mu-ḫul (15-side) 4

17. Fish, *CST* 468, collated by Gomi, *MVN* 12, p. 114 with copy of traces on plate cvi (AS [6]/iv/1$^{!}$)
(1) 1 udu-[niga] (2) KA-[....]-šè (3) ^{d}šul-[gi]-uru-mu maškim (4) 1 máš-gal-niga li-pá-an-aš-ku$_5$-pí [l]ú-kin-gi$_4$-a li-pá-nu-uk-[š]a-pá-aš énsi-mar-ḫa-ši^{ki} (5) [gì]ri šu-^{d}suen sukkal (6) 1 udu-

[77] This transliteration is based on Dhorme's description which did not provide a line by line transliteration nor an accompanying copy.

[78] Following the reading of Fish which is not confirmed by Gomi's collation. The plural ending, -me, at the end of line 5 requires a second PN at this point. The only name compounded with ^{d}Šulgi other than ^{d}Šulgi-palil and associated with him occurs in Nies, *UDT* 92, and Sigrist, apud Spar, *CTMMA* 1 17 which are the basis for the tentative restoration here. Note, however, that neither text qualifies the PNs as coming from Mari.

niga **ì-lí-^{d}da-gan lú-eb-la^{ki}** (7) gìri na-bí-^{d}suen sukkal (8) 1 máš-gal-niga (9) **šu-^{d}iš-ḫa-ra lú-ma-rí^{ki}** (10) gìri ši$_{x}$(SIG$_{4}$)-te-li sukkal (11) 1 udu-niga (12) [....-g]i-zi lú-kin-gi$_{4}$-a énsi-a-bar-ni-um^{ki} (13) [gìri nam]-ḫa-ni sukkal (14) [ár]ad-mu maškim (15) iti u$_{4}$-1 ba-zal (16) ki a-ḫu-we-er-ta ba-zi (17) [it]i ki-síg-^{d}nin-a-zu (18-side) 5 udu

18. *Gelb, "Mari and the Kish Civilization," p. 161, Dawson 9[79] (date unknown)

19. *de Genouillac, *TCL* 5 6063 (AS 4/i/6)

20. de Genouillac, *TrD* 18 (ŠS 1/iii/17)
(1) 1 gu$_{4}$-niga (2) é-muḫaldim (3) mu-kaš$_{4}$-e-ne-šè (4) 1 udu-niga (5) **a-bu-DU$_{10}$ lú-ma-rí^{ki}** (6) gìri ^{d}nanna-ul$_{4}$-gal (7) árad-mu$^{!}$ maškim (8) šà nibru^{ki} (9) iti u$_{4}$-17 ba-zal (10) ki igi-^{d}en-líl-šè-ta (11) ba-zi (12) gìri ma-n[úm-ki]-^{d}šul-gi (13) iti u$_{5}$-bí-kú (14) mu ^{d}šu-^{d}suen / lugal

21. de Genouillac, *TrD* 54 (date lost)
(I+x) (1) [x] udu-ú (2) 9 máš-gal-ú (3) **éren-te-er-qà^{ki}** (4) šeš-kal-la (5) [x+]10 udu-ú (6) [ugula ^{d}iškur]-da-ni (7) [x ....]-ú (II+x) (1) šà 1 (2) éren-da-ši-il^{ki} (3) ugula ^{d}iškur-da-ni (4) 10 udu-ú u$_{4}$-20 (5) 1 si-zum (6) 10 udu-ú (5) KWU769-da-bi-u-ši-šè (6) 2 gu$_{4}$-ú šà-a (7) 14 udu-ú (8) 5 máš-gal (9) [remainder broken] (III+x) (x+1) 2 [....] (x+2) 27 udu-ú (x+3) 3 máš-gal-ú (x+4) éren-ur-gu-ḫa-lam^{ki} (x+5) 1 gu$_{4}$-ú (x+6) 9 udu-ú (x+7) 1 máš-gal-ú (x+8) éren-maš-gán-ga-raš$_{x}$(KASKAL-*gunû*)$^{sar\ ki}$ (x+8) udu-a-mur-àm (x+9) 10 udu-ú (x+10) puzur$_{4}$-ḫa-ìa (x+11) 10 udu-ú (IV+x) (x+1) [....]-mu-um / [....]-ši-šè (x+2) [x g]u$_{4}$-ú (x+3) [x+]5 udu-ú (x+4) [x] máš-ú (x+5) [éren-a]-šur$_{5}$^{ki} (x+6) [ugula nu]-úr-eš$_{4}$-tár / [lú-kin]-gi$_{4}$-/a [remainder broken]

22. Goetze, *JCS* 7 (1953) 104 Smith College 473 (AS 6/iv/1)
(1) 2 udu-niga (2) ^{d}inanna-unug^{ki}-šè (3) gìri nu-úr-^{d}suen sagi (4) 2 udu-niga ^{d}nin-tin-ug$_{5}$⟨-ga⟩-/ì-si^{ki}-šè gin-né (5) gìri ur-^{d}lama sagi (6) 1 udu-niga (7) li-pá-an-aš-ku$_{8}$-pí lú-kin$_{4}$-/gi$_{4}$-a li-pá-nu-uk-ša-pá-aš / énsi-mar-ḫa-ši^{ki} (8) gìri šu-^{d}šul-gi sukkal (9) 1 udu-niga **ì-lí-^{d}da-gan / lú-eb-la^{ki}** (10) gìri na-bí-^{d}suen [sukka]l (11) 1 udu-niga **šu-^{d}iš-ḫa-⌜ra⌝ / lú ma-rí^{ki}** (12) gìri ši$_{x}$(SIG$_{4}$)-te-li sukkal (13) 2 udu-niga **i-din-AG** (14) **lú-ma-rí^{ki}** u$_{4}$ uru-ni-⌜ta⌝ / ì-im-gin-na-a (15) gìri lú-^{d}da-mu sukkal (16) ilum-dan sukkal maškim (17) iti u$_{4}$-10-lá-1 ba-zal (18) ki a-ḫu-we-er-ta ba-[z]i (19) iti ki-síg-^{d}nin-a-[z]u (20) mu ša-aš-ru^{ki} ba-ḫul (21-side) 10-lá-1 udu

23. Goetze, *JCS* 7 (1953) 104 St. Louis City Art Museum 61:27 (AS 2/iii/20)
(1) 1 máš-gal-niga **puzur$_{4}$-/ma-ma lú-ma-rí^{ki}** (2) 1 máš-gal-niga **ì-lí-/^{d}da-gan lú-eb-la^{ki}** (3) 1 máš-gal-niga na-na-ù / lú-ur-šu^{ki} (4) é-a-ne-ne-šè (5) lugal-má-gur$_{8}$-re šabra (6) iti u$_{4}$-20 ba-zal (7) ki ^{d}šul-gi-a-a-/mu-ta ba-zi (8) iti ne-ne-kú (9) mu ^{d}amar-^{d}suen / lugal-e ur-bí-lum/^{ki} mu-ḫul

---

[79] The whereabouts of this text are unknown.

24. Goetze, *JCS* 7 (1953) 105 NCBT 1593 [collated] (AS 2/viii/-)
(1) 2 dúsu-níta (2) **puzur$_4$-ma-ma** (3) **lú-ma-rí^{ki}** (4) 2 dúsu-níta (5) **ì-lí-^{d}da-gan** (6) **lú-eb-la^{ki}** (7) 1 dúsu-níta (8) **dú-ul-qá-núm / mar-tu** (9) **ìa-a-ma-dì** (10) árad-mu maškim (11) iti šu-eš-ša (12) mu ^{d}amar-^{d}suen / lugal-e ur-bí-lum^{ki} / mu-ḫul

25. Goetze, *JCS* 7 (1953) 106 Kenrick 72 = Jean, *ŠA* LXXI:85 ([ŠS 6/?/?] [date restored from Buccellati, *Amorites*, plate xi-xii, no. 22])
(I.) (1) [1 gú ^{giš}ma]-nu / [... sìla kaš-sig$_5$ 4 sìla / zì-gu-ta] (2) [10 guruš 2 sìla kaš 2 sìla zì-ta] (3) [lú-SU.KI-me-šè] (4) [1 guruš 6 sìla kaš-sig$_5$ 4 sìla / z]ì-gu (5) [lú-ša-ri-it]-ḫi^{ki}⟨-šè⟩ (6) [2 guru]š 2 sìla kaš 2 sìla zì-ta (7) lú-ḫu-u[r-t]i^{ki}-me⟨-šè⟩ (8) 10 sa gi (9) kaš$_4$-me⟨-šè⟩ šà en-nu-gá (10) gìri be-lí-šar (11) ki na-wi-ir-ilum (12) 0.1.0. kaš-sig$_5$ 0.2.0. kaš-gin (13) 0.1.0. zì-gu-sig$_5$ (14) 0.0.5. sìla zì-še sa (15) 20 sa gi 1 gú ^{giš}ma-nu (16) pá-na-na lú-mar-ḫa-ši^{ki} (17) 1 guruš 0.0.1. kaš-sig$_5$ 0.0.1. zì-/gu (18) 2 guruš 0.0.1. kaš-sig$_5$ 5 sìla zì-/gu-ta (19) sukkal-eme-bal ⟨ki⟩ lú-/mar-ḫa-ši^{ki} gub-ba-m[e-⟨šè⟩] (20) 0.0.2. kaš-sig$_5$ 0.0.1. zì-gu-sig$_5$ (21) [10] sa gi (II.) (1) [....] (2) [....] (3) [19 guruš 0.0.2. zì-ta] (4) lú-u[r-bí-lum^{ki}] (5) 7 guruš (6) 2 [....] (7) lú-ḫu-[....] (8) 2 guruš 4 [sìla zì-ta] (9) lú-MÙŠ.ERIN.[KI] (10) 0.0.2. kaš-sig$_5$ 0.0.1. [zì-gu-sig$_5$] (11) 3 s[a gi] (12) ḫu-un-z[i-ib-tum] (13) 0.0.1. kaš 0.0.1. zì 2 [sìla zì-gu] (14) šu-ab-ba m[ar-tu] (15) 5 sìla kaš 5$^{!}$ sìla [zì-gu$^{?}$] (16) ša$^{!}$-pu-n[úm SAG.X] (17) 20 guruš [0.0.2.$^{!}$ zì-ta] (18) lú-[a-la^{ki}-me-šè] (19) guruš a[d-da] (20) 5 lú-ús-sa-ni-me / [62 sìla kaš 2 sìla zì-ta] (21) 0.0.2. kaš-sig$_5$ 0.0.2. kaš-[gin] (III.) (1) 0.0.1. z[ì]-gu-sig$_5$ 10 sa g[i] (2) **a-bu-DU$_{10}$ lú-ma-r[í^{ki}]** (3) 2 ab-ba 5 (Bucc. 0.0.1. kaš) sìla kaš 5 sìla z[ì 1 sa gi] (4) 15 lú-ús-sa-ni 2 sìla-[ta] (5) 0.0.2. kaš-sig$_5$ 0.0.2. kaš-gin (6) 0.0.1. zì-gu-sig$_5$ 10 sa gi (7) **i-zi-in-^{d}da-[gan]** (8) 0.0.1. kaš-sig$_5$ (9) 5 sa-gi (10) **kur-bi-la-ak** (11) 15 guruš 2 sìla kaš 2 [sìla zì-ta] (12) **lú-eb-la^{ki}-[me-šè]** (13) 0.0.2. kaš-sig$_5$ [5] sa g[i] (14) **i-pí-iq-re-e-ú** (15) **m[ar]-tu ìa-a-ma-d[ì-um$^{?}$]** (16) 4 sìla zì lú-ús-s[a-ni-me-šè] (17) 4 sìla zì kí-ba-a-[tal] lú-/ur-bí-lum^{k}[^{i}-šè] (18) 4 sìla zì si-mu lú-[....] (19) 0.0.1. kaš-sig$_5$ 5 sìla [zì-gu$^{?}$] (20) 10 s[a gi] (21) é-gi$_4$-a [....] (22) 4 guruš 2 [sìla zì$^{?}$-ta] (23) 10 géme 1 sìla kaš 1 sìla [zì$^{?}$-ta] (24) [lú-ús-sa-ni-me-šè] (25) [0.0.2. kaš-sig$_5$ 0.0.2. kaš-gin] (26) [0.0.1. zì-gu-sig$_5$] (27) [10 sa gi] (IV.) (1) [ni]-im-sí lú-ìa-[a]b-ra-at^{ki} (2) [7 l]ú-ús-sa-ni 2 / sìla kaš-ta (3) [šu-a]-gi-na (0) BLANK SPACE (4) šu+nígin 0.2.0. zì 2 sìla kaš-sig$_5$ (5) šu+nígin 1.1.3.1 sìla kaš-gin gur (6) šu+nígin 0.1.1.5 sìla zì-gu-sig$_5$ (7) šu+nígin 0.0$^{!}$.5$^{!}$.8 sìla zì-gu-gin (8) [šu+nígi]n [10$^{?}$].3.3.9 sìla zì-še ⟨gur$^{?}$⟩ (9) [šu+nígin] 0.0.5. zì-še sa (10) [š]e-bi 4.0.3.3 ½ sìla / gur (11) [šu+nígin 1]02 sa gi (12) [šu+nígin 1 g]ú ^{giš}ma-nu (13) [u$_4$-x-kam] (14) [gìri lú-^{d}en-líl-lá] (15) [mu ^{d}šu-^{d}suen lugal-e / na-rú-a-maḫ-^{d}en-líl-/^{d}nin-líl-ra mu-na-dù]

26. Gomi, *Orient* 16 (1980) 40, no. 7 Liverpool Merseyside County Museums 51-63-51 = Fish, *MCS* 7 (1957) 19-20 Liverpool 51-63-51 (Š 46/vi/28)
(1) 1 sila$_4$ ^{d}en-líl (2) 1 sila$_4$ ^{d}nin-líl (3) mu-DU en-^{d}inanna (4) 1 sila$_4$ ^{d}en-líl (5) 1 sila$_4$ ^{d}nin-líl (6) mu-DU šeš-da-da sanga (7) 1 sila$_4$ ^{d}inanna (8) mu-DU ur-ni$_9$-gar ka-gur$_7$ (9) 1 udu-niga 1 sila$_4$ ^{d}en-líl (10) 1 udu-niga 1 sila$_4$ ^{d}nin-líl (11) mu-DU énsi-marad^{ki} (12) zabar-dab$_5$ maškim (13) 1 ^{mí}ešgar-niga é-uzu-ga (14) mu-DU énsi-nibru^{ki} (15) da-a-a-ni maškim (16) 1 gu$_4$-niga 5 udu-niga **zu-ri-im / lú-kin-gi$_4$-a lú-eb-la^{ki}** (17) mu-DU á-da-a (18) árad-mu maškim (19) 2 gu$_4$ 2 áb 24 udu (20) 13 u$_8$ 8 máš (21) šu-gíd é-muḫaldim-šè (22) BLANK LINE (23) zi-ga u$_4$-28-kam (24) iti šeš-da-kú (25) mu ki-maš^{ki} ù ḫu-/ur$_5$-ti^{ki} ba-ḫul

27. Gomi, *Orient* 16 (1980) 42, no. 10 Liverpool Merseyside County Museums 51-63-122 (Š 46/viii/3)
(1) 2 udu-niga (2) 2 máš-gal-niga (3) **mu lú-kin-gi$_4$-a / lú-ìa-ma$^{!?}$(⌈AB⌉)-dì-um** (4) ù **lú-kin-gi$_4$-a / lú-ma-rí^{ki}-šè** (5) šà nibru^{ki} (6) 2 gu$_4$ (7) 1 áb (8) 22 udu (9) 18 u$_8$ (10) 1 udu-ge$_6$ (11) 1 u$_8$-ge$_6$ (12) 4 máš-gal (13) 23 ùz (14) šu-gíd é-muḫaldim-šè (15) mu àga-ús-e-ne-šè (16) árad-mu maškim (17) iti u$_4$-3 ba-zal (18) zi-ga ki lú-dingir-ra (19) iti šu-eš$_5$-[ša] (20) mu ki-maš^{ki} ù ḫu-ur$_5$-/ti^{ki} ba-ḫul

28. Gomi, Hirose, *Hirose* 231 (AS 6/iv/23)
(1) 1 máš-gal-niga (2) li-pá-an-aš-ku$_8$-pí / lú-kin-gi$_4$-a li-pá-nu-uk-/ša-pá-aš énsi-mar-ḫa-ši^{ki} (3) gìri lú-^{d}da-mu sukkal (4) 1 máš-gal-niga (5) **ì-lí-^{d}da-gan / lú-eb-la^{ki}** (6) gìri na-bí-^{d}suen sukkal (7) 1 máš-gal-niga (8) **šu-^{d}iš-ḫa-ra lú-/ma-rí^{ki}** (9) gìri ši$_x$(SIG$_4$)-te-li sukkal (10) árad-mu maškim (11) iti ud-23-ba-zal (12) ki a-ḫu-we-er-ta (13) ba-zi (14) iti ki-síg-^{d}nina-a-zu (15) mu ša-aš-ru^{ki} ba-ḫul

29. Hallo, NCBT 1669 (AS 3/iv/14)
(1) [1] máš-gal-niga (2) **puzur$_4$-ma-ma / lú-ma-rí^{ki}** (3) 1 máš-gal-niga (4) **ì-lí-^{d}da-gan / lú-eb-la^{ki}** (5) 1 máš-gal-niga (6) **na-na-ù lú-[ur]-šu^{ki}** (7) ⌈gìri lugal-inim-gi-na sukkal⌉ (8) árad-mu maškim (9) ⌈iti u$_4$-14⌉ ba-zal (10) ⌈ki lú-dingir-ra⌉-ta ba-zi (11) ⌈iti ki-síg-^{d}nin-a-zu⌉ (12) ⌈mu⌉ gu-[za]-^{d}en-[líl-lá] / mu-ne-in-[dím] (13-side) 3

30. Hallo, *TLB* 3 (1963-73) 24 = Weidner, *RSO* 9 (1921-23) 472 P370 (AS 4/iii/22)
(1) 1 udu-niga a-mur-ilum lú-kin-gi$_4$-/a li-pá-nu-uk-ša-pá-aš / énsi-mar-ḫa-ši^{ki} (2) 1 udu-niga **gu-ra-a lú-ur$^{!}$-šu$^{!ki}$**[80] (3) 1 udu-niga **'à-um lú-ma-rí^{ki}** (4) gìri ḫu-zi-ri sukkal (5) árad-mu maškim (6) iti u$_4$-22 ba-zal (7) ki ^{d}šul-gi-a-a-mu-/ta ba-zi (8) BLANK SPACE (9) iti u$_5$-bí-kú (10) mu ús-sa gu-za-/^{d}en-líl-lá ba-dím (11-side) 3 udu[81]

31. Jean, *ŠA* VI:2[82] (AS 5/x/18)
(1) 2 udu-niga [....] (2) gìri x-zi$^{?}$ (3) še-le-pu-tum maškim (4) 3 udu **šu-^{d}da-gan / lú-ma-rí^{ki}** (5) gìri ilum-ba-ni sukkal (6) 4 máš-gal ši$_x$(SIG$_4$)-te-li / u$_4$ nam-érim in-ku$_5$-rá-a (7) gìri lú-^{d}en-ki sukkal (8) árad-mu maškim (9) u$_4$-18-kam (10) ki in-ta-è-a-ta / ba-zi (11) iti ezem-an-na (12) mu en-unu$_6$-gal-/^{d}inanna ba-ḫ[un]

32. Jones and Snyder, *SET* 59 (AS 3/i/3)
(1) 5 udu-niga má-an-na (2) 2 udu-niga a-rá-1-kam (3) 2 udu-niga a-rá-2-kam (4) ^{d}nanna (5) lugal ku$_4$-ra (6) 2 udu-niga du$_6$-ùr (7) 1 udu-niga má-an-na a-rá-3-kam (8) 1 udu-niga ^{d}nin-

---

80 Hallo's copy shows the signs clearly as ur-šu while Weidner's shows an equally clear eb-la. A similar confusion may also exist in text 12:6 where Kurb-ilak, otherwise known from Ebla, is qualified as coming from Uršu. See above note 46.

81 Only Hallo's copy indicates a total on the side of the tablet, not indicated in Weidner's copy. But such oversights by copyists are not uncommon in Ur III publications with respect to notations on the edges or sides of tablets.

82 On this text see J. Klein, "Šeleppūtum a Hitherto Unknown Ur III Princess," *ZA* 80 (1990) 39.

ḫur-sag-ga (9) a-tu sagi maškim (10) 1 udu-niga ra-ši lú-zi$^{!}$-da-nu-um^{ki} (11) 1 udu-niga **tù{-a}-ra-am-^{d}da-gan / lú-ma-rí$^{!ki}$** (12) árad-mu maškim (13) iti u$_4$-3 ba-zal (14) ki na-lu$_5$-ta ba-zi (15) šà á-ki-ti (16) iti maš-dù-kú (17) mu ^{giš}gu-za-^{d}en-líl-lá ba-dím (18-side) 15

33. Keiser and Kang, *BIN* 3 221 (ŠS 2/vi/30)
(1) 1 gu$_4$-niga 4-kam-ús 4 gu$_4$ (2) 5 áb 1 udu-niga-si[g$_5$] (3) 1 udu-niga 3-kam-ús ^{d}en-lí[l] (4) 1 gu$_4$-niga 3 kam-ús ^{d}gu-[la] (5) 1 gu$_4$-niga ḫur-sag-kà-lam-m[a] (6) šà é-^{d}en-líl-lá (7) 2 gu$_4$-niga 4-kam-ús (8) 1 gu$_4$-niga 4 gu$_4$ 3 áb (9) 1 udu-niga-sig$_5$ 1 udu-niga 3-kam-ús (10) ^{d}nin-líl (11) 1 udu-niga 4-kam-ús ^{d}nin-tin-ug$_5$-ga (12) šà é-^{d}nin-líl-lá (13) 1 gu$_4$ ^{d}nin-ḫur-sag (14) 1 gu$_4$-niga ^{d}nuska (15) 1 gu$_4$-niga ^{d}utu (16) 1 gu$_4$-niga ^{d}nin-urta (17) 1 gu$_4$-niga ^{d}inanna (18) 1 gu$_4$ ^{d}šu-^{d}suen (19) 1 gu$_4$-niga 3-kam-ús ^{d}suen (20) 1 gu$_4$-niga ^{d}šul-gi (21) 1 gu$_4$-niga ^{d}nin-sún (22) 1 gu$_4$-niga ^{d}lugal-bàn-da (23) 1 gu$_4$-niga ^{d}nin-im-ma (24) 1 gu$_4$ ^{d}lugal-gu$_4$-si-su (25) 1 gu$_4$-niga ^{d}[....] (26) 1 gu$_4$-niga [4$^{?}$ udu$^{?}$-niga$^{?}$ 3-kam-ú]s (27) ^{d}nin-[tin-ug$_5$-g]a (28) 1 gu$_4$-niga an-[nu-ni-t]um (29) [è]š-èš u[$_4$-sa]kar (30) 3 udu-niga-sig$_5$ 1 máš-gal-niga-sig$_5$ (31) ^{d}nanna sískur šà é-gal (32) [l]ugal ku$_4$-ra (33) šà nibru^{ki} (34) 1 máš-gal-niga **'à-um lú-ma-rí^{ki}** (35) 1 máš-gal-niga **da-sal-ib-ri / lú-ur-šu^{ki}** (36) gìri ì-lí-be-lí sukkal (37) árad-mu maškim (38) iti u$_4$-30 ba-zal (39) ki a-ḫu-we-er-ta ba-zi (40) gìri ur-^{d}lugal-bàn-da š[a$_{13}$-dub-ba] (41) ù ad-da-kal-la šár-ra-a[b-du] (42) iti á-ki-t[i] (43) mu má-dàra-[ab]zu / ba-a[b-du$_8$] (44-side) 37 gu$_4$ 15$^{?}$ udu (45) (46)

34. King, *CT* 32 (1912), Plate 23 BM 104458 (AS 8/viii/11)
(1) 1 gu$_4$ 3 udu 2 máš-gal (2) ^{d}en-líl ^{d}nin-líl (3) lugal ku$_4$-ra (4) 1 udu 1 máš-gal (5) gu-za-^{d}šul-gi-ra (6) ur-^{d}šul-pa-è muḫaldim maškim (7) 1 máš-gal ki a-nag-ur-^{d}nammu (8) ur-^{d}ba-ba$_6$ muḫaldim maškim (9) 1 gu$_4$-niga 3 udu 2 máš-gal (10) ur-^{d}nin-gublaga nar (11) gìri ur-me-me sukkal (12) ú-la-ì-ni-iš maškim (13) 30 udu 20 máš-gal (14) lugal-má-gur$_8$-re (15) ú-tá-mi-šar-ra-am maškim (16) 2 udu 1 máš-gal (17) **a-mur-^{d}šul-gi** (18) 1 udu 1 máš-gal (19) **^{d}šul-gi-pa-lí-il** (20)1 udu 1 máš-gal **aq$^{!}$(APIN)-ba-ìa** (21) **lú-ma-rí^{ki}-me** (22) 1 gu$_4$-niga 5 udu 5 máš-gal (23) tá-din-eš$_4$-tár (24) 5 udu 5 máš-gal UM.ME-da 2-a-bi (25) gìri ur-me-lám-an-na sukkal (26) árad-mu maškim (27) 1 máš-gal mu$_7$-mu$_7$-šè (28) ši$_x$(SIG$_4$)-te-li maškim (29) šà mu-DU-ra-ta (30) u$_4$-21-kam (31) ki ab-ba-sa$_6$-ga-ta ba-zi (32) iti šu-eš$_5$-ša (33) mu en-eridu^{ki} ba-ḫun (34-side) 3 gu$_4$ 91 udu

35. Legrain, *TRU* 305 (AS 2/vi/4)
(1) 2 udu-niga (2) é-muḫaldim-šè (3) mu mar-tu maš-maš tilmun$^{\langle ki\rangle}$⟨-ta⟩/ e-ra-ne-šè (4) 1 udu-niga (5) ra-ši lú-zi-da-núm^{ki} (6) 1 udu-niga (7) **puzur$_4$-ma-ma lú-ma-rí^{ki}** (8) 1 udu-niga (9) **ì-lí-^{d}da-gan lú/-eb-la^{ki}** (10) gìri lugal-inim-gi-na sukkal (11) lugal-má-gur$_8$-re maškim (12) iti u$_4$-4 ba-zal (13) ki lú-dingir-ra-ta (14) ba-zi (15) blank line (16) iti á-ki-ti (17) mu ^{d}amar-^{d}suen lugal-/e ur-bí-lum^{ki} mu-ḫul (18-side) 5

36. Legrain, *TRU* 344 (Š 46/iv/6)
(1) 2 udu-niga (2) 3 máš-gal-niga (3) mu-kaš$_4$-e-ne-šè (4) gìri ^{d}šul-gi-uru-mu ⟨sukkal⟩ (5) 1 udu-niga-gu$_4$-e-ús-sa (6) mu géme-^{d}nanna é-gi$_4$-a / bù-ú-du-šè (6) gìri kù-^{d}nanna sukkal (7) 1 udu-niga (8) li-pá-an-aš-ku$_8$-pí / lú-kin-gi$_4$-a li-pá-nu-uk-/ša-pá-aš énsi-mar-ḫa-ši^{ki} (9) gìri šu-^{d}šul-gi sukkal (10) 1 máš-gal-niga (11) **ì-lí-^{d}da-gan / lú-eb-la^{ki}** (12) gìri na-bí-^{d}suen sukkal

(13) 1 máš-gal-niga **šu-^{d}iš-ḫa-ra lú-ma-rí^{ki}** (14) gìri ši$_{x}$(SIG$_{4}$)-te-li sukkal (15) árad-mu maškim (16) iti u$_{4}$-6 ba-zal (17) ki a-ḫu-we-er-ta (18) ba-zi (19) iti ki-síg-^{d}nin-a-zu (20) mu ša-aš-ru^{ki} ba-ḫul (21-side) 10-lá-1 udu

37. Luckenbill, *AJSL* 39 (1922-24) 65-66 (Š 46/?/?)
(1) 1 sila$_{4}$ ^{d}en-líl (2) 1 sila$_{4}$ ^{d}nin-líl (3) mu-DU en-^{d}inanna (4) 1 sila$_{4}$ (undetermined gap) (5+x) 1 máš-nita (6+x) 5 udu-nita (7+x) **zu$^{!}$-ri-im lú-kin-gi$_{4}$-a lú-eb-la^{ki}** (undetermined gap) (8+x) mu ki-maš^{ki} ù ḫu-ur$_{5}$-ti^{ki} ba-ḫul

38. Myhrman, *BE* 3 46 [= CBS 10230, collated] (AS 8/viii/-)
(1) 1 ^{dug}dida 0.0.3. (2) 0.0.2. zì-še (3) 4 kuš-tur-gíd-sa-ba (4) 3 kuš-bi-šè (5) **lú-ma$^{!}$-⌈ri$^{!}$⌉-ke$_{4}$-ne** (5a-env.) ki lú-^{d}nin-š[ubur]-/ta (6) **puzur$_{4}$-^{d}adad** (7) **lú-kin-gi$_{4}$-a** (8) **lú-má$^{!}$-ri$^{!}$-ke$_{4}$$^{[k]i}$** (9) šu ba-ti (10) i-šar-ì-si (11) lú-kin-gi$_{4}$-a / lugal maškim$^{!}$ (12) iti šu-eš:ša (13) [m]u en-eridu^{ki} ba-ḫun

39. Nesbit, iii (Š 31/vii/9)
(1) 1 géme (2) **lú-ur-šu^{ki}** (3) nì-šu-ús-sa-lugal (4) mu-DU (5) ki lugal-si-sá-ta (6) en-dingir-mu (7) BLANK LINE (8) iti ezen-^{d}šul-gi-/ta u$_{4}$-9 ba-zal (9) mu a-rá-2-kam-aš / kára-ḫar^{ki} ba-ḫul

40. Nies, *UDT* 29 (Š 46/ix/-)
(1) 2 še BE gur-lugal (2) **sipa-lú-ma-rí^{ki}-ta** (3) ì-dub-é-bil-li (4) ki ba-zi-ta (5) kìšib ur-^{d}ba-ba$_{6}$ dumu na-di {li} (6) iti mu-šu-du$_{7}$ (7) mu ki-maš^{ki} ba-ḫul (seal) ur-^{d}ba-ba$_{6}$ / dumu na-di / lunga

41. Nies, *UDT* 92[83] (AS 8/xii/29)
(1) 1 udu-niga ^{d}inanna (2) 1 udu-niga ^{d}nin-gal (3) gìri kàs-pu-ša sagi (4) ^{d}en-líl-zi-šà-gál maškim (5) 4 udu-niga-sig$_{5}$-ús bu-ú-du (6) tu-ra-am-^{d}da-gan maškim (7) 1 udu-niga ^{giš}gu-za-^{d}šul-gi-ra (8) 1 udu-niga ^{giš}gu-za-ur-^{d}nammu (9) ur-^{d}ba-ba$_{6}$ muḫaldim maškim (10) 2 gu$_{4}$-niga 2 udu-niga-sig$_{5}$ (11) 5 udu-niga-gu$_{4}$-e-ús-sa (12) 5 udu (13) 5 máš-gal (14) na-ap-la-núm mar-tu (15) 2 [erasure] udu-niga (16) 2 udu 1 máš-gal (17) a-ri-ip-a-tal dumu pu-ša-am lú-ši-ma-nu-um^{ki} (18) 1 udu-niga-gu$_{5}$-e-ús-sa 1 udu (19) a-ri-ip-ḫu-up-pí lú-/tal-muš^{ki} (20) [1] udu-niga-gu$_{4}$-e-ús-sa (21) [1] udu (22) ku$_{8}$-sú-sú lú-ma-ar-/da-ma-an^{ki} (23) 2 udu-niga (24) 2 udu (25) 1 máš-gal (26) lú-tilmun^{ki} (27) 1 udu pa$_{4}$-pa$_{4}$ nin$_{9}$ kiš-er (28) 2 udu (29) ^{d}šul-gi-a-bí (30) 1 udu **^{d}šul-gi-pa-lí-il** (31) [1 udu] **aq-ba-ìa** (32) [1 udu] **^{d}šul-gi-ì-lí** (33) gìri ^{d}nanna-kam sukkal (34) árad-mu maškim (35) u$_{4}$-30-lá-1-kam (36) ki ab-ba-sa$_{6}$-ga-ta (37) ba-zi (38) šà uri$_{5}$^{ki}-ma (39) gìri lú-sa$_{6}$ dub-/sar (40) mu en-eridu^{ki} ba-ḫun (41-side) 2 gu$_{4}$ 45 udu [....]

42. *Oppenheim, *AOS* 32 C 1 = Sauren, *PIOL* 19 373 (date lost)

43. Oppenheim, *AOS* 32 R 11 = Sauren, *PIOL* 19 274 (ŠS 2/iv/6)
(1) 1 udu-niga (2) **'à-um lú-ma-rí^{ki}** (3) 1 udu-niga (4) **da-sal-ib-ri lú-ur-šu$^{\langle ki \rangle}$** (5) gìri ḫu-zi-ri sukkal (6) árad-mu maškim (7) iti u$_{4}$-6 ba-zal (8) ki a-ḫu-we-er-ta (9) ba-zi (10) gìri ur-

[83] This text is included because it contains the names of three Mariotes among other foreigners.

^{d}lugal-bàn/-da ša$_{13}$-dub-⟨ba⟩ (11) ù ad-da-kal-la / šár-ra-ab-du (12) iti ki-síg-^{d}nin-a-zu (13) mu má-dàra-abzu-/^{d}en-ki ba-ab-du$_{8}$ (14-side) 2 udu

44. Owen, A.2852 (AS 9/xi/3)
(1) 1 udu-niga (2) ki-ri-ib-ul-me lú-si-mu-ru-um^{ki} (3) gìri ḫu-zi-ri sukkal (4) [1] udu-niga (5) **ga-ba-ba lú-mu-ki-iš^{ki}** (6) gìri kir-ba-tal sukkal (7) árad-mu maškim (8) iti u$_{4}$-3-ba-zal (9) ki zu-ba-ga-ta ba-zi (10) gìri ad-da-kal-la dub-sar (11) iti ezem-me-ki-gál (12) mu en-^{d}nanna-kar-zi-da ba-ḫun (13) 2 udu

45. Owen, A.3188 (Š 45/x/6)
(1) 1 gu$_{4}$-niga (2) 10-lá-1 udu 1 máš (3) **a-da-tum / lú-ma-rí$^{k[i]}$** (4) 1 sila$_{4}$ (5) [gìri$^{?}$] du-uk-r[a] (6) mu-DU iti ezem-an-[na] (7) mu ^{d}š[ul-gi lugal / ur-bí-[lum^{ki} lu-lu-bu^{ki}...]/ [dil-šè sag-du-bi] šu-b[úr-r]a / [...] bí-ra-a (8-side) u$_{4}$-6-kam

46. Owen, Anonymous 1[84] (ŠS 3/iii/6)
(1) [1 gu$_{4}$-niga] (2) [^{d}en-líl] (3) [1 g]u$_{4}$-niga] (4) ^{d}nin-líl (5) sískur gu-la (6) lugal-ku$_{9}$-ra (7) 1 gu$_{4}$-niga ^{d}inanna (8) gìri a-bí-sí-im-[ti] (9) šà nibru^{ki} (l0) 1 udu-niga (11) **a-bu-DU$_{10}$ lú-ma-rí^{ki}** (12) 1 udu-niga (13) **e-zu-un-^{d}da-gan / lú-eb-la^{ki}** (14) [gì]ri na-ra-am-^{d}adad / sukkal (15) árad-mu maškim (16) iti u$_{4}$-6 ba-zal (17) ki a-ḫu-we-er-ta (18) ba-z[i] (19) gìri ur-^{d}lugal-b[àn-da] / dub-s[ar] (20) ù lú-^{d}nanna / šár-ra-ab-d[u] (21) iti u$_{5}$-bí-kú (22) mu ús-sa má-dàra-/[abzu ba-du$_{8}$] (23-side) 3 gu$_{4}$ 2 udu

47. Owen, *Hallo AV*, Owen, Anonymous 3 (AS 2/vii/21)
(1) 5 udu-niga-sig$_{5}$ (2) 1 udu-niga (3) ezem-má-an-na (4) 2 udu-niga ^{d}inanna-unug^{ki}-šè (5) gìri lugal-ì-maḫ sagi (6) zabar-dab$_{5}$ maškim (7) 1 udu-niga sískur-šà-é-gal (8) èr-ra-na-da maškim (9) 1 udu-niga **ì-lí-^{d}da-/gan lú-eb-la^{ki}** (10) 1 udu-niga **puzur$_{4}$-ma/-ma lú-ma-rí^{ki}** (11) ⌜1⌝ máš-gal-niga **du-ul-qá-/nu-um lú-ìa-a-ma-dì-um^{ki}** (12) árad-mu maškim (13) iti u$_{4}$-21 ba-zal (14) ki-^{d}šul-gi-a-a-mu-ta (15) ba-zi (16) iti ezem-^{d}šul-gi (17) mu ^{d}amar-^{d}suen lugal-e/ ur-bí-lum^{ki} ba-ḫul

48. Owen, *MVN* 3 384 [= FLP 1383] ([AS 4]/iii/7)
(1) [....] (2) [....] (3) gìri ur-^{d}[...] (4) 2 udu-niga mu kaš$_{4}$-e-ne (5) 2 udu 2 u$_{8}$ (6) 1 máš-gal (7) šu-gíd mu àga-ús-e-ne (8) é-muḫaldim-šè (9) gìri ^{d}šul-gi-uru-mu / rá-gaba (10) 1 udu [a-mur]-ilum lú-kin-gi$_{4}$-a / li-[pá-nu-u]k-ša-pá-aš / é[nsi]-mar-ḫa-ši^{ki} (11) gìri lú-^{d}da-mu (12) 1 udu-niga **gu-ra-a lú-/ur-šu^{ki}** (13) 1 udu-niga **'à-um lú-ma-/rí^{ki}** (14) gìri ḫu-zi-ri sukkal (15) árad-mu maškim (16) iti u$_{4}$-7 ba-zal (17) ki ^{d}šul-gi-a-a-mu⟨-ta⟩ / ba-zi (18) [iti] u$_{5}$-bí-k[ú] (19) [mu ....]

49. Owen, *MVN* 11 146 [= HSM 911.3.31] (AS 6/iv/26)
(1) 3 udu-niga (2) sískur-^{d}ma-al-kum-ma (3) ur-^{d}ba-ba$_{6}$ muḫaldim maškim (4) 1 máš-gal-niga-sig$_{5}$ (5) u$_{4}$-ná-a-ka é-gal-la ba-an-ku$_{9}$ (6) a-bí-sí-im-ti (7) gìri a-ḫu-we-er (8) 1 máš-gal-niga

---

[84] The transliteration of this text is published with the kind permission of its owner. The text is in a European private collection.

(9) li-pá-an-aš-ku$_8$-pí lú/-kin-gi$_4$-a li-pá-nu-uk-ša-pá-aš / énsi-mar-ḫa-ši^{ki} (10) gìri lú-^{d}da-mu sukkal (11) 1 máš-gal-niga **ì-lí-^{d}da-gan / lú-e[b-l]a^{ki}** (12) gìri na-bí-^{d}suen sukkal (13) 1 máš-gal-niga (14) **šu-^{d}iš-ḫa-ra lú-/ma-rí^{ki}** (15) gìri ši$_x$(SIG$_4$)-te-li (16) árad-mu maškim (17) iti u$_4$-26 ba-zal (18) ki a-ḫu-we-er-ta (19) ba-zi (20) iti ki-síg-^{d}nin-a-zu (21) mu ša-aš-ru^{ki} ba-ḫul (22-side) 7 udu

50. Owen, *MVN* 11 152 [= HSM 911.3.48] (AS 5/iv/19)
(1) 13 gukkal (2) 1 gukkal giš-dù (3) 26 udu-a-lum (4) šà-kà-na-kum (5) 1 sila$_4$ da-da-ni / dub-sar (6) 1 máš-gal **aq-ba-ìa / lú-ma-rí^{ki}** (7) 1 máš nu-úr-zu nu-bànda (8) 1 más SUḪUŠ-ki-in nu-bànda (9) 1 máš ir-du-a nu-bànda (10) 1 gu$_4$ 4 udu (11) 1 sila$_4$ 1 máš (12) a-da-na-aḫ sipa-/ur-ra (13) 2 sila$_4$ énsi-nibru^{ki} (14) u$_4$-19-kam (15) mu-DU (16) ab-ba-sa$_6$-ga ì-dab$_5$ (17) iti ki-síg-^{d}nin-a-zu (18) mu en-unu$_6$-gal / ^{d}inanna ba-ḫun (19-side) 54

51. Owen, *MVN* 15 189 [= Kelsey Museum 89125] (Š 47/viii/28)
(1) 2 u[du$^?$]-niga-sig$_5$-nita (2) 3 [udu$^?$]-niga (3) ^{d}nin-líl (4) 2 udu-niga ^{d}en-ki (5) ^{d}nanše-ul$_4$-gal maškim (6) 2 udu-niga (7) sískur ^{d}inanna-šà-unug^{ki} (8) zabar-dab$_5$ maškim (9) gìri lugal-ì-maḫ sagi (10) 1 udu-niga ì-si-in^{ki} (11) kur-gìri-ni-šè maškim (12) 4 udu-niga (13) 1 máš-gal-niga (14) **a-mi-ir-^{d}šul-gi** (15) 4 udu-niga (16) **^{d}šul-gi-pa-lí-il / lú-ma-rí^{ki}-me** (17) u$_4$ a-ḫu-ti^{ki} (18) a-šà dab$_5$-dè ì-re$^!$-eš-ša-a (19) diri ba-ne-DU (20) gìri kù-^{d}nanna sukkal (21) 1 gu$_4$-niga NÌ.MÍ.ÚS.SÁ / árad-mu dumu ad-da-bi gala (22) árad-mu maškim (23) iti u$_4$-28 ba-zal šà tum-ma-al^{ki} (24) [z]i-[g]a ki lú-dingir-ra⟨-ta⟩ (25) iti šu-eš-ša (26) mu ús-sa ki-maš^{ki} ba-ḫul

52. Owen, *MVN* 15 204 [= Kelsey Museum 89234][85] (AS 8/v/28)
(1) 1 udu-a-udu-ḫur-sag-niga (2) 1 máš-gal-a-dara$_4$-niga (3) ^{d}en-líl (4) 1 udu-a-lu-ḫur-sag-niga (5) 1 máš-gal-a-síg-niga (6) ^{d}nin-líl (7) lugal-ku$_9$-r[a] (8) a-tu sag[i] (9) šà nibru[^{ki}] (10) 2 udu šu-gíd [é-muḫaldim] (11) mu gàr-du-e-n[e-šè] (12) gìri ^{d}šul-gi-[...] (13) 1 udu-niga **la-qì-pu-[um] / lú-ma-rí[^{ki}]** (14) gìri šu-ab-ba [...] (15) árad-mu maškim (16) iti u$_4$-28 ba-zal (17) ki igi-^{d}en-líl-šè-ta (18) ba-zi (19) iti ezem-^{d}nin-a-zu (20) mu en-eridu^{ki} ba-ḫun (21-side) 7

53. Owen, *MVN* 15 360 [= Birmingham (Alabama) Art Museum 56.86.1 = Dhorme, *RA* 9 (1912) 59 SA 79] (AS 2/iii/13)
(1) 1 udu-niga (2) **puzur$_4$-ma-ma lú-/ma-rí-ki^{ki}** (3) 1 udu-niga **ì-lí-^{d}da-gan lú-/eb-la^{ki}** (4) 1 udu-niga (5) **na-na-ù lú$^!$-ur-šu^{ki}** (6) é-a-ne-ne-a$^!$ (7) lugal-má-gur$_8$-re / maškim (8) iti u$_4$-13 ba-zal (9) ki ^{d}šul-gi-a-a-mu-ta$^!$ (10) ba-zi (11) iti u$_5$-bí-kú (12) mu ^{d}amar-^{d}suen lugal-e / ur-bí-lum^{ki} mu-ḫul (13-side) 3$^!$

54. Owen, Newell 1978, collated (ŠS 1/vi/24)
(1) 3 gu$_4$ 5 udu-a-lum 5 gukkal (2) na-ap-la-núm (3) 1 udu-a-lum 3 gukkal (4) ì-lí-a-ḫu (5) 3 gukkal a-ḫi-a-ù$^!$ (6) 3 gukkal-ú e-a-ḫu-um (7) 1 gukkal 1 máš-gal (8) ìa-a-ma-dú (9) 2 gukkal tuš-a-me (10) 2 gukkal e-ša-nu-um (11) 1 udu-a-lum 1 máš-gal (12) la-ḫi-a-nu-um

---

[85] Note that in Owen, *MVN* 15, p. 81, the Kelsey Museum numbers on texts 203 and 204 were inadvertantly reversed. They are correct in the catalogue and on the copies.

(13) 1 gukkal 1 máš-gal (14) nu-gi-ra-nu-um (15) 1 gukkal 1 máš-gal (16) al-lu-ri-núm (17) mar-tu-me (18) 1 ^{mí}ešgar-niga lugal-má-gur$_8$-re (19) 1 sila$_4$ ḫu-un-ḫu-ub-še (20) 1 sila$_4$ lugal-á-zi-da šabra (21) 1 sila$_4$ šà-kal-la (22) 1 sila$_4$ ^{d}utu-kam (23) 1 sila$_4$ ur-mes (24) u$_4$-24-kam (25) mu-DU (26) in-ta-è-a ì-dab$_5$ (27) gìri ^{d}nanna-ma-ba dub-sar (28) šà uri$_5$^{ki}-ma (29) iti á-ki-ti (30) mu ^{d}šu-^{d}suen lugal (31) 41

55. Owen and Veenker, "MeGum," p. 267 Trout 1 (AS 7/v/21)
(1) 3 udu-niga (2) 2 máš-gal-niga (3) é-muḫaldim (4) mu kaš$_4$-e-ne-šè (5) gìri ur-^{d}šar-ru-gin$_7$ sukkal (6) 1 máš-gal-niga (7) **[a-b]u-DU$_{10}$ lú-ma-rí^{ki}** (8) [1] udu-niga (9) **[e$^{?}$-r]i-iš-ti-ar lú-ur-šu^{ki}** (10) [1] udu-niga (11) **puzur$_4$-^{d}da-gan / lú-tu-tu-ul^{ki}** (12) gì[ri š]i$_x$(SIG$_4$)-te-li sukkal (13) [1] udu-niga (14) **z[u$^{?}$-ri$^{?}$-im$^{?}$] lú-kin-gi$_4$-a** (15) **me-GU-um énsi-eb-la^{ki}** (16) gìri na-bí-^{d}suen sukkal (17) 1 udu-niga ga-da-ad-du (18) 1 máš-gal-niga zu-bu-uš (19) lú-kin-gi$_4$-a ìa-a-ab-/ra-ad lú-SU.A.KI-me (20) gìri ^{d}nanna-ì-gi sukkal (21) árad-mu maškim (22) [it]i u$_4$-21 ba-zal (23) [k]i a-ḫu-we-er-ta (24) [ba]-zi (25) [iti ezem]-^{d}nin-a-zu (26) [mu ḫ]u-úḫ-nu-ri^{ki} / ba-ḫul (27-side) 11 [ud]u

56. Pettinato, *MVN* 6 100 [= *ITT* 4 7101] (no date)
(1) 2 ma-na nagga-zabar (2) [....] lugal (3) ⌈½⌉ ma-na (4) ⌈puzur$_4$⌉-da-ga-an (5) **⅓ ŠA lú-eb-la$^{\langle ki \rangle}$** (6) ½ ma-na (7) ḪA.⌈AD⌉.ḪI.IŠ (8) 10 gín GAL.ŠÈ (9) eren-da (10) šu ba-ti

57. *Pettinato, *MVN* 6 110 [= *ITT* 4 7111] (no date)

58. *Pettinato, *MVN* 6 247 [= *ITT* 4 7253] (no date)

59. Pohl, *TMH NF* 1/2 313 (Š 46/iii/1)
(1) 500 illar(GIŠ.ŠUB) / ṣu-ti-a-núm[86] (2) 500 ^{giš}káb(NAG)-gúl(NUMUN)[87] (3) gún **lú-eb-la^{ki}** (4) gìri zu-rí-im lú-na (5) ù lugal-pa-è (6) mu-DU (7) ilum-ba-ni 8) šu ba-ti (9) iti u$_5$-bí-kú / u$_4$-1-kam (10) mu ki-maš^{ki} ba-ḫul

60. Schneider, *AnOr* 7 (1932) 99; collated and transliterated by L. Cagni, *OA* 22 (1983) 90-91 with suggested corrections by E. Arcari, *Or* 53 (1984) 442-443. Transliterated from new copy by M. Molina, unpublished (AS 4/v/6)
(1) [2] udu-niga (2) [1] máš-gal-niga (3) IGI.KÁR u$_4$ ^{d}nin-líl-e-ma-ki-ág / u$_4$ dumu in-tu-da-a (4) gìri lugal-inim-gi-na sukkal (5) 1 udu-niga mu ama-ki-kal-ki-šè (6) gìri ur-^{d}dumu-zi-da sukkal (7) é-muḫaldim-šè (8) 5 udu-niga (9) ki na-ap-la-núm mar-tu-šè (10) gìri ad-da-sa$_6$-ga àga-ús (11) 2 udu-niga-gu$_4$-e-ús-sa (12) ^{d}nin-tu (13) gìri kur-gìr-ì-ni-šè (14) 1 máš-gal-niga a-mur-ilum lú-kin-/gi$_4$-a li-pá-nu-uk-ša-pá-aš énsi-/mar-ḫa-ši^{ki} (15) 1 máš-gal-niga **gu-ra-a lú-**

---

[86] *CAD* Ṣ 228 s.v. *ṣudānu*, (a tree) does not list this citation, only *MSL* V 133. See now the references and discussion by Steinkeller, "Container" (1991).

[87] Steinkeller reads ^{giš}káb-kul with discussion in "Container" (1991). See also W. Sallaberger, "Zur Lesung der Bewässerungseinrichtung NAG-kud = káb-kud," *NABU* 1991/47. However, note the attestations with GUL as pointed out by J. Bauer, *Altorientalistische Notizen* 1 (1992) No. 46 and H. Waetzoldt, "Zu P. Steinkeller," *NABU* 1992/15. On the basis of these spellings I read the sign tentatively as gúl.

ur-[šu]^{ki} (16) 1 máš-gal-niga **'à-um ⌜lú⌝-ma-/rí^{ki}** (17) gìri ḫu-zi-ri sukkal (18) 1 máš-gal-niga **^{d}da-gan-a-bu / lú-kin-gi$_4$-a ìa-ši-li-im / énsi-tu-tu-la^{ki}** (19) 1 máš-gal-niga **i-ba-ti lú-kin-gi$_4$-/a ib-da-ti énsi-gu$_5$-ub-la^{ki}** (20) gìri pù-ša-am sukkal (21) árad-mu maškim (22) iti u$_4$-6 ba-zal (23) ki ^{d}šul-gi-a-a-mu-ta (24) ba-zi (25) ⌜iti⌝ ezem-^{d}nin-a-zu (26) [m]u en-maḫ-gal-an-na / [e]n-^{d}nanna ba-ḫun (27-side) 16 udu

61. Schneider, *Or*SP 18 (1925) 17 (Š 48/ix/9)
(1) 1 [si]la$_4$ ^{d}utu (2) mu-DU ur-^{d}nin-gublaga (3) 1 sila$_4$ mu-DU énsi-gír-su^{ki} (4) 1 sila$_4$ mu-DU en-šà-kù-ge / sanga-^{d}nin-giš-zi-da (5) 1 sila$_4$-niga mu-DU árad-mu (6) 1 sila$_4$-niga mu-DU lú-^{d}nin-šubur (7) ^{d}nanna (8) èr-ra-na-da maškim (9) 1 máš-niga 1 sila$_4$ mu-DU é-a-ì-lí (10) 1 sila$_4$ mu-DU lugal-má-gur$_8$-re sukkal (11) é-ùzu-ga (12) a-a-kal-la maškim (13) 8 gu$_4$ sískur-^{d}nanna (14) 2 gu$_4$ 50$^{?}$ udu 4 máš nin-kal-la (15) igi-kár dag-ga-šè (16) 3 udu 2 máš ur-^{d}šul-pa-/è ù numun (17) u$_4$ nam-gala in-ku$_4$-ra⟨-a⟩ (18) 2 udu-niga-gu$_4$-e-ús-sa (19) 1 udu 2 máš-gal (20) **a-mi-ir-^{d}šul-gi** (21) 2 udu-niga-gu$_4$-e-ús-sa (22) 1 [udu 2 máš-gal] (23) **^{d}š[ul-gi-pa-lí-il]** (24) 2 udu-gu$_4$-e-ús-sa (25) 1 udu 2 máš-gal (26) **aq-ba-ìa** (27) 2 udu-niga-gu$_4$-e-ús-sa (28) 1 udu 2 máš:gal (29) **ì-lí-iš-ti-kál** (30) **lú-ma-rí^{ki}-me** (31) 2 udu-niga-gu$_4$-e-ús-sa (32) 1 udu 2 máš-gal (33) KA-ú-KA nar$^{?}$ (34) árad-mu maškim (35) u$_4$-10-lá-1-kam (36) ki na-sa$_6$-ta ba-zi (37) iti ezem-maḫ (38) mu ḫa-ar-ši^{ki} ù / ki-maš^{ki} ba-ḫul

62. Sigrist, *AUCT* 1 494 [= AUAM 73.1362] (ŠS 1/iv/9)
(1) 14 udu (2) 38 u$_8$ (3) 4 máš 9 ùz (4) é-muḫaldim (5) 10 máš **lú-ma-rí^{ki}** (6) 10 máš **lú-ur-šu^{ki}** (7) 10 máš **lú-eb-la^{ki}** (8) u$_4$-9-kam (9) zi-ga (10) ki ur-kù-nun-na (11) iti ezem-maḫ (12) mu ús-sa ki-maš^{ki} / ba-ḫul

63. Sigrist, *AUCT* 3 294 [= AUAM 73.1024] (ŠS 1/iv/1)
(1) 1 gu$_4$-niga 4-[kam-ús] (2) ^{d}en-[líl] (3) 1 gu$_4$-niga 4-kam-[ús] (4) ^{d}nin-lí[l] (5) sískur-gu-[la] (6) lugal ku$_4$-[ra] (7) 1 gu$_4$-niga a-tu$_5$-^{d}nin-tin-ug$_5$-[ga] (8) šu-a-gi-na (9) 1 udu-niga ar-ba-tal lú-[ši-ma-núm^{ki}] (10) 1 udu-niga gu$_4$-e-ús-sa (11) ku-un-ši-ma-tum é-g[i$_4$-a] ar-ba-tal lú-ši-ma-núm^{ki} (12) gìri èr-ra-a sukkal (13) šà$^{!}$ nibru^{ki} (14) 1 udu-niga ^{d}geštin-an-na (15) 1 udu bu-ga-šur-ra (16) 1 udu-niga ^{d}nun-gal (17) a-tu sagi maškim (18) 1 udu-niga 4-kam-ús (19) 2 udu niga-gu$_4$-e-ús-sa (20) 3 silá išib-^{d}ištaran (21) nu-úr-^{d}šamaš rá-gaba maškim (22) 1 udu-niga KA.NE-šè (23) šà é-duru$_5$-šè (24) gìri ur-šu-mu (25) 1 udu-niga **a-bu-DU$_{10}$ lú-ma-rí^{ki}** (26) gìri ì-lí-be-lí suk[kal] (27) iti ud-1 ba-[zal] (28) ki zu-ba-ga-ta b[a-zi] (29) iti ki-síg-^{d}nin-[a-zu] (30) mu ^{d}šu-^{d}suen [lugal] (31-side) 3 gu$_4$ 13! udu

64. Sigrist, *AUCT* 3 480 [= AUAM 73.1323] ([IS(?) ?]/i/19)[88]
(1) [x udu-nig]a-gu$_4$-e-ús-s[a] (2) 1 udu-niga ^{d}gu-la (3) 1 udu-niga gú-NE (4) 5 udu-niga-gu$_4$-e-ús-sa alan-lugal (5) šà ^{d}en-líl-lá (6) 1 udu-niga 3-kam-ús 2 udu-niga-gu$_4$-e-ús-sa (7) 1 ^{mí}ešgar-niga-sig$_4$-ús ^{d}nin-líl (8) 1 udu-niga-gu$_4$-e-ús-sa ^{d}nanna (9) 1 udu-niga gú-NE (10) 5 udu-niga gu$_4$-e-ús-sa alan-lugal (11) šà é-^{d}nin-líl-lá (12) uzu-a-bala (13) 1 udu-niga-sig$_5$-ús 2 udu-niga-gu$_4$-e-ús-sa (14) ^{d}en-líl (15) 1 udu-niga ^{d}gu-za (16) 1 udu-niga ḫur-sag-kà-lam-ma

[88] For the basis of the dating of this text, see above n. 62. Note that the name read ba-za-za in line 38 may be the same as the name read ba-a-a in other texts such as no. 15:7 (Fish, *CST* 190:7) above.

(17) šà é-^{d}en-líl-lá (18) 1 udu-niga-sig$_5$-ús 2 udu-niga-gu$_4$-e-ús-sa (19) ^{d}nin-líl (20) 1 udu-niga ^{d}nanna (21) šà é-^{d}nin-líl-lá (22) lugal ku$_4$-ra sískur-gu-la (23) [1] udu-niga-gu$_4$-e-ús-sa du$_6$-kù (24) [1] udu-niga-gu$_4$-e-ús-sa ^{d}nin-ḫur-sag (25) [1] udu-niga-gu$_4$-e-ús-sa ^{d}nuska (26) 1 udu-niga-gu$_4$-e-ús-sa ^{d}nin-urta (27) 1 udu-niga-gu$_4$-e-ús-sa ^{d}inanna (28) 1 udu-niga-gu$_4$-e-ús-sa ^{d}šu-^{d}suen (29) 1 udu-niga-gu$_4$-e-ús-sa ^{d}suen (30) 1 udu-niga-gu$_4$-e-ús-sa ^{d}šul-gi (31) 1 udu-niga-gu$_4$-e-ús-sa ^{d}nin-sún (32) 1 udu-niga-gu$_4$-e-ús-sa ^{d}lugal-bàn-da (33) 1 udu-niga-gu$_4$-e-ús-sa ^{d}en-ki (34) 1 udu-niga-gu$_4$-e-ús-sa ^{d}nin-ḫur-sag-ga (35) sískur-ge$_6$ (36) a-tu sagi maškim (37) 5 udu-niga **x-[G]I$^{?}$-ŠI$^{?}$ lú-ma-rí^{ki}** (38) gìri ba-za-za sukkal (39) ^{d}nanna-kam sukkal maškim (40) [šà] nibru^{ki} (41) [ur-^{d}]en-líl-lá dub-sar (42) [iti maš-d]ù-kú (43) [mu ....] (44-side) 50-lá-1 (seal) ur-^{d}en-líl-lá / dub-sar / dumu lugal-úr-ra-ni

65. Sigrist, *TPTS* 1 73 [= PTS 312] (AS 8/v/15)
(1) 1 udu[-niga] (2) m[u....] / taḫ-ša-tal maškim (3) 1 udu-niga (4) **la-qì-ip / lú-ma-rí^{ki}** (5) ilum-dan sukkal maškim (6) iti u$_4$-15 ba-zal (7) ki-na-lu$_5$-ta (8) ba-zi (9) šà nibru^{ki} (10) iti ezem-^{d}nin-a-zu (11) mu en-NU[N.KI / ba-ḫun] (12-side) 2

66. Sigrist, *Toronto* 279 [= ROM 925×62.267] (Š 43/i/-)
(1) 72 gu$_4$ (2) kìšib si-dù (3) 1 gu$_4$ **lú-ma-rí^{ki}** (4) 1 gu$_4$ na-kab-tum-šè (5) 6 gu$_4$ kìšib ^{d}en-líl-lá--ì-ša$_6$ (6) zi-ga (7) ^{d}en-líl-lá (8) iti maš-dù-kú (9) mu en-^{d}nanna maš-e ì-pàd (10-side) 80

67. Sigrist, *Toronto* 287 [= ROM 925×62.275] (Š 44/iii/18)
(1) 1 sila$_4$ ^{d}en-líl (2) 1 sila$_4$ ^{d}nin-líl (3) mu-DU šeš-da-da sanga (4) 1 sila$_4$ ^{d}utu (5) mu-DU an-ni-a (6) zabar-dab$_5$ maškim (7) 1 áb 4 u$_8$ (8) 1 udu 4 sila$_4$ (9) šu-gíd é-muḫaldim-šè (10) 1 dúsu-nita (11) **ì-lí-^{d}da-gan** (12) **lú-kin-gi$_4$-a-lú-eb-la^{ki}** (13) árad-mu maškim (14) zi-ga u$_4$-18-kam (15) iti u$_5$-bí-kú (16) mu si-mu-ru-um^{ki} ù lu-lu-bu^{ki} / a-rá-10-lá-1-kam ba-ḫul

68. Sigrist, Owen, Young, *MVN* 13 635 [= FLP 277] (AS 6/iv/5)
(1) 1 máš-gal-niga (2) li-pá-an-aš-ku$_8$-pí lú-/kin-gi$_4$-a li-pá-nu-uk-ša-/pá-aš énsi-mar-ḫa-ši^{ki} (3) gìri šu-^{d}šul-gi sukkal (4) 1 udu-niga (5) **ì-lí-^{d}da-gan lú-/eb-la^{ki}** (6) [g]ìri na-bí-^{d}suen ⟨sukkal⟩ (7) [1 m]áš-gal-niga **šu-^{d}iš-ḫa-ra / lú-ma-rí^{ki}** (8) [gìri š]i$_x$(SIG$_4$)-te-li sukkal (9) [1 ud]u-niga (10) [géme-é]-an-na é-gi$_4$-a [sukka]l-ma[ḫ u]$_4$ tu-ra ì-me-a (11) árad-mu maškim (12) iti u$_4$-5 ba-zal (13) ki a-ḫu-we-er-ta (14) ba-zi (15) iti ki-síg-^{d}nin-a-zu (16) mu ša-aš-ru^{ki} ba-[ḫul] (17-side) 6 udu

69. Sigrist, apud Spar, *CTMMA* 1 17 (AS 4/vii/1)
(1) 1 udu-niga-gu$_4$-e-ús-sa (2) 1 máš-gal (3) ^{giš}gu-za-^{d}šul-gi (4) šá-ta-kù-zu maškim (5) 1 gu$_4$-niga (6) 3 udu-niga-gu$_4$-e-ús-sa (7) 7 udu (8) tá-din-eš$_4$-tár (9) 1 gu$_4$-niga (10) 2 udu-niga-gu$_4$-e-ús-sa (11) 1 udu 2 máš-gal (12) ^{d}nin-líl-tu-kul-ti (13) 1 gu$_4$-niga (14) 2 udu-niga-gu$_4$-e-ús-sa (15) 1 udu 2 máš-gal (16) géme-^{d}nanna (17) 1 gu$_4$-niga (18) 2 udu-niga-gu$_4$-e-ús-sa (19) 1 udu 2 máš-gal (20) pa$_4$-ki-na-na (21) 1 gu$_4$-niga (22) 2 udu-niga-gu$_4$-e-ús-sa (23) 1 udu 2 máš-gal (24) ša-at-^{d}ma-mi (25) 1 gu$_4$-niga (26) 2 udu-niga-gu$_4$-e-ús-sa (27) 1 udu 2 máš-gal (28) nin-ḫé-du$_7$ (29) 1 gu$_4$-niga (30) 2 udu-niga-gu$_4$-e-ús-sa (31) 1 udu 2 máš-gal (32) géme-é-an-[na] (33) 1 gu$_4$-niga 2 udu-niga-[gu$_4$-e-ús-sa] (34) 1 udu 2 máš-[gal] (35) te-ṣe-in-ma-ma$^{!}$ (36) 1 gu$_4$-niga 2 udu-niga-gu$_4$-e-ús-sa (37) 1 udu 2 máš-gal (38) dam-lugal-má-gur$_8$-re (39)

1 gu$_4$-niga 2 udu-niga-gu$_4$-e-ús-sa (40) 1 udu 2 máš-gal (41) išib-^{d}ištaran (42) 1 gu$_4$-niga 1 udu-niga-gu$_4$-e-ús-sa (43) 2 udu 1 máš-gal (44) dam-šar-ru-um-ba-ni (45) 1 gu$_4$-niga 2 udu-niga-gu$_4$-e-ús-sa (46) 2 udu 1 máš-gal (47) dam-lú-^{d}nanna dumu ur-ni$_9$-gar (48) dumu-mí-lugal-me (49) 2 udu-niga (50) 2 udu 1 máš-gal (51) ki-na-at-nu-nu (52) 2 udu-niga-gu$_4$-e-ús-sa (53) 2 udu 1 máš-gal (54) ku$_8$-ba-tum (55) UM+ME-da-lugal-me (56) ri-iṣ-ilum rá-gaba maškim (57) 2 gu$_4$-niga 2 udu-niga-sig$_5$ (58) 5 udu-niga-gu$_4$-e-ús-sa (59) 3 udu 2 máš-gal (60) na-ap-la-nu-um (61) 2 udu a-bí-iš-ki-il (62) 2 udu dan-núm šeš-a-ni (63) 2 udu ^{d}šul-gi-a-bí (64) mar-tu-me (65) 1 máš-gal i-šar-li-bur (66) 1 udu ki-ma-ni (67) 1 máš-gal si-ni-ni (68) 1 máš-gal ba-da-ti-na (69) 1 máš-gal pu-ul-ba-at (70) 1 máš-gal dan-ḫa-la-aḫ (71) 1 udu ḫu-un-ki-ib-ri (72) 1 udu ḫu-un-^{d}šul-gi (73) 1 máš-gal **^{d}šul-gi-ì-lí** (74) 2 udu 1 máš-gal (75) **a-mur-^{d}šul-gi** (76) 1 udu 1 máš-gal (77) **^{d}šul-gi-pa-lí-il** (78) 1 udu 1 máš-gal (79) **aq-ba-ìa** (80) 1 udu ba-ša-an-ti-ba-at (81) 1 udu mu-lu-uš (82) 1 gu$_4$-niga (83) 3 udu 2 máš-gal (84) we-du-um lú-kin-gi$_4$-a na-du-be-lí énsi-má-gan^{ki} (85) 3 udu 2 máš-gal (86) má-za lú-kin-gi$_4$-a ì-še-bu lú-da-ri-ba^{ki} (87) 1 gu$_4$-niga (88) 3 udu 2 máš-gal (89) ši-ba-ra-aq lú-zi-da-⟨aḫ-⟩ri^{ki} (90) 1 gu$_4$-niga (91) 3 u[du] 2 máš-gal (92) **še-da-ku-ku lú-ma-rí^{ki}** (93) 1 udu 1 máš-gal (94) zi-nu-gi lú-ḫi-bí-la-ti^{ki} (95) gìri ne-ni-la sukkal (96) 1 gu$_4$-niga 10 udu (97) ur-^{d}ba-ba$_6$ muḫaldim (98) 1 gu$_4$-niga (99) 2 udu-niga-sig$_5$ (100) 3 udu-niga-gu$_4$-e-ús-sa (101) 5 udu (102) en-^{d}inanna (103) árad-mu maškim (104) šà-me-túm á-ki-ti-šu-numun (105) ud-1-kam (106) ki ab-ba-sa$_6$-ga-ta (107) ba-zi (108) iti ezem-^{d}šul-gi (109) mu en-maḫ-gal-an-na en-^{d}nanna ba-ḫun (110) 174

70. Sollberger, *AfO* 19 (1959-60) 120-121 Pinches Manuscript 82 = idem, *MVN* 5 (1978) 111 (AS 4/v/9)
(1) 2 udu-niga ^{d}inanna-unug^{ki}-šè (2) gìri ^{d}šul-gi-ad-gur sagi (3) 1 udu-niga ^{d}nun-gal (4) ^{d}nanše-ul$_4$-gal maškim (5) 1 udu-niga-gu$_4$-e-ús-sa (6) 2[89] máš-gal-niga-gu$_4$-e-ús-sa (7) a-rá-1-kam (8) 6 udu (9) 4 sila$_4$ (10) 10 más-g[al$^{!?}$-niga$^{?}$] (11) a-rá-2-kam (12) šu-gíd é-muḫaldim-šè (13) mu àga-ús-ke$_4$-ne-šè (14) gìri ^{d}šul-gi-uru-mu rá-gaba (15) 1 udu-niga a-mur-ilum lú-kin-gi$_4$-a / li-pá-nu-uk-ša-pá-aš énsi-mar-ḫa-ši^{ki} (16) 1 udu-niga **gu-ra-a lú-ur$^{!}$-šu$^{!ki}$** (17) 1 udu-niga **'à-um lú-ma-rí^{ki}** (18) 1 udu-niga **^{d}da-gan-a-bu lú-kin-gi$_4$-a / ìa-ši-li-im énsi-tu-tu-la^{ki}** (19) 1 udu-niga **i-ba-ti lú-kin-gi$_4$-a ib-da-ti / énsi-gu$_5$-ub-la^{ki}** (20) gìri pù-ša-am sukkal (21) árad-mu maškim (22) iti u$_4$-10-lá-1 ba-zal (23) ki ^{d}šul-gi-a-a-mu-ta ba-zi (24) iti ezem-^{d}nin-a-zu (25) mu en-maḫ-gal-an-na en-^{d}nanna ba-ḫun (26-side) 31 udu

71. *Virolleaud, *TEL* 46 (ŠS 8/i-xii/-)

72. Watson, *Birmingham* 1 77[90] (AS 2/vii/6)
(51) 1 udu 1 máš (2) UM+ME-da-lugal (3) šà mu-DU éren-ni-da-ra-/aš-we^{ki} (4) puzur$_4$-èr-ra šu-i maškim (5) 1 udu iš-me-ilum mar-tu (6) 3 udu 2 máš (7) **aq-ba-ìa lú-ma-rí^{ki}** (8) u$_4$ nam-gala-šè ì-in-ku$_4$-ra⟨-a⟩ (9) šà mu-DU-[ra-t]a$^{!}$ (10) 1 áb 18 u[du] (11) 8 u$_8$ 10-lá-1 ^{mí}sila$_4$-gukkal (12) 12 máš 8 ùz (13) šu-gíd é-muḫaldim-šè (14) árad-mu maškim (15) u$_4$-6-kam (16) ki ab-

[89] Note that the number here, 2, is correct as indicated in Sollberger, *AfO* 19 (1959-60) 120 but incorrectly written as 1 in idem, *MVN* 5 (1978) 111. The total of 31, written on the side, suggests that 2 is required.

[90] For this text see Owen, [review of Watson, *Neo-Sumerian Texts from Drehem* (1986)], *JAOS* 108 (1988) 113.

ba-sa$_6$-ga-ta / ba-zi (17) iti šu-eš$_5$-ša (18) mu ^{d}amar-^{d}suen lugal-e / ur-bí-lum^{ki} mu-ḫul (19-side) 64

73. Watson, *Birmingham* 1 95 (ŠS 1/vi/21)
(1) 1 udu-niga (2) **a-bu-DU$_{10}$ lú-ma-rí^{ki}** (3) gìri ì-lí-be-lí sukkal (4) šà unug^{ki}-ga (5) 1 udu-niga (6) ar-ba-tal lú-ši-ma-núm^{ki} (7) gìri šu-eš$_4$-tár sukkal (8) šà nibru^{ki} (9) árad-mu maškim (10) iti u$_4$-21 ba-zal (11) ki zu-ba-ga-ta ba-zi (12) gìri ad-da-kal-la / dub-sar (13) iti á-ki-ti (14) mu ^{d}šu-^{d}suen / lugal (15-side) 2 udu

74. *YBC 3635 (AS 2/xi/-)

75. *Yıldız and Gomi, *PDT* 2 959 ([AS 8$^{?}$/?/?])

76. Young, Wabash 1 (AS 1/ii/26)
(1) 1 gu$_4$-niga (2) 5 udu-niga 3 máš$^{!}$-nita (3) ki na-ap-la-núm mar-tu-šè (4) kur mar-tu-šè má-a ba-a-DU (5) 1 udu-niga **ì-lí-^{d}da-gan / lú-eb-la^{ki}** (6) 1 máš-gal-niga **bu-du-úr / lú-ur-šu^{ki}** (7) 1 máš-gal-niga (8) **iš-me-^{d}da-gan / lú-ma-rí^{ki}** (9) gìri lugal-inim-gi-/na sukkal (10) 1 udu eš$_4$-tár-nu-ri (11) árad-mu maškim (12) iti u$_4$-26 ba-zal (13) ki a-ḫu-ni-ta ba-/zi (14) mu ^{d}amar-^{d}suen / lugal

77. Molina, MM 1103 (AS 8/[i]v/[?])[91]
(1) 2 udu-niga (2) ^{d}inanna-unug^{ki}-šè (3) a$^{!}$-ḫu$^{!}$-ni sagi maškim (4) 1 máš-gal-niga (5) **la-qì-pu-um / lú-ma-rí^{ki}** (6) gìri šu-ab-ba sukkal (7) ilum-dan sukkal maškim (8) it[i u$_4$-x ba-za]l (9) k[i ...-t]a (10) [ba-z]i (11) [iti ki-síg-^{d}nin-a]-zu (12) m[u ^{d}amar-^{d}suen] ki-/ág-en-[erid]u^{ki} ba-ḫun (13-side) 3 udu (seal) ad-da / dub-sar / dumu [....]

[91] Unpublished from a copy courtesy of M. Molina. This text records the same transaction for Laqipum as in No. 9 above.

Index of Personal Names[92]

’à-um (lú-ma-rí^{ki}) 30:3; 33:34; 43:2; 48:13; 60:16 (’à-um ⌜lú⌝-ma-rí^{ki}); 70:17

a-a-kal-la (maškim) 61:12

a-an-[...] 11:18

ab-ba-sa$_6$-ga 34:31; 41:36; 50:16; 69:106; 72:16

a-bí-iš-ki-il (b. dan-núm) 69:61

a-bí-sí-im-ti 4:27; 49:6; a-bí-sí-im-[ti] (gìri) 46:8

a-bu-*ṭab*(DU$_{10}$) (lú-ma-rí^{ki}) 4:15; 5:II.19; 10:6; 20:5; 25:III.2 (lú-ma-r[í^{ki}]); 46:11; 55:7 ([a-b]u-*ṭab*); 63:25; 73:2

á-da-a 26:17

a-da-na-aḫ (sipa-ur-ra) 50:12

a-da-tum (lú-ma-rí$^{k[i]}$) 45:3

ad-da[-....] (dub-sar [....]) 9:seal; 77:seal

ad-da 5:II.13; 25:II.19 (a[d-da])

ad-da-bi (f. árad-mu) 51:21

ad-da-kal-la (gìri, dub-sar) 1:12; 10:12; 44:10; 73:12

ad-da-kal-la (šár-ra-ab-du) 33:41 (šár-ra-a[b-du]); 43:11

ad-da-kal-la (dub-sar dumu nì-érim-e-du$_{10}^{?}$) 10:15

ad-da-sa$_6$-ga (gìri, àga-ús) 60:10

ad-da-tur *Toronto* 639:2

a-ḫi-a-ù$^{!}$ 54:5

a-ḫu-ni 76:13

a-ḫu-ni (sukkal) 6:17

a-ḫu-ni (gìri, [sukkal]) 6:27

a$^{!}$-ḫu$^{!}$-ni (sagi maškim) 77:3

a-ḫu-we-er 22:18; 28:12; 33:39; 36:17; 43:8; 46:17; 49:18; 55:23; 68:13; 76:13

a-ḫu-we-er (gìri) 49:7

al-lu-ri-núm (mar-tu-me) 54:16-17

ama-úg-ga 11:22

a-mi-ir-^{d}šul-gi (lú-ma-rí^{ki}) 51:14; 61:20

a-mur-é-a *Toronto* 639:7

a-mur-ilum (lú-kin-gi$_4$-a) 30:1; 48:10 ([a-mur]-ilum); 60:14 (lú-kin-gi$_4$-a); 70:15

a-mur-^{d}šul-gi (lú-ma-rí^{ki}) 34:17 (lú-ma-rí^{ki}-me); 69:75

an-ni-a 67:5

[92] Includes all texts cited in this article.

aq-ba-ìa (lú-ma-rí^{ki}) 6:38 (aq$^{!}$-ba$^{!}$-ìa); 34:20-21 (aq$^{!}$(APIN)-ba-ìa lú-ma-rí^{ki}-me); 41:31; 50:6; 61:26; 69:79; 72:7

árad-mu 61:5

árad-mu (maškim) 1:9; 2:12; 4:24; 10:8; 11:28; 15:8; 17:14 ([ár]ad-mu); 20:7 (árad-mu$^{!}$) 24:10; 26:18; 27:16; 28:10; 29:8; 30:5; 31:8; 32:12; 33:37; 34:26; 36:15; 41:34; 43:6; 44:7; 46:15; 47:12; 48:15; 49:16; 51:22; 52:15; 55:21; 60:21; 61:34; 67:13; 68:11; 69:103; 70:21; 72:14; 73:9; 76:11

árad-mu (dumu ad-da-bi) 51:21

ar-ba-tal (lú-ši-ma-núm^{ki}) 63:9 (lú-[ši-ma-núm^{ki}]); 63:11; 73:6

a-ri-du-bu-uk 5:I.24-25

a-rí-ip$^{?}$[-....] 5:III.30

a-ri-ip-a-tal (dumu pu-ša-am lú-ši-ma-nu-um^{ki}) 41:17

a-ri-ip-ḫu-up-pí (lú-tal-muš^{ki}) 41:19

a-tu (sagi maškim) 32:9; 63:17; 64:36; a-tu (sag[i]) 52:8

ba-a-a (gìri, sukkal) 15:7

ba-da-du (lú-S[U]) *Toronto* 639:1

ba-da-ti-na 69:68

ba-ša-an-ti-ba-at 69:80

ba-za-za (gìri, sukkal) 64:38

be-lí-šar (gìri) 5:I.10; 25:I.10

bí-ša-za-núm (ur-^{d}šul-gi-ra...eger-a-na) 6:9

bu-du-úr (lú-ur-šu^{ki}) 11:14; 76:6

bu-ga-šur-ra 63:15

da-a-a-ni (maškim) 26:15

^{d}da-gan-a-bu (lú-kin-gi$_{4}$-a) 60:18; 70:18

dam-lugal-má-gur$_{8}$-re 69:38

dam-lú-^{d}nanna (dumu ur-ni$_{9}$-gar) 69:47

dam-šar-ru-um-ba-ni 69:44

dan-ḫa-la-aḫ 69:70

dan-núm (šeš a-bí-iš-ki-il) 69:62

da-sal-ib-ri (lú-ur-šu^{ki}) 33:35; 43:4 (lú-ur-šu$^{(ki)}$)

du-uk-r[a] ([gìri$^{?}$]) 45:5

dú-ul-qá-núm (mar-tu ìa-a-ma-dì) 24:8-9

du-ul-qá-nu-um (lú-ìa-a-ma-dì-um^{ki}) 47:11

du$_{11}$-ga-zi-da *Toronto* 639:4

e-a-ḫu-um 54:6

é-a-ì-lí 61:9

en-^{d}inanna 8:8; 69:102

^{d}en-líl (ugula) *Toronto* 639:16

^{d}en-líl-lá-maḫ (sagi maškim) 1:3

^{d}en-líl-lá-ì-ša$_{6}$ 66:5

^{d}en-líl-zi-šà-gál (maškim) 41:4

en-šà-kù-ge (sanga-^{d}nin-giš-zi-da) 61:4

[e$^{?}$-r]i-iš-ti-ar (lú-ur-šu^{ki}) 55:9

èr-ra-a (gìri, sukkal) 10:3; 63:12

èr-ra-na-da (maškim) 47:8; 61:8

e-ša-nu-um 54:10

eš$_{4}$-tár-nu-ri 76:10

e-zu-un-^{d}da-gan (lú-eb-la^{ki}) 46:13

ga$^{?}$-ba$^{?}$-a 5:III.17

ga-ba-ba (lú-mu-ki-iš^{ki}) 1:7; 44:4

ga-da-ad-du 55:17

géme-é-an-[na] 69:32

géme-^{d}nanna 69:16

^{d}geštin-an-na 63:14

gu-ra-a (lú-ur-šu^{ki}) 30:2 (lú-ur$^{!}$-šu$^{!ki}$); 48:12; 60:15 (gu-ra-a lú-ur-[šu]^{ki}); 70:16 (lú-ur$^{!}$-šu$^{!ki}$)

ḫa-ar-me-me (ki-iz-zi lú-) *Toronto* 639:19

ḪAR-ti (lú-ši-ik-ri-[i]š$^{[ki]}$) 5:III.15

ḫu-un-ḫu-ub-še 54:19

ḫu-un-ki-ib-ri 69:71

ḫu-un-^{d}šul-gi 69:72

ḫu-un-ti-pá (lú-kin-gi$_{4}$-a, lú-du$_{8}$-du$_{8}$-lí$^{!ki}$) 11:25

ḫu-un-zi-ib-tum 5:II.6 (ḫu-un-zi-[ib-tum]); 25:II.12 (ḫu-un-z[i-ib-tum])

ḫu-uz-taḫ (lú-ḫu-na-t[al]) 5:III.13

ḫu-zi-ri (gìri, sukkal) 1:6; 30:4; 43:5; 44:3; 48:14; 60:17

ìa-a-ab-ra-ad (lú-SU.A.KI-me) 55:19

ìa-a-ma-dú (mar-tu) 54:8

ìa-ši-li-im (énsi-tu-tu-la^{ki}) 60:18; 70:18

ìa-ù-ša (dumu me-ša-[nu-n]u lú-simaški(SU)) 4:22

i-ba-ti (lú-kin-gi$_{4}$-a) 60:19; 70:19

ib-da-ti (énsi-gu$_{5}$-ub-la^{ki}) 60:19 (énsi-gu$_{5}$-⌜ub-la^{ki}⌝); 70:19

ib-ni-ilum (sukkal) 6:5

[i]b-ni-^{d}šu-^{d}suen 5:III.11 (lú-)

i-din-AG (lú-ma-rí$^{!ki}$) 22:13-14

igi-^{d}en-líl 52:17 (igi-^{d}en-líl-šè)

ì-lí-a-ḫu$^{!}$ 54:4

ì-lí-be-lí (gìri, sukkal) 10:7; 33:36; 63:26 (suk[kal]); 73:3

ì-lí-^{d}da-gan (lú-eb-la^{ki}) 3:12; 11:16; 13; 16:8; 17:6; 22:9; 23:2; 24:5-6; 28:5; 29:4; 35:9; 36:11; 47:9; 49:11 (lú-e[b]-la^{ki}); 53:3; 68:5; 76:5

ì-lí-^{d}da-gan (lú-kin-gi$_{4}$-a lú-eb-la^{ki}) 67:11-12

ì-lí-iš-ti-kál (lú-ma-rí^{ki}-me) 61:30

ì-lum-a-bi$^{!}$ (gìri, lú-ma-rí^{ki}) 14:5-6

ilum-ba-ni 59:7

ilum-ba-ni (dub-sar-kaš$_{4}$) 6:14

ilum-ba-ni (gìri, sukkal) 31:5

ilum-dan (maškim) 9:4

ilum-dan (sukkal maškim) 22:16; 65:5; 77:7

i-na-LUM 5:III.24

in-ta-è-a 31:10

i-pí-iq-re-e-ú (mar-tu ìa-a-ma-dì-um) 4:17; 5:II.31 (ìa-a-ma-dì-[um$^{?}$]; 25:III.15 (m[ar]-tu ìa-a-ma-d[ì-um$^{?}$])

ir-du-a (nu-bànda) 50:9

is-ga-ga (maš-en-kak lú-ì-lí-am-ra^{ki}) *Toronto* 639:20

i-šar-ì-ši (lú-kin-gi$_{4}$-a) 38:11

i-šar-li-bur 69:65

ì-še-bu (lú-da-ri-ba^{ki}) 69:86

išib-^{d}ištaran 63:20; 69:41

^{d}iškur-da-ni (ugula) 21:I+x.6 ([ugula ^{d}iškur]-da-ni), II+x.3

iš-me-^{d}da-gan (lú-ma-rí^{ki}) 11:12; 76:8

iš-me-ilum (mar-tu) 72:5

i$^{!}$(TUR)-ti-é-a *Toronto* 639:6

[it-r]a-ak-ì-lí (lú-ma-rí^{ki}) 8:10

i-zi-in-^{d}da-gan (lú-eb-la^{ki}) 4:9; 5:II.25 (i-zi-in-^{d}da-[gan]); 25:III.7

kàs-pu-ša (gìri, sagi) 41:3

KA-ú-KA (nar$^{?}$) 61:33

kí-ba-a-tal (lú-ur-bí-lum^{ki}) 5:II.33 (kí-ba-a-[tal] lú-ur-bí-[lum^{ki}-šè]); 25:III.17 (kí-ba-a-[tal] lú-ur-bí-lum^{k}[^{i}-šè])

ki-iz-zi (lú-ḫa-ar-me-me) *Toronto* 639:19

ki-ma-ni 69:66

ki-na-lu$_{5}$ 65:7

ki-na-at-nu-nu 69:51

kir-ba-tal (gìri, sukkal) 1:8; 44:6

ki-ri-ib-ul-me (lú-si-mu-ru-um^{ki}) 1:5; 44:2

kiš (b. pa$_{4}$-pa$_{4}$) 41:27

ku$_{8}$-ba-tum 69:54

kù-^{d}nanna (gìri, sukkal) 36:6; 51:20

kù-^{d}nanna (sukkal) 6:19

ku-un-ši-ma-tum 63:11

kur-bi-la-ak (lú-eb-la^{ki}-me-šè) 4:11

kur-bi-la-ak (lú-ur-šu^{ki}) 12:6

kur-gìr-ì-ni (gìri) 60:13 (kur-gìr-ì-ni-šè)

kur-gìri-ni (maškim) 51:11 (kur-gìri-ni-šè)

ku$_8$-sú-sú (lú-ma-ar-da-ma-an^{ki}) 41:22

la-ḫi-a-nu-um 54:12

la-qì-pu-um (lú-ma-rí^{ki}) 9:2; 52:13 (la-qì-pu-[um] lú-ma-rí[^{ki}]); 65:4 (la-qì-ip); 77:4

li-pá-an-aš-ku$_5$-pí (lú-kin-gi$_4$-a) 17:4 ([l]ú-kin-gi$_4$-a); 28:2; 36:8; 49:9; 68:2

li-pá-nu-uk-ša-pá-aš (énsi-mar-ḫa-ši^{ki}) 17:4 (li-pá-nu-uk-[š]a-pá-aš); 28:2; 30:1; 36:8; 48:10 (li-[pá-nu-u]k-ša-pá-aš é[nsi]-mar-ḫa-ši^{ki}); 49:9; 60:14; 68:2; 70:15

lú-dam-a-ḫu-a 5:III.28

lú-an-dùl (rá-gaba, maškim) 2:14

lú-^{d}da-mu (gìri) 48:11

lú-^{d}da-mu (gìri, sukkal) 22:15; 28:3; 49:10

lú-^{d}da-ni (gìri, sukkal) 6:21

lú-dingir-ra 14:7; 16:12; 29:10 (⌈lú-dingir-ra⌉); 35:13; 51:24

lú-^{d}en-ki (gìri, sukkal) 31:7

lú-^{d}en-líl-lá (gìri) 5:IV.13; 25:IV.14 ([gìri lú-^{d}en-líl-lá])

lugal-á-zi-da (šabra) 54:20

lugal-dal[la] (gìri) *Toronto* 639:28

lugal-gu$_4$-si-su 33:24

lugal-dingir-[ra] *Toronto* 639:30

lugal-ì-maḫ (gìri, sagi) 47:5; 51:9

lugal-inim-gi-na (gìri, sukkal) 11:23; 16:9; 29:7 (⌈gìri lugal-inim-gi-na sukkal⌉); 35:10; 60:4; 76:9

lugal-má-gur$_8$-re 34:14; 54:18; 69:38 (dam-)

lugal-má-gur$_8$-re (maškim) 3:15; 16:10; 35:11; 53:7

lugal-má-gur$_8$-re (sukkal) 61:10

lugal-má-gur$_8$-re (šabra) 23:5

lugal-nir-gál 8:5

lugal-pa-è 59:5

lugal-si-sá 39:5

lugal-úr-ra-ni (f. ur-^{d}en-líl-lá dub-sar) 64:44

lú-ḫu-[...] 5:II.1 (l[ú-ḫu...]); 25:II.7 (lú-ḫu-[...])

lú-igi-ma (dub-sar) 7:seal

lú-^{d}nanna (dumu ur-ni$_9$-gar) 69:47

lú-^{d}nanna (šár-ra-ab-d[u]) 46:20

lú-^{d}nin-šubur 61:6

lú-^{d}nin-šubur (gìri, dub-sar) 4:34

lú-sa$_6$ (gìri, dub-sar) 41:39

lú-sukkal-an-dùl *Toronto* 639:27

lú-ša-lim (ḫa-za-núm gar-ša-na^{ki}-ka) 6:11

ma-n[úm-ki]-^{d}šul-gi (gìri) 20:12

má-za (lú-kin-gi$_4$-a) 69:86

me-me-šu-ra (lú-eb-la^{ki}) 12:3

me-ša-[nu-n]u (lú-simaški(SU), f. ìa-ù-ša) 4:22

mu-lu-uš 69:81

na-[...] (sukkal) 6:25

na-bí-^{d}suen (gìri, sukkal) 17:7; 22:10 ([sukka]l); 28:6; 36:12; 49:12; 55:16; 68:6 ([g]ìri na-bí-^{d}suen ⟨sukkal⟩)

na-di (lunga, f. ur-^{d}ba-ba$_6$) 40:5,7

na-du-be-lí (ensi-má-gan^{ki}) 69:84

nam-ḫa-ni (gìri, sukkal) 17:13 ([gìri n]am-ḫa-ni)

na-[na$^{?}$-ù$^{?}$] (⸢lú-kin⸣-gi$_4$-a ⸢lú⸣-[ur$^{?}$-šu$^{?ki}$]) 11:20

na-na-ù (lú-ur-šu^{ki}) 23:3; 29:6 (lú-[ur]-šu^{ki}); 53:5 (lú$^{!}$-ur-šu^{ki})

^{d}nanna-ì-gi (gìri, sukkal) 55:20

^{d}nanna-kam (gìri, sukkal) 41:33

^{d}nanna-kam (sukkal maškim) 64:39

^{d}nanna-ma-ba (gìri, dub-sar) 54:27

^{d}nanna-palil (sagi maškim) 4:5

^{d}nanna-ul$_4$-gal (gìri) 20:6

^{d}nanše-ul$_4$-gal (maškim) 51:5; 70:4

na-ap-la-núm (mar-tu) 41:14; 54:2 (mar-tu-me); 60:9 (mar-tu-šè); 76:3 (mar-tu-šè)

na-ap-la-nu-um (mar-tu) 69:60 (mar-tu-me)

na-ra-am-^{d}adad ([gì]ri, sukkal) 46:14

na-sa$_6$ 61:36

ne-ni-la (gìri, sukkal) 69:95

nì-érim-e-du$_{10}^{?}$ (f. ad-da-kal-la dub-sar) 10:15

ni-im-sí (lú-ìa-ab-ra-at^{ki}) 5:III.8; 25:IV:1

ni-la-lum 13

nin-ḫé-du$_7$ 69:28

^{d}nin-im-ma 33:23

nin-kal-la 61:14

^{d}nin-líl-tu-kul-ti 69:12

^{d}nin-[tin-ug$_5$-g]a 33:27

^{d}nin-tin-ug$_5$⟨-ga⟩-ì-si^{ki}-šè 22:4

nu-gi-ra-nu-um 54:14

^{d}nun-gal 63:16

[nu]-úr-eš$_4$-tár ([ugula], [lú-kin]-gi$_4$-a) 21:IV+x;x+6

nu-úr-^{d}suen (gìri, sagi) 22:3

nu-úr-^{d}šamaš (rá-gaba maškim) 63:21

nu-úr-zu (nu-bànda) 50:7

pa$_4$-ki-na-na 69:20

pá-na-na (lú-mar-ḫa-ši^{ki}) 5:I.18; 25:I.16

pa$_4$-pa$_4$ (nin$_9$ kiš-er) 41:27

pù-ša-am (gìri, sukkal) 60:20; 70:20

pu-ša-am (lú-ši-ma-nu-um^{ki}, f. a-ri-ip-a-tal) 41:17

pu-ú-la 5:III.21

pu-ul-ba-at 69:69

puzur$_4$-^{d}adad (lú-kin-gi$_4$-a lú-ma$^{!}$-⌈ri⌉-ke$_4$$^{[k]i}$) 38:6-8

⌈puzur$_4$⌉-da-ga-an 56:4

puzur$_4$-^{d}da-gan (lú-tu-tu-ul^{ki}) 55:11

puzur$_4$-èr-ra (šu-i maškim) 72:4

puzur$_4$-ḫa-ìa 21:III+x.x+10

puzur$_4$-ma-ma (lú-ma-rí^{ki}) 3:14; 13; 16:6; 23:1; 24:2-3; 29:2; 35:7; 47:10; 53:2 (lú-ma-rí-ki^{ki})

ra-ši (lú-zi-da-núm^{ki}) 2:11 (lú-⌈zi-da-núm^{ki}⌉); 3:10; 16:4; 32:10 (lú-zi$^{!}$-da-nu-um^{ki}); 35:5

ri-iṣ-ilum (rá-gaba maškim) 69:56

si-mu (lú-[...]) 5:II.34

SIG$_4$-te-li → ši$_x$(SIG$_4$)-te-li

si-ni-ni 69:67

SUḪUŠ-ki-in (nu-bànda) 50:8

ša-at-^{d}ma-mi 69:24

šà-kal-la 54:21

ša-lim-be-lí 5:III.20

šà-me-túm (á-ki-ti-šu-numun) 69:104

ša-pu-núm (SAG.X) 5:II.10 (SAG.[X]); 25:II.16 (ša$^{!}$-pu-n[úm SAG.X])

šar-ri-a 5:III.18

šar-ru-um-ì-lí *Toronto* 639:5

šá-ta-kù-zu (maškim) 69:4

ša-za-núm (eger-a-na) 6:9

še-da-ku-ku (lú-ma-rí^{ki}) 69:92

še-le-pu-tum (maškim) 31:3

šeš-da-da *Toronto* 639:29

šeš-da-da (sanga) 26:6; 67:3

šeš-kal-la 21:4

ši-ba-ra-aq (lú-zi-da-⟨aḫ-⟩ri^{ki}) 69:89

ši$_x$(SIG$_4$)-te-li 31:6

ši$_x$(SIG$_4$)-te-li (gìri) 49:15

ši$_x$(SIG$_4$)-te-li (gìri, sukkal) 17:10; 22:12; 28:9; 36:14; 55:12 (gì[ri S]IG$_4$-te-li); 68:8 ([gìri S]IG$_4$-te-li)

ši$_x$(SIG$_4$)-te-li (maškim) 34:28

šu-ab-ba (gìri) 52:14

šu-ab-ba (mar-tu) 5:II.8 (mar-[tu]); 25:II.14 (m[ar-tu])

šu-ab-ba (gìri, sukkal) 9:3; 77:6

šu-^{d}adad (gìri, sipa-gú-gur$_5$) 11:26

šu-^{d}da-gan (lú-ma-rí^{ki}) 31:4

šu-eš$_4$-tár (gìri, sukkal) 73:7

šu-eš$_4$-tár (šagina-gú-du$_8$-a$^{\langle ki\rangle}$-ka) 6:7

šu-ì-lí (gìri, nu-bànda) *Toronto* 639:15

šu-ì-lí (gìri, sukkal-lugal) 6:12

šu-ì-lí (sukkal) 6:10

šu-^{d}iš-ḫa-ra (lú-ma-rí^{ki}) 17:9; 22:11 (šu-^{d}iš-ḫa-⌈ra⌉); 28:8; 36:13; 49:14; 68:7

šu-ku$_8$-[bu]-um 6:36

^{d}šul-gi-[...] (gìri) 52:12

^{d}šul-gi-a-a-mu 23:7; 30:7; 47:14; 48:17; 53:9; 60:23; 70:23

^{d}šul-gi-a-bí 41:29

^{d}šul-gi-a-bí (mar-tu-me) 69:63-64

^{d}šul-gi-ì-lí (lú-ma-rí^{ki}) 15:2 ($^{d!}$š[ul$^{?}$-gi$^{?}$-ì$^{?}$-lí$^{?}$], lú-ma-rí^{ki}-me); 41:32; 69:73

^{d}šul-gi-pa-lí-il (lú-ma-rí^{ki}) 15:4 (lú-ma-rí^{ki}-me); 34:19; 41:30; 51:16 (lú-ma-rí^{ki}-me); 61:23 (^{d}š[ul-gi-pa-lí-il]); 69:77

^{d}šul-gi-uru-mu (gìri, rá-gaba) 48:9; 70:14

^{d}šul-gi-uru-mu (gìri, ⟨sukkal⟩) 36:4

^{d}šul-[gi]-uru-mu (maškim) 17:3

šu-^{d}šul-gi (gìri, sukkal) 22:8; 36:9; 68:3

šu-ma-ma (lú-ma-rí^{ki}) 2:9

[šu$^{?}$-^{d}suen$^{?}$] *Toronto* 639:31

šu-^{d}suen (sukkal) 6:37

šu-^{d}suen ([gì]ri, sukkal) 17:5

šuruš(SUḪUŠ)-ki-in (nu-bànda) 50:8

šu-ru-uš-kí-in (lú-) 5:III.27

ṣi-il-be-lí (sukkal) 6:13

tá-din-eš$_4$-tár 69:8

taḫ-ša-tal (maškim) 65:2

tap$_x$(MAN)-pá-an-da-ra-aḫ (lú-si-mu-ru-um^{ki}) 10:2

te-ṣe-in-ma-ma$^{!}$ 69:35

tu-ra-am-^{d}da-gan (maškim) 4:28; 41:6

tù{-a}-ra-am-^{d}da-gan (lú-ma-rí^{ki}) 32:11

ṭab(DU$_{10}$)-bi-tum 5:III.25

ú-la-ì-ni-iš (maškim) 34:12

ú-NE-nu-um 5:III.19

ur-^{d}[....] (gìri) 48:3

ur-^{d}[....] (sukkal) 6:28 (ur-^{d}[....] sukkal])

ur-^{d}ba-ba$_6$ (dumu na-di) 40:5,7

ur-^{d}ba-ba$_{6}$ (muḫaldim) 69:97

ur-^{d}ba-ba$_{6}$ (muḫaldim maškim) 34:8; 41:9; 49:3

ur-^{d}dumu-zi-da (gìri, sukkal) 60:6

[ur-^{d}]en-líl-lá (dub-sar) 64:41

ur-^{d}en-líl-lá (dub-sar dumu lugal-úr-ra-ni) 64:44

ur-kù-nun-na 62:10

ur-^{d}lama (gìri, sagi) 22:5

ur-^{d}lugal-bàn-da (gìri, dub-sar) 46:19

ur-^{d}lugal-bàn-da (gìri, ša$_{13}$-dub-ba) 33:40 (š[a$_{13}$-dub-ba]); 43:10 (ša$_{13}$-dub-⟨ba⟩)

ur-me-lám-an-na (gìri, sukkal) 34:25

ur-me-me (gìri, sukkal) 34:11

ur-mes 54:23

ur-mes (sagi) 8:2

ur-^{d}nammu 34:7 (a-nag-)

ur-^{d}nanše (lú-énsi[-ka]) 6:24

ur-ni$_{9}$-gar (ka-gur$_{7}$) 26:8

ur-ni$_{9}$-gar (maškim) 2:6

ur-ni$_{9}$-gar (f. lú-^{d}nanna) 69:47

ur-^{d}nin-gublaga 61:2

ur-^{d}nin-gublaga (nar) 34:10

ur-sukkal (gìri, sukkal) 4:23

ur-šar-ru-gin$_{7}$ (sukkal) 6:20

ur-^{d}šar-ru-gin$_{7}$ (gìri, sukkal) 55:5

ur-^{d}šul-gi-ra (šagina) 6:8

ur-^{d}šul-pa-è 61:16

ur-^{d}šul-pa-è (muḫaldim maškim) 34:6

ur-šu-mu (gìri) 63:24

ur-^{d}tílla 8:6

ú-tá-mi-šar-ra-am (maškim) 34:15

^{d}utu-kam 54:22

^{d}utu-mu (gìri, sukkal) 6:15

we-du-um (lú-kin-gi$_{4}$-a) 69:84

zabar-dab$_{5}$ (maškim) 26:12; 47:6; 51:8; 67:6

zi-nu-gi (lú-ḫi-bí-la-ti^{ki}) 69:94

zu-ba-ga 44:9; 63:28; 73:11

zu-bu-uš (lú-kin-gi$_{4}$-a) 55:18-19

zu-rí-im (gìri, lú-na) 59:4 z[u$^{?}$-rí$^{?}$-im$^{?}$] (lú-kin-gi$_{4}$-a) 55:14

zu-ri-im (lú-kin-gi$_{4}$-a-lú-eb-la^{ki}) 26:16; 37:7+x (zu$^{!}$-ri-im)

^{d}[...] 33:25

[....-g]i-zi (lú-kin-gi$_{4}$-a) 17

x-[G]I$^{?}$-ŠI$^{?}$ (lú-ma-rí^{ki}) 64:37

x-zi$^{?}$ (gìri) 31:2

[...]-mu-um ([...]-ši-šè) 21:IV+x;x+1

Index of Professions, Titles, Etc.

àga-ús
ad-da-sa$_6$-ga (gìri) 60:10

dam
dam-lugal-má-gur$_8$-re 69:38
dam-lú-^{d}nanna dumu ur-ni$_9$-gar 69:47
dam-šar-ru-um-ba-ni 69:44

dub-sar
ad-da-[....] 9:seal
ad-da-kal-la (gìri) 1:12; 10:12; 44:10; 73:12
ad-da-kal-la dumu nì-érim-e-du$_{10}$$^{?}$ 10:15
ilum-ba-ni (dub-sar-kaš$_4$) 6:14
lú-igi-ma 7:seal
lú-^{d}nin-šubur (gìri) 4:34
lú-sa$_6$ (gìri) 41:39
^{d}nanna-ma-ba (gìri) 54:27
[ur-^{d}]en-líl-lá 64:41
ur-^{d}en-líl-lá dumu lugal-úr-ra-ni 64:44
ur-^{d}lugal-b[àn-da] (gìri) 46:19

eger
bí-ša-za-núm (ur-^{d}šul-gi-ra...eger-a-na) 6:9

eme-bal → sukkal-eme-bal

énsi
énsi-a-bar-ni-um^{ki} 17:12
énsi-eb-la^{ki}
me-GU-um 55:15
énsi-gír-su^{ki} 61:3
énsi-gu$_5$-ub-la^{ki}
ib-da-ti 60:19; 70:19
énsi-má-gan^{ki}
na-du-be-lí 69:84
énsi-marad^{ki} 26:11
énsi-mar-ḫa-ši^{ki}
li-pá-nu-uk-ša-pá-aš 17:4 (li-pá-nu-uk-[š]a-pá-aš); 28:2; 30:1; 36:8; 48:10 (li-[pá-nu-u]k-ša-pá-aš é[nsi]-mar-ḫa-ši^{ki}); 49:9; 60:14; 68:2; 70:15
énsi-nibru^{ki} 26:14; 50:13
énsi-umma^{ki} 6:47
énsi-tu-tu-la^{ki}
ìa-ši-li-im 60:18; 70:18

éren
[éren-a]-šur$_5$^{ki} 21:IV+x.x+5
éren-da-ši-il^{ki} 21:II+x.2
éren-maš-gán-ga-raš$_x$(KASKAL-*gunû*)$^{sar\ ki}$ 21:III+x.x+7
éren-ni-da-ra-aš-we^{ki} 72:3
éren-te-er-qà^{ki} 21:I+x.3
éren-ur-gu-ḫa-lam^{ki} 21:III+x.x+4

gìri
a-bí-sí-im-[ti] 46:8-9
ad-da-kal-la (dub-sar) 1:12; 10:12; 44:10; 73:12
ad-da-sa$_6$-ga (àga-ús) 60:10
a-ḫu-ni ([sukkal]) 6:27
a-ḫu-we-er 49:7
ba-a-a (sukkal) 15:7
ba-za-za (sukkal) 64:38
be-lí-šar 5:I.10; 25:I.10
du-uk-r[a] 45:5 ([gìri$^{?}$])

èr-ra-a (sukkal) 10:3; 63:12
ḫu-zi-ri (sukkal) 1:6; 30:4; 43:5; 44:3; 48:14; 60:17
ì-lí-be-lí (sukkal) 10:7; 33:36; 63:26 (suk[kal])
ì-lí-be-lí (sukkal) 73:3
ì-lum-a-bi$^{!}$ (lú-ma-rí^{ki}) 14:5-6
ilum-ba-ni (sukkal) 31:5
kàš-pu-ša (sagi) 41:3
kir-ba-tal (sukkal) 1:8; 44:6
kù-^{d}nanna (sukkal) 36:6; 51:20
kur-gìr-ì-ni 60:13 (kur-gìr-ì-ni-šè)
lú-^{d}da-mu 48:11
lú-^{d}da-mu (sukkal) 22:15; 28:3; 49:10
lú-^{d}da-ni (sukkal) 6:21
lú-^{d}en-ki (sukkal) 31:7
lú-^{d}en-líl-lá 5:IV.13; 25:IV.14 ([gìri lú-^{d}en-líl-lá])
lugal-dal[la] *Toronto* 639:28
lugal-ì-maḫ (sagi) 47:5; 51:9
lugal-inim-gi-na (sukkal) 11:23; 16:9; 29:7 (⌈gìri lugal-inim-gi-na sukkal⌉); 35:10; 60:4; 76:9
lú-^{d}nin-šubur (dub-sar) 4:34
lú-sa$_{6}$ (dub-sar) 41:39
ma-n[úm-ki]-^{d}šul-gi 20:12
na-bí-^{d}suen (sukkal) 17:7; 22:10 ([sukka]l); 28:6; 36:12; 49:12; 55:16; 68:6 ([g]ìri na-bí-^{d}suen ⟨sukkal⟩)
[n]am-ḫa-ni (sukkal) 17:13 ([gìri n]am-ḫa-ni)
^{d}nanna-ì-gi (sukkal) 55:20
^{d}nanna-kam (sukkal) 41:33
^{d}nanna-ma-ba (dub-sar) 54:27
^{d}nanna-ul$_{4}$-gal 20:6
na-ra-am-^{d}adad (sukkal) 46:14 ([gì]ri)
nu-úr-^{d}suen (sagi) 22:3
pù-ša-am (sukkal) 60:20; 70:20
ši$_{x}$(SIG$_{4}$)-te-li 49:15
ši$_{x}$(SIG$_{4}$)-te-li (sukkal) 17:10; 22:12; 28:9; 36:14; 55:12 (gì[ri S]IG$_{4}$-te-li); 68:8 ([gìri S]IG$_{4}$-te-li)
šu-ab-ba 52:14
šu-ab-ba (sukkal) 9:3
šu-^{d}adad (sipa-gú-gur$_{5}$) 11:26
šu-eš$_{4}$-tár (sukkal) 73:7
šu-ì-lí (nu-bànda) *Toronto* 639:15
šu-ì-lí (sukkal-lugal) 6:12
^{d}šul-gi-[...] 52:12
^{d}šul-gi-uru-mu (rá-gaba) 48:9; 70:14
^{d}šul-gi-uru-mu (⟨sukkal⟩) 36:4
šu-^{d}šul-gi (sukkal) 22:8; 36:9; 68:3
šu-^{d}suen (sukkal) 17:5 ([gì]ri)
ur-^{d}[...] 48:3
ur-^{d}dumu-zi-da (sukkal) 60:6
ur-^{d}lama (sagi) 22:5
ur-^{d}lugal-bàn-da (dub-sar) 46:19
ur-^{d}lugal-bàn-da (ša$_{13}$-dub-ba) 33:40 (š[a$_{13}$-dub-ba]); 43:10 (ša$_{13}$-dub-⟨ba⟩)
ur-^{d}me-lám-an-na (sukkal) 34:25
ur-me-me (sukkal) 34:11
ur-sukkal (sukkal) 4:23
ur-^{d}šar-ru-gin$_{7}$ (sukkal) 55:5
ur-šu-mu 63:24
^{d}utu-mu (sukkal) 6:15
zu-rí-im (lú-na) 59:4
x-zi$^{?}$ 31:2

ḫa-za-núm

lú-ša-lim (gar-ša-na^{ki}-ka) 6:11

ka-gur$_{7}$

ur-ni$_{9}$-gar 26:8

kaš$_{4}$

ilum-ba-ni (dub-sar-kaš$_{4}$) 6:14
kaš$_{4}$-lú-ma-rí^{ki} 78:28

lú-énsi

ur-^{d}nanše (lú-énsi[-ka]) 6:24

lú-kin-gi$_{4}$-a

lú-ìa-ma$^{!?}$(⌈AB⌉)-dì-um 27:3
lú-ma-rí^{ki}-šè 27:4
[....-g]i-zi 17:12
a-mur-ilum 30:1; 48:10 ([a-mur]-ilum); 60:14 (lú-kin-gi$_{4}$-a); 70:15
^{d}da-gan-a-bu 60:18; 70:18
ḫu-un-ti-pá (lú-du$_{8}$-du$_{8}$-lí^{ki}) 11:25
i-ba-ti 60:19; 70:19
ì-lí-^{d}da-gan (lú-eb-la^{ki}) 67:11-12
i-šar-ì-si 38:10
li-pá-an-aš-ku$_{8}$-pí 17:4 ([l]ú-kin-gi$_{4}$-a); 28:2; 36:8; 49:9; 68:2
má-za 69:86
na-[na$^{?}$-ù$^{?}$] (⌈lú-kin⌉-gi$_{4}$-a ⌈lú⌉-[ur$^{?}$-šu$^{?ki}$]) 11:20
[nu]-úr-eš$_{4}$-tár ([ugula], [lú-kin]-gi$_{4}$-a) 21:IV+x.x+6
puzur$_{4}$-^{d}adad (lú-ma$^{!}$-⌈ri$^{!}$⌉-ke$_{4}$$^{[k]i}$) 38:6-8
we-du-um 69:84
zu-bu-uš 55:18-19
z[u$^{?}$-rí$^{?}$-im$^{?}$] 55:14
zu-ri-im (lú-eb-la^{ki}) 26:16; 37:7+x (zu$^{!}$-ri-im)

lunga

na-di f. ur-^{d}ba-ba$_{6}$ 40:5,7

maš-en-kak

is-ga-ga *Toronto* 639:20

maškim

árad-mu 1:9; 2:12; 4:24; 10:8; 11:28; 15:9; 17:14 ([ár]ad-mu); 20:8 (árad-mu$^{!}$) 24:10; 26:18; 27:16; 28:10; 29:830:5; 31:8; 32:12; 33:37; 34:26; 36:15; 41:34; 43:6; 44:7 46:15; 47:12; 48:15; 49:16; 51:22; 52:15; 55:21; 60:21; 61:34; 67:13; 68:11; 69:103; 70:21; 72:14; 73:9; 76:11
a-tu (sagi) 32:9; 63:17; 64:36
da-a-a-ni 26:15
^{d}en-líl-á-maḫ (sagi) 1:3
^{d}en-líl-zi-šà-gál 41:4
èr-ra-na-da 47:8; 61:8
ilum-dan 9:4
ilum-dan (sukkal) 22:16; 65:5
i-šar-i-ši 38:11 (lugal maškim$^{!}$) 38:11
kur-gìri-ni 51:11 (kur-gìri-ni-šè)
lú-an-dùl (rá-gaba) 2:14
lugal-má-gur$_{8}$-re 3:15; 16:10; 35:11; 53:7
^{d}nanna-kam (sukkal) 64:39
^{d}nanna-palil (sagi) 4:5
^{d}nanše-ul$_{4}$-gal 51:5; 70:4
nu-úr-^{d}šamaš (rá-gaba) 63:21
puzur$_{4}$-èr-ra (šu-i) 72:4
ri-iṣ-ilum (rá-gaba) 69:56
ši$_{x}$(SIG$_{4}$)-te-li 34:28
šá-ta-kù-zu 69:4
še-le-pu-tum 31:3
^{d}šul-[gi]-uru-mu 17:3
taḫ-ša-tal 65:2
tu-ra-am-^{d}da-gan 4:28; 41:6
ú-la-ì-ni-iš 34:12
ur-^{d}ba-ba$_{6}$ (muḫaldim) 34:8; 41:9; 49:3
ur-ni$_{9}$-gar 2:6
ur-^{d}šul-pa-è (muḫaldim) 34:6
ú-tá-mi-šar-ra-am 34:15
zabar-dab$_{5}$ 26:12; 47:6; 51:8; 67:6

muḫaldim

ur-^{d}ba-ba$_{6}$ 69:97
ur-^{d}ba-ba$_{6}$ (maškim) 34:8; 41:9; 49:3
ur-^{d}šul-pa-è (maškim) 34:6

nar

KA-ú-KA 61:33 (nar$^{?}$)

ur-^{d}nin-gublaga 34:10

nì-mussa (NÍ.MÍ.ÚS.SÁ)
 nì-mussa árad-mu dumu ad-da-bi 51:21

nin$_9$
 pa$_4$-pa$_4$ nin$_9$ kiš-er 41:27

nu-bànda
 ir-du-a 50:9
 nu-úr-zu 50:7
 šu-ì-lí (gìri) *Toronto* 639:15
 šuruš(SUḪUŠ)-ki-in 50:8

rá-gaba
 lú-an-dùl (maškim) 2:14
 nu-úr-^{d}šamaš (maškim) 63:21
 ri-iṣ-ilum (maškim) 69:56
 ^{d}šul-gi-uru-mu (gìri) 48:9; 70:14

sagi
 a-tu (maškim) 32:9; 63:17; 64:36
 a-tu (sag[i]) 52:8
 ^{d}en-líl-á-maḫ (maškim) 1:3
 kàš-pu-ša (gìri) 41:3
 lugal-ì-maḫ (gìri) 47:5; 51:9
 ^{d}nanna-palil (maškim) 4:5
 nu-úr-^{d}suen (gìri) 22:3
 ur-^{d}lama (gìri) 22:5
 ur-mes 8:2

sanga
 šeš-da-da 26:6; 67:3

sanga-^{d}nin-giš-zi-da
 en-šà-kù-ge 61:4

sipa-gú-gur$_5$
 šu-^{d}adad (gìri) 11:26

sipa-lú-ma-rí^{ki}
 40:2 (sipa-lú-ma-rí^{ki}-ta)

sipa-ur-ra
 a-da-na-aḫ 50:12

sukkal
 a-ḫu-ni 6:17
 a-ḫu-ni (gìri, [sukkal]) 6:27
 ba-a-a (gìri) 15:7
 ba-za-za (gìri) 64:38
 èr-ra-a (gìri) 10:3-4; 63:12-13
 ḫu-zi-ri (gìri) 1:6; 30:4; 43:5; 44:3; 48:14; 60:17
 ib-ni-ilum 6:5
 ì-lí-be-lí (gìri) 10:7; 33:36; 63:26 (suk[kal])
 ì-lí-be-lí (gìri) 73:3
 ilum-ba-ni (gìri) 31:5
 ilum-dan (maškim) 65:5
 kir-ba-tal (gìri) 1:8; 44:6
 kù-^{d}nanna (gìri) 36:6; 51:20
 kù-^{d}nanna 6:19
 lú-^{d}da-mu (gìri) 22:15; 28:3; 49:10
 lú-^{d}da-ni (gìri) 6:21
 lú-^{d}en-ki (gìri) 31:7
 lugal-inim-gi-na (gìri) 11:23; 16:9; 29:7 (⸢gìri lugal-inim-gi-na sukkal⸣); 35:10; 60:4; 76:9
 lugal-má-gur$_8$-re 60:11
 na-[...] 6:25
 na-bí-^{d}suen (gìri) 17:7; 22:10 ([sukka]l); 28:6; 36:12; 49:12; 55:16; 68:6 ([g]ìri na-bí-^{d}suen ⟨sukkal⟩)
 [nam]-ḫa-ni (gìri) 17:13 ([gìri nam]-ḫa-ni)
 ^{d}nanna-ì-gi (gìri) 55:20
 ^{d}nanna-kam (gìri) 41:33
 ^{d}nanna-kam (maškim) 64:39
 na-ra-am-^{d}adad (gìri) 46:14 ([gì]ri)
 ne-ni-la (gìri) 69:95
 pù-ša-am (gìri) 60:20; 70:20
 ši$_x$(SIG$_4$)-te-li (gìri) 17:10; 22:12; 28:9; 36:14; 55:12 (gì[ri S]IG$_4$-te-li); 68:8 ([gìri S]IG$_4$-te-li)

šu-ab-ba (gìri) 9:3
šu-eš$_4$-tár (gìri) 73:7
šu-ì-lí 6:10
^{d}šul-gi-uru-mu (gìri) 36:4 (⟨sukkal⟩)
šu-^{d}šul-gi (gìri) 22:8; 36:9; 68:3
šu-^{d}suen 6:37
šu-^{d}suen ([gì]ri) 17:5
ṣi-il-be-lí 6:13
ur-^{d}[...] 6:28 (ur-^{d}[... sukkal])
ur-^{d}dumu-zi-da (gìri) 60:6
ur-me-lám-an-na (gìri) 34:25
ur-me-me (gìri) 34:11
ur-sukkal (gìri) 4:23
ur-šar-ru-gin$_7$ 6:20
ur-^{d}šar-ru-gin$_7$ (gìri, sukkal) 55:5
^{d}utu-mu (gìri) 6:15

sukkal-eme-bal 5:I.21 ([sukkal]-eme-bal); 25:I.19

sukkal-maḫ 6:3

sukkal-lugal
šu-ì-lí (gìri) 6:12

šabra
lugal-má-gur$_8$-re 23:5
lugal-á-zi-da 54:20

ša$_{13}$-dub-ba
ur-^{d}lugal-bàn-da (gìri) 33:40 (š[a$_{13}$-dub-ba]); 43:10 (ša$_{13}$-dub-⟨ba⟩)

šagina
ur-^{d}šul-gi-ra 6:8

šagina-gú-du$_8$-a^{ki}
šu-eš$_4$-tár 6:7 (šagina-gú-du$_8$-a$^{⟨ki⟩}$-ka) šár-ra-ab-du
ad-da-kal-la 33:41 (šár-ra-a[b-du]); 43:11
lú-^{d}nanna 46:20 (šár-ra-ab-d[u])

šu-i
puzur$_4$-èr-ra (maškim) 72:4

ugula
^{d}en-líl *Toronto* 639:16
^{d}iškur-da-ni 21:I+x.6 ([ugula ^{d}iškur]-da-ni), II+x.3 [nu]-úr-eš$_4$-tár ([ugula], [lú-kin]-gi$_4$-a) 21: IV+x;+6

UM.ME-da 34:24

UM+ME-da-lugal 69:55 (UM+ME-da-lugal-me); 72:2

zabar-dab$_5$
(maškim) 26:12; 47:6; 51:8; 67:6

Index of Geographical Names and Gentilics

a-bar-ni-um^{ki}
→ énsi

a-ḫu-ti^{ki}
51:17

a-la^{ki}
→ lú-a-la^{ki}

a-nag-ur-^{d}nammu 34:7

a-šur$_5$^{ki}
→ éren

da-ri-ba^{ki}
→ lú-da-ri-ba^{ki}

da-ši-il^{ki}
→ éren

du$_8$-du$_8$-lí^{ki}
→ lú-du$_8$-du$_8$-lí^{ki}

eb-la^{ki}
→ énsi-eb-la^{ki}
→ lú-eb-la^{ki}

gar-ša-na^{ki}
lú-ša-lim (ḫa-za-núm gar-ša-na^{ki}-ka) 6:11

gu$_5$-ub-la^{ki}
→ énsi

gú-du$_8$-a^{ki}
→ šagin-gú-du$_8$-a^{ki}

ḫi-bí-la-ti^{ki}
zi-nu-gi 69:94

ḫu-ur-ti^{ki}
→ lú-ḫu-ur-ti^{ki}

ìa-ab-ra-at^{ki}
→ lú-ìa-ab-ra-at^{ki}

ìa-a-ma-dì-um^{ki}
→ lú-ìa-ma-dì-um^{ki}
dú-ul-qá-núm (mar-tu) 24:9 (ìa-a-ma-dì)
i-pí-iq-re-e-ú (mar-tu) 4:17; 5:II.31 (ìa-a-ma-dì-[um$^?$]; 25:III.15 (m[ar]-tu ìa-a-ma-d[ì-um$^?$])

ì-si-in^{ki}
51:10

kur-mar-tu
nam-ra-ak *Toronto* 639:14

larsa^{ki}
14:4 (larsa(UD.UNU)^{ki}-šè)

lú-[...]
si-mu 25.iii.18; 5:II.34

lú-a-la^{ki}
lú-a-la^{ki} 5:III.23 (lú-a-la^{ki}-me-šè); 25:II.18 (lú-[a-la^{ki}-me-šè])

lú-du$_8$-du$_8$-lí^{ki}
ḫu-un-ti-pá (lú-kin-gi$_4$-a) 11:25

lú-da-ri-ba^{ki}
ì-še-bu 69:86

lú-eb-la^{ki}
5:II.29 (lú-eb-la^{ki}-me-šè); 25:III.12 (lú-eb-la^{ki}-[me-šè]); 56:5 (lú-eb-la$^{\langle ki \rangle}$); 59:3; 62:7
e-zu-un-^{d}da-gan 46:13
ì-lí-^{d}da-gan 3:12; 11:16; 13; 16:8; 17:6; 22:9; 23:2; 24:5-6; 28:5; 29:4; 35:9; 36:11; 47:9;

49:11 (lú-e[b]l]a^{ki}); 53:3; 68:5; 76:5
ì-lí-^{d}da-gan (lú-kin-gi$_4$-a) 67:11-12
i-zi-in-^{d}da-gan 4:9; 5:II.25 (i-zi-in-^{d}da-[gan]); 25:III.7
kur-bi-la-ak 4:12 (lú-eb-la^{ki}-me-šè); 5:II.27; 25:III.10
me-me-šu-ra 12:3
zu-ri-im (lú-kin-gi$_4$-a) 26:16; 37:7+x (zu$^{!}$-ri-im)

lú-ḫa-ar-me-me
ki-iz-zi *Toronto* 639:19

lú-ḫi-bí-la-ti^{ki}
zi-nu-gi 69:94

lú-ḫu-na-tal
ḫu-uz-taḫ (lú-ḫu-na-t[al]) 5:III.13

lú-ḫu-ur-ti^{ki}
5:I.7 (lú-ḫu-ur-ti^{ki}-me-šè); 25:I.7 (lú-ḫu-u[r-t]i^{ki}-me⟨-šè⟩)

lú-ìa-ab-ra-at^{ki}
ni-im-sí 5:III.8; 25:IV.1

lú-ìa-a-ma-dì-um^{ki}
du-ul-qá-nu-um 47:11
ìa-a-ma-dú 54:8
i-pí-iq-re-e-ú (mar-tu ìa-a-ma-dì-um) 4:17; 5:II.31 (ìa-a-ma-dì-[um$^{?}$]; 25:III.15 (m[ar]-tu ìa-a-ma-d[ì-um$^{?}$])
lú-kin-gi$_4$-a (lú-ìa-ma$^{!?}$(⌜AB⌝)-dì-um) 27:3

lú-ì-lí-am-ra^{ki}
is-ga-ga (maš-en-kak) *Toronto* 639:20

lú-ma-ar-da-ma-an^{ki}
ku$_8$-sú-sú 41:22

lú-mar-ḫa-ši^{ki}
pá-na-na 5:I.18; 25:I.16
sukkal-eme-bal (ki lú-mar-ḫa-ši^{ki}, f. a-ri-du-bu-uk) 5:I.21 ([sukkal]-eme-bal); 25:I.19 (⟨ki⟩ lú-mar-ḫa-ši^{ki})

lú-ma-rí^{ki}
7 (lú-ma-rí^{ki}-me); 62:5; 66:3
a-bu-*ṭab*(DU$_{10}$) 4:15; 5:II.19; 10:6; 20:5; 25:III.2 (lú-ma-r[í^{ki}]); 46:11; 55:7 ([a-b]u-*ṭab*(DU$_{10}$)); 63:25; 73:2
a-da-tum 45:3
a-mi-ir-^{d}šul-gi 51:14; 61:20
a-mur-^{d}šul-gi 34:17 (lú-ma-rí^{ki}-me); 69:75
aq-ba-ìa 6:38 (aq$^{!}$-ba$^{!}$-ìa); 34:20-21 (aq$^{!}$(APIN)-ba-ìa lú-ma-rí^{ki}-me); 50:6; 72:7
i-din-AG 22:13-14
ì-lí-iš-ti-kál 61:29-30 (lú-ma-rí^{ki}-me)
ì-lum-a-bi$^{!}$ (gìri) 14:5-6
iš-me-^{d}da-gan 11:12; 76:8
[it-r]a-ak-ì-lí 8:10
la-qì-ip 65:4
la-qì-pu-um 9:2; 52:13 (la-qì-pu-[um] lú-ma-rí[^{ki}]); 65:4; 77:5
puzur$_4$-^{d}adad (lú-kin-gi$_4$-a) 38:6-8 (lú-ma-ri-ke$_4$$^{[k]i}$)
puzur$_4$-ma-ma 3:14; 13; 16:6; 23:1; 24:2-3; 29:2; 35:7; 47:10; 53:2 (lú-ma-rí-ki^{ki})
sipa-lú-ma-rí^{ki} 40:2 (sipa-lú-ma-rí^{ki}-ta)
še-da-ku-ku 69:92
šu-^{d}da-gan 31:4
šu-^{d}iš-ḫa-ra 17:9; 22:11 (šu-^{d}iš-ḫa-⌜ra⌝); 28:8; 36:13; 49:14; 68:7
^{d}šul-gi-pa-lí-il 15:4 (lú-ma-rí^{ki}-me); 34:19; 41:30; 51:16 (lú-ma-

rí^{ki}-me); 61:23 (^{d}š[ul-gi-pa-lí-il]); 69:77
šu-ma-ma 2:9
tù{-a}-ra-am-^{d}da-gan 32:11
x-[G]I$^{?}$-ŠI$^{?}$ 64:37

lú-mu-ki-iš^{ki}
ga-ba-ba 1:7; 44:5

lú-simaški(SU)
→ lú-SU(.A.KI)
me-ša-[nu-n]u (f. ìa-ù-ša) 4:22

lú-si-mu-ru-um^{ki}
ki-ri-ib-ul-me 1:5; 44:2
tap$_{x}$(MAN)-pá-an-da-ra-aḫ 10:1

lú-SU.A.KI
→ lú-simaški
ìa-a-ab-ra-ad 55:19 (lú-SU.A.KI-me)

lú-SU.KI
→ lú-simaški
5:I.3 (lú-SU.KI-me-šè); 25:I.3 ([lú-SU.KI-me-šè])

lú-ša-ri-it-ḫi^{ki}
5:I.5 (lú-ša-ri-it-ḫi$^{!ki}$); 25:I.5 ([lú-ša-ri-it]-ḫi^{ki}⟨-šè⟩)

lú-ši-ik-ri-iš^{ki}
ḪAR-ti (lú-ši-ik-ri-[i]š$^{[ki]}$) 5:III.15

lú-ši-ma-núm^{ki}
ar-ba-tal 63:9 (lú-[ši-ma-núm^{ki}]); 63:11; 73:6
a-ri-ip-a-tal dumu pu-ša-am 41:17
pu-ša-am f. a-ri-ip-a-tal 41:17 (lú-ši-ma-nu-um^{ki})

lú-tal-muš^{ki}
a-ri-ip-ḫu-up-pí 41:19

lú-tu-tu-ul^{ki}
puzur$_{4}$-^{d}da-gan 55:11

lú-ur-bí-lum^{ki}
kí-ba-a-tal 5:II.33 (kí-ba-a-[tal] lú-ur]-bí-[lum^{ki}-šè]); 25:III.17 (kí-ba-a-[tal] lú-ur-bí-lum^{k}[^{i}-šè])

lú-ur-šu^{ki}
bu-du-úr 11:14; 76:6
da-sal-ib-ri 33:35; 43:4 (lú-ur-šu$^{⟨ki⟩}$)
[e$^{?}$-r]i-iš-ti-ar 55:9
gu-ra-a 30:2 (lú-ur$^{!}$-šu$^{!ki}$); 48:12; 60:15 (gu-ra-a lú-ur-[šu]^{ki}); 70:16 (lú-ur$^{!}$-šu$^{!ki}$)
kur-bi-la-ak 12:6
na-[na$^{?}$-ù$^{?}$] (⌈lú-kin⌉-gi$_{4}$-a ⌈lú⌉-[ur$^{?}$-šu$^{?ki}$]) 11:20
na-na-ù 23:3; 53:5 (lú$^{!}$-ur-šu^{ki})

lú-zi-da-aḫ-ri^{ki}
ši-ba-ra-aq 69:89 (lú-zi-da⟨-aḫ⟩-ri^{ki})

lú-zi-da-núm^{ki}
ra-ši 2:11 (lú-⌈zi-da-núm^{ki}⌉); 3:10; 16:4; 32:10 (lú-zi$^{!}$-da-nu-um^{ki}); 35:5

má-gan^{ki}
→ énsi-má-gan^{ki}

marad^{ki}
→ énsi-marad^{ki}

ma-ar-da-ma-an^{ki}
→ lú-ma-ar-da-ma-an^{ki}

mar-ḫa-ši^{ki}
→ énsi
→ lú-mar-ḫa-ši^{ki}

ma-rí^{ki}

→ lú-ma-rí^{ki}

mar-tu
→ kur-mar-tu
al-lu-ri-núm 54:17 (mar-tu-me)
dú-ul-qá-núm (ìa-a-ma-dì) 24:8
i-pí-iq-re-e-ú (ìa-a-ma-dì-um) 4:17; 5:II.31 (ìa-a-ma-dì-[um$^{?}$]; 25:III.15 (m[ar]-tu ìa-a-ma-d[ì-um$^{?}$])
iš-me-ilum 72:5
na-ap-la-núm 41:14; 54:2 (mar-tu-me); 60:9 (mar-tu-šè); 76:3 (mar-tu-šè)
na-ap-la-nu-um 69:60 (mar-tu-me)
šu-ab-ba 5:II.8 (mar-[tu]); 25:II.14 (m[ar-tu])
^{d}šul-gi-a-bí 69:63-64 (mar-tu-me)

maš-gán-ga-raš$_{x}$(KASKAL-*gunû*)$^{sar\ ki}$
→ éren

mu-ki-iš^{ki}
→ lú-mu-ki-iš^{ki}

nibru^{ki}
→ énsi-nibru^{ki}
4:33; 10:4; 11:29; 20:8; 27:5; 33:33; 46:9; 52:9 (nibru[^{ki}]); 63:13; 64:40; 65:9; 73:8

ni-da-ra-aš-we
→ éren

simaški(SU[.A.KI])
→ lú-SU(.A.KI)

si-mu-ru-um^{ki}
→ lú-si-mu-ru-um^{ki}

SU.KI (=Simaški)
→ lú-SU.KI

ša-ri-it-ḫi^{ki}
→ lú-ša-ri-it-ḫi^{ki}

ši-ik-ri-iš^{ki}
→ lú-ši-ik-ri-iš^{ki}

ši-ma-núm^{ki}
→ lú-ši-ma-núm^{ki}

SU(.A.KI)
→ lú-SU(.A.KI)
→ lú-simaški

tal-muš^{ki}
→ lú-tal-muš^{ki}

te-er-qà^{ki}
→ éren

tilmun^{ki}
→ lú-tilmun^{ki}
maš-maš-tilmun^{ki} 3:3 (tilmun$^{\langle ki \rangle}$); 16:2 (tilmum$^{\langle ki \rangle}$); 35:3 (tilmun$^{\langle ki \rangle}$)

tum-ma-al^{ki}
51:23

tu-tu-la^{ki}
→ énsi

tu-tu-ul^{ki}
→ lú-tu-tu-ul^{ki}

umma^{ki}
→ énsi

unu^{ki}-ga
15:9; 73:4
^{d}inanna-šà-unug^{ki} 51:7; 47:4 (^{d}inanna-unug^{ki}-šè); 70:1 (^{d}inanna-unug^{ki}-šè); 77:2 (^{d}inanna-unug^{ki}-šè);

ur-bí-lum^{ki}
→ lú-ur-bí-lum^{ki}
nam-ra-ak *Toronto* 639:18

ur-gu-ḫa-lam^{ki}
→ éren

uri$_5$^{ki}
41:38 (uri$_5$^{ki}-ma); 54:28 (uri$_5$^{ki}-ma)

ur-šu^{ki}
→ lú-ur-šu^{ki}

zi-da-aḫ-ri^{ki}
→ lú-zi-da-aḫ-ri^{ki}

zi-da-núm^{ki}
→ lú-zi-da-núm^{ki}

Appendix: Wabash 1 and a Note on Ur III Syria[1]

Gordon D. Young

Purdue University

The tablet published in autograph copy here is in the possession of Wabash College, Crawfordsville, Indiana, but the circumstances of its arrival at Wabash College are unknown. A Drehem text dated to Amar-Suena 1/ii/26, Wabash 1 measures 40 × 49 mm, is buff-pink in color, and is in excellent condition although not recently baked or cleaned. The text has been transliterated from this copy in Owen and Veenker, "MeGum," Appendix II as text K and again above in slightly corrected form as No. 79.[2] The text records the expenditure of an ox, sheep and goats to four Syrians and one other person of unspecified origin.

Wabash 1 (= Text No. 79)

obv. rev.

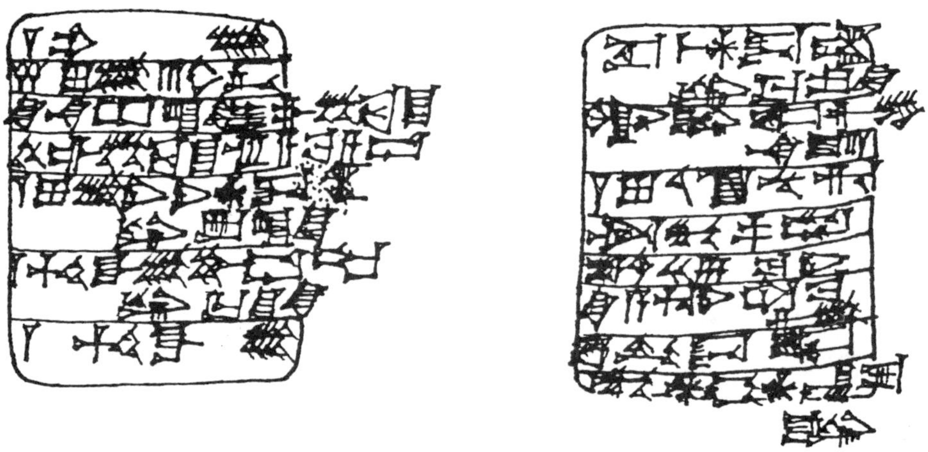

Translation: 1 fattened ox, 5 fattened sheep (and) 3 male goats for Naplanum, the Amorite, sent by boat to KUR MAR.TU. 1 fattened sheep for Ili-Dagan, the man of Ebla. 1 mature fattened goat for Budur, the man of Uršu. 1 mature fattened goat for Išme-Dagan, the man of Mari. The gíri-official was Lugal-inimgina, the sukkal. 1 sheep for Eštar-nuri. Arad-mu was the maškim. (The animals were) expended by Aḫuni at the end of the 26th day, second month of the year Amar-Suena became king.

Comments: The synchronism of Naplanum, the Amorite, Ili-Dagan, the Eblaite, Budur the Uršuite and Išme-Dagan, the Mariote is unique, to my knowledge, in a single inscription. The reference to KUR MAR.TU, however is of far greater interest in view of the long-term debate over its location. Two points about this text should be noted: (1) the initial entry of Naplanum, followed by the notation that the delivery was sent by boat to KUR MAR.TU, is grouped together with those of the other Syrians, all under the supervision (gíri) of Lugal-inimgina. (2) The final entry, that of Eštar-nuri, follows but is kept distinct from the foregoing. By ordering the text in this fashion, the scribe has differentiated the transaction of Eštar-nuri from the others. Thus the grouping of Naplanum and KUR MAR.TU with the other Syrians clearly implies that the four transactions supervised by Lugal-inimgina had Syrian destinations. This being the case, Wabash 1 adds additional Ur III evidence for the location of KUR MAR.TU in Syria.

[1] It was planned to publish this text in Gordon D. Young, *Mari in Retrospect: Fifty Years of Mari and Mari Studies* (Eisenbrauns: Winona Lake, 1992), but that proved impossible. I thank David I. Owen for the opportunity to include the copy and accompanying note here.

[2] Note that the personal name in line 13 is to be read as *a-ḫu-ni* and not *a-ḫu-we-er* and that the text was incorrectly cited as VAB 1 by G. Pettinato, in *RLA* 5 10a.

ABBREVIATIONS

AAAS	*Annales archéologiques arabes syriennes*
AASOR	*Annual of the American Schools of Oriental Research*
AASOR 44	Freedman 1979
AbN	*Abr-Nahrain*
AfO	*Archiv für Orientforschung*
AION	*Annali dell'Istituto Orientale di Napoli*
AJA	*American Journal of Archaeology*
AJSL	*American Journal of Semitic Languages*
ANET	Pritchard 1955
AnOr	*Analecta Orientalia*
AnOr 7	Schneider 1932
AnOr 26	O'Callaghan 1948
AnSt	*Anatolian Studies*
AOAT	*Alter Orient und Altes Testament*
AOAT 1	Dietrich and Röllig 1969
AOAT 3/1	Loretz 1969
AOAT 12	Römer 1971
AOAT 25	Eichler 1976
AOAT 212	Caquot and Delcor 1981
AOAT 216	Tsukimoto 1985
AoF	*Altorientalische Forschungen*
AOS	*American Oriental Series*
AOS 32	Oppenheim 1948
AR	Kohler and Ungnad 1913
ARES	*Archivi Reali di Ebla: Studi*
ARES 1	Archi 1985
ARET	*Archivi Reali di Ebla: Testi*
ARET 1	Archi 1985
ARET 2	Edzard 1981
ARET 3	Archi and Biga 1982
ARET 4	Biga and Milano 1984
ARET 5	Edzard 1984
ARET 7	Archi 1988
ARET 8	Sollberger 1986
ARET 9	Milano 1990
ARI	*Assyrian Royal Inscriptions*
ARI 2	Grayson 1976
ARM	*Archives royales de Mari*
ARM 16/1	Birot, Kupper and Rouault 1979
ARM 19	Limet 1976
ArOr	*Archiv Orientální*
AS	*Assyriological Studies*

AS 11	Jacobsen 1939
AS 21	Gelb 1980
AS 23	Hoffner and Beckman 1986
ASJ	*Acta Sumerologica*
AUCT	*Andrews University Cuneiform Texts*
AUCT 1	Sigrist 1984
AUCT 2	Sigrist 1988
AUCT 3	Sigrist and Gavin 1988
AuOr	*Aula Orientalis*
BA	*Biblical Archaeologist*
BagM	*Baghdader Mitteilungen*
BAH	*Bibliothèque archéologique et historique*
BAH 16	Thureau-Dangin et al. 1931
BAH 23	Thureau-Dangin et al. 1936
BAH 65	Parrot 1956
BAH 80	Nougayrol 1968
BAH 81	Schaeffer 1969
BAH 86	Parrot 1967
BASOR	*Bulletin of the American Schools of Oriental Research*
BE	*The Babylonian Expedition of the University of Pennsylvania Series A: Cuneiform Texts*
BE 3	Myhrman 1910
BIN	*Babylonian Inscriptions in the Collection of James B. Nies*
BIN 3	Keiser and Kang 1971
BM	*Bibliotheca Mesopotamica*
BM 3	Biggs 1976
BM 10	Buccellati 1979
BM 16	Rouault 1984
BM 20	Buccellati and Kelly-Buccellati 1988
BM 21	Kelly-Buccellati 1986
CAH	*Cambridge Ancient History*
CRAIBL	*Comptes Rendus des Séances de l'Académie des Inscriptions et Belles-Lettres*
CST	Fish 1932
CT	*Cuneiform Texts from Babylonian Tablets in the British Museum*
CTH	Laroche 1971
CTMMA	Spar 1988
DamM	*Damaszener Mitteilungen*
DV	*Drevnosti Vostocnyja, Trudy Vostocno*
DV 5	Nikol'skij 1915
HO	*Handbuch der Orientalistik*
HSAO	*Heidelberger Studien zum Alten Orient*
HSAO 2	Waetzoldt and Hauptmann 1988
HSM	*Harvard Semitic Monographs*
HSM 45	Meier 1988
HSS	*Harvard Semitic Series*
HSS 10	Meek 1935

HSS 42	Fleming 1992
HUCA	*Hebrew Union College Annual*
IBoT	*Istanbul Arkeoloji Müzelerinde Bulunan Boğazköy Tabletleri*
IEJ	*Israel Exploration Journal*
IOS	*Israel Oriental Studies*
IRSA	Solberger and Kupper 1971
ISET	*Istanbul Arkeoloji Müzelerinde Bulunan Sumer Edebi Tablet ve Parçalari*
JANES	*Journal of the Ancient Near Eastern Society*
JAOS	*Journal of the American Oriental Society*
JBL	*Journal of Biblical Literature*
JCS	*Journal of Cuneiform Studies*
JEOL	*Jaarbericht Ex Oriente Lux*
JESHO	*Journal of the Economic and Social History of the Orient*
JKF	*Jahrbuch für kleinasiatische Forschung*
JSS	*Journal of Semitic Studies*
KAV	Schroeder 1920
KBo	*Keilschrifttexte aus Boghazköi*
KUB	*Keilschrifturkunden aus Boghazköi*
LAK	Deimel 1922
MAD	*Materials for the Assyrian Dictionary*
MAD 1	Gelb 1952
MAD 3	Gelb 1957
MAM	*Mission Archéologique de Mari*
MAM 1	Parrot 1956
MAM 3	Parrot 1967
MCS	*Manchester Cuneiform Studies*
MDOG	*Mitteilungen der Deutschen Orient-Gesellschaft zu Berlin*
MDP	*Mémoires de la Délégation en Perse*
MEE	*Materiali Epigrafici di Ebla*
MEE 1	Pettinato 1979
MEE 3	Pettinato 1981
MEE 4	Pettinato 1982
MIO	*Mitteilungen des Instituts für Orientforschung*
MRS	*Mission de Ras Shamra*
MRS VI	Nougayrol 1955
MRS IX	Nougayrol 1956
MRS XII	Nougayrol 1970
MRS XVI	Nougayrol 1968
MRS XVII	Schaeffer 1969
MSL	*Materials for the Sumerian Lexicon*
MSL V	Landsberger 1957
MSL XI	Reiner and Civil 1974
MSL XIV	Civil, Green, and Lambert 1979
MVAG	*Mitteilungen der Vorderasiatischen Gesellschaft*
MVN	*Materiali per il vocabolario neosumerico*
MVN 1	Pettinato and Waetzoldt 1974

MVN 3	Owen 1975
MVN 4	Cagni and Pettinato 1976
MVN 5	Sollberger 1978
MVN 6	Pettinato 1977
MVN 11	Owen 1982
MVN 12	Gomi 1982
MVN 13	Sigrist, Owen, and Young 1984
MVN 15	Owen 1991
NPN	Gelb et al. 1943
OA	*Oriens Antiquus*
OIP	*Oriental Institute Publications*
OIP 57	Gelb et al. 1957
OIP 61	Braidwood and Braidwood 1960
OIP 79	McEwan et al. 1958
OIP 99	Biggs 1974
OLP	*Orientalia Lovaniensia Periodica*
OLZ	*Orientalistische Literaturzeitung*
PBS	*Publications of the Babylonian Section. The Museum, University of Pennsylvania*
Or	*Orientalia*
PDK	Weidner 1923
PDT	*Die Puzriš-Dagan Texte*
PDT 1	Çığ, Kızılyay, and Salonen 1954
PDT 2	Yıldız and Gomi 1988
PIOL	*Publications de l'Institut Orientaliste de Louvain*
PIOL 6	Kestemont 1974
PIOL 11	Lebrun 1976
PIOL 19	Sauren 1978
PRU	*Le Palais royal d'Ugarit*
PRU III	Nougayrol 1955
PRU IV	Nougayrol 1956
PRU VI	Nougayrol 1970
QS	*Quaderni di Semitistica*
QS 13	Fronzaroli 1984
R	Rawlinson 1861
RA	*Revue d'Assyriologie*
RAI	*Rencontre Assyriologique Internationale*
RBI	*Rivista Biblica*
RGTC	*Répertoire Géographique des Textes Cunéiformes*
RGTC 2	Edzard and Farber 1974
RGTC 4	Nashef 1991
RGTC 5	Nashef 1982
RGTC 6	del Monte and Tischler 1978
RHA	*Revue Hittite et Asianique*
RLA	*Reallexikon der Assyriologie*
RSO	*Rivista degli Studi Orientali*
SAKI	Thureau-Dangin 1907

SAOC	*Studies in Ancient Oriental Civilization*
SAOC 36	Young et al. 1984
SAOC 42	Murnane 1985
SAOC 44	Stone 1987
SAOC 47	Leonard and Williams 47
SBT	*Studien zu den Boğazköy-Texten*
SBT 4	Werner 1967
SBT 18	Neu 1974
SBT 27-28	Singer 1983-84
SCCNH	*Studies on the Civilization and Culture of Nuzi and the Hurrians*
SCCNH 1	Morrison and Owen 1981
SEb	*Studi Eblaiti*
SET	Jones and Snyder 1961
SH	*Scripta Hierosolymitana*
SH 33	Cogan and Eph'al 1991
SMEA	*Studi micenei ed egeo-anatolici*
SMS	*Syro-Mesopotamian Studies*
SS	*Studi Semitici*
SS 6	Liverani 1962
SS 26	Buccellati 1967
SS 54	Xella 1981
SVT	*Supplements to Vetus Testamentum*
ŠA	Jean 1923
TA	*Tel-Aviv*
TCL	*Textes cunéiformes du Louvre*
TCL 2	de Genouillac 1911
TCL 5	de Genouillac 1922
TCL 21	J. Lewy 1937
TCS	*Texts from Cuneiform Sources*
TCS 2	Biggs 1967
TCS 5	Grayson 1975
TCSD	Boson 1936
TEL	Virolleaud 1968
TH	*Texte der Hethiter*
TH 5	Bin-Nun 1975
TH 10	Košak 1982
TLB	*Tabulae Cuneiformes a F.M.Th. de Liagre Böhl Collectae*
TLB 3	Hallo 1963-73
TPTS	Sigrist 1990
TRD	de Genouillac 1911
TRU	Legrain 1912
TSO	*Texte und Studien zur Orientalistik*
TSO 2	Krebernik 1984
TSO 4	Harrak 1987
TSŠ	Jestin 1937
TMH NF	*Texte und Materialien der Frau Professor Hilprecht Collection of Babylonian Antiquities im Eigentum der Universität Iena, Neue Folge*

UCP	*University of California Publications in Semitic Philology*
UCP 9/4	Lutz 1929
UDT	Nies 1920
UDU	Contenau 1916
UET	*Ur Excavations. Texts*
UET 1	Gadd 1928
UF	*Ugarit-Forschungen*
Ug	*Ugaritica*
Ug 5	Nougayrol 1968
Ug 6	Schaeffer 1969
VO	*Vicino Oriente*
WO	*Die Welt des Orients*
WVDOG	*Wissenschaftliche Veröffentlichungen der Deutschen Orient-Gesellschaft*
YOS	*Yale Oriental Studies*
YOS 11	van Dijk, Goetze, and Hussey 1985
YOS 18	Snell and Lager 1991
ZA	*Zeitschrift für Assyriologie*
ZDMG	*Zeitschrift der Deutschen Morgenländischen Gesellschaft*
ZDPV	*Zeitschrift des Deutschen Palästina-Vereins*

BIBLIOGRAPHY

Abou-Assaf, Ali et al.

1982 *La statue de Tell Fekherye et son inscription bilingue assyro-araméenne*. Paris: Editions Recherche sur les civilisations. *Etudes Assyriologiques*.

Akkermans, Peter M.M.G.

1984 "Archäologische Geländebegehung im Baliḫ-Tal." *AfO* 31:188-190.

1988 "An Updated Chronology for the Northern Ubaid and Late Chalcolithic Periods in Syria: New Evidence from Tell Hammam Et-Turkman." *Iraq* 50:109-145.

Alberti, Amedeo

1990 "AN.BU = *a-nu-bu*$_x$." *NABU* 1990/124.

Albright, W.F.

1940 "New Light on the History of Western Asia in the Second Millennium B.C. [I]." *BASOR* 77:20-32.

1940 "New Light on the History of Western Asia in the Second Millennium B.C. (continued)." *BASOR* 78:23-31.

Al-Fouadi, Abdul-Hadi

1976 "Bassetki Statue with an Old Akkadian Royal Inscription of Narām-Sin of Agade (B.C. 2291-2255)." *Sumer* 32:63-75.

Algaze, Guillermo

1986 *Mesopotamian Expansion and its Consequences: Informal Empire in the Late Fourth Millennium B.C.* Dissertation: University of Chicago.

1989 "The Uruk Expansion: Cross-cultural Exchange in Early Mesopotamian Civilization." *Current Anthropology* 30:571-608.

Alp, Sedat

1950 "Die soziale Klasse der NAM.RA-Leute und ihre hethitische Bezeichnung." *JKF* 1:113-135.

1991 *Maşat-Höyükte Bulunan Çivi Yazılı Hitit Tabletleri = Hethitische Keilschrifttafeln aus Maşat-Höyük* (Ankara: Türk Tarih Kurumu Basımevi).

Alster, Bendt

1975 "Paradoxical Proverbs and Satire in Sumerian Literature." *JCS* 27:201-230.

1980 (ed) *Death in Mesopotamia: Papers read at the XXVI*[e] *Rencontre assyriologique internationale*. Copenhagen: Akademisk Forlag. *Mesopotamia* 8. *RAI* 26.

1990 "A duplicate to 'Enlil and Namzitarra'." *NABU* 1990/102.

1990 "The Sumerian Poem of Early Rulers and Related Poems." *OLP* 21:5-25.

1991 "The Instructions of Urninurta and Related Compositions." *Or* 60:141-157.

1991 "Väterliche Weisheit in Mesopotamien." In *Weisheit: Beiträge zur Archäologie der literarischen Kommunikation* III, edited by Aleida Assmann. München: W. Fink. 103-115.

Anbar (Bernstein), M.

1973 "Le début du règne de Šamši-Addu Ier." *IOS* 3:1-33.

Anbar, Moshe and Nadav Na'aman

1986-87 "An Account Tablet of Sheep from Ancient Hebron." *TA* 13-14:3-12.

Arcari, Elena
1984 "Remarks on AnOr 7, 99 and Parallel Texts." *Or* 53:442-443.
Archi, Alfonso
1979 "The Epigraphic Evidence from Ebla and the Old Testament." *Biblica* 60:556-566.
1980 "Notes on Eblaite Geography [I]." *SEb* 2:1-16.
1980 "Le testimonianze oracolari per la regina Tawannanna." *SMEA* 22:19-29. *Incunabula Graeca* 73.
1981 "Kiš nei testi di Ebla." *SEb* 4:77-87.
1981 "La 'Lista di nomi e professioni' ad Ebla." *SEb* 4:177-204.
1981 "A Mythologem in Eblaitology: Mesilim of Kish at Ebla." *SEb* 4:227-230.
1981 "Notes on Eblaite Geography II." *SEb* 4:1-17.
1981 "I rapporti tra Ebla e Mari." *SEb* 4:129-166.
1982 "About the Organization of the Eblaite State." *SEb* 5:201-220.
1984 "Anatolia in the Second Millennium B.C." In *Circulation of Goods in Non-Palatial Context in the Ancient Near East*, edited by idem. Roma: Edizioni Dell'Ateneo. *Incunabula Graeca* 82. 195-206.
1984 (ed) *Circulation of Goods in Non-Palatial Context in the Ancient Near East*. Roma: Edizioni Dell'Ateneo. *Incunabula Graeca* 82.
1984 "The 'Names and Professions List': more fragments from Ebla." *RA* 78:171-174.
1985 "Les rapports politiques et économiques entre Ebla et Mari." *MARI* 4:63-83.
1985 "Le synchronisme entre les rois de Mari et les rois d'Ebla au IIIe millénaire." *MARI* 4:47-51.
1985 *Testi amministrativi: Assegnazioni di tessuti (Archivio L. 2769).* Roma: Missione Archeologica Italiana in Siria. *ARET* 1.
1986 "Die ersten zehn Könige von Ebla." *ZA* 76:213-217.
1987 "More on Ebla and Kish." *Eblaitica* 1:125-140.
1987 "The 'Sign-list' from Ebla." *Eblaitica* 1:91-113.
1988 "Cult of the Ancestors and Tutelary God at Ebla." In *Fucus: A Semitic/Afrasian Gathering in Remembrance of Albert Ehrman*, edited by Yoël L. Arbeitman. Amsterdam: John Benjamins. *Current Issues in Linguistic Theory* 58. 103-112.
1988 (ed) *Eblaite Personal Names and Semitic Name-giving*. Roma: Missione Archeologica Italiana in Siria. *ARES* 1.
1988 "Ḫarran in the III Millennium B.C." *UF* 20:1-8.
1988 "Prices, Workers' Wages and Maintenance at Ebla." *AoF* 15:24-29.
1988 *Testi amministrativi: Registrazioni di metalli e tessuti (Archivio L. 2769).* Roma: Missione Archeologica Italiana in Siria. *ARET* 7.
1989 "Tables de comptes eblaïtes." *RA* 83:1-6.
1990 "Imâr au IIIème millénaire d'après les archives d'Ebla." *MARI* 6:21-38.
1990 "Tuttul-sur-Baliḫ à l'âge d'Ebla." In *De la Babylonie à la Syrie, en passant par Mari: Mélanges offerts a Monsieur J.-R. Kupper*, edited by Ö. Tunca. Liège: Université de Liège. 197-207.
1991 "Ebla: la formazione di uno Stato del III millennio a.C." *La Parola del Passato* 46:195-219.
Archi, Alfonso and Maria Giovanna Biga
1982 *Testi amministrativi di vario contenuto (Archivo L. 2769: TM.75.G.3000-4101).* Roma: Missione Archeologica Italiana in Siria. *ARET* 3.
Archi, Alfonso and Francesco Pomponio

1990 *Testi cuneiformi neo-sumerici da Drehem, 1-142*. Milano: Cisalpino Istituto Editoriale Universitario.

Arnaud, Daniel

1975 "Catalogue des textes cunéiformes trouvés au cours des trois premières campagnes à Meskéné Qadimé Quest (Chantiers A, C, E, et trouvaille de surface)." *AAAS* 25:87-93.

1975 "Les textes d'Emar et la chronologie de la fin du Bronze Récent." *Syria* 52:87-92.

1976-77 "Religion assyro-babylonienne." *École pratique des Hautes Études, Vᵉ Section (Sciences Religieuses)* 84:221-228.

1980 "La bibliothèque d'un devin syrien à Meskéné-Emar (Syrie)." *CRAIBL* 375-388.

1980 "Traditions urbaines et influences semi-nomades à Emar, à l'âge du bronze récent." In *Le Moyen Euphrate*, edited by Jean-Claude Margueron. Leiden: E.J. Brill. 245-264.

1981 "Humbles et superbes à Emar (Syrie) à la fin de l'âge du Bronze récent." In *Mélanges bibliques et orientaux en l'honneur de M. Henri Cazelles*, edited by A. Caquot and M. Delcor. Kevelaer: Verlag Butzon & Bercker. *AOAT* 212. 2-14.

1982 "Les textes cunéiformes suméro-accadiens des campagnes 1979-1980 à Ras Shamra-Ougarit." *Syria* 59:199-222.

1982 "Les textes suméro-accadiens: un florilège." In *Meskéné-Emar: Dix ans de travaux 1972-1982*, edited by Dominique Beyer. Paris: Editions Recherche sur les civilisations. 43-52.

1984 "La Syrie du moyen-Euphrate sous le protectorat hittite: l'administration d'après trois lettres inédites." *AuOr* 2:179-188.

1985-87 *Recherches au Pays d'Aštata: Emar VI.1-4. Les textes sumériens et accadiens*. Paris: Editions Recherche sur les civilisations.

1987 "La Syrie du moyen-Euphrate sous le protectorat hittite: contrats de droit privé." *AuOr* 5:211-241.

Artzi, Pinḥas

1985 "Observations on the 'Library' of the Amarna Archives." In *Cuneiform Archives and Libraries: Papers read at the 30ᵉ Rencontre Assyriologique Internationale*, edited by Klaas R. Veenhof. Istanbul: Nederlands Historisch-Archaeologisch Instituut te Istanbul. *Uitgaven van het Nederlands Historisch-Archaeologisch Instituut te Istanbul* 57. 210-212.

1990 "Studies in the Library of the Amarna Archive." In *Bar-Ilan Studies in Assyriology dedicated to Pinḥas Artzi*, edited by Jacob Klein and Aaron Skaist. Ramat-Gan: Bar-Ilan University Press. 139-156.

Astour, Michael C.

1969 "The Partition of the Confederacy of Mukiš-Nuḫašše-Nii by Šuppiluliuma." *Or* 38:381-414.

1971 "Tell Mardīḫ and Ebla." *UF* 3:9-19.

1972 "Some Recent Works on Ancient Syria and the Sea People." *JAOS* 92:447-459.

1977 "Continuité et changement dans la toponymie de la Syrie du Nord." In *La Toponymie Antique*, org. by T. Fahd. Leiden: E.J. Brill. 117-141.

1977 "Tunip-Hamath and Its Region: A Contribution to the Historical Geography of Central Syria." *Or* 46:51-64.

1978 "Les Hourrites en Syrie du Nord: rapport sommaire." *RHA* 36 (= Actes de la XXIVᵉ Rencontre Assyriologique Internationale, Paris 1977). *RAI* 24. 1-22.

1979 "The Kingdom of Siyannu-Ušnatu." *UF* 11:13-28.

1980 "King Ammurapi and the Hittite Princess." *UF* 12:103-108.

1981 "Toponymic Parallels Between the Nuzi Area and Northern Syria, with an appendix:

Nuzi Place Names in Egyptian Topographic Lists." *SCCNH* 1:11-26.
1981 "Ugarit and the Great Powers." In *Ugarit in Retrospect*, edited by Gordon Douglas Young. Winona Lake: Eisenbrauns. 3-29.
1988 "The Geographical and Political Structure of the Ebla Empire." In *Wirtschaft und Gesellschaft von Ebla*, edited by Hartmut Waetzoldt and Harald Hauptmann. Heidelberg: Heidelberger Orientverlag. *HSAO* 2. 139-158.
1988 "Toponymy of Ebla and Ethnohistory of Northern Syria: A Preliminary Survey." *JAOS* 108:545-555.
1989 *Hittite History and Absolute Chronology of the Bronze Age*. Partille, Sweden: Paul Åströms förlag. *Studies in Mediterranean Archaeology, Pocket-book* 73.
1992 "An Outline of the History of Ebla (Part 1)." *Eblaitica* 3:3-82.

Åström, Paul
1989 (ed) *High, Middle or Low? Acts of an International Colloquium on Absolute Chronology held at the University of Gothenburg 20th-22nd August 1987. Part 3.* Gothenburg: Paul Åströms förlag. *Studies in Mediterranean Archaeology and Literature, Pocket-book* 80.

Badian, Ernst
1958 *Foreign Clientelae (264-70 B.C.)*. Oxford: Clarendon Press. Reprinted 1967.

Batto, Bernard Frank
1974 *Studies on Women at Mari*. Baltimore: The Johns Hopkins University Press.

Beckman, Gary
1983 "Mesopotamians and Mesopotamian Learning at Ḫattuša." *JCS* 35:97-114.
1988 "Three Tablets from the Vicinity of Emar." *JCS* 40:61-68.
1990 "Medizin. B. Bei der Hethitern." *RLA* 7:629-631.

Behrens, Hermann, Darlene Loding, and Martha T. Roth
1989 *DUMU-E$_2$-DUB-BA-A: Studies in Honor of Åke W. Sjöberg*. Philadelphia: The University Museum. *Occasional Publications of the Samuel Noah Kramer Fund* 11.

Beyer, Dominique
1982 (ed) *Meskéné-Emar: Dix ans de travaux 1972-1982*. Paris: Editions Recherche sur les civilisations.
1990 "Quelques vestiges de l'imagerie émariote du Bronze Moyen." *MARI* 6:93-102.

Biga, Maria Giovanna and Lucio Milano
1984 *Testi amministrativi: Assegnazioni di tessuti (Archivio L. 2769)*. Roma: Missione Archeologica Italiana in Siria. *ARET* 4.

Biga, Maria Giovanna and Francesco Pomponio
1990 "Elements for a Chronological Division of the Administrative Documentation of Ebla." *JCS* 42:179-201.
1992 "Critères de rédaction compatable et chronologie relative des textes d'Ebla." *MARI* 7:1-22.

Biggs, Robert D.
1966 "The Abū Ṣalābīkh Tablets: A Preliminary Survey." *JCS* 20:73-88.
1967 *ŠÀ.ZI.GA: Ancient Mesopotamian Potency Incantations*. Locust Valley: J.J. Augustin. *TCS* 2.
1974 *Inscriptions from Tell Abū Ṣalābīkh*. Chicago: The University of Chicago Press. *OIP* 99.
1976 *Inscriptions from Al-Hiba—Lagash: The First and Second Seasons*. Malibu: Undena Publications. *BM* 3. Reprinted 1992 with Addenda.
1981 "Ebla and Abu Salabikh: The Linguistic and Literary Aspects." In *La lingua di Ebla*,

edited by Luigi Cagni. Napoli: Istituto Universitario Orientale. 121-133.

Biggs, Robert D. and J.N. Postgate
1978 "Inscriptions from Abu Salabikh, 1975." *Iraq* 40:101-117.

Bin-Nin, Shoshana R.
1975 *The Tawananna in the Hittite Kingdom.* Heidelberg: Carl Winter Universitätsverlag. *TH* 5.

Birot, Maurice
1980 "Fragment de rituel de Mari relatif au *kispum.*" In *Death in Mesopotamia: Papers read at the XXVI*[e] *Rencontre assyriologique internationale*, edited by Bendt Alster. Copenhagen: Akademisk Forlag. *Mesopotamia* 8. *RAI* 26. 139-150.

Birot, Maurice, Jean-Robert Kupper and Olivier Rouault
1979 *Répertoire analytique (2*[e] *volume).* Paris: Paul Geuthner. *ARM* 16/1.

Bonechi, Marco
1990 "Aleppo in età arcaica. A proposito di un'opera recente." *SEL* 7:15-37.
1991 "Onomastica dei testi di Ebla: nomi propri come fossili-guida?" *SEL* 8:59-79.

Borger, R.
1970 "Sur le récit du Déluge RS 22421." *RA* 64:189.

Boson, Giustino
1936 *Tavolette cuneiformi sumere, degli archivi di Drehem e di Djoha.* Milano: Società Editrice Vita e Pensiero. *Pubblicazioni della Università Cattolica del Sacro Cuore.*

Bottéro, Jean
1971 "Syria at the Time of the Kings of Agade." *CAH*[3] I/2:321-327.
1971 "Syria During the Third Dynasty of Ur." *CAH*[3] I/2:559-566.

Bottéro, Jean et al.
1967 (ed) *The Near East: The Early Civilizations.* New York: Delacorte Press.

Bounni, Adnan and Paolo Matthiae
1980 "Tell Fray, ville frontière entre hittites et assyriens au XIIIe siècle av. J.C." *Archéologica* 140:30-39.

Braidwood, Robert J. and Linda S. Braidwood
1960 *Excavations in the Plain of Antioch I: The Earlier Assemblages Phases A-J.* Chicago: The University of Chicago Press. *OIP* 61.

Breniquet, C.
1989 "Les origines de la culture d'Obeid en Mésopotamie du nord." In *Upon this Foundation—The 'Ubaid Reconsidered*, edited by Elizabeth F. Henrickson and Ingolf Thuesen. København: Museum Tusculanum Press. 325-338.

Brugnatelli, Vermondo
1982 "Per un'interpretazione di TM.75.G.1392." *OA* 21:31-32.
1988 "Sprachwissenschaftliche Überlegungen zu einem literarischen Text aus Ebla." In *Wirtschaft und Gesellschaft von Ebla*, edited by Hartmut Waetzoldt and Harald Hauptmann. Heidelberg: Heidelberger Orientverlag. *HSAO* 2. 173-178.

Bryce, T.R.
1988 "Tette and the Rebellions in Nuhassi." *AnSt* 38:21-28.

Buccellati, Giorgio
1966 *The Amorites of the Ur III Period.* Napoli: Istituto Orientale di Napoli.
1967 *Cities and Nations of Ancient Syria.* Roma: Università di Roma. *SS* 26.
1979 *Terqa Preliminary Reports No. 10: The Fourth Season: Introduction and the Stratigraphic Record.* Malibu: Undena Publications. *BM* 10.

1988 "The Kingdom and Period of Khana." *BASOR* 270:43-61.

1990 "'River Bank,' 'High Country,' and 'Pasture Land': The Growth of Nomadism on the Middle Euphrates and the Khabur." In *Tall al-Ḥamīdīya* 2, edited by Seyyare Eichler et al. Frieburg, Schweiz: Universitätsverlag. 87-117.

Buccellati, Giorgio and Marilyn Kelly-Buccellati

1977 "Syro-Mesopotamian Studies: A Preface." *SMS* 1/1:1-2.

1988 *Mozan 1: The Soundings of the First Two Seasons*. Malibu: Undena Publications. *BM* 20.

Bunnens, Guy

1989 "Emar on the Euphrates in the 13th Century B.C. Some Thoughts about Newly Published Cuneiform Texts." *AbN* 27:23-36.

1989 "Tell Ahmar on the Euphrates. A New Research Project of the University of Melbourne." *Akkadica* 63:1-11.

1990 (ed) *Tell Ahmar: 1988 Season*. Leiden: E.J. Brill. *AbN Supplement* 2.

Cagni, Luigi

1981 (ed) *La lingua di Ebla*. Napoli: Istituto Universitario Orientale.

1982 "Miscellanea neo-sumerica, IX: collazioni a N. Schneider, *Die Drehem- und Djoḫa-Texte im Kloster Montserrat (Barcelona) (Analecta Orientalia* 7), Roma 1932." *OA* 22:73-118.

1984 (ed) *Il bilinguismo a Ebla*. Napoli: Istituto Universitario Orientale.

1987 (ed) *Ebla 1975-1985: Dieci anni di studi linguistici e filologici*. Napoli: Istituto Universitario Orientale.

Cagni, Luigi and Giovanni Pettinato

1976 *La Collezione del Pontificio Istituto Biblico—Roma; La Collezione della Collegiata dei SS. Pietro e Orso—Aosta*. Roma: Multigrafica Editrice. *MVN* 4.

Carruba, Onofrio

1977 "Beiträge zur mittelhethitischen Geschichte I. *Die Tutḫalijas und die Arnuwandas*." *SMEA* 18:137-74. *Incunabula Graeca* 67.

Carter, Charles

1962 *Hittite Cult Inventories*. Dissertation: University of Chicago.

Carter, Elizabeth and Matthew W. Stolper

1984 *Elam: Surveys of Political History and Archaeology*. Berkeley: University of California Press. *University of California Publications: Near Eastern Studies* 25.

Cauvin, Jacques

1979 "Les fouilles de Mureybet (1971-1974) et leur signification pour les origines de la sedentarisation au Proche-Orient." In *Archaeological Reports from the Tabqa Dam Project—Euphrates Valley, Syria*, edited by David Noel Freedman. Cambridge: American Schools of Oriental Research. *AASOR* 44. 19-48.

1980 "Le Moyen-Euphrate au VIIIe millénaire d'après Mureybet et Cheikh Hassan." In *Le Moyen Euphrate*, edited by Jean-Claude Margueron. Leiden: E.J. Brill. 21-34.

Cauvin, Jacques and Danielle Stordeur

1985 "Une occupation d'époque Uruk en Palmyrène: le niveau supérieur d'El Kowm 2—Caracol." *Cahiers de l'Euphrate* 4:191-205.

Charpin, Dominique

1982 "Mari et le calendrier d'Ebla." *RA* 76:1-6.

1987 "Šubat-Enlil et le pays d'Apum." *MARI* 5:129-140.

1987 "Tablettes présargoniques de Mari." *MARI* 5:65-127.

1989 "Tuttul et It d'après les archives de Mari." *NABU* 1989/16.

1990 "A Contribution to the Geography and History of the Kingdom of Kaḫat." In *Tall al-Ḥamīdīya* 2, edited by Seyyare Eichler et al. Freiburg, Schweiz: Universitätsverlag. 67-85.

Chiera, Edward

1921 *Selected Temple Accounts from Telloh, Yokha and Drehem: Cuneiform Tablets in the Library of Princeton University*. Philadelphia.

Çığ, M., H. Kızılyay and A. Salonen

1954 *Die Puzriš-Dagan-Texte der Istanbuler Archäologischen Museen Teil I: Nrr. 1-725*. Helsinki: *Annales Academiae Scientiarum Fennicae* 92.

Civil, Miguel

1964 "The 'Message of Lú-dingir-ra to his Mother' and a Group of Akkado-Hittite 'Proverbs'." *JNES* 23:1-11.

1967 "Šū-Sîn's Historical Inscriptions: Collection B." *JCS* 21:24-38.

1974-77 "Enlil and Namzitarra." *AfO* 25:65-71.

1982 "Studies on Early Dynastic Lexicography. I." *OA* 21:1-26.

1984 "Bilingualism in Logographically Written Languages: Sumerian in Ebla." In *Il bilinguismo a Ebla*, edited by Luigi Cagni. Napoli: Istituto Universitario Orientale. 75-97.

1984 "Studies in Early Dynastic Lexicography II: 3. Word List D 50-57 (ARET 5 No. 23)." *ZA* 74:161-163.

1985 "On Some Texts Mentioning Ur-Namma." *Or* 54:27-45.

1987 "The Early History of HAR-ra: The Ebla Link." In *Ebla 1975-1985: Dieci anni di studi linguistici e filologici*, edited by Luigi Cagni. Napoli: Istituto Universitario Orientale. 131-158.

1987 "[Note]." *RA* 81:187-188.

1989 "The Texts from Meskene-Emar." *AuOr* 7:5-25.

Civil, Miguel, Margaret W. Green, and Wilfred G. Lambert

1979 *Ea A* = nâqu, *Aa A* = nâqu, *with their Forerunners and Related Texts*. Roma: Pontificium Istitutum Biblicum. *MSL* XIV.

Clay, Albert T.

1919 *Neo-Babylonian Letters from Erech*. New Haven: Yale University Press. *YOS Babylonian Texts* 3.

Cogan, Mordechai and Israel Eph'al

1991 (eds) *Ah, Assyria...: Studies in Assyrian History and Ancient Near Eastern Historiography Presented to Hayim Tadmor*. Jerusalem: The Magnes Press, The Hebrew University. *SH* 33.

Cohen, Mark E.

1976 "Literary Texts from the Andrews University Archaeological Museum." *RA* 70:129-144.

Cohen, Mark E., D. Snell, and D.B. Weisberg

forth (eds) *The Temple and the Book: Ancient Near Eastern Studies in Honor of William W. Hallo*. Bethesda: CDL Press.

Contenau, G.

1916 *Umma Sous la Dynastie d'Ur*. Paris: Paul Geuthner.

de Contenson, Henri and Willem J. van Liere

1966 "Premier sondage à Bouqras en 1965: Rapport préliminaire." *AAAS* 16:181-192.

de Contenson, Henri et al.

1979 "Tell Aswad (Damascene)." *Paléorient* 5:153-156.

Cooper, Jerrold S.
1971 "New Cuneiform Parallels to the Song of Songs." *JBL* 90:157-162.

Cooper, Jerrold S. and Wolfgang Heimpel
1983 "The Sumerian Sargon Legend." *JAOS* 103:67-82.

Danmanville, Jenny
1965 "Anatolie hittite." In *Histoire mondiale de la femme*, edited by Pierre Grimal. Paris: Nouvelle Librarie de France. Vol. 1. 248-266.

Deimel, Anton
1922 *Liste der archäischen Keilschriftzeichen*. Leipzig: J.C. Hinrichs'sche Buchhandlung. *WVDOG* 40.
1923 *Schultexte aus Fara*. Leipzig: J.C. Hinrichs'sche Buchhandlung. *WVDOG* 43.

Demsky, Aaron
1990 "The Education of Canaanite Scribes in the Mesopotamian Cuneiform Tradition." In *Bar-Ilan Studies in Assyriology dedicated to Pinḥas Artzi*, edited by Jacob Klein and Aaron Skaist. Ramat-Gan: Bar-Ilan University Press. 157-170.

Dever, William G.
1980 "New Vistas on the EB IV ('MB I') Horizon in Syria-Palestine." *BASOR* 237:35-64.

Dhorme, P.
1912 "Tablettes de Dréhem à Jérusalem." *RA* 9:39-63.

Diakonoff, I.M.
1959 *Obščestvennyj i gosudarstvennyj stroj drevnego Dvureč'ja: Šumer* [*Society and State in Ancient Mesopotamia: Sumer*]. Moscow: Nauka.
1985 (ed) *Drevnjaja Èbla (Raskopki v Sirii)* (*Ancient Ebla [Excavations in Syria]*). Moscow: Progress.
1990 "The Importance of Ebla for History and Linguistics." *Eblaitica* 2:3-29.

Dietrich, Manfred
1989 "Das Einsetzungsritual der Entu von Emar (Emar VI/3, 369)." *UF* 21:47-100.
1990 "Die akkadischen Texte der Archive und Bibliotheken von Emar." *UF* 22:25-48.
1991 "Der Dialog zwischen Šūpē-amēli und seinem 'Vater': die Tradition babylonischer Weisheitsgesprüche im Westen." *UF* 23:33-68.

Dietrich, Manfred and Wolfgang Röllig
1969 (eds) *Lišān mitḫurti: Festschrift Wolfram Freiherr von Soden*. Kevelaer: Verlag Butzon & Bercker. *AOAT* 1.

van Dijk, Jan
1982 "Fremdsprachige Beschwörungstexte in der Südmesopotamischen literarischen Überlieferung." In *Mesopotamien und seine Nachbarn: Politische und kulturelle Wechselbeziehungen im Alten Vorderasien vom 4. bis 1. Jahrtausend v. Chr.*, edited by Hans-Jörg Nissen and Johannes Renger. *Berliner Beiträge zum Vorderen Orient* 1. *RAI* 25. 97-110.

van Dijk, Jan, A. Goetze, and M.I. Hussey
1985 *Early Mesopotamian Incantations and Rituals*. New Haven: Yale University Press. *YOS* 11.

Dobel, Allan, Frank Asaro, and H.V. Michel
1977 "Neutron Activation Analysis and the Location of Waššukanni." *Or* 46:375-382.

Dornemann, Rudolph H.
1979 "Tell Hadidi: A Millennium of Bronze Age City Occupation." In *Archaeological*

Reports from the Tabqa Dam Project—Euphrates Valley, Syria, edited by David Noel Freedman. Cambridge: American Schools of Oriental Research. *AASOR* 44. 113-151.

1980 "Tell Hadidi: an Important Center of the Mitannian Period and Earlier." In *Le Moyen Euphrate*, edited by Jean-Claude Margueron. Leiden: E.J. Brill. 217-234.

1988 "Tell Hadidi: One Bronze Age Site Among Many in the Tabqa Dam Salvage Area." *BASOR* 270:13-42.

Dossin, Georges

1938 "Aplaḫanda, roi de Carkémiš." *RA* 35:115-121.

1938 "Les Archives épistolaires du Palais de Mari." *Syria* 19:105-126.

1938 "Un rituel du culte d'Ištar provenant de Mari." *RA* 35:1-13.

1939 "Iamḫad et Qatanum." *RA* 36:46-54.

1952 "Le royaume d'Alep au XVIIIe siècle avant notre ère d'après les 'Archives de Mari'." *Académie royale de Belgique, Bulletin de la Classe des Lettres et des Sciences Morales et Politiques, 5e Série* 38:229-239.

1954 "Le royaume de Qatna au XVIIIe siècle avant notre ère d'après les 'Archives royales de Mari'." *Académie royale de Belgique, Bulletin de la Classe des Lettres et des Sciences Morales et Politiques, 5e Série* 40:417-425.

van Driel, Govert

1980 "The Uruk Settlement on Jebel Aruda: a Preliminary Report." In *Le Moyen Euphrate*, edited by Jean-Claude Margueron. Leiden: E.J. Brill. 75-93.

1982 "Tablets from Jebel Aruda." In *Zikir Šumim: Assyriological Studies Presented to F.R. Kraus*, edited by idem et al. Leiden: E.J. Brill. 12-25.

1983 "Seals and Sealings from Jebel Aruda 1974-1978." *Akkadica* 33:34-62.

van Driel, Govert and Carol van Driel-Murray

1979 "Jebel Aruda 1977-1978." *Akkadica* 12:2-28.

1983 "Jebel Aruda, The 1982 Season of Excavation, interim report." *Akkadica* 33:1-26.

Drower, Margaret S.

1971 "Syria Before 2200 B.C." *CAH*3 I/2:315-321; 328-362.

1973 "Syria *c.* 1550-1400 B.C." *CAH*3 II/1:417-525.

Du Mesnil du Buisson, Robert

1935 *Le site archéologique de Mishrifé/Qaṭna*. Paris: E. de Boccard.

Dunand, Maurice

1939-58 *Fouilles de Byblos* I-II. Paris: Paul Geuthner.

Dunand, Maurice, Adnan Bounni, and Nessib Saliby

1964 "Fouilles de Tell Kazel, Rapport préliminaire." *AAAS* 14:3-14.

Durand, Jean-Marie

1985 "La situation historique des Šakkanakku: nouvelle approche." *MARI* 4:147-172.

1989 [review of Daniel Arnaud, *Recherches au Pays d'Aštata: Emar VI. Les textes sumériens et accadiens*. Paris, 1986]. *RA* 83:163-191.

1990 "La cité-état d'Imâr à l'époque des rois de Mari." *MARI* 6:39-92.

Durand, Jean-Marie and J.-R. Kupper

1985 (eds) *Miscellanea Babylonica: Mélanges offerts à Maurice Birot*. Paris: Editions Recherche sur les civilisations.

Edel, Elmar

1976 *Ägyptische Ärtzte und ägyptische Medizin am hethitischen Königshof. Neue Funde von Keilschriftbriefen Ramses' II. aus Bogazköy*. Opladen: Westdeutscher Verlag. *Rheinisch-Westfälische Akademie der Wissenschaften Vorträge* G205.

Edzard, Dietz Otto
1980 "Ein neues Tontafelfragment (Nr. 7) aus Kāmid al-Lōz." *ZA* 70:52-54.
1980 "Sumerisch 1 bis 10 in Ebla." *SEb* 3:121-127.
1981 "Neue Erwägungen zum Brief des Enna-Dagan von Mari (TM.75.G.2367)." *SEb* 4:89-97.
1981 *Verwaltungstexte verschiedenen Inhalts aus dem Archiv L2769.* Roma: Missione Archeologica Italiana in Siria. *ARET* 2.
1984 *Hymnen, Beschwörungen und Verwandtes aus dem Archiv L. 2769.* Roma: Missione Archeologica Italiana in Siria. *ARET* 5.
1984 "Zur Syntax der Ebla-Texte." In *Studies on the Language of Ebla*, edited by Pelio Fronzaroli. Firenze: Istituto di Linguistica e di Lingue Orientali. *QS* 13. 101-116.

Edzard, Dietz Otto and Gertrud Farber
1974 *Die Orts- und Gewässernamen der Zeit der 3. Dynastie von Ur.* Wiesbaden: Dr. Ludwig Reichert Verlag. *RGTC* 2.

Ehrich, Robert W.
forth *Chronologies in Old World Archaeology*^{3}. Chicago: The University of Chicago Press. 2 vols. Third edition.

Eichler, Barry L.
1976 (ed) *Kramer Anniversary Volume: Cuneiform Studies in Honor of Samuel Noah Kramer.* Kevelaer: Verlag Butzon & Bercker. *AOAT* 25.

Eichler, Seyyare et al.
1982 (eds) *Tall al-Ḥamīdīya I: Vorbericht 1984.* Freiburg, Schweitz: Universitätsverlag. *Orbis biblicus et orientalis: Series archaeologica* 4.
1990 (eds) *Tall al-Ḥamīdīya* 2. Freiburg, Schweiz: Universitätsverlag.

Fahd, T.
1977 (org) *La Toponymie Antique: Actes du Colloque de Strasbourg 12-14 juin 1975.* Leiden: E.J. Brill.

Fales, Mario
1984 "An Archaic Text from Mari." *MARI* 3:269-270.
1984 "*(L)Arugatu*^{ki} in a Ugaritic Text?" *SEb* 7:83-85.
1988 (ed) *Prima dell'alfabeto. La storia della scrittura attraverso testi cuneiformi inediti.* Venezia: Erizzo Editrice. *Studi e documenti* 4.

Fales, Mario and Th.J.H. Krispijn
1979-80 "An Early Ur III Copy of the Abū Ṣalābīkh 'Names and Professions' List." *JEOL* 26:39-46.

Fielden, Kate
1977 "Tell Brak 1976: The Pottery." *Iraq* 39:245-255.

Finet, André
1975 "Les Temples Sumériens du Tell Kannâs." *Syria* 52:157-174.
1979 "Bilan provisoire des fouilles belges du Tell Kannâs." In *Archaeological Reports from the Tabqa Dam Project—Euphrates Valley, Syria*, edited by David Noel Freedman. Cambridge: American Schools of Oriental Research. *AASOR* 44. 79-94.
1982 *"Lorsque la royauté descendit du ciel...": Les fouilles belges du Tell Kannâs sur l'Euphrate en Syrie.* Morlanwelz: Musée royal de Mariemont.
1982 (ed) *Les pouvoirs locaux en Mésopotamie et dans les regions adjacentes.* Bruxelles: Institut des Hautes Études de Belgique.
1985 "Le port d'Emar sur l'Euphrate, entre le royaume de Mari et le pays de Canaan." In

The Land of Israel: Cross-roads of Civilizations, edited by E. Lipiński. Leuven: Uitgeverij Peeters. *Orientalia Lovaniensia Analecta* 19. 27-38.

Finkbeiner, Uwe and Wolfgang Röllig

1986 (eds) *Ǧamdat Naṣr: Period or Regional Style?* Wiesbaden: Dr. Ludwig Reichert Verlag. *Beihefte zum Tübinger Atlas des Vorderen Orients, Reihe B (Geisteswissenschaften)* 62.

Finkel, Irving L.

1985 "Inscriptions from Tell Brak 1984." *Iraq* 47:187-201.

1986 "On the Series of Sidu." *ZA* 76:250-253.

Finkelstein, J.J.

1956 "A Hittite *mandattu*-Text." *JCS* 10:101-105.

Fish, T.

1932 *Catalogue of Sumerian Tablets in The John Rylands Library*. Manchester: The Manchester University Press.

1957 "Some Place Names and Their Contexts." *MCS* 7:15-24.

Fisher, Loren R.

1959 *Nuzi Geographical Names*. Dissertation: Brandeis University.

Fitz, Stephan

1984 "Steinzeug vom Tell Ḫuēra: Das früheste Beispiel für die Herstellung dichtgebrannter Keramik." *ZA* 74:123-132.

Fleming, Daniel E.

1992 *The Installation of Baal's High Priestess at Emar: a Window on Ancient Syrian Religion*. Atlanta: Scholars Press. *HSS* 42.

Fortin, M.

1988 "Rapport préliminaire sur la seconde campagne de fouilles à Tell ᵓAtij et la première à Tell Gudeda (Automne 1987), sur le Moyen Euphrate." *Syria* 67:219-256.

Foster, Benjamin R.

1982 "The Siege of Armanum." *JANES* 14:27-36.

1990 "Naram-Sin in Martu and Magan." *Annual Review of the Royal Inscriptions of Mesopotamia Project* 8:25-44.

Frayne, Douglas R.

forth *The Early Dynastic List of Geographical Names*. New Haven. *AOS*.

Freedman, David Noel

1979 (ed) *Archaeological Reports from the Tabqa Dam Project—Euphrates Valley, Syria*. Cambridge: American Schools of Oriental Research. *AASOR* 44.

Friberg, J.

1990 "Mathematik." *RLA* 7:531-585.

Friedrich, Johannes

1925 *Aus dem hethitischen Schrifttum, 2. Heft: Religiöse Texte*. Leipzig: J.C. Hinrichs'sche Buchhandlung. *Der Alte Orient* 25/2.

1926 *Staatsverträge des Ḫatti-Reiches in hethitischer Sprache, 1. Teil*. Leipzig: J.C. Hinrichs'sche Buchhandlung. *Hethitische Texte in Umschrift* 2. *MVAG* 31.

1930 *Staatsverträge des Ḫatti-Reiches in hethitischer Sprache, 2. Teil*. Leipzig: J.C. Hinrichs'sche Buchhandlung. *Hethitische Texte in Umschrift* 4. *MVAG* 34.

Friedrich, Johannes and Annelies Kammenhuber

1975ff *Hethitisches Wörterbuch*[2]. Heidelberg: Carl Winter Universitätsverlag.

Fronzaroli, Pelio

1977 "West Semitic Toponymy in Northern Syria in the Third Millennium B.C." *JSS* 22:145-

166.
1984 (ed) *Studies on the Language of Ebla*. Firenze: Istituto di Linguistica e di Lingue Orientali. *QS* 13.

Fugmann, E.
1958 *Hama: Fouilles et recherches de la Fondation Carlsberg 1931-38*. København: Nationalmuseet.

Gadd, C.J.
1928 *Royal Inscriptions*. London: The British Museum. *UET* 1.
1937 "Tablets from Chagar Bazar, 1936." *Iraq* 4:178-185.
1940 "Tablets from Chagar Bazar and Tall Brak, 1937-38." *Iraq* 7:22-61.
1971 "The Dynasty of Agade and the Gutian Invastion." *CAH*[3] I/2:417-463.

Gamkrelidze, T.V.
1961 "The Akkado-Hittite Syllabary and the Problem of the Origin of the Hittite Script." *ArOr* 29:406-418.

Garelli, Paul
1969 *Le Proche-Orient Asiatique des origines aux invasions des peuples de la mer*. Paris: Presses Universitaires de France. *Nouvelle Clio* 2.
1982 "Les pouvoirs locaux en Assyrie." In *Les pouvoirs locaux en Mésopotamie et dans les regions adjacentes*, edited by André Finet. Bruxelles: Institut des Hautes Études de Belgique. 76-91.

Gates, M
1981 "Alalakh Levels VI and V: A Chronological Reassessment." *SMS* 4:11-50.

Gelb, Ignace J.
1938 "Studies in the Topography of Western Asia." *AJSL* 55:66-85.
1952 *Sargonic Texts from the Diyala Region*. Chicago: The University of Chicago Press. *MAD* 1. Second impression, 1961.
1956 "On the Recently Published Economic Texts from Mari." *RA* 50:1-10.
1957 *Glossary of Old Akkadian*. Chicago: The University of Chicago Press. *MAD* 3. Second impression, 1973.
1977 "Thoughts About Ibla: A Preliminary Evaluation, March 1977." *SMS* 1/1:3-30.
1980 *Computer-aided Analysis of Amorite*. Chicago: The Oriental Institute. *AS* 21.
1981 "Ebla and the Kish Civilization." In *La lingua di Ebla*, edited by Luigi Cagni. Napoli: Istituto Universitario Orientale. 9-73.
1992 "Mari and the Kish Civilization." In *Mari in Retrospect*, edited by Gordon D. Young. Winona Lake: Eisenbrauns. 121-202.

Gelb, Ignace J., Pierre M. Purves, and Allan A. MacRae
1943 *Nuzi Personal Names*. Chicago: The University of Chicago. *OIP* 57.

Geller, M.J.
1987 "The Lugal of Mari at Ebla and the Sumerian King List." *Eblaitica* 1:141-145.

de Genouillac, H.
1911 *La trouvaille de Dréhem: Étude avec un choix de textes de Constantinople et Bruxelles*. Paris: Paul Geuthner.
1911 *Tablettes de Dréhem*. Paris: Paul Geuthner. *TCL* 2.
1922 *Textes économiques d'Oumma*. Paris: Paul Geuthner. *TCL* 5.

Geyer, Bernard and Jean-Yves Monchambert
1987 "Prospection de la moyenne vallée de l'Euphrate: rapport préliminaire: 1982-1985." *MARI* 5:293-344.

Goetze, Albrecht
1933 *Die Annalen des Muršilis.* Leipzig: J.C. Hinrichs'sche Buchhandlung. *MVAG* 38/6. Reprinted Darmstadt, 1967.
1953 "Four Ur Dynasty Tablets Mentioning Foreigners." *JCS* 7:103-107.
1953 "Ḫulibar of Duddul." *JNES* 12:114-123.
1953 "An Old Babylonian Itinerary." *JCS* 7:51-72.
1956 "The Inventory IBoT I 31." *JCS* 10:32-38.
1957 *Kleinasien*². München: C.H. Beck'sche Verlagsbuchhandlung. *Handbuch der Altertumswissenschaft* 3:1:3:3:1. Second edition.
1968 [review of Johannes Friedrich, *Hethitisches Wörterbuch. 3. Ergänzungsheft*. Heidelberg, 1966]. *JCS* 22:16-24.
1975 "The Hittites and Syria (1300-1200 B.C.)." *CAH*³ II/2: 252-273.

Gomi, Tohru
1980 "Administrative Texts of the Third Dynasty of Ur in the Merseyside County Museums, Liverpool." *Orient* 16:1-110.
1982 *Wirtschaftstexte der Ur III—Zeit aus dem British Museum.* Roma: Multigrafica Editrice. *MVN* 12.

Gomi, Tohru, Yoko Hirose, and Kazutaka Hirose
1990 *Neo-Sumerian Administrative Texts of the Hirose Collection.* Bethesda: CDL Press.

Gordon, Cyrus H.
1958 "Abraham and the Merchants of Ura." *JNES* 17:28-31.
1987 "Eblaitica." *Eblaitica* 1:19-28.
1990 "Eblaite and Northwest Semitic." *Eblaitica* 2:127-144.

Gorney, Ronald L.
1989 (ed) "Reflections of a Late Bronze Age Empire: The Hittites." *BA* 52/2-3.

Grayson, Albert Kirk
1974-77 "The Empire of Sargon of Akkad." *AfO* 25:56-64.
1975 *Assyrian and Babylonian Chronicles.* Locust Valley: J.J. Augustin. *TCS* 5.
1976 *Assyrian Royal Inscriptions, Part 2: From Tiglath-pileser I to Ashur-nasir-apli II.* Wiesbaden: Otto Harrassowitz. *ARI* 2.

Grayson, Albert Kirk and E. Sollberger
1976 "L'insurrection générale contre Narām-Suen." *RA* 70:103-128.

Greengus, Samuel
1990 "Bridewealth in Sumerian Sources." *HUCA* 61:25-88.

Gurney, O.R.
1952 *The Hittites.* Harmondsworth: Penguin. 2nd ed. 1954; reprinted with revisions 1990.

Güterbock, Hans Gustav
1936 "Die historische Tradition und ihre literarische Gestaltung bei Babyloniern und Hethitern bis 1200 (2. Teil)." *ZA* 44:45-149.
1956 "The Deeds of Suppiluliuma as Told by His Son, Mursili II." *JCS* 10:41-68; 75-98; 107-130.
1958 "The Composition of Hittite Prayers to the Sun." *JAOS* 78:237-245.
1958 "The Cuneiform Tablets." In *Soundings at Tell Fakhariyah*, edited by Calvin W. McEwan et al. Chicago: The University of Chicago Press. *OIP* 79. 86-90.
1962 "Hittite Medicine." *Bulletin of the History of Medicine* 36:109-113.
1978 "Hethitische Literatur." In *Altorientalische Literaturen*, edited by Wolfgang Röllig. Wiesbaden: Akademische Verlagsgesellschaft Athenaion. *Neues Handbuch der Litera-*

turwissenschaft 1. 211-253.

1978 "Some Aspects of Hittite Prayers." In *The Frontiers of Human Knowledge: Lectures held at the Quincentenary Celebrations of Uppsala University 1977*, edited by Torgny T. Segerstedt. Uppsala: Uppsala University. 125-139.

1980 "Randbemerkungen zu einigen hethitischen Gesetzen." *WO* 11:90-92.

1983 "A Hurro-Hittite Hymn to Ishtar." *JAOS* 103:155-164.

Hachmann, Rolf

1980 *Bericht über die Ergebnisse der Ausgrabungen in Kāmid el-Lōz in den Jahren 1968 bis 1970.* Bonn: Rudolf Habelt Verlag Gmbh. *Saarbrücker Beiträge zur Altertumskunde* 22.

1980-83 "Kumidi (Tell Kāmid al-Lōz)." *RLA* 6:330-334.

1982 *Bericht über die Ergebnisse der Ausgrabungen in Kāmid el-Lōz in den Jahren 1971 bis 1974.* Bonn: Rudolf Habelt Verlag Gmbh. *Saarbrücker Beiträge zur Altertumskunde* 32.

Hallo, William W.

1963-73 *Sumerian Archival Texts.* Leiden: Nederlands Instituut voor het Nabije Oosten. *TLB* 3.

1964 "The Road to Emar." *JCS* 18:57-88.

1967 "New Texts from the Reign of Sin-iddinam." *JCS* 21:95-99.

1972 "*Ḫabil-kīn." *RLA* 4:13-14.

1973 "The Date of the Fara Period: A Case Study in the Historiography of Early Mesopotamia." *Or* 42:228-238.

1977 "New Moons and Sabbaths: A Case-study in the Contrastive Approach." *HUCA* 48:1-18.

1978 [review of Alster, *Instructions of Suruppak* (1974) and *Studies in Sumerian Proverbs* (1975)]. *JNES* 37:54-66.

1978 "Simurrum and the Hurrian Frontier." *RHA* 36 (= Actes de 1a XXIV[e] Rencontre Assyriologique Internationale, Paris, 1977). *RAI* 24. 71-83.

1980 "The Expansion of Cuneiform Literature." *PAAJR* 46-47:307-322.

1980 "Royal Titles from the Mesopotamian Periphery." *AnSt* 30:189-195.

1982 "Notes from the Babylonian Collection, II: Old Babylonian HAR-ra." *JCS* 34:81-93.

1985 "Biblical Abominations and Sumerian Taboos." *JQR* 76:21-40.

1987 "The Birth of Kings." In *Love and Death in the Ancient Near East: Essays in Honor of Marvin H. Pope*, edited by John H. Marks and Robert M. Good. Guilford: Four Quarters Publishing Company. 45-52.

1988 "Texts, Statues and the Cult of the Divine King." *SVT* 40:54-66.

1989 "Nippur Originals." In *DUMU-E$_2$-DUB-BA-A: Studies in Honor of Åke W. Sjöberg*, edited by Hermann Behrens, Darlene Loding, and Martha T. Roth. Philadelphia: The University Museum. *Occasional Publications of the Samuel Noah Kramer Fund* 11. 237-247.

1991 "The Death of Kings: Traditional Historiography in Contextual Perspective." In *Ah, Assyria...: Studies in Assyrian History and Ancient Near Eastern Historiography Presented to Hayim Tadmor*, edited by Mordechai Cogan and Israel Eph'al. Jerusalem: The Magnes Press, The Hebrew University. *SH* 33. 148-165.

1992 "Royal Ancestor Worship in the Biblical World." In *Shaarey Talmon: Studies in the Bible, Qumran, and the Ancient Near East Presented to Shemaryahu Talmon.* Winona Lake: Eisenbrauns. 381-401.

1992 “Trade and traders in the Ancient Near East: some new perspectives.” In *La circulation des biens, des personnes et des idées dans le Proche Orient ancien: Actes de la XXXVIIIe Rencontre Assyriologique Internationale*, edited by D. Charpin and F. Joannès. Paris: Editions Recherche sur les civilisations. *RAI* 38. 351-356.

Hallo, William W. and William Kelly Simpson

1971 *The Ancient Near East: A History*. New York: Harcourt Brace Jovanovich.

Hallo, William W. et al.

1990 *The Bible in the Light of Cuneiform Literature: Scripture in Context* III. Lewiston: The Edwin Mellen Press. *Ancient Near Eastern Texts and Studies* 8.

Harrak, Amir

1987 *Assyria and Hanigalbat. A Historical Reconstruction of Bilateral Relations from the Middle of the Fourteenth to the End of the Twelfth Centuries B.C.* Hildesheim: Georg Olms Verlag. *TSO* 4.

Hawkins, J.D.

1980 “Karkamiš.” *RLA* 5:426-446.

1982 “The Neo-Hittite States in Syria and Anatolia.” *CAH*[2] III/1:372-441.

Hayes, W.C.

1970 “Chronology I. Egypt—To End of Twentieth Dynasty.” *CAH*[3] I/1:173-193.

Hecker, Karl and Walter Sommerfeld

1986 (eds) *Keilschriftliche Literaturen: ausgewählte Vorträge der XXXII. Rencontre Assyriologique Internationale*. Berlin: Dietrich Reimer Verlag. *Berliner Beiträge zum Vorderen Orient* 6. *RAI* 32.

Heinrich, Ernst et al.

1969 “Bericht über die von der Deutschen Orient-Gesellschaft mit Mitteln der Stiftung Volkswagenwerk im Euphrattal bei Aleppo begonnenen archäologischen Untersuchungen, erstattet von Mitgliedern der Expedition.” *MDOG* 101:27-67.

1970 “Bericht über die von der Deutschen Orient-Gesellschaft mit Mitteln der Stiftung Volkswagenwerk in Habuba Kabira and in Mumbaqat unternommenen archäologischen Untersuchungen.” *AAAS* 20:25-47.

1970 “Zweiter vorläufiger Bericht über die von der Deutschen Orient-Gesellschaft mit Mitteln der Stiftung Volkswagenwerk in Ḥabuba Kabira und in Mumbaqat unternommenen archäologischen Untersuchungen (Herbstkampagne 1969), erstattet von Mitgliedern der Mission.” *MDOG* 102:27-85.

1971 “Dritter vorläufiger Bericht über die von der Deutschen Orient-Gesellschaft mit Mitteln der Stiftung Volkswagenwerk in Ḥabūba Kabira und in Mumbaqat unternommenen archäologischen Untersuchungen (Herbstkampagne 1970), erstattet von Mitgliedern der Mission.” *MDOG* 103:5-58.

1973 “Vierter vorläufiger Bericht über die von der Deutschen Orient-Gesellschaft mit Mitteln der Stiftung Volkswagenwerk in Ḥabuba Kabira (Ḥububa Kabira, Herbstkampagnen 1971 und 1972 sowie Testgrabung Frühjahr 1973) und in Mumbaqat (Tall Munbaqa, Herbstkampagne 1971) unternommenen archäologischen Untersuchungen, erstattet von Mitgliedern der Mission.” *MDOG* 105:5-68.

Helck, Wolfgang

1963 “Urḫi-Tešup in Ägypten.” *JCS* 17:87-97.

Heltzer, Michael

1976 *The Rural Community in Ancient Ugarit*. Wiesbaden: Dr. Ludwig Reichert Verlag.

1982 *The Internal Organization of the Kingdom of Ugarit*. Wiesbaden: Dr. Ludwig Reichert Verlag.

Henrickson, Elizabeth F. and Ingolf Thuesen

1989 *Upon this Foundation—The 'Ubaid Reconsidered*. København: Museum Tusculanum Press.

Hirsch, Hans

1963 "Die Inschriften der Könige von Agade." *AfO* 20:1-82.

Hitti, Philip K.

1951 *History of Syria*. London: MacMillan & Co. Second edition, 1957.

Hoffner, Harry A., Jr.

1965 "The Elkunirsa Myth Reconsidered." *RHA* 23 (= Fascicule 76):5-16.

1968 "A Hittite Text in Epic Style about Merchants." *JCS* 22:34-45.

1969 "Some Contributions of Hittitology to Old Testament Study." *Tyndale Bulletin* 20:27-55.

1980 "Histories and Historians of the Ancient Near East: The Hittites." *Or* 49:283-332.

1983 "A Prayer of Muršili II about his Stepmother." *JAOS* 103:187-192.

1990 *Hittite Myths*. Atlanta: Scholars Press. *Writings from the Ancient World* 2.

forth "The Last Days of Ḫattuša." *Berytus* 39/40.

Hoffner, Harry A., Jr. and Gary M. Beckman

1986 (eds) *Kaniššuwar: A Tribute to Hans G. Güterbock*. Chicago: The Oriental Institute. *AS* 23.

Hogarth, D.G. and C.L. Woolley

1914-52 (eds) *Carchemish: Report on the Excavations at Djerablus on Behalf of the British Museum* I-III. London: British Museum.

Holland, T.A.

1976 "Preliminary Report on Excavations at Tell es-Sweyhat, Syria, 1973-4." *Levant* 8:36-70.

1977 "Preliminary Report on Excavations at Tell es-Sweyhat, Syria 1975." *Levant* 9:36-65.

Hoskisson, P.Y.

forth "Emar as an Empirical Model of the Transmission of Canon." In *The Biblical Canon in Comparative Perspective: Scripture in Context* IV, edited by K.L. Younger, Jr. et al. Lewiston: The Edwin Mellen Press. *Ancient Near Eastern Texts and Studies* 11.

Hrouda, Barthel

1958 "Waššukanni, Urkiš, Šubat-Enlil: Ein Beitrag zur historischen Geographie des nördlichen Zweistromlandes." *MDOG* 90:22-35.

1985 "Zum Problem der Hurriter." *MARI* 4:595-613.

Hrozný, Bedřich

1931 "L'entraînement des chevaux chez les anciens Indo-Européens d'après un texte mîtannien-hittite provenant du 14ᵉ siècle av. J.-C." *ArOr* 3:438-441.

Huehnergard, John

1983 "Five Tablets from the Vicinity of Emar." *RA* 77:11-43.

Hutchinson, R.W.

1962 *Prehistoric Crete*. Harmondsworth: Penguin Books.

Imparati, Fiorella

1975 "'Signori' e 'figli del re'." *Or* 44:80-95.

Izre'el, Shlomo

1991 *Amurru Akkadian: A Linguistic Study*. Atlanta: Scholars Press. 2 vols.

Jacobsen, Thorkild

1939 *The Sumerian King List*. Chicago: The University of Chicago Press. *AS* 11.

1989 "Lugalbanda and Ninsuna." *JCS* 41:69-86.

Jean, Charles-F.

1923 *Šumer et Akkad*. Paris: Paul Geuthner.

Jestin, Raymond

1937 *Tablettes Sumériennes de Šuruppak*. Paris: E. De Boccard. *Mémoires de l'Institut Français d'Archéologie de Stamboul* 3.

Jones, Tom B. and John W. Snyder

1961 *Sumerian Economic Texts from the Third Ur Dynasty*. Minneapolis: University of Minnesota Press.

Kammenhuber, Annelies

1961 *Hippologia Hethitica*. Wiesbaden: Otto Harrassowitz.

Keiser, Clarence Elwood and Shin Theke Kang

1971 *Neo-Sumerian Account Texts from Drehem*. New Haven: Yale University Press. *BIN* 3.

Kelly-Buccellati, Marilyn

1986 (ed) *Insight Through Images: Studies in Honor of Edith Porada*. Malibu: Undena Publications. *BM* 21.

1989 "A New Third Millennium Sculpture from Mozan." In *Essays in Ancient Civilization Presented to Helene J. Kantor*, edited by Albert Leonard, Jr. and Bruce B. Williams. Chicago: The Oriental Institute. *SAOC* 47. 149-155.

1990 "Three Seasons of Excavation at Tell Mozan." In *Tall al-Hamīdīya* 2, edited by Seyyare Eichler et al. Freiburg, Schweiz: Universitätsverlag. 119-132.

Kempinski, Aharon

1983 "Die hethitischen und akkadischen Dokumente aus Boğazköy." In *Syrien und Palästina (Kanaan) in der letzten Phase der Mittelbronze IIB-Zeit (1650-1570 v. Chr.)*, edited by idem. Wiesbaden: Otto Harrassowitz. *Ägypten und Altes Testament* 4. 14-57, 197-229.

Kenyon, K.M.

1971 "Syria: The Sites." *CAH*[3] I/2:583-594.

Kessler, Karlheinz

1984 "Nilabšinu und der altorientalische Name des Tell Brak." *SMEA* 24:21-31. *Incunabula Graeca* 81.

Kestemont, Guy

1974 *Diplomatique et droit international en Asie occidentale (1600-1200 av. J.C.)*. Louvain-la-Neuve: Institut Orientaliste de l'Université Catholique de Louvain. *PIOL* 6.

Kienast, Burkhart

1980 "Der Feldzugsbericht des Ennadagān in literarhistorischer Sicht." *OA* 19:247-261.

Kienast, Burkhart and H. Waetzoldt

1990 "Zwölf Jahre Ebla: Versuch einer Bestandsaufnahme." *Eblaitica* 2:31-77.

King, Leonard W.

1907 *Chronicles Concerning Early Babylonian Kings*. London: Luzac and Co. 2 vols.

Kingsbury, Edwin C.

1963 "A Seven Day Ritual in the Old Babylonian Cult at Larsa." *HUCA* 34:1-34.

Kitchen, K.A.

1962 *Suppiluliuma and the Amarna Pharaohs*. Liverpool: Liverpool University Press.

Klein, Jacob

1990 "The 'Bane' of Humanity: A Lifespan of One Hundred Twenty Years." *ASJ* 12:57-70.

1990 "Šeleppūtum a Hitherto Unknown Ur III Princess." *ZA* 80:20-39.

Klengel, Horst

1963 "Der Schiedsspruch des Muršili II. hinsichtlich Barga und seine Übereinkunft mit Duppi-

Tešup von Amurru (KBo III 3)." *Or* 32:32-55.
1965 *Geschichte und Kultur Altsyriens*. Leipzig: Koehler & Amelang. Second edition 1979.
1965 "Der Wettergott von Ḫalab." *JCS* 19:87-93.
1965-70 *Geschichte Syriens im 2. Jahrtausend v.u.Z.* I-III. Berlin: Akademie-Verlag. *Deutsche Akademie der Wissenschaften zu Berlin, Institut für Orientforschung, Veröffentlichung* 40.
1975 "Ḫalab." *RLA* 4:50-53.
1975 "Neue Quellen zur Geschichte Nordsyriens im 2. Jahrtausend v. u. Z." *AoF* 2:47-64.
1979 "Handel und Kaufleute im hethitischen Reich." *AoF* 6:69-80.
1988 "Die Keilschrifttexte von Meskene und die Geschichte von Aštata/Emar." *OLZ* 83:645-653.
1989 (ed) *Kulturgeschichte des alten Vorderasien*. Berlin: Akademie-Verlag.

Kohler, Josef and Arthur Ungnad
1913 *Assyrische Rechtsurkunden in Umschrift und Übersetzung nebst einem Index der Personen-namen und Rechtserläuterungen*. Leipzig: Eduard Pfeiffer.

Kohlmeyer, Kay
1984 "Euphrat-Survey: Die mit Mitteln der Gerda Henkel Stiftung durchgeführte archäologische Geländebegehung im syrischen Euphrattal." *MDOG* 116:95-118.

König, Friedrich Wilhelm
1965 *Die elamischen Königsinschriften*. Graz: Ernst Weidner. *AfO* Beiheft 16.

Korošec, Viktor
1931 *Hethitische Staatsverträge: ein Beitrag zu ihrer juristischen Wertung*. Leipzig: T. Weicher.

Košak, Silvin
1982 *Hittite inventory texts (CTH 241-250)*. Heidelberg: Carl Winter Universitätsverlag. *TH* 10.

Kraus, F.R.
1948 "Ein altakkadisches Festungsbild." *Iraq* 10:81-92.

Krebernik, Manfred
1984 *Die Beschwörungen aus Fara und Ebla*. Hildesheim: Georg Olms Verlag. *TSO* 2.

Krecher, Joachim
1966 *Sumerische Kultlyrik*. Wiesbaden: Otto Harrassowitz.
1969 "Schreiberschulung in Ugarit: Die Tradition von Listen und sumerischen Texten." *UF* 1:131-158.
1983 "Eine unorthographische sumerische Wortliste aus Ebla." *OA* 22:179-189.

Krispijn, Th.J.H.
1981-82 "Die Identifikation zweier lexikalischen Texte aus Ebla: *MEE* III Nr. 62 und 63." *JEOL* 27:47-59.

Kühne, Hartmut
1978 "Vorläufiger Bericht über die erste Grabungskampagne auf dem Tall Šeḫ Ḥamad am Unteren Ḫabur." *Akkadica* 10:16-23.
1983 "Tell Šēḫ Ḥamad/Dūr-Katlimmu, die Wiederentdeckung einer mittelassyrischen Stadt." *DamM* 1:149-163.
1984 "Tell Šēḫ Ḥamad/Dur Katlimmu: The Assyrian Provincial Capital in the Mohafazat Deir Az-Zor." *AAAS* 34:160-179.
1990 "Gedanken zur historischen und städtebaulichen Entwicklung der assyrischen Stadt Dūr-katlimmu." In *Resurrecting the Past: A Joint Tribute to Adnan Bounni*, edited by Paolo Matthiae, Maurits van Loon and Harvey Weiss. Istanbul: Nederlands Historisch-

Archaeologisch Instituut te Istanbul. *Uitgaven van het Nederlands Historisch-Archaeologisch Instituut te Istanbul* 67. 153-169.

Kümmel, Hans Martin

1989 "Ein Kaufvertrag aus Ḫana mit mittelassyrischer *līmu*-Datierung." *ZA* 79:191-200.

Kupper, J.-R.

1956 *Les nomades en Mésopotamie au temps des rois de Mari*. Paris: Société d'Edition "Les Belles Lettres." *Bibliothèque de la Faculté de Philosophie et Lettres de l'Université de Liège* 142. Third printing, 1982.

1967 (ed) *XV*[e] *Rencontre Assyriologique Internationale: La Civilisation de Mari*. Liège: Université de Liège. *Les Congrès et Colloques de l'Université de Liège* 42. *RAI* 15.

1973 "Northern Mesopotamia and Syria." *CAH*[3] II/1:1-41.

1980 "Une tablettte paléo-babylonienne de Mardikh III." *SEb* 2:49-51.

Lacheman, E.R.

1940 "Nuzi Geographical Names I." *BASOR* 78:18-23.

Lackenbacher, Sylvie

1982 "Nouveaux documents d'Ugarit I.—Une lettre royale." *RA* 76:141-156.

Læssøe, Jørgen

1959 *The Shemshāra Tablets: A Preliminary Report*. København: I kommission hos Ejnar Munksgaard. *Arkæologisk-kunsthistoriske Meddelelser udgivet af Det Kongelige Danske Videnskabernes Selskab* 4/3.

Lafont, Bertrand

1984 "Le roi de Mari et les prophètes du dieu Adad." *RA* 78:7-18.

Lambert, Maurice

1968 "Masses d'armes de pierre au nom de Naramsîn." *Or* 37:85-86.

1970 "Les inscriptions des temples d'Ishtarat et de Ninni-zaza." *RA* 64:168-171.

Lambert, W.G.

1960 *Babylonian Wisdom Literature*. Oxford: The Clarendon Press.

1976 "A Late Assyrian Catalogue of Literary and Scholarly Texts." In *Kramer Anniversary Volume: Cuneiform Studies in Honor of Samuel Noah Kramer*, edited by Barry L. Eichler. Kevelaer: Verlag Butzon & Bercker. *AOAT* 25. 313-318.

1985 "A list of Gods' Names found at Mari." In *Miscellanea Babylonica: Mélanges offerts à Maurice Birot*, edited by J.-M. Durand and J.-R. Kupper. Paris: Editions Recherche sur les civilisations. 181-190.

1989 "Notes on a Work of the Most Ancient Semitic Literature." *JCS* 41:1-33.

1990 "Ḫalam, Il-Ḫalam and Aleppo." *MARI* 6:641-643.

Lambert, W.G. and A.R. Millard

1969 *Atra-ḫasīs: The Babylonian Story of the Flood*. Oxford: The Clarendon Press.

Landsberger, Benno

1957 *The Series ḪAR-ra = ḫubullu: Tablets I-IV*. Roma: Pontificium Institutum Biblicum. *MSL* V.

Laroche, Emmanuel

1957 "Fragment hourrite provenant de Mâri." *RA* 51:104-106.

1958 "Études sur les hiéroglyphes hittites [III]." *Syria* 35:252-283.

1958 "Lécanomancie hittite." *RA* 52:150-162.

1966 *Les noms des Hittites*. Paris: Librairie C. Klincksieck. *Études linguistiques* 4.

1971 *Catalogue des textes hittites*. Paris: Éditions Klincksieck. *Études et commentaires* 75.

1980 "Emar, étape entre Babylone et le Hatti." In *Le Moyen Euphrate*, edited by Jean-Claude

Margueron. Leiden: E.J. Brill. 235-244.
1982 "Documents hittites et hourrites." In *Meskéné-Emar: Dix ans de travaux 1972-1982*, edited by Dominique Beyer. Paris: Editions Recherche sur les civilisations. 53-60.
1988 "Observations sur le rituel anatolien provenant de Meskéné-Emar." In *Studi di storia e di filologia anatolica dedicati a Giovanni Pugliese Carratelli*, edited by Fiorella Imparati. Firenze: Elite. 111-117.

Laroche, Emmanuel and Mirjo Salvini
forth *Recherches au Pays d'Aštata: Emar VII. Les textes hourrites*. Paris: Editions Recherche sur les civilisations.

Lebeau, Marc
1985 "Rapport préliminaire sur la céramique du Bronze Ancien IVa découverte au 'Palais Présargonique l' de Mari." *MARI* 4:127-136.
1985 "Rapport préliminaire sur la séquence céramique du chantier B de Mari (IIIe millénaire)." *MARI* 4:93-126.

Lebrun, René
1976 *Samuha: foyer religieux de l'empire hittite*. Louvain-la-Neuve: Institut Orientaliste de l'Université Catholique de Louvain. *PIOL* 11.
1979 "Considérations sur la femme dans la société hittite." *Hethitica* 3:109-125.
1988 "Divinites louvites et hourrites des rituels anatoliens en langue akkadienne provenant de Meskéné." *Hethitica* 9:147-155.

Leemans, W.F.
1988 "Aperçu sur les textes juridiques d'Emar." *JESHO* 31:207-242.

Levine, Baruch A.
1983 "The Descriptive Ritual Texts from Ugarit: Some Formal and Functional Features of the *Genre*." In *The Word of the Lord Shall Go Forth: Essays in Honor of David Noel Freedman*, edited by Carol L. Meyers and M. O'Connor. Winona Lake: Eisenbrauns. 467-475.

Legrain, L.
1912 *Le temps des rois d'Ur*. Paris: Librarie Honoré Champion. *Bibliothèque de l'École des Hautes Études, Sciences philologiques et historiques* 199.

Lewy, Hildegard
1967 "The Chronology of the Mari Texts." In *XVe Rencontre Assyriologique Internationale: La Civilisation de Mari*, edited by J.-R. Kupper. Liège: Université de Liège. *Les Congrès et Colloques de l'Université de Liège* 42. *RAI* 15. 13-28.
1968 "A Contribution to the Historical Geography of the Nuzi Texts." *JAOS* 88:150-162.

Lewy, J.
1937 *Tablettes cappadociennes, troisième série, troisième partie*. Paris: Paul Geuthner. *TCL* 21.

van Liere, W.J.
1963 "Capitals and citadels of Bronze-Iron Age Syria in their relationship to land and water." *AAAS* 13:107-122.

van Liere, W.J. and J. Lauffray
1954-55 "Nouvelle prospection archéologique dans la Haute Jézireh syrienne (Compte-rendu provisiore)." *AAAS* 4-5:129-148.

Limet, Henri
1976 *Textes administratifs de l'époque des šakkanakku*. Paris: Paul Geuthner. *ARM* 19.

Liverani, Mario

1962 *Storia di Ugarit nell'età degli archivi politici*. Roma: Università di Roma. *SS* 6.

1965 "I tell pre-classici." *Missione Archeologica Italiana in Siria, Rapporto preliminare della Campagna 1964*. Roma: Università di Roma—Centro di Studi Semitici, *Serie archeologica* 8. 107-133.

van Loon, Maurits

1964 *The Tabqa Reservoir Survey 1964*. Damascus: Direction générale des antiquités et des musées.

1968 "The Oriental Institute Excavations at Mureybiṭ, Syria: Preliminary Report on the 1965 Campaign. Part I: Architecture and General Finds." *JNES* 27:265-282.

1975-76 "First Results of the 1974 and 1975 Excavations at Selenkahiye near Meskene, Syria." *AAAS* 27-8:165-185.

1979 "1974 and 1975 Preliminary Results of the Excavations at Selenkahiye Near Meskene, Syria." In *Archaeological Reports from the Tabqa Dam Project—Euphrates Valley, Syria*, edited by David Noel Freedman. Cambridge: American Schools of Oriental Research. *AASOR* 44. 97-112.

1983 "Hammâm et-Turkmân on the Balikh: First results of the University of Amsterdam's 1982 Excavation." *Akkadica* 35:1-23.

1988 (ed) *Hammam et-Turkman 1: Preliminary Report on the 1981-84 Seasons*. Istanbul: Nederlands Historisch-Archaeologisch Instituut te Istanbul.

1988 "New Evidence for North Syrian Chronology from Hammam et-Turkman." *AJA* 92:582-587.

Loretz, Oswald

1969 "Texte aus Chagar Bazar." In *Lišān mitḫurti: Festschrift Wolfram Freiherr von Soden*, edited by M. Dietrich and W. Röllig. Kevelaer: Verlag Butzon & Bercker. *AOAT* 1. 199-260.

1969 *Texte aus Chagar Bazar und Tell Brak, Teil 1*. Kevelaer: Verlag Butzon & Bercker. *AOAT* 3/1.

Luckenbill, D.D.

1922 "A Messenger from Ibla." *AJSL* 39:65-66.

Luke, J.T.

1965 *Pastoralism and Politics in the Mari Period: A Re-examination of the Character and Political Significance of the Major West Semitic Tribal Groups on the Middle Euphrates, ca. 1828-1758 B.C.* Dissertation: University of Michigan. UMI 66-5094.

von Luschan, Felix

1893-1911 *Ausgrabungen in Sendschirli*. Berlin: W. Spemann. *Mitteilungen aus den orientalischen Sammlungen* 15.

Lutz, Henry Frederick

1929 *Old Babylonian Letters*. Berkeley: University of California Press. *UCP* 9/4.

Machinist, Peter

1982 "Provincial Governance in Middle Assyria and Some New Texts from Yale." *Assur* 3/2:67-101.

McClellan, T. and A. Porter

forth "Archaeological Surveys of the Tishreen Dam Flood Zone." *AAAS*.

McClellan, T. et al.

forth "The Tishreen Salvage Excavations, 1989." *AAAS*.

McEwan, Calvin W. et al.

1958 *Soundings at Tell Fakhariyah*. Chicago: The University of Chicago Press. *OIP* 79.

Macqueen, J.G.
1975 *The Hittites and Their Contemporaries in Asia Minor*. London: Thames and Hudson. Second edition 1986.

Malamat, A.
1982 "Longevity: Biblical Concepts and Some Ancient Near Eastern Parallels." In *Vorträge gehalten auf der 28. Rencontre Assyriologique Internationale in Wien*. Horn: Verlag Ferdinand Berger & Söhne. *AfO* Beiheft 19. *RAI* 28. 215-224.

Mallowan, M.E.L.
1936 "The Excavations at Tall Chagar Bazar, and an Archaeological Survey of the Ḫabur Region, 1934-5." *Iraq* 3:1-86.
1937 "The Excavations at Tall Chagar Bazar and an Archaeological Survey of the Ḫabur Region. Second Campaign, 1936." *Iraq* 4:91-117.
1947 "Excavations at Brak and Chagar Bazar." *Iraq* 9:1-266.
1971 "The Early Dynastic Period in Mesopotamia." *CAH*[3] I/2:238-314.

Margueron, Jean-Claude
1975 "Les fouilles françaises de Meskéné-Émar (Syrie)." *CRAIBL* 201-213.
1975 "Quatre campagnes de fouilles à Emar (1972-1974): un bilan provisoire." *Syria* 52:53-85.
1975 "Rapport préliminaire sur les deux premières campagnes de fouilles à Meskéné-Emar (1972-1973)." *AAAS* 25:73-86.
1980 "Emar: Un exemple d'implantation hittite en terre syrienne." In *Le Moyen Euphrate*, edited by idem. Leiden: E.J. Brill. 285-312.
1980 (ed) *Le Moyen Euphrate: Zone de contacts et d'échanges: Actes du Colloque de Strasbourg 10-12 mars 1977*. Leiden: E.J. Brill.
1982 "Aux marches de l'empire hittite: une campagne de fouille à Tell Faq'ous (Syrie), citadelle du pays d'Aštata." In *La Syrie au Bronze Récent*, edited by Marguerite Yon. Paris: Editions Recherche sur les civilisations. Extraits de la XXVIIe R.A.I., Paris 1980. 47-66.
1982 "Rapport préliminaire sur les 3e, 4e, 5e, et 6e campagnes de fouilles à Meskéné-Emar." *AAAS* 32:233-249.

de Martino, S.
1991 "I Hurriti nei testi dell'Antico Regno." *Seminari dello Istituto per gli studi micenei et egeo-anatolici anno 1990*. Roma: 1991. 71-83.

Matthiae, Paolo
1976 "Ébla à l'époque d'Akkad: archéologie et histoire." *CRAIBL* 1976 190-215.
1976 "Ebla in the Late Early Syrian Period: The Royal Palace and the State Archives." *BA* 39:94-113.
1977 *Ebla: Un impero ritrovato*. Torino: Giulio Einaudi editore.
1977 "Le palais royal protosyrien d'Ébla: nouvelles recherches archéologiques à Tell Mardikh en 1976." *CRAIBL* 1977 148-174.
1977 "Tell Mardikh: The Archives and Palace." *Archaeology* 30:244-253.
1978 "Recherches archéologiques à Ébla, 1977: le quartier administratif du palais royal G." *CRAIBL* 1978 204-236.
1979 "*DU-UB*[ki] di Mardikh IIBI = *TU-BA*[ki] di Alalakh VII." *SEb* 1:115-118.
1980 "Ittiti ed Assiri a Tell Fray: Lo scavo di una città medio-siriana sull'Eufrate." *SMEA* 22:35-51. *Incunabula Graeca* 73.
1981 *Ebla: An Empire Rediscovered*. Garden City: Doubleday.

1982 "Il Palazzo Reale G di Ebla e la tradizione architettonica protosiriana." *SEb* 5:75-92.

1982 "The Problem of the Relations Between Ebla and Mesopotamia in the Time of the Royal Palace of Mardikh IIB1 (ca. 2400-2250 B.C.)." In *Mesopotamien und seine Nachbarn: Politische und kulturelle Wechselbeziehungen im Alten Vorderasien vom 4. bis 1. Jahrtausend v. Chr.*, edited by Hans-Jörg Nissen and Johannes Renger. *Berliner Beiträge zum Vorderen Orient* 1. *RAI* 25. 111-123.

1984 *I tesori di Ebla.* Bari: Editori Laterza.

1985 "Carskij dvorec G v Èble i protosirijskie arxitekturnye tradicii" ("The Royal Palace G at Ebla and the Protosyrian Architectural Traditions"). In *Drevnjaja Èbla (Raskopki v Sirii) (Ancient Ebla [Excavations in Syria])*, edited by I.M. Diakonoff. Moscow: Progress. 34-51.

1985 "Ebla Recovered." In *Ebla to Damascus: Art and Archaeology of Ancient Syria*, edited by Harvey Weiss. Washington, D.C.: Smithsonian Institution. 134-139.

1987 "Les dernières découvertes d'Ébla en 1983-1986." *CRAIBL* 1987 135-161.

1988 "On the Economic Foundations of the Early Syrian Culture of Ebla." In *Wirtschaft und Gesellschaft von Ebla*, edited by Hartmut Waetzoldt and Harald Hauptmann. Heidelberg: Heidelberger Orientverlag. *HSAO* 2. 75-80.

1989 "The Destruction of Ebla Royal Palace; Interconnections between Syria, Mesopotamia and Egypt in the Late EB IVA." In *High, Middle or Low?*, edited by Paul Åstöm. Gothenburg: Paul Åströms förlag. *Studies in Mediterranean Archaeology and Literature, Pocket-book* 80. 163-169.

1990 "Nouvelles fouilles à Ébla en 1987-1989." *CRAIBL* 1990 384-431.

1991 "Architettura e urbanistica di Ebla paleosiriana." *La Parola del Passato* 46:304-371.

forth (ed) *L'Archéologie et l'histoire de la Syrie I: De la préhistoire aux royaumes araméens.* Damascus.

Matthiae, Paolo, Maurits van Loon and Harvey Weiss

1990 *Resurrecting the Past: A Joint Tribute to Adnan Bounni.* Istanbul: Nederlands Historisch-Archaeologisch Instituut te Istanbul. *Uitgaven ven het Nederlands Historisch-Archaeologisch Instituut te Istanbul* 67.

Mattingly, Gerald L.

1990 "The Pious Sufferer: Mesopotamia's Traditional Theodicy and Job's Counselors." In *The Bible in the Light of Cuneiform Literature: Scripture in Context* III, edited by William W. Hallo et al. Lewiston: The Edwin Mellen Press. *Ancient Near Eastern Texts and Studies* 8. 305-348.

Mayer, Walter

1987 "Grundzüge der Geschichte der Stadt Tuttul im 2. Jt. v. Chr." *UF* 19:121-160.

Mazzoni, Stefania

1985 "Elements of the Ceramic Culture of Early Syrian Ebla in Comparison with Syro-Palestinian EB IV." *BASOR* 257:1-18.

1991 "Ebla e la formazione della cultura urbana in Siria." *La Parola del Passato* 46:163-194.

Meek, Theophile James

1935 *Old Akkadian, Sumerian, and Cappadocian Texts from Nuzi.* Cambridge: Harvard University Press. *Excavations at Nuzi* 3. *HSS* 10. Reprinted 1968, Johnson Reprint Company.

Meier, Samuel A.

1988 *The Messenger in the Ancient Semitic World.* Atlanta: Scholars Press. *HSM* 45.

1991 "Women and Communication in the Ancient Near East." *JAOS* 111:540-547.

Meijer, D.J.
1990 "An Archaeological Surface Survey: Some Assumptions and Ideas." In *Tall al-Ḥamīdīya* 2, edited by Seyyare Eichler et al. Freiburg, Schweiz: Universitätsverlag. 31-45.

Meyer, Jan-Waalke and Gernot Wilhelm
1983 "Eine spätbronzezeitliche Keilschrifturkunde aus Syrien." *DamM* 1:249-261.

Michalowski, Piotr
1976 *The Royal Correspondence of Ur.* Dissertation: Yale University.
1978 "Foreign Tribute to Sumer during the Ur III Period." *ZA* 68:34-49.
1981 "Carminative Magic: Towards an Understanding of Sumerian Poetics." *ZA* 71:1-18.
1985 "Third Millennium Contacts: Observations on the Relationships between Mari and Ebla." *JAOS* 105:293-302.
1987 "Language, Literature, and Writing at Ebla." In *Ebla 1975-1985: Dieci anni di studi linguistici e filologici*, edited by Luigi Cagni. Napoli: Istituto Universitario Orientale. 165-175.
1987 "On the Early History of the Ershahunga Prayer." *JCS* 39:37-48.

Milano, Lucio
1990 *Testi amministrativi: Assegnazioni di prodotti alimentari (Archivio L. 2712-Parte I).* Roma: Missione Archeologica Italiana in Siria. *ARET* 9.
1991 "Mozan 2: The Epigraphic Finds of the Sixth Season." *SMS* 5/1:1-34.

Millard, A.R.
1981 "Strays From a 'Nuzi' Archive, with an appendix: Two 'Nuzi' Texts in the Wellcome Institute for the History of Medicine." *SCCNH* 1:433-441.

Monchambert, Jean-Yves
1984 "Le futur lac du Moyen Khabour: Rapport sur la prospection archéologique menée en 1983." *Syria* 61:181-218.
1984 "Prospection archéologique sur l'emplacement du futur lac du Moyen Khabour." *Akkadica* 39:1-7.

del Monte, Giuseppe F. and Johann Tischler
1978 *Die Orts- und Gewässernamen der hethitischen Texte.* Wiesbaden: Dr. Ludwig Reichert Verlag. *RGTC* 6.

Moore, Andrew M.T.
1975 "The Excavation of Tell Abu Hureyra in Syria: A Preliminary Report." *Proceedings of the Prehistoric Society* 41:50-77.
1988 "The Prehistory of Syria." *BASOR* 270:3-12.

Moorey, P.R.S.
1966 "A Re-Consideration of the Excavations on Tell Ingharra (East Kish), 1923-33." *Iraq* 28:18-51.
1981 "Abu Salabikh, Kish, Mari and Ebla: Mid-third Millennium Archaeological Interconnections." *AJA* 85:447-448.

Moortgat, Anton
1960ff *Tell Chuēra in Nordost-Syrien.* Köln: Westdeutscher Verlag.
1969 *The Art of Ancient Mesopotamia: The Classical Art of the Near East.* London: Phaidon.

Moortgat-Correns, Ursula
1972 *Die Bildwerke vom Djeblet el-Bēḍā in ihrer räumlichen und zeitlichen Umwelt.* Berlin: de Gruyter.

Morrison, M.A. and David I. Owen
1981 (eds) *Studies on the Civilization and Culture of Nuzi and the Hurrians In Honor of Ernest R.*

Lacheman. Winona Lake: Eisenbrauns. *SCCNH* 1.

Murnane, William J.
1985 *The Road to Kadesh*. Chicago: The Oriental Institute. *SAOC* 42. Second revised edition 1990.

Myhrman, David W.
1910 *Sumerian Administrative Documents Dated in the Reigns of the Kings of the Second Dynasty of Ur*. Philadelphia: University of Pennsylvania. *BE* 3.

Nashef, Khaled
1982 *Die Orts- und Gewässernamen der mittelbabylonischen und mittelassyrischen Zeit*. Wiesbaden: Dr. Ludwig Reichert Verlag. *RGTC* 5.
1991 *Die Orts- und Gewässernamen der altassyrischen Zeit*. Wiesbaden: Dr. Ludwig Reichert Verlag. *RGTC* 4.

Neu, Erich
1974 *Der Anitta-Text*. Wiesbaden: Otto Harrassowitz. *SBT* 18.
1986 "Zur Datierung der Hethitischen Pferdetexte." In *Kaniššuwar: A Tribute to Hans G. Güterbock*, edited by Harry A. Hoffner, Jr. and Gary M. Beckman. Chicago: The Oriental Institute. *AS* 23. 151-163.
1988 *Das Hurritische: Eine altorientalische Sprache in neuem Licht*. Mainz: Akademie der Wissenschaften und der Literatur. *Abhandlungen der geistes- und sozialwissenschaftlichen Klasse* 3.
1988 "Varia Hurritica: Sprachliche Beobachtungen an der hurritisch-hethitischen Bilingue aus Ḫattuša." In *Documentum Asiae minoris antiquae: Festschrift für Heinrich Otten*, edited by Erich Neu and Christel Rüster. Wiesbaden: Otto Harrassowitz. 235-254.
1989 "Neue Wege im Hurritischen." Stuttgart: Franz Steiner Verlag. *XXIII. Deutscher Orientalistentag*. *ZDMG* Supplement 7. 293-303.

Neu, Erich and Wolfgang Meid
1979 *Hethitisch und indogermanisch: Vergleichende Studien zur historischen Grammatik und zur dialektgeographischen Stellung der Indogermanischen Sprachgruppe Altkleinasiens*. Innsbruck: Institut für Sprachwissenschaft der Universität Innsbruck. *Innsbrucker Beiträge zur Sprachwissenschaft* 25.

Niebuhr, C.
1896 "Das Land Jarimuta." *MVAG* 1:208-212.

Nies, James B.
1920 *Ur Dynasty Tablets*. Leipzig: J.C. Hinrichs'sche Buchhandlung.

Nikol'skij, Michail Vasil'evic
1915 *Dokumenty chozjajstvennoj otčetnosti drevnej Chaldei iz sobranija N.P. Lichačeva, Čast' II: Epocha dinastii Agade i epoche dinastii Ura [Documents of Economic Accounting from Ancient Chaldea in the Collection of N.P. Lichacev. Volume 2: The Dynasty of Akkad and the Dynasty of Ur III]*. Moscow: G. Lissnyera i D. Cosko. *DV* 5.

Nissen, Hans-Jörg
1981 "Bemerkungen zur Listenliteratur Vorderasiens im 3. Jahrtausend." In *La lingua di Ebla*, edited by Luigi Cagni. Napoli: Istituto Universitario Orientale. 99-108.

Nissen, Hans-Jörg and Johannes Renger
1982 (eds) *Mesopotamien und seine Nachbarn: Politische und kulturelle Wechselbeziehungen im Alten Vorderasien vom 4. bis 1. Jahrtausend v. Chr. Berliner Beiträge zum Vorderen Orient* 1. *RAI* 25.

Nougayrol, Jean
1955 *Le Palais royal d'Ugarit, III. Textes accadiens et hourrites des Archives Est, Ouest et Centrales*. Paris: Imprimerie nationale. *PRU* III; *MRS* VI.
1956 *Le Palais royal d'Ugarit, IV. Textes accadiens des Archives Sud (Archives internationales)*. Paris: Imprimerie nationale. *PRU* IV; *MRS* IX.
1968 *Ugaritica* 5. Paris: Imprimerie nationale. *Ug* V; *BAH* 80; *MRS* XVI.
1970 *Le Palais royal d'Ugarit, VI. Textes en cunéiformes babyloniens des Archives du Grand Palais et du Palais Sud d'Ugarit*. Paris: Imprimerie nationale. *PRU* VI; *MRS* XII.

Oates, David
1977 "The Excavations at Tell Brak, 1976." *Iraq* 39:233-244.
1985 "Walled Cities in Northern Mesopotamia in the Mari Period." *MARI* 4:585-594.
1990 "Tell Brak: The Mitanni Palace and Temple." In *Tall al-Ḥamīdīya* 2, edited by Seyyare Eichler et al. Freiburg, Schweiz: Universitätsverlag. 149-157.

Oates, Joan
1984 "Ubaid Mesopotamia Reconsidered." In *The Hilly Flanks and Beyond: Essays in the Prehistory of Southwestern Asia Presented to Robert J. Braidwood*, edited by T. Cuyler Young, Jr. et al. Chicago: The University of Chicago Press. *SAOC* 36. 251-281.
1985 "Tell Brak and Chronology: the Third Millennium." *MARI* 4:137-144.
1985 "Tell Brak: Uruk Pottery from the 1984 Season." *Iraq* 47:175-186.
1986 "Tell Brak: The Uruk/Early Dynastic Sequence." In *Ǧamdat Naṣr: Period or Regional Style?*, edited by Uwe Finkbeiner and Wolfgang Röllig. Wiesbaden: Dr. Ludwig Reichert Verlag. *Beihefte zum Tübinger Atlas des Vorderen Orients, Reihe B (Geisteswissenschaften)* 62. 245-273.
1990 "Tell Brak in the Fourth and Third Millennia: From Uruk to Ur III." In *Tall al-Ḥamīdīya* 2, edited by Seyyare Eichler et al. Freiburg, Schweiz: Universitätsverlag. 133-147.

O'Callaghan, Roger T.
1948 *Aram Naharaim: A Contribution to the History of Upper Mesopotamia in the Second Millennium B.C.* Roma: Pontificium Institutum Biblicum. *AnOr* 26.

Oelsner, Joachim
1989 "Zu einer Schülertafel aus Mari." *NABU* 1989/33.

Oettinger, Norbert
1980 [review of Johann Tischler, *Hethitisches Etymologisches Glossar* (Innsbruck, 1977)]. *ZDMG* 130:589-593.
1990 "Die *n*-Stämme des Hethitischen und ihre indogermanischen Ausgangspunkte." *Zeitschrift für vergleichende Sprachforschung* 94:44-63.

del Olmo Lete, G.
1984 "Ritual regio ugarítico de evocación/adivinación (KTU 1.112)." *AuOr* 2:197-206.
1986 "The Cultic Literature of Ugarit: Hermeneutical Issues and Their Application to KTU 1.112." In *Keilschriftliche Literaturen: ausgewählte Vorträge der XXXII. Rencontre Assyriologique Internationale*, edited by Karl Hecker and Walter Sommerfeld. Berlin: Dietrich Reimer Verlag. *Berliner Beiträge zum Vorderen Orient* 6. *RAI* 32. 155-164.

Oppenheim, A. Leo
1948 *Catalogue of the Cuneiform Tablets of the Wilberforce Eames Babylonian Collection in The New York Public Library*. New Haven: American Oriental Society. *AOS* 32.
1977 *Ancient Mesopotamia: Portrait of a Dead Civilization*. Revised ed. Chicago: University of Chicago Press. First edition 1964.

von Oppenheim, Max Freiherrn
1931 *Der Tell Halaf: Eine neue Kultur im ältesten Mesopotamien.* Leipzig: F.A. Brockhaus.
1943-62 *Tell Halaf* I-IV. Berlin: de Gruyter.

Orlin, Louis Lawrence
1970 *Assyrian Colonies in Cappadocia.* The Hague: Mouton. *Studies in Ancient History* 1.

Orthmann, Winfried
1971 *Untersuchungen zur späthethitischen Kunst.* Bonn: Rudolf Habelt Verlag. *Saarbrücker Beiträge zur Altertumskunde* 8.
1986 "The Origin of Tell Chuera." In *The Origins of Cities in Dry-Farming Syria and Mesopotamia in the Third Millennium B.C.*, edited by Harvey Weiss. Guillford: Four Quarters Publishing Co. 61-70.

Otten, Heinrich
1953 "Ein kanaanäischer Mythus aus Boğazköy." *MIO* 1:125-150.
1959 "Zur Kontinuität eines altanatolischen Kultes." *ZA* 53:174-184.
1975 *Puduḫepa: Eine hethitische Königin in ihren Textzeugnissen.* Mainz: Akademie der Wissenschaften und der Literature. *Abhandlungen der Geistes- und Sozialwissenschaftlichen Klassen* 1.
1981 "Bemerkungen zum Hethitischen Wörterbuch II." *ZA* 71:135-143.
1984 "Blick in die altorientalische Geisteswelt: Neufund einer hethitischen Tempelbibliothek." *Jahrbuch der Akademie der Wissenschaften in Göttingen.* 50-60.
1984 "Die Tontafelfunde aus Haus 16." *Archäologischer Anzeiger* 372-375.
1988 *Die Bronzetafel aus Boğazköy. Ein Staatsvertrag Tutḫalijas IV.* Wiesbaden: Otto Harrassowitz. *SBT* Beiheft 1.
1988 "Ebla in der hurritisch-hethitischen Bilingue aus Boğazköy." In *Wirtschaft und Gesellschaft von Ebla*, edited by Hartmut Waetzoldt and Harald Hauptmann. Heidelberg: Heidelberger Orientverlag. *HSAO* 2. 291-292.

Owen, David I.
1975 *The John Frederick Lewis Collection.* Roma: Multigrafica Editrice. *MVN* 3.
1981 [review of Edzard and Farber, *RGTC* 2]. *JCS* 33:244-269.
1982 *Selected Ur III Texts from the Harvard Semitic Museum.* Roma: Multigrafica Editrice. *MVN* 11.
1988 "Random Notes on a Recent Ur III Volume." *JAOS* 108:111-122.
1991 *Neo-Sumerian Texts from American Collections.* Roma: Multigrafica Editrice. *MVN* 15.
1992 "Exit Gura'a from Ebla!" *NABU* 1992/3.
forth "Some New Evidence on Yaḫmadiu = Aḫlamû." In *The Temple and the Book: Ancient Near Eastern Studies in Honor of William W. Hallo*, edited by M. Cohen, D. Snell, and D.B. Weisberg. Bethesda: CDL Press.

Owen, David and Ron Veenker
1987 "MeGum, the First Ur III Ensi of Ebla." In *Ebla 1975-1985: Dieci anni di studi linguistici e filologici*, edited by Luigi Cagni. Napoli: Istituto Universitario Orientale. 263-291.

Özdoğan, Mehmet
1977 *Lower Euphrates Basin 1977 Survey.* Istanbul: Middle East Technical University. *Lower Euphrates Project Publications*, Series 1, No. 2.

Özten, Aliye
1976-77 "Two Pots Recovered in the Excavations at Samsat Belonging to the Late Chalcolitic Period." *Anadolu* 20:267-271.

Parayre, D.

forth "The Ninevite 5 Period Seal Impressions Retrieved at Tell Leilan in 1987." In *The Origins of North Mesopotamian Civilization: Ninevite 5 Chronology, Economy, Society*, edited by Harvey Weiss. New Haven: Yale University Press.

Parpola, Simo

1983 "Assyrian Library Records." *JNES* 42:1-29.

Parr, P.

1968 "The Origins of the Rampart Fortifications of Middle Bronze Age Palestine and Syria." *ZDPV* 84:18-45.

Parrot, André

1953 "Les fouilles de Mari: Huitième campagne (automne 1952)." *Syria* 30:196-221.

1956 *Le temple d'Ishtar*. Paris: Paul Geuthner. *MAM* 1. *BAH* 65.

1967 *Les temples d'Ishtarat et de Ninni-zaza*. Paris: Paul Geuthner. *MAM* 3. *BAH* 86.

1974 *Mari: capitale fabuleuse*. Paris: Payot. *Bibliothèque historique*.

Parrot, André and Jean Nougayrol

1948 "Un document de fondation hurrite." *RA* 42:1-20.

Payne, Joan Crowfoot

1968 "Lapis Lazuli in Early Egypt." *Iraq* 30:58-61.

Pecchioli Daddi, Franca

1982 *Mestieri, professioni e dignità nell'Anatolia ittita*. Roma: Edizioni dell'Ateneo. *Incunabula Graeca* 79.

Pecchioli Daddi, Franca, and Anna Maria Polvani

1990 *La mitologia ittita*. Brescia: Paideia Editrice. *Testi del Vicino Oriente antico* 4.1.

Pecorella, Paolo Emilio

1990 "The Italian Excavations at Tell Barri (Kaḫat)." In *Tall al-Ḥamīdīya* 2, edited by Seyyare Eichler et al. Freiburg, Schweiz: Universitätsverlag. 47-66.

1990 "Tell Barri/Kahat durante il II millennio." In *Resurrecting the Past: A Joint Tribute to Adnan Bounni*, edited by Paolo Matthiae, Maurits van Loon and Harvey Weiss. Istanbul: Nederlands Historisch-Archaeologisch Instituut te Istanbul. *Uitgaven van het Nederlands Historisch-Archaeologisch Instituut te Istanbul* 67. 259-275.

Pecorella, Paolo Emilio and Mirjo Salvini

1982 *Tell Barri/Kahat 1: Relazione preliminare sulle Campagne 1980 e 1981 a Tell Barri/Kahat nel bacino del Habur*. Roma: Istituto per gli studi micenei ed egeo-anatolici.

Pettinato, Giovanni

1976-80 "Ibla (Ebla). A. Philologisch." *RLA* 5:9-13.

1977 "Gli archivi reali di Tell Mardikh-Ebla: Riflessioni e prospettive." *RBI* 25:225-243.

1977 *Testi economici di Lagaš del Museo di Istanbul Parte I: La. 7001-7600*. Roma: Multigrafica Editrice. *MVN* 6.

1978 "L'Atlante Geografico del Vicino Oriente Antico attestato ad Ebla e ad Abū Ṣalābīkh (I)." *Or* 47:50-73.

1978 "Liste presargoniche di uccelli nella documentazione di Fara ed Ebla." *OA* 17:165-178.

1979 *Catalogo dei testi cuneiformi di Tell Mardikh-Ebla*. Napoli: Istituto Universitario Orientale. *MEE* 1.

1979 "Le collezioni én-é-nu-ru di Ebla." *OA* 18:329-351.

1979 *Ebla: Un impero inciso nell'argilla*. Milano: Arnoldo Mondadori Editore.

1980 "Bollettino militare della campagna di Ebla contro la città di Mari." *OA* 19:231-245.

1980 "Ebla and the Bible." *BA* 43:203-216.

1980 "Ebla e la Bibbia." *OA* 19:49-72.

1981 *The Archives of Ebla: An Empire Inscribed in Clay*. Garden City: Doubleday.

1981 "Gasur nella documentazione epigrafica di Ebla." In *Studies on the Civilization and Culture of Nuzi and the Hurrians in Honor of Ernest R. Lacheman*, edited by M.A. Morrison and D.I. Owen. Winona Lake: Eisenbrauns. *SCCNH* 1. 297-304.

1981 "La pronuncia sumerica dei numeri da 1 a 10 in un testo lessicale di Ebla." *AION* 41:141-143.

1981 *Testi lessicali monolingui della Biblioteca L. 2769*. Napoli: Istituto Universitario Orientale. *MEE* 3.

1981 "I vocabolari bilingui di Ebla: Problemi di traduzione e di lessicografia sumerico-eblaita." In *La lingua di Ebla*, edited by Luigi Cagni. Napoli: Istituto Universitario Orientale. 241-276.

1982 *Testi lessicali bilingui della Biblioteca L. 2769*. Napoli: Istituto Universitario Orientale. *MEE* 4.

1986 *Ebla: Nuovi orizzonti della storia*. Milano: Rusconi.

1991 *Ebla: A New Look at History*. Baltimore: The Johns Hopkins University Press.

Pettinato, Giovanni and Hartmut Waetzoldt

1974 *La Collezione Schollmeyer*. Roma: Multigrafica Editrice. *MVN* 1.

Picchioni, Sergio Angelo

1975 "Miscellanea neo-sumerica, II: Collazione a M. Çığ - H. Kızılyay - A. Salonen, *Die Puzriš-Dagan-Texte der Istanbuler Archäologischen Museen. Teil I:* Nrr. 1-725." *OA* 14:153-168.

1987 "Le liste monolingui sumeriche šè.bar.kin$_x$ di Ebla: Studio preliminare." In *Ebla 1975-1985: Dieci anni di studi linguistici e filologici*, edited by Luigi Cagni. Napoli: Istituto Universitario Orientale. 159-164.

Pinnock, Frances

1985 "About the Trade of Early Syrian Ebla." *MARI* 4:85-92.

1986 "The Lapis Lazuli Trade in the Third Millennium B.C. and the Evidence from the Royal Palace G of Ebla." In *Insight Through Images: Studies in Honor of Edith Porada*, edited by Marilyn Kelly-Buccellati. Malibu: Undena Publications. *BM* 21. 221-228.

1987 "The Lapis Lazuli in the Royal Palace of Ebla." *Studies in the History and Archaeology of Palestine* 2. Aleppo. 65-71.

1988 "Observations on the Trade of Lapis Lazuli in the IIIrd Millennium B.C." In *Wirtschaft und Gesellschaft von Ebla*, edited by Hartmut Waetzoldt and Harald Hauptmann. Heidelberg: Heidelberger Orientverlag. *HSAO* 2. 107-110.

1991 "Considerazioni sul sistema commerciale di Ebla protosiriana (c. 2350-200 A.C.)." *La Parola del Passato* 46:270-284.

Pintore, Franco

1978 *Il matrimonio interdinastico nel Vicino Oriente durante i secoli xv-xiii*. Roma: Istituto per l'Oriente. *Orientis Antiqui collectio* 14.

Pitard, Wayne T.

1987 *Ancient Damascus: A Historical Study of the Syrian City-State from Earliest Times Until its Fall to the Assyrians in 732 B.C.E.* Winona Lake: Eisenbrauns.

Podany, Amanda

forth *Kings of Ḫana: An Analysis of their Time and Place in Syro-Mesopotamian History*. Malibu: Undena Publications. *BM*.

Poetto, Massimo
1977 [review of Johann Tischler, *Hethitisches Etymologisches Glossar* (Innsbruck, 1977)]. *Paideia* 32:314-321.
Pohl, Alfred
1937 *Rechts- und Verwaltungsurkunden der III. Dynastie von Ur*. Leipzig. *TMH NF* 1/2.
1952 "Personalnachrichten." *Or* 21:493-509.
Pomponio, Francesco
1983 "The Meaning of the Term uštil in the Ebla Documents." *ArOr* 51:372-377.
1983 "Notes on the Lexical Texts from Abū Ṣalābīkh and Ebla." *JNES* 42:285-290.
1990 "Exit Kiš dagli orizzonti di Ebla." *Mesopotamia*[T] 25:175-184.
Posener, G.
1971 "Syria and Palestine *c.* 2160-1780 B.C.: Relations with Egypt." *CAH*[3] I/2:532-558.
Postgate, John N.
1986 "Abu Essalabikh and Tell Mardikh: Sumer and Ebla." *Sumer* 42:68-70.
Potratz, Hanns A.
1938 *Das Pferd in der Frühzeit*. Rostock: Carl Hinstorffs Verlag.
Pritchard, James B.
1955 (ed) *Ancient Near Eastern Texts Relating to the Old Testament*. Princeton: Princeton University Press. Second edition. First edition 1950.
Puhvel, Jaan
1984ff. *Hittite Etymological Dictionary*. Berlin: Mouton. *Trends in Linguistics Documentation* 1.
Rabin, Chaim
1963 "Hittite Words in Hebrew." *Or* 32:113-139.
Rainey, A.F.
1970 "The Order of Sacrifices in Old Testament Ritual Texts." *Biblica* 51:485-498.
Rashīd [Reschid], Fawzi
1976 "Dirāsa awwaliyya litimthāl Bāsaṭkı" ["Preliminary Study of the Bassetki Statue"]. *Sumer* 32:49-58 [Arabic part].
Rawlinson, Sir Henry
1861-84 *The Cuneiform Inscriptions of Western Asia*. London: British Museum.
Reimer, Steve
1989 "Tell Qraya on the Middle Euphrates." In "Complexity in Peripheral Mesopotamia During the Uruk Period. Workshop Summary." *Paléorient* 15:279-290.
Reiner, Erica and Miguel Civil
1974 *The Series ḪAR-ra* = ḫubullu: *Tablets XX-XXIV*. Roma: Pontificium Institutum Biblicum. *MSL* XI.
Renan, Ernest
1864 *Mission de Phénicie*. Paris: Imprimerie impériale.
Rochberg-Halton, Francesca and Paul Zimansky
1979 "The University of Iowa Cuneiform Texts." *JCS* 31:127-148.
Röllig, Wolfgang and Hartmut Kühne
1977-78 "The Lower Habur: A Preliminary Report on a Survey Conducted by the Tübinger Atlas des Vorderen Orients in 1975." *AAAS* 27-8:115-140.
Römer, Willem H.Ph.
1971 *Frauenbriefe über Religion, Politik und Privatleben in Mari*. Kevelaer: Verlag Butzon & Bercker. *AOAT* 12.

Rothman, Mitchell S.
1989 (ed) "Out of the Heartland: The Evolution of Complexity in Peripheral Mesopotamia During the Uruk Period. Workshop Summary." *Paléorient* 15:279-290.
Rouault, Olivier
1984 *Terqa Final Reports No. 1: L'Archive de Puzurum*. Malibu: Undena Publications. *BM* 16.
Rutten, Maggie
1938 "Trente-deux modèles de foies en argile inscrits provenant de Tell-Hariri (Mari)." *RA* 35:36-70.
Sader, Hélène S.
1987 *Les états araméens de Syrie depuis leur fondation jusqu'à leur transformation en provinces assyriennes*. Beirut: Orient-Institut der Deutschen Morgenländischen Gesellschaft. *Beiruter Texte und Studien* 36.
Sallaberger, W.
1991 "Zur Lesung der Bewässerungseinrichtung NAG-kud = káb-kud." *NABU* 1991/47.
Salvini, Mirjo
1988 "Un texte hourrite nommant Zimrilim." *RA* 82:59-69.
Sasson, Jack M.
1974 "Ḫurrians and Ḫurrian Names in the Mari Texts." *UF* 6:353-400.
forth (ed) *Civilizations of the Ancient Near East*. New York: Scribners.
Sauren, H.
1978 *Les tablettes cuneiformes de l'époque d'Ur des collections de la New York Public Library*. Louvain: Institut Orientaliste de l'Université Catholique de Louvain. *PIOL* 19.
Scandone Matthiae, Gabriella
1979 "Vasi iscritti di Chefren e Pepi I nel Palazzo Reale G di Ebla." *SEb* 1:33-43.
1981 "I vasi egiziani in pietra dal Palazzo Reale G." *SEb* 4:99-127.
1988 "Les Relations entre Ébla et l'Égypte au IIIème et au IIème Millénaire av. J.-Chr." In *Wirtschaft und Gesellschaft von Ebla*, edited by Hartmut Waetzoldt and Harald Hauptmann. Heidelberg: Heidelberger Orientverlag. *HSAO* 2. 67-73.
Schaeffer, Claude F.A.
1969 *Ugaritica 6: Publié à l'occasion de la XXXe campagne de fouilles à Ras Shamra (1968) sous la direction de Claude F.A. Schaeffer*. Paris: Paul Geuthner. *BAH* 81. *MRS* XVII.
Schmandt-Besserat, Denise
1992 *Before Writing*. Austin: University of Texas Press. 2 vols.
Schmökel, Hartmut
1957 *Geschichte des alten Vorderasien*. Leiden: E.J. Brill. *HO*, 2 Band, 3 Abschnitt.
Schneider, Nikolaus
1925 "Das Drehem- und Djoḫaarchiv, 2. Heft." *Or* SP 18:1-118.
1932 *Die Drehem- und Djoḫa-Texte im Kloster Montserrat (Barcelona)*. Roma: Pontificio Istituto Biblico. *AnOr* 7.
Schroeder, Otto
1920 *Keilschrifttexte aus Assur verschiedenen Inhalts*. Leipzig: J.C. Hinrichs'sche Buchhandlung. *WVDOG* 35.
von Schuler, Einar
1957 *Hethitische Dienstanweisungen für höhere Hof- und Staatsbeamte. Ein Beitrag zum antiken Recht Kleinasiens*. Graz: Ernst Weidner. *AfO* Beiheft 10.
1963 "Hethitische Kultbräuche in dem Brief eines ugaritischen Gesandten." *RHA* 21 (=

Fascicule 72):43-46.

Schwartz, G. and Harvey Weiss

forth "Syria: ca. 10,000-2,000 B.C." In *Chronologies in Old World Archaeology*[3], edited by Robert Ehrich. Chicago: The University of Chicago Press. Third edition. 2 vols.

Shea, William H.

1983 "Two Palestinian Segments From the Eblaite Geographical Atlas." In *The Word of the Lord Shall Go Forth: Essays in Honor of David Noel Freedman*, edited by Carol L. Meyers and M. O'Connor. Winona Lake: Eisenbrauns. 589-612.

Siegelová, Jana

1986 *Hethitische Verwaltungspraxis im Lichte der Wirtschafts- und Inventardokumente*. Praha: Národní muzeum.

Sigrist, Marcel

1977 "Offrandes dans le temple de Nusku à Nippur." *JCS* 29:169-183.

1979 "Nouveaux noms géographiques de l'empire d'Ur III." *JCS* 31:166-170.

1982 "Miscellanea." *JCS* 34:242-252.

1984 *Neo-Sumerian Account Texts in the Horn Archaeological Museum*. Berrien Springs: Andrews University Press. *AUCT* 1.

1988 *Neo-Sumerian Account Texts in the Horn Archaeological Museum*. Berrien Springs: Andrews University Press. *AUCT* 2.

1990 *Tablettes du Princeton Theological Seminary: Époque d'Ur 3*. Pennsylvania: The University Museum. *Occasional Publications of the Samuel Noah Kramer Fund* 10.

forth *Ur III Texts in the Royal Ontario Museum, Toronto*.

Sigrist, Marcel and C.E.S. Gavin

1988 *Neo-Sumerian Account Texts in the Horn Archaeological Museum*. Berrien Springs: Andrews University Press. *AUCT* 3.

Sigrist, Marcel and Tohru Gomi

1992 *The Comprehensive Catalogue of Published Ur III Tablets*. Bethesda: CDL Press.

Sigrist, Marcel, David I. Owen, and Gordon D. Young

1984 *The John Frederick Lewis Collection Part II*. Roma: Multigrafica Editrice. *MVN* 13.

Simpson, K.

1988 "Qraya Modular Reports 1: The Early Soundings." *SMS* 4/4:1-44.

Singer, Itamar

1977 "A Hittite Hieroglyphic Seal Impression from Tel Aphek." *TA* 4:178-190.

1983-84 *The Hittite KI.LAM Festival*. Wiesbaden: Otto Harrassowitz. 2 vols. *SBT* 27-28.

1985 "The Battle of Niḫriya and the End of the Hittite Empire." *ZA* 75:100-123.

1987 "Dating the End of the Hittite Empire." *Hethitica* 8:413-421.

1991 "A Concise History of Amurru." In *Amurru Akkadian: A Linguistic Study*, by Shlomo Izre'el. Atlanta: Scholars Press. Vol. 2:135-195.

Skinner, James H.

1968 "The Oriental Institute Excavations at Mureybiṭ, Syria: Preliminary Report on the 1965 Campaign. Part II: Chipped Stone Finds." *JNES* 27:282-290.

Smith, Sidney

1957 "Yarim-Lim of Yamḫad." *RSO* 32:155-184.

Snell, Daniel C. and Carl H. Lager

1991 *Economic Texts from Sumer*. New Haven: Yale University Press. *YOS* 18.

von Soden, Wolfram

1969 "Bemerkungen zu einigen literarischen Texten in akkadischer Sprache aus Ugarit." *UF*

1:189-195.
1988 "Ebla, die früheste Schriftkultur Syriens." In *Wirtschaft und Gesellschaft von Ebla*, edited by Hartmut Waetzoldt and Harald Hauptmann. Heidelberg: Heidelberger Orientverlag. *HSAO* 2. 325-332.

Sollberger, Edmond
1959-60 "Byblos sous les rois d'Ur." *AfO* 19:120-122.
1978 *The Pinches Manuscript*. Roma: Multigrafica Editrice. *MVN* 5.
1982 "Notes sur la paléographie des textes d'Ebla." *SEb* 5:221-228.
1986 *Administrative Texts Chiefly Concerning Textiles (L. 2752)*. Roma: Missione Archeologica Italiana in Siria. *ARET* 8.
1990 "Une tablette d'Ibla." *MARI* 6:647-648.

Sollberger, Edmond and Jean-Robert Kupper
1971 *Inscriptions royales sumériennes et akkadiennes*. Paris: Les Éditions du Cerf.

Sommer, Ferdinand
1932 *Die Aḫḫijavā-Urkunden*. München: Verlag der Bayerischen Akademie der Wissenschaften. *Abhandlungen der Bayerischen Akademie der Wissenschaften: Philosophisch-historische Abteilung Neue Folge* 6.

Souček, Vladimir and Jana Siegelová
1974 "Der Kult des Wettergottes von Ḫalap in Ḫatti." *ArOr* 42:39-52.

Spar, Ira
1988 *Cuneiform Texts in The Metropolitan Museum of Art*. Volume 1. New York: The Metropolitan Museum of Art.

Stefanini, Ruggero
1964 "Una lettera della Regina Puduhepa al Re di Alasija (KUB XXI 38)." *Atti e memorie dell'Accademia Toscana di Scienze e Lettere "La Colombaria"* 29:1-69.

Steinkeller, Piotr
1982 "The Question of Marḫaši: A Contribution to the Historical Geography of Iran in the Third Millennium B.C." *ZA* 72:237-265.
1986 "Seal of Išma-ilum, Son of the Governor of Matar." *VO* 6:27-40.
1989 *Sale Documents of the Ur-III-Period*. Stuttgart: Franz Steiner Verlag. *Freiburger Altorientalische Studien* 17.
1991 "The Container *kabkūru*." *NABU* 1991/4.

Stieglitz, Robert R.
1990 "Ebla and the Gods of Canaan." *Eblaitica* 2:79-89.

Stol, Martin
1991 "Old Babylonian Personal Names." *SEL* 8:191-212.

Stone, Elizabeth C.
1987 *Nippur Neighborhoods*. Chicago: The Oriental Institute. *SAOC* 44.

Strommenger, Eva
1960 "Das Menschenbild in der altmesopotamischen Rundplastik von Mesilim bis Hammurapi." *BagM* 1:1-103.
1976 "Fünfter vorläufiger Bericht über die von der Deutschen Orient-Gesellschaft mit Mitteln der Stiftung Volkswagenwerk in Ḥabūba Kabīra unternommenen archäologischen Untersuchungen (Kampagnen 1974, 1974, 1975)." *MDOG* 108:5-22.
1979 "Ausgrabungen der Deutschen Orient-Gesellschaft in Ḥabuba Kabira." In *Archaeological Reports from the Tabqa Dam Project—Euphrates Valley, Syria*, edited by David Noel Freedman. Cambridge: American Schools of Oriental Research. *AASOR* 44. 63-78.

1980 *Habuba Kabira: Eine Stadt vor 5000 Jahren*. Mainz am Rhein: Verlag Philipp von Zabern.

Sturtevant, Edgar H. and George Bechtel

1935 *A Hittite Chrestomathy*. Philadelphia: Linguistic Society of America. Second printing, corrected, 1952.

Süel, Aygül

1976-77 "In den Urkunden von Boğazköy verwendete Wort ^{LÚ}*UBĀRU*." *Anadolu* 20:131-140.

Sürenhagen, Dietrich

1986 "The Dry-Farming Belt: The Uruk Period and Subsequent Developments." In *The Origins of Cities in Dry-Farming Syria and Mesopotamia in the Third Millennium B.C.*, edited by Harvey Weiss. Guilford: Four Quarters Publishing Co. 7-43.

Tadmor, Hayim

1977 "A Lexicographical Text from Hazor." *IEJ* 27:98-102.

Thuesen, Ingolf

1989 "Diffusion of Ubaid Pottery into Western Syria." In *Upon this Foundation—The 'Ubaid Reconsidered*, edited by Elizabeth F. Henrickson and Ingolf Theusen. København: Museum Tusculanum Press. 419-440.

Thureau-Dangin, François

1897 "Tablettes chaldéennes inédites." *RA* 4:69-86.

1907 *Die sumerischen und akkadischen Königsinschriften*. Leipzig: J.C. Hinrichs'sche Buchhandlung.

1934 "Inscriptions votives sur des statuettes de Ma'eri." *RA* 31:137-144.

1939 "Tablettes ḫurrites provenant de Mâri." *RA* 36:1-28.

Thureau-Dangin, François et al.

1931 *Arslan-Tash*. Paris: Paul Geuthner. *BAH* 16.

1936 *Til-Barsib*. Paris: Paul Geuthner. *BAH* 23.

Tsukimoto, Akio

1984 "Eine neue Urkunde des *Tili-Šarruma*, Sohn des Königs von Karkamiš." *ASJ* 6:65-74.

1985 *Untersuchungen zur Totenpflege (kispum) im alten Mesopotamien*. Kevelaer: Verlag Butzon & Bercker. *AOAT* 216.

1988 "Sieben spätbronzezeitliche Urkunden aus Syrien." *ASJ* 10:153-189.

1990 "Akkadian Tablets in the Hirayama Collection (I)." *ASJ* 12:177-259.

1991 "Akkadian Tablets in the Hirayama Collection (II)." *ASJ* 13:277-333.

Vanstiphout, H.L.J.

1980 "Some Notes on 'Enlil and Namzitarra'." *RA* 74:67-71.

Veenhof, Klaas R.

1986 *Cuneiform Archives and Libraries: Papers read at the 30^{e} Rencontre Assyriologique Internationale*. Istanbul: Nederlands Historisch-Archaeologisch Instituut te Istanbul. *Uitgaven van het Nederlands Historisch-Archaeologisch Instituut te Istanbul* 57. *RAI* 30.

Vincente, Claudine

1990 "Tell Leilan Recension of the Sumerian King List." *NABU* 1990/11.

Virolleaud, Charles

1968 *Tablettes économiques de Lagash*. Paris: Imprimerie nationale. *Cahiers de la Société Asiatique* 19.

Waetzoldt, Hartmut

1992 "Zu P. Steinkeller." *NABU* 1992/15.

Waetzoldt, Hartmut and Harald Hauptmann
1988 (eds) *Wirtschaft und Gesellschaft von Ebla: Akten der Internationalen Tagung Heidelberg 4.-7. November 1986*. Heidelberg: Heidelberger Orientverlag. *HSAO* 2.

Wäfler, M.
1990 "The Excavations at Tell Hamidi." In *Tall al-Ḥamīdīya* 2, edited by Seyyare Eichler et al. Freiburg, Schweiz: Universitätsverlag. 219-228.

Warburton, David
1985 "Previous archaeological work in the Ḫābūr region." In *Tall al-Ḥamīdīya 1: Vorbericht 1984*, edited by Seyyare Eichler et al. Freiburg, Schweitz: Universitätsverlag. *Orbis biblicus et orientalis: Series archaeologica* 4. 13-30.

Watanabe, Kazuko
1987 "Freiburger Vorläufer zu ḪAR-ra = *ḫubullu* XI und XII." *ASJ* 9:277-291.

Waterhouse, Samuel Douglas
1965 *Syria in the Amarna Age: A Borderland between Conflicting Empires*. Dissertation: University of Michigan. UMI 66-6734.

Watkins, Calvert
1979 "NAM.RA GUD UDU in Hittite: Indo-European poetic language and the folk taxonomy of wealth." In *Hethitisch und Indogermanisch: Vergleichende Studien zur historischen Grammatik und zur dialektgeographischen Stellung der indogermanischen Sprachgruppe Altkleinasiens*, edited by Erich Neu and Wolfgang Meid. Innsbruck: Institut für Sprachwissenschaft der Universität Innsbruck. *Innsbrucker Beiträge zur Sprachwissenschaft* 25. 269-287.

Weidner, Ernst F.
1921-23 "Assyriologische Studien." *RSO* 9:469-479.
1923 *Politische Dokumente aus Kleinasien: Die Staatsverträge in akkadischer Sprache aus dem Archiv von Boghazköi*. Leipzig: J.C. Hinrichs'sche Buchhandlung. 2 vols. *Boghazköi-Studien* 8-9.
1953 "Das Reich Sargons von Akkad." *AfO* 16:1-24.
1958 "Die Feldzüge und Bauten Tiglatpilesers I." *AfO* 18:342-360.
1969 "Assyrien und Hanigalbat." *Ug* 6:519-531.

Weiss, Harvey
1983 "Excavations at Tell Leilan and Third Millennium Urbanization." *Paléorient* 9:42-52.
1985 (ed) *Ebla to Damascus: Art and Archaeology of Ancient Syria*. Washington, D.C.: Smithsonian Institution.
1985 "Introduction." In *Ebla to Damascus: Art and Archaeology of Ancient Syria*, edited by idem. Washington, D.C.: Smithsonian Institution. 30-43.
1985 [review of John Curtis, *Fifty Years of Mesopotamian Discovery* (1982)]. *JAOS* 105:327-330.
1985 "Tell Leilan and Shubat Enlil." *MARI* 4:269-292.
1985 "Tell Leilan on the Habur Plains of Syria." *BA* 48:5-35.
1986 "Introduction: The Origins of Cities in Dry-Farming Syria and Mesopotamia in the Third Millennium B.C." In *The Origins of Cities in Dry-Farming Syria and Mesopotamia in the Third Millennium B.C.*, edited by idem. Guilford: Four Quarters Publishing Co. 1-6.
1986 (ed) *The Origins of Cities in Dry-Farming Syria and Mesopotamia in the Third Millennium B.C.* Guilford: Four Quarters Publishing Co.
1986 "The Origins of Tell Leilan and the Conquest of Space in Third Millennium

Mesopotamia." In *The Origins of Cities in Dry-Farming Syria and Mesopotamia in the Third Millennium B.C.*, edited by idem. Guilford: Four Quarters Publishing Co. 1-6.
1990 "'Civilizing' the Habur Plains: Mid-Third Millennium State Formation at Tell Leilan." In *Resurrecting the Past: A Joint Tribute to Adnan Bounni*, edited by Paolo Matthiae, Maurits van Loon and Harvey Weiss. Istanbul: Nederlands Historisch-Archaeologisch Instituut. *Uitgaven van het Nederlands Historisch-Archaeologisch Instituut te Istanbul* 67. 387-407.
1990 "The Identification of Tell Leilan as Šubat-Enlil." *AJA* 94:573-575.
1990 "Tell Leilan 1989: New Data for Mid-Third Millennium Urbanization and State Formation." *MDOG* 122:193-218.
1990 "Third Millennium Urbanization: A Perspective from Tell Leilan." In *Tall al-Ḥamīdīya* 2, edited by Seyyare Eichler et al. Freiburg, Schweiz: Universitätsverlag. 159-166.
1990 "1985 Excavations at Tell Leilan, Syria." *AJA* 94:529-582.
1991 "Archaeology in Syria." *AJA* 95:683-740.
forth (ed) *The Origins of North Mesopotamia Civilization: Ninevite 5 Chronology, Economy, Society*. New Haven: Yale University Press.
forth "Archaeology in Syria." *AJA* 97.

Werner, Rudolf
1967 *Hethitische Gerichtsprotokolle*. Wiesbaden: Otto Harrassowitz. *SBT* 4.

Westenholz, Aage
1988 "Personal Names in Ebla and in Pre-Sargonic Babylonia." In *Eblaite Personal Names and Semitic Name-giving*, edited by A. Archi. Roma: Missione Archeologica Italiana in Siria. *ARES* 1. 99-117.

Westenholz, Joan and Aage
1977 "Help for Rejected Suitors: The Old Akkadian Love Incantation MAD V 8." *Or* 46:198-219.

Whiting, Robert M.
1976 "Tiš-atal of Nineveh and Babati, Uncle of Šu-Sin." *JCS* 28:173-182.
1990 "Tell Leilan/Šubat-Enlil: Chronological Problems and Perspectives." In *Tall al-Ḥamīdīya* 2, edited by Seyyare Eichler et al. Freiburg, Schweiz: Universitätsverlag. 167-218.

Wilcke, Claus
1970 "Drei Phasen des Niedergangs des Reiches von Ur III." *ZA* 60:54-69.
1988 "Anmerkungen zum 'Konjugationspräfix' /i/- und zur These vom 'silbischen Charakter der sumerischen Morpheme' anhand neusumerischer Verbalformen beginnend mit ì-íb-, ì-im- und ì-in-." *ZA* 78:1-49.
1988 "Die Sumerische Königsliste und erzählte Vergangenheit." In *Vergangenheit in mündlicher Überlieferung*, edited by Jürgen von Ungern-Sternberg and Hansjörg Reinau. Stuttgart: B.G. Teuber. *Colloquium Rauricum* 1. 113-140.
1989 "Die Emar-Version von 'Dattelpalme und Tamariske'—ein Rekonstruktionsversuch." *ZA* 79:161-190.
1989 "Genealogical and Geographical Thought in the Sumerian King List." In *DUMU-E$_2$-DUB-BA-A: Studies in Honor of Åke W. Sjöberg*, edited by Hermann Behrens, Darlene Loding, and Martha T. Roth. Philadelphia: The University Museum. *Occasional Publications of the Samuel Noah Kramer Fund* 11. 556-571.
1990 "Kudurmabuk in Terqa." In *De la Babylonie à la Syrie, en passant par Mari: Mélanges offerts à Monsieur J.-R. Kupper*, edited by Ö. Tunca. Liège: Université de Liège. 179-181.

1990 "Zur Rekonstruktion der Šū-Sîn Inschriften-Sammlung B." *NABU* 1990/33.

Wilhelm, Gernot

1982 *Grundzüge der Geschichte und Kultur der Hurriter.* Darmstadt: Wissenschaftliche Buchgesellschaft. Tr. by Jennifer Barnes: *The Hurrians.* Warminster: Aris & Phillips. 1989.

Wirth, Eugen

1971 *Syrien: Eine geographische Landeskunde.* Darmstadt: Wissenschaftliche Buchgesellschaft. *Wissenschaftliche Länderkunden* 4/5.

Wiseman, D.J.

1953 *The Alalakh Tablets.* London: The British Institute of Archaeology at Ankara. *Occasional Publications of the British Institute of Archaeology at Ankara* 2.

Woolley, C.L.

1953 *A Forgotten Kingdom: Being a Record of the Results Obtained from the Excavation of Two Mounds Atchana and Al Mina, in the Turkish Hatay.* London: Harmondsworth.

1955 *Alalakh: An Account of the Excavations at Tell Atchana in the Hatay 1937-49.* Oxford: Oxford University Press.

Wyatt, Nicolas

1980 "The Relationship of the Deities Dagan and Hadad." *UF* 12:375-379.

Xella, Paolo.

1981 *I testi rituali di Ugarit - 1. Testi.* Roma: Consiglio Nazionale delle Ricerche. *SS* 54.

Yıldız, Fatma and Tohru Gomi

1988 *Die Puzriš-Dagan-Texte der Istanbuler Archäologischen Museen, Teil 2: Nr. 726-1379.* Stuttgart: Franz Steiner Verlag. *Freiburger altorientalische Studien* 16.

Yon, Marguerite

1982 (ed) *La Syrie au Bronze Récent.* Paris: Editions Recherche sur les civilisations. Extraits de la XXVIIe Recontre Assyriologique Internationale, Paris 1980.

1985 "La ville d'Ougarit au XIIIe siècle av. J.-C." *CRAIBL* 1985 705-723.

Young, Gordon Douglas

1981 (ed) *Ugarit in Retrospect: Fifty Years of Ugarit and Ugaritic.* Winona Lake: Eisenbrauns.

1992 (ed) *Mari in Retrospect: Fifty Years of Mari and Mari Studies.* Winona Lake: Eisenbrauns.

Young, T. Cuyler, Jr. et al.

1984 (ed) *The Hilly Flanks and Beyond: Essays on the Prehistory of Southwestern Asia Presented to Robert J. Braidwood.* Chicago: The University of Chicago Press. *SAOC* 36.

Zadok, R.

1991 "Elamite Onomastics." *SEL* 8. 225-237.

INDICES

N.B. This set of indices does not duplicate the indices in Owen; it does include all items cited in the text and footnotes of Owen which are not included in his indices.

Personal Names

Abi-ešuḫ 85
Adad-Narari I 30n40
Alulu 84
Amar-Suen 125n57
Ammiṣaduqa 15
ᶜAmmistamru II 46
ᶜAmmurapi 46
Anu-šar-ilani 94
Anubu 24n9
Apil-kin 78n85, 110
Arennum 23
Arnuwanda I 92, 105
Assurbanipal 85
Asuka 24n8
Ašmunikal 105
Azzari 93
Baᶜal-malik 49n74
Bar-za-ma-li 26n17
Bazi 84, 85
Bentešina 46, 90, 106
Chephren 25, 26
Duppi-Teššup 90
Eannatum 26n17, 27n24, 35n61, 71
Ebdamu [Ibdamu] 120n50
Eḫal-Teššup 102
Eḫli-Nikkalu 46
Enkidu 84
Enlil-ibni 85
Enannatum I 27n24, 71
Enna-Dagan 27-28, 28
EN.ZI-Da-mu 84
Etana 84
Gilgamesh 63, 82, 84, 86
Gudea 13n121, 112
Ḫalpaḫi 94
Ḫalpaili 94
Ḫalpamuwa 94
Ḫalparunta 94
Ḫalpašulupi 94
Ḫalpaziti 94
Ḫammurapi 14, 32n47, 41, 68, 77, 80
Ḫaranamuwa 94
Ḫaššiuman 94
Ḫaššuili 94
Ḫataniš 84
Ḫattušili I 41, 98, 98n55, 100, 102, 104
Ḫattušili III 45, 46, 90, 91, 93, 94, 105
Ḫidar 28, 34
Ibbi-Sin 131n64
Ibbi-Zikir 23, 24, 30n38
Ibdamu [Ebdamu] 120n50
ᶜIbiranu 47
Iblul-Il 24, 24n8, 27, 28n26
Ibrium 23
Idrimi 31n43
Igriš-Ḫalam 23
Iku-(I)šar 28
Iku-Šamagan 24n8
Iku-Šamaš 24n8
Ikum-Mari 24n8
Ini-Teššup 44n23, 46
Irkab-Damu 23
Iršappa 95
Iṣi-Dagan 78n86
Išᵓar-Damu 23
Išbi-Irra 79, 85
Iški-Mari [Lamgi-Mari] 24n8, 24n9, 27, 28
Ištup-Šar 27
Kadašman-Enlil 93
Kantuzzili 105
Karpani 92
Kikkuli 105
Kudur-mabuk 80
Kurunta 94
Lamgi-Mari [Iški-Mari] 24n8, 24n9, 27, 28
Lugalbanda 73
Lugalzagesi 9, 26n17, 27, 27n23, 29n30, 32n46, 35, 35n60, 35n61, 36, 109n6
Maništušu 29n30
Mār-ešrē 94n34

Melišiḫu 51n3, 83
Melišipak 51n3, 83
Mesalim 26n17
Muliyaziti 93
Muršili I 41
Muršili II 42, 45, 46n40, 51n3, 90, 91, 93, 94, 104, 105
Muwatalli II 42, 90, 105
Naram-Sin 9, 25, 28, 28n27, 28n28, 29, 29n30, 30, 31, 31n42, 31n43, 31n44, 32n46, 32n47, 35, 79, 110n8, 112, 112n19
Nazimurattaš 30n40
Nerikkaili 46
Nizi 27, 28, 28n26
Nur-Dagan 95
Pepi I 25, 25n10, 26, 26n17, 28n27, 35, 37, 67
Pilsu-Dagan 44n23
Piyaššili 43
Puduḫepa 90
Ramses II 45, 90
Rapᵓanu 81
Rib-Addi 33n49
Rim-Sin 80
Riš-Adad 28, 30, 30n37
Sargon 9, 25, 26, 27, 27n18, 28n29, 29n30, 31, 31n44, 32, 32n46, 32n47, 33, 33n49, 34, 34n51, 35, 36, 37, 67, 70, 70n5, 79, 109n6, 112, 112n19
Samsuditana 15
Samsuiluna 77
Saᵓumu 24n9, 27
Sin-iddinam 86
Sin-iribam 28n28
Sin-muballiṭ 32n47
Ša-nam-gi-nu 28n29
Šaḫli 92
Šalmaneser I 19
Šamši-Adad I 14, 15n132, 16
Šapili 90
Šarkališarri 112
Šarri-Kušuḫ 43
Šattiwazza 46
Šaušgamuwa 46
Šilḫak-Inšušnak 30n40
Šimti-šilḫak 80
Šu-Suen 110, 113, 114, 114n27, 117n44, 131n64
Šube-awilim 82n123, 86
Šulgi 77, 113n24, 125n57
Šuppiluliuma I 16, 18, 42, 42n5, 43, 44, 45, 46, 89, 90, 91, 102, 103, 105, 106
Šuppiluliuma II 46, 106
Taram-Uram 78n85
Targasnalli 93
Tiglath-Pileser III 30n40
Tiqqa-UR.MAḪ 92n20
Tudḫaliya 42
Tudḫaliya IV 42, 44n23, 46, 94, 106
Tukulti-Ninurta I 15n139
Tura-Dagan 78n86
Ur-Nammu 78n85, 110, 110n8, 112
Ur-Nanše 27, 71
Ur-Zababa 29n30
Urukagina 9, 35
Utuk 35n61
Warad-Sin 80
Wen-Amon 103
Yaggid-Lim 78n86
Yaḫdun-Lim 32n47
Yarim-Lim 98n58
Yibbiṭ-Lim 115n36, 120n50
Zimri-Lim 78
Ziusudra 84
Zizi 84, 85
Zukraši 98n58

Geographical Names and Peoples

A-ru$_{12}$-ga-tù^{ki} 28n29, 65
AB 74n47
Abarnium, Abarnum 30n33, 117n44
Abu Hureyra 3, 5n35
Abu Ṣalabikh 63, 73, 74, 75, 75n59, 76, 85n145
ABZU 30n33
Adab 34n56, 74n47
Ahmar 20, 20n193
Akkad 9, 12, 28, 28n27, 28n29, 29, 29n30, 30, 32, 32n47, 34n56, 35, 67, 79
Akšak 34n56, 74n47
Alalakh 14, 17, 17n156, 31n43, 66, 70, 103 [see also Tell Atchana]
Aleppo 8, 13, 14, 17, 43, 59, 64, 64n6, 67, 68, 70, 89, 94, 97, 98, 102, 102n74, 106 [see also Ḫalab; see also Yamkhad]
Alše 103
Amanus Mts. 1, 31, 31n43, 33 [see also Cedar Mountains]
Amarna 33n49, 64, 65, 80
Amida 117n44
Amorites 13, 14, 67, 113n26, 116
ᶜAmqa 103
Amuda 20, 20n190
Amuq 113n26

Amurru 14, 14n130, 17, 43, 45, 45n30, 45n33, 46, 66, 90, 98, 103, 106
Anatolia 1, 6, 16, 18, 19, 41, 44, 48n59, 49, 52, 80, 81, 89-106 passim
Anšan 30n33
Antioch 4
Aphek 80
Aram 97
Arameans 16
Aratta 63, 73
Arg/qa/u 64, 67
Armanum 28, 28n27, 28n28, 29, 30, 30n37, 30n38, 31, 31n44, 64, 112
Armi 30n38, 64, 64n6, 65, 115n34
Arrapḫa 30, 30n40, 103
Arslan Tash 20, 20n194
Arugatu 28n29, 65
Ashara 10, 15, 132n67 [see also Terqa]
Ashdod 66
Assur 110n8
Assyria, Assyrians 2, 14, 15n139, 17, 19, 20, 30, 30n40, 42, 42n8, 44, 52, 54, 66, 92, 94
Aswad 4, 111n14
Aštata 17, 43, 44, 45n33, 47, 103
Atchana 17, 70 [see also Alalakh]
A'ur [Awur] 74n47
Azu 16 [see also Tell Hadidi]
Babylon, Babylonia 14, 15, 16, 17, 30n40, 32n47, 34n56, 41, 44, 46n37, 54, 77, 80, 83, 85, 90, 91, 93, 94, 94n34, 110, 111n14
Badar [Matar] 74n47
Balikh 1, 3, 6, 32n47, 33n50, 64, 66, 72
Banat 10
Barri 6, 11, 11n98, 21, 111n14 [see also Kaḫat]
Bazey 10
Beqᶜa 42
Bit-Nanip 30, 30n36
Boghazköy 42, 55, 99, 101
Bouqras 4
Brak 3, 4, 4n23, 6, 6n42, 7, 7n56, 8, 13n119, 16, 21, 29n30, 31n42, 110n8, 111n14 [see also Taᵓidu]
Byblos 2, 8, 33n49, 65, 72, 103 [see also Gubla]
Canaan 60, 81, 92, 103, 113n26, 114
Carchemish 2, 4, 6, 7, 10, 14, 14n130, 17, 20, 43, 44, 44n23, 45, 45n33, 46, 46n40, 47, 47n47, 49, 51n3, 60, 65, 89, 97, 106, 112n21 [see also Jerablus]
Cedar Lands 97
Cedar Mountains 31, 32, 33, 112 [see also Amanus Mts.]
Çermük 117n44
Chagar Bazar 3, 15, 16, 77
Choga Mish 5
Chuera 8, 11, 21, 112n21
Cyprus 81
Damascus 13
Deir Alla 72n26
Diniktum 30n33
Diyala 29n32, 30, 30n40, 132n67
Drehem 113, 116, 116n43, 141n74 [see also Puzriš-Dagan]
DUlu 115n34
Dunanapa 103
Dur-Ebla 29n32, 120n51
Durubla 29n32
Durum 74n47
É-a-(a) 66
Eanna 32n47
Ebla 3, 8, 8n63, 8n67, 9, 9n71, 10, 11, 13n118, 14, 21, 23-37 passim, 51, 60, 61n48, 63-68 passim, 69-77 passim, 78, 81, 84, 88, 109, 109n5, 110, 110n11, 111, 111n13, 111n14, 111n15, 112, 112n21, 113n26, 115, 115n33, 115n34, 115n36, 117n47, 120n50, 120n51, 121n53, 133n68, 134n71, 147n80 [see also Tell Mardikh]
Egypt 1, 3, 7, 9, 13, 16, 17, 25, 25n12, 26, 26n14, 33n49, 34n56, 36n69, 41, 42, 42n7, 44, 45, 46n37, 52, 60, 60n43, 67, 70, 80, 81, 90, 93, 110n11, 114, 114n28
Ekron 66
Elam 28n28, 30n40, 70, 110, 113, 116, 116n43
Emar 14, 16, 17, 18, 18n175, 19, 42, 43n11, 43n12, 43n13, 44, 44n23, 46, 46n46, 47, 47n47, 48, 48n66, 48n67, 48n68, 49, 49n74, 51-61 passim, 64, 66, 78, 82, 83, 83n130, 84, 85, 86, 102, 103 [see also Meskeneh]
Eridu 32n47
Euphrates 1, 1n4, 5, 6, 8, 10, 14, 15, 19, 20, 31, 32n47, 33, 34n56, 35n61, 43, 49, 52, 56, 59, 64, 65, 66, 67, 79, 83, 110, 110n11, 112n21, 114, 132n67
Fakhariyah 16, 20, 20n189
Faqᵓous 44
Fara 71, 76 [see also Šuruppak]
Fray 19, 19n187
Gasur 29n32, 31, 66, 66n17
Gatanna 103
Gezer 80
Godin Tepe 5
Gubla 72, 116 [see also Byblos]
Gudeda 10

Gú-nu 65
Gutium [Quti] 30, 112
Habuba Kabira 4, 5, 6, 7, 70
Hadidi 5, 10, 16 [see also Azu]
Halaf 2, 2n11, 3
Hama 4, 6, 64, 65, 113n26
Hamidi 16
Hammam et-Turkman 4, 6, 21
Hamoukar 6, 8, 12
Hazor 80, 80n108
Hebron 80
al-Hiba 71 [see also Lagaš]
Hit 32n47
Hittites 2, 16, 16n151, 17, 19, 41-49 passim, 51-61 passim, 65, 66, 81, 89-106 passim
Homs 8
Hurrians 11, 11n94, 12, 12n103, 15, 16, 17, 19, 41, 42, 44, 44n23, 51-61 passim, 78, 89-106 passim, 108n4
Ḫaḫḫum 98, 98n55, 100
Ḫakmiš 90
Ḫalab 14, 17, 41, 42, 43, 45n33, 102 [see also Aleppo; see also Yamkhad]
Ḫalam 64n6
Ḫamazi 84
Ḫanigalbat 19, 44
Ḫapalla 93
Ḫarbe 32n47
Ḫarḫar 132n67
Ḫarran 33n50, 64, 65, 94, 112n21
Ḫaššu 94, 98
Ḫatra 98, 100
Ḫatti 17, 18, 41-49 passim, 53, 53n11, 54, 55, 55n22, 57, 60, 61, 81, 89-106 passim
Ḫattuša 41-49 passim, 65, 80, 81, 82, 82n119, 89-106 passim
Ḫemuwa 100
Ibratum 30n33
Idarukatta 103
Id 32n47
Imar 52, 52n5, 52n6, 61n48, 64, 65, 66, 112n21
Ingharra 35
Irbil 30n34
Isin 79, 85
Iškar 74n47
Ištanuwa 103n83
Išuwa 101
Jebel Aruda 5, 5n32
Jebel Belene 6
Jebel Ḥamrin 30, 30n40 [see also Mt. Ebiḫ]
Jerablus 43, 65 [see also Carchemish]
Jerusalem 65, 67
Judaidah 7
Kadesh 42n7, 90, 103
Kaḫat 6, 15 [see also Tell Barri]
Kalzi 30n34
Kaniš 120n50
Kannas 4, 70
Karaḫar 132n67
KAS_4 30n33
Kassites 51n3, 83
Kazel 43
Keš 32n47
Khabur 1, 3, 6, 6n40, 8, 11, 12, 14, 15, 15n132, 15n133, 16, 21, 29n30, 33, 33n49, 34n56, 42, 108, 108n4, 111n14, 112n21, 113n26
Khafaje 6
Khana 15, 15n139, 69, 79
Khorsabad 2n13
Khoshi 12
Kinza 43, 45, 45n33
Kirkuk 66, 66n17
Kiš 9, 13n118, 26n17, 29, 29n30, 34, 34n56, 35, 35n60, 35n61, 36, 65, 111, 111n13, 111n14
Kiškiš 34n56
Kizzuwatna 104
Kulab 33n50, 73, 73n36
Kumidi 80
Kummiya 100
Kutha 32n47
Laban-e 30n33
Lachish 67
Lagaš 27, 26n17, 27n22, 27n24, 28, 32n46, 35n61, 71, 71n19, 76, 76n65 [see also al-Hiba]
Lake Assad 52, 52n6
Larsa 14, 28n28, 79, 80, 86
Leilan 4, 6, 8, 12, 13, 14, 14n131, 16, 24n9, 77, 108n4, 113n26 [see also Šubat-Enlil]
Little Zab 30, 32n47
Lrgt 65
Lubdi 30
Lulubu 30
Ma-ba-ra-at/Má-bar-du 67
Maḫ(i)li 30n33, 129n63
Malatya 117n44
Mardikh 8, 23-37 passim, 63, 70 [see also Ebla]
Mardu 66, 110, 112, 113, 113n24, 114, 114n27, 115, 115n35, 115n37, 116, 127n62
Marḫaši 116n43
Mari 3, 8n63, 9, 10, 13, 13n118, 14, 15, 16, 21, 23, 24, 24n8, 24n9, 26n17, 27, 28, 28n26, 29, 29n30, 31n44, 32, 32n47, 33, 34,

34n56, 35, 36, 52, 54n14, 59, 61n48, 63, 65, 68, 77, 78, 78n84, 79, 80, 81, 85, 108n1, 110, 110n8, 110n9, 110n11, 111, 111n14, 111n15, 112, 112n17, 112n21, 116, 123n55, 126n59, 126n60, 127n61, 129n63, 132n67
Maṣat 94, 94n34
Maš-bar-tu 67
Maśśa 67
Maškan-Dūr-Ebla 31
Matar [Badar] 74n47
Megiddo 80
Meluḫḫa 33n49
Meskeneh 42, 44, 51-61 passim, 64, 66, 102, 103 [see also Emar]
Mitanni 15, 16, 16n146, 16n147, 17, 42, 43, 44, 45n33, 46, 52, 89, 103
Mount Basar 112
Mount Ebiḫ 30, 30n40 [see also Jebel Ḥamrim]
Mount Lebanon 31n43
Mozan 8, 11, 12, 12n103, 21, 108n4 [see also Urkiš]
Mukiš 43, 45, 97, 132n65
Mureybiṭ 3, 5n35
Nagar 29, 29n30, 34n56, 111n14
Naḫur 29n30
Neribtum 30n33
Nimrud 2n13
Nineveh 2n13, 103
Nippur 32n47, 56, 56n25, 77, 81
Niya 43
Nuḫašše 43, 45n33, 97, 103
Nuza 30n40
Nuzi 29n32, 30n34, 30n36, 30n40, 31, 32n47, 66, 83, 120n51
Orontes 6, 7, 14, 64
Purušḫanda 95
Puzriš-Dagan 116, 141n74 [see also Drehem]
Qaṣr Šemamuk 30n34
Qatna 8, 14, 14n130, 64
Qraya 5-6
Quti [Gutium] 30, 112
Radanu River 30
Rapiqum 32n47
Ramadi 6
Ras Shamra 42 [see also Ugarit]
Retenu 97
Sa-na-ru$_{12}$-gu 67
Samsat 4, 6, 7
Sanapzugum 64
Saza 63, 64
Selenkahiye 10
Shechem 80
Sheikh Hamad 20, 20n188, 21
Sidon 2, 103
Sikumanum 28n28
Silver Mountains 32, 33 [see also Taurus Mts.]
Simurrum 30n33
Sippar 32n47, 74, 74n47, 84, 85
Siyannu 45, 46, 64
Sodom 67
Sultan Tepe 70
Sumer 7, 13, 32, 32n47, 63, 76, 109, 110, 111, 113, 117n44, 120n51
Sumurunu 30n34
Susa 5, 71n17
Sweyhat 10
Ṣumur 43 [see also Tell Kazel]
Šatappi 54, 59
Šimerunni 30n34
Šubat-Enlil 14, 14n131 [see also Tell Leilan]
Šuruppak 71, 76 [see also Fara]
Šušarra 30n34
Taanach 80
Taʾidu 16 [see also Tell Brak]
Tamalki 100
Tapikka 94
Tarḫuntaša 94
Tašḫiniya 100
Taurus Mts. 1, 33, 44 [see also Silver Mountains]
Tell Abu Hureyra 3, 5n35
Tell Abu Ṣalabikh 63, 73, 74, 75, 75n59, 76, 85n145
Tell Ahmar 20, 20n193
Tell Amuda 20, 20n190
Tell Ashara 10, 15, 132n67 [see also Terqa]
Tell Aswad 4, 111n14
Tell Atchana 17, 70 [see also Alalakh]
Tell Banat 10
Tell Barri 6, 11, 11n98, 21, 111n14 [see also Kaḫat]
Tell Bazey 10
Tell Bouqras 4
Tell Brak 3, 4, 4n23, 6, 6n42, 7, 7n56, 8, 13n119, 16, 21, 29n30, 31n42, 110n8, 111n14 [see also Taʾidu]
Tell Chagar Bazar 3, 15, 16, 77
Tell Chuera 8, 11, 21, 112n21
Tell Fakhariyah 16, 20, 20n189
Tell Faqʾous 44
Tell Fray 19, 19n187
Tell Gudeda 10
Tell Habuba Kabira 4, 5, 6, 7, 70
Tell Hadidi 5, 10, 16 [see also Azu]

Tell Halaf 2, 2n11, 3
Tell Hamidi 16
Tell Hammam et-Turkman 4, 6, 21
Tell Hamoukar 6, 8, 12
Tell Ingharra 35
Tell Kannas 4, 70
Tell Kazel 43 [see also Ṣumer]
Tell Khoshi 12
Tell Leilan 4, 6, 8, 12, 13, 14, 14n131, 16, 24n9, 77, 108n4, 113n26 [see also Šubat-Enlil]
Tell Mardikh 8, 23-37 passim, 63, 70 [see also Ebla]
Tell Mozan 8, 11, 12, 12n103, 21, 108n4 [see also Urkiš]
Tell Mureybiṭ 3, 5n35
Tell Qraya 5-6
Tell Ramadi 6
Tell Sheikh Hamad 20, 20n188, 21
Tell Sweyhat 10
Terqa 13, 15, 15n137, 16, 34n56, 77, 79, 132n67 [see also Tell Ashara]
Tishreen Dam 10, 20
Tuba 65, 66
Tunip 43, 64, 103
Tuttul 32, 32n47, 65, 133n68
Tyre 2, 103
Ṭawuq 30
Ṭawuq Çay 30
Ù-ti-gú/ig 67
Ugar-Sali 30, 30n40, 31
Ugarit 3, 8n63, 14, 16, 18, 18n168, 18n170, 19, 21, 42, 42n8, 43, 44, 45, 45n33, 46, 46n46, 47, 49, 51, 52, 53, 54, 57, 57n30, 60, 60n43, 61, 61n46, 64, 65, 66, 67n19, 69, 72n26, 81, 82, 82n119, 83, 84, 86, 86n158, 91, 94, 96, 97, 99n63, 103 [see also Ras Shamra]
Ugulzit 103
Ulisum 31, 31n43
Ullaza 31n43
Ullu 120n51
Ulma 98
Uluzina 31n43
Umm el-Jir 29n30
Umma 29n32, 32n46
Upper Sea 31
Ur 13, 26, 32n46, 32n47, 77, 78n85, 112, 116
Ura 91, 92n20
Urbilum 113n24
Urkiš 12n103, 108n4 [see also Tell Mozan]
Uršu 65, 97, 110, 110n9, 117n47, 134n71, 147n80
Urua 74n47
Uruk 5, 6, 6n40, 7, 11, 12, 26n17, 32n47, 35n60, 73, 74n47, 76
Usdum 67
Ušnatu 45, 46
ᶜUẓaym 30
Waššukkanni 17, 43
Yabliya 32n47
Yamkhad 13, 14, 112n21 [see also Aleppo; see also Ḫalab]
Yarmuti 32, 32n47, 33, 33n49
Yazilikaya 101, 106
ZA 74n47
Zagros 110, 113
Zaidan 4, 6
Zalpa 100
Zinjirli 2
Zinzira 103
Zunzurḫa 103

Divine Names

Adad 72
Adar-wa-An 72
Alalu 99
Ama-Ušum 73
Ama-Ušumgal 73
Amar-Utu 101
An 73
ᶜAnat 101
Anu 99
Asherah 101
Astarte 101
Ašertu 60n43, 99n63
Aštart 54n19, 58, 58n37, 59, 60, 60n44
Aštart of Battle 54, 58n33, 59
Baᶜal 48n66, 54n19, 58, 58n33, 58n37, 59, 59n38, 60, 60n44, 101
Balikh 63, 66, 72
Dagan 32, 32n47, 48n66, 54n19, 56, 58, 58n33, 59, 59n41, 60, 60n44, 95
Dumuzi 73
Ea 54n19, 59, 102
Eblaitu 30n34
El 60, 63, 101
Elkuniрša 60n43, 101
Enki 32n47
Enlil 32n47, 35n61, 56, 73
Ereškigal 59
Ḫebat 54n19, 57, 58, 59, 95, 101, 102, 102n74, 105

Ḫedammu 99
ÍD 66
IM 58n33, 59n38, 60n43
Inanna 73
Išḫara 54n19, 59
Ištar 24n8, 32n47, 60n43, 103
Ištarat 24n8
Kemosh 72
Kothar-wa-Ḫasis 72n26
Kumarbi 18n165, 99, 99n61, 105
LAMMA 99
Marduk 101
Nanna 73
Nergal 32n47
Nin-girim 71, 71n17
Ninḫursag 32n47
NIN.KUR 54n19
Ninni-zaza 24n8
NIN.URTA 48, 48n66, 48n67, 48n68, 53n8, 54n19, 56, 56n25, 59
Ninurta 56, 56n25
Rasap-Gunu 65
Resheph 65, 95
Ršp-Gn 65
Sin 6, 32n47, 67
Šagar-wa-Ištar 72n26
Šamaš 32n47, 73, 74
Šarruma 105
Šaušga 105
Stormgod of Aleppo 59, 102
Teššup 95, 99, 100, 101, 102, 102n74, 105
Ullikummi 99
Utu 73
Yamm 66
Yrḫ 65

Texts

A-Tablet 81, 84
Animal List A 76
Ašertu Myth 99n63, 101
Atra-ḫasis 82
Ballade des héros du temps jadis 84
Cannibal Tale 98
Chronicle 20 32n46
Chronicle 21 30n40
Chronicle of Early Kings 32n46
Code of Ḫammurapi 66
Diri 81, 84
Ea 84n136
Elkuniřša Myth 99, 99n62
Empire of Sargon of Akkad 30
Enlil and Namzitarra 85
Enmerkar and the Lord of Aratta 74
Evil Spirits 84
Fowler and his Wife 86
Gilgamesh 82, 86
Gilgamesh and Aratta 63
Headache 84
Ḫamazi Letter 84
ḪAR-ra 81, 83n130, 84
Idrimi 31n43
Instructions of Šube-awilim 82n123
iqqur ippuš 84
Izi 84
King of Battle 33n49, 95
Kumarbi 18n165, 99, 99n61, 105
Lord of Heaven and Earth 73
lú=ša 81, 84
Message of Lu-dingira to his Mother 82
Names and Professions List 74, 74n45
Níg-ga 84
Omens Collection 32n46
Ritual to Ištar 78, 79
Sag B 84
sag-gig 84
Scribal Letter B 20 81
Second Training Regimen 105
Si-du 81, 85
Signalement Lyrique 99n63
Silbenalphabet A 81, 83
Song of Ḫedammu 99
Song of Kumarbi 99
Song of LAMMA 99
Song of Silver 99
Song of Ullikummi 99
Sumerian King List 9, 16, 24n9, 29n30, 35n60, 77, 78n84, 84
Sumerian Sargon Legend 29n30
Syllabary A 81, 83
Syllabary of Ebla 75
Syllabic Vocabulary A 83
Synchronistic History 30n40
Tamarisk and the Palm 86
Third Training Regimen 105
udug-ḫul 84
tu-ta-ti 81, 84
Vocabulary of Ebla 74, 85n145
Vocabulary S(a) 83
Wen-Amon 103
Wordlist D 76

Genesis 6:3 86

Genesis 10:17 67
Judges 11:3 66
Judges 11:5 66
Proverbs 30:1 67
Proverbs 31:1 67
II Samuel 10:6 66
II Samuel 10:8 66

AR 145 30n34
ARET 2:22 33n49
ARET 5:1-5 71n7, 71n8, 71n9
ARET 5:4 72
ARET 5:6 73
ARET 5:7 73
ARET 5:8-19 71n8
ARET 5:16 71n9, 72
ARET 5:20ff 73
ARET 5:22 72, 75n51
ARET 5:23 72
ARET 5:24-26 72
ARET 7:151 75n56
ARET 7:152 75n55
ARET 8:524 66
ARI II §98 30n40
ARI II §520 30n40
CT 1 BU.91-5-9 588 29n30
CT 1 BU.91-5-9 590 29n30
CT 44:30 71n18
CTH 4 98n55
CTH 14 98n58
CTH 15 98n58
CTH 40 42n5
CTH 42 102n72
CTH 46 45n33
CTH 49 45n33
CTH 50 45n33
CTH 51 45n33
CTH 52 45n33
CTH 53 45n33
CTH 61 42n6
CTH 62 45n33
CTH 63 46n40
CTH 66 45n33
CTH 75 42n4, 45n33
CTH 76 102n72
CTH 92 45n33
CTH 93 91n8
CTH 105 45n33
CTH 122 45n33
CTH 180f 102n77
CTH 223 93n28
CTH 241 93n27
CTH 241.6 98n53
CTH 241.12 98n53
CTH 242 97n43, 97n45, 98n50
CTH 243 93n27
CTH 247 94n29
CTH 247.4 98n53
CTH 250 94n32
CTH 261 48n59
CTH 277.4 102n77
CTH 279.1 102n77
CTH 285 105
CTH 286 105
CTH 315 99n63
CTH 483 103
CTH 490 93n26
CTH 510 101n68
CTH 570 103n81
CTH 575 102n73
CTH 584 94n31
CTH 616.3 102
CTH 625 98n56
CTH 698 102n74
CTH 698C 102n78
CTH 698.1A 102n78
CTH 698.1F 102n79
CTH 716 103
CTH 777 95n37
DV 5 Nr. 10: 29n32
Emar VI, 1-4 53n8
Emar VI, 9 53n8
Emar VI, 18 46n46, 49n72
Emar VI, 19 49n72
Emar VI, 25-27 44n25
Emar VI, 28 48n70
Emar VI, 31 49n72
Emar VI, 42 44n23
Emar VI, 90 48n57, 48n62, 49n74
Emar VI, 130 49n73
Emar VI, 143-155 48n67
Emar VI, 144 49n73
Emar VI, 144-155 53n8
Emar VI, 148 49n73, 49n77
Emar VI, 149 49n77
Emar VI, 150 49n77
Emar VI, 157 49n77
Emar VI, 177 46n46, 49n72
Emar VI, 181 48n57, 48n62
Emar VI, 182 47n54
Emar VI, 186 49n78
Emar VI, 194 49n72

Emar VI, 199-226 53n8
Emar VI, 201 49n72, 49n76
Emar VI, 202 46n46, 49n72
Emar VI, 211 47n55
Emar VI, 212 48n69, 49n75, 49n78
Emar VI, 252 48n57, 48n62, 48n70
Emar VI, 253 49n77
Emar VI, 254 49n77
Emar VI, 259 48n57
Emar VI, 262 48n57, 48n61
Emar VI, 263 48n57, 48n60
Emar VI, 289 48n57
Emar VI, 315 49n75
Emar VI, 369 53
Emar VI, 369-535 53n9, 87
Emar VI, 370 54, 59n38
Emar VI, 373 54
Emar VI, 385-388 54
Emar VI, 392 61
Emar VI, 446 54
Emar VI, 446-451 57n31
Emar VI, 452 54, 57n30
Emar VI, 453-459 57n30
Emar VI, 460 48n57, 48n63
Emar VI, 463 57n30
Emar VI, 563 84n136
Emar VI, 592 85n149
Emar VI, 767 84
Emar VI, 768f 86
Emar VI, 771-774 85n149
Emar VI, 775 86
Emar VI, 778-780 86
Emar VI, 781f 86
Emar VI, 783f 86
F.1153:2 29n30
Fales No. 66 48n57, 48n62
Hirayama 3 47n54
Hirayama 5 47n47
Hirayama 7 44n23
HSS 10 1 29n32, 31n41
IAS 33 75
IAS 37 75
IAS 278 73n35, 73n36
IAS 326 73
IAS 342 73
IAS 523 76n66
IBoT 1.31 97n45, 98n53
IBoT 1.33 102n73
IBoT 2.116 93n26
ISET I:217 No. 4176 71n19
KAV 92 30n35, 32n47
KAV 107 30n34
KAV 183 32n47, 132n67
KBo 1.6 42n4
KBo 4.13 98n56
KBo 5.3 102n72
KBo 5.4 93n23
KBo 5.7 93n28
KBo 7.24 98n48
KBo 10.1 98n55, 100n65, 102n71
KBo 10.2 98n55, 100n66, 102n71
KBo 11.45 102
KBo 14.142 102n78
KBo 16.63 94n32
KBo 18.88 92
KBo 18.153 97n43
KBo 18.156 97n43
KBo 18.164 97n43
KBo 18.175 93n27
KBo 18.181 93n27
KBo 26.156 102n79
KBo 27.55 103n83
Krebernik 1 71, 71n16
Krebernik 2 71n16
Krebernik 3 71n16
Krebernik 21 71n15
Krebernik 26 72
Krebernik 27 71
Krebernik 28 71n15
Krebernik 29 71n9
Krebernik 30 71n15
Krebernik 35 71n15
Krebernik 37 71n15
Krebernik 38 71n15
KTU 1.112 57n30
KUB 1.14 103n83
KUB 5.3 102n76
KUB 5.6 103n81
KUB 10.82 98n56
KUB 13.33 94n36
KUB 13.34 92n20, 92n21
KUB 13.4 91n13
KUB 15.23 94n31
KUB 18.54 103n81
KUB 21.1 102n72
KUB 21.38 90n4
KUB 26.66 98n50
KUB 27.15 102n78
KUB 30.42 93n26
KUB 30.51 102n77
KUB 30.56 102n77
KUB 34.45 94n32

KUB 38.10 101n68
KUB 41.15 103n83
KUB 42.18 98n53
KUB 42.20 98n53
KUB 42.22 98n53
KUB 42.28 98n47, 98n49
KUB 42.29 97n46
KUB 42.65 98n53
KUB 42.67 94n32
KUB 42.81 97n45
KUB 42.84 94n29
KUB 42.106 93n27
KUB 53.15 103n83
KUB 55.5 102n76
KUB 59.56 98n52
MAD 1 52 29n32
MDP 14:91 71n17
ME 110 102n69
MEE 3:12-17 76
MEE 3:39 76
MEE 3:45 75
MEE 3:46 75
MEE 3:47 65n15
MEE 3:48 76
MEE 3:50 65n15
MEE 3:51f 75
MEE 3:54 76
MEE 3:55 75n56
MEE 3:56 75
MEE 3:57 75n56
MEE 3:61 75
MEE 3:62 75
MEE 3:63 76
MEE 3:64 76
MEE 3:68 76, 85n145
MEE 3:72 76
MEE 3:73f 76
MEE 3:74 76n73
MEE 4:3-90 75n49
MEE 4:78 76
MEE 4:91-113 75n51
MEE 4:118-130 75n50
MEE 4:336 67
MSL XI:35 32n47
MSL XI:104 30n33
Naram-Sin b 5 28, 28n28
NBC 3842 98n54
OBGT XIV 81
PBS 13:27 34n51
PBS 13:35 71n19
PRU III, 6f 47n51
PRU III, 6-7 46n44
PRU IV, 103ff 91n8
PRU IV, 134ff 46n41
PRU IV, 152ff 46n43
PRU IV, 161ff 46n42
PRU IV, 165-169 46n46
PRU IV, 188 46n44
PRU IV, 189 47n52
PRU IV, 191 47n53
PRU IV, 292-293 46n46
PRU VI, 35-38 46n45
III *R* 66 30n34
RE 16 49n77
RE 19 44n26
RE 21 48n69
RE 24 49n77
RE 34 49n77
RE 39 49n77
RE 54 46n46, 49n72
RE 55 46n46, 49n72
RE 56 48n57, 48n62
RE 85 49n72
Sargon b 1 32n46, 35n57
Sargon b 2 32, 32n46
Sargon b 13 32n46
SH 867 30n34
TM.75.G.1435 26n17
TM.75.G.2268 34n56
TM.75.G.2367 24n9
TM.75.G.2422 75n50
TM.75.G.2628 115n33
TM.76.G.412 26n17
TSŠ 170 72n21
TSŠ 190 76
UCP 9/4 32n47
UET 1 80 31n43
UET 1 275 28n28, 30n37
Ug 5:15 81, 82n119
Ug 5:16 82
Ug 5:17 82
Ug 5:162 82
Ug 5:163 82
Ug 5:164-6 81
Ug 5:167 82
Ug 5:168 82
Ug 5:169 82
VAT 12598 71n10, 71n16, 72n21
YOS 11:81 71n19

Languages

Akkadian 11, 16, 19, 20, 29n30, 42-43, 51, 52, 53, 54, 55, 56, 56n26, 57, 65, 72, 73, 74, 74n43, 78, 78n86, 79, 80, 81, 83, 83n132, 86, 100, 102, 104, 105, 106, 127n62
Amorite 66, 127n62
Aramaic 20, 69, 82
Eblaite 8, 63-67 passim, 71, 72, 75, 115, 115n36
Elamite 72
Greek 93, 93n22
Hattic 103n83
Hebrew 95-96
Hieroglyphic Hittite 69, 82, 99
Hittite 18, 18n175, 19, 44, 52, 53, 55, 70, 83, 89-106 passim
Hurrian 11, 11n94, 15, 16, 17, 18, 19, 30n36, 44, 51n2, 52, 53, 53n8, 55, 70, 72, 78, 81, 83, 88, 89-106 passim
Luwian 96, 103n83
Sumerian 11, 16, 56, 71, 72, 73, 77, 78, 80, 81, 83, 85, 86, 86n150, 87
Ugaritic 18, 81, 96

Words

Akkadian

abarakku 84
andurāru 100
āšipu 94
bārû 94
bēl qāti 93
entu 57, 87
galābu 57n28
gipāru 57n29
ḫazannu 49, 49n73
ikkibu 86n150
isinnu 56
kissu 54, 54n15, 54n18, 58n33, 59, 59n42
malāku 57n28, 58
mandattu 96, 97
mār šipri 91
maš$^{\supset}$*artu* 54, 54n13, 54n18, 56n26, 57n28, 58, 58n33, 59, 60
meKim eblaim 120n50
naḫlaptu 93
naptanu 56n27
purû 57n29
qadāšu 57n28
šakkanakku 29n30, 78n87, 123n55
šibūtu 48n67
ubāru 90, 91, 91n12
zukru 54, 54n14, 54n18, 58n33, 59, 60

Eblaite

abarakku 84
ba-da-lum 64
bu-la-tim 67
di-mu-mu 85n145
DUB-SAR 65n15
É/^{c}*A-lu* 67
EN 64
sukkal-du$_8$ 84
ti-É/ha-ma-tum 67
U$_9$*-ra/ru*$_{12}$ 67

Greek

dēmioergi 93, 93n22
metoikos 90n7
paroikos 90n7

Hebrew

^{c}*arqī* 64, 67
d^e*ror* 100
gēr 90n7
ha^c*îrā* 67
koba^c 96
šeber 67
ṭôb 66

Hittite

aḫrušḫi 95
ang/kurinu 98n49
ANTAḪŠUM 98, 102
araḫzenaš 91n12
argaman 96, 96n39
arnuwalaš 89
^{LÚ}A.ZU 93, 103n83
BĒL MADGALTI 48n59
dumu.lugal 47
EZEN 53, 55, 55n23, 56
gurta 96
^{lú}ḪAL 102
ḫila 96
ḫuḫupal 103n83
itgaḫiyaš 95
itkalziyaš 95

kariulli 96
keldiya 95
kubaḫi 96
kullupi 96
lappiya 96
LÚ.MEŠ É.GAL ^{URU}*ḪALAB* 102
lú.meš gal 48
luzzi 100
maššiya 96
nu=za=kan ḫatta 103n83
SISKUR 55n23, 95
šaḫḫan 100
tawannanna 91
tuwarša 96
^{lú}ugula 48
ugula.kalam.ma 48
wiyana 96
zapzigi 96
zilipuriyatalla 103n83

Hurrian

aḫrušḫi 95
itgaḫiyaš 95
itkalziyaš 95
keldiya 95

Luwian

tuwarša 96

Sumerian

AMA.AR.GI 100
ANTAḪŠUM 98, 102
^{LÚ}A.ZU 93, 103
DU_{11}.UD 72
dumu.lugal 47
EZEN 53, 55, 55n23, 56
garaš 74
^{LÚ}ḪAL 102
KÙ.GI GAR.RA 94
lú.meš gal 48
NAM.RA 89
níg-gig 86n150
NIN.DINGIR 53, 57, 57n28, 57n29, 58, 58n33, 59, 61
SISKUR 55n23, 95
sukkal-du_8 84
^{giš}šudul 72n25
TÚG.GÚ.É.A ḪURRI 93
^{lú}ugula 48
ugula.kalam.ma 48
^{giš}uštil 72

Ugaritic

ṯpṭ nhr 66